MERCHANTS MAKE HISTORY

ERNST SAMHABER

MERCHANTS MAKE HISTORY

How Trade has influenced the Course
of History throughout the World

TRANSLATED BY E. OSERS

THE JOHN DAY COMPANY
NEW YORK

First American Edition 1964

© 1960 by Verlag Heinrich Scheffler. English translation © 1963 by
George G. Harrap & Co., Ltd. All rights reserved. This book, or parts
thereof, must not be reproduced in any form without permission. Published by The John Day Co., Inc., 62 West 45th St., New York 36, N. Y.

Library of Congress Catalogue
Card Number: 63-15903

Printed in the United States of America

Contents

1. World without Merchants   13
2. First Journeys into the Unknown   25
3. Athens lives by its Grain Trade   43
4. The Fall of Rome   65
5. The Man from the East   84
6. The Italian Cities: Trade becomes Business   102
7. Strength through Unity: the Hanseatic League   126
8. The Fuggers, Kings and Slaves of Credit   150
9. The Elusive Treasure of El Dorado   178
10. War, Commerce, and Piracy   200
11. Paper Money, Illusions, and Speculations   231
12. Triangular Trade: England, Africa, the West Indies   262
13. Bills of Exchange open up the Continental Market   277
14. Machines need New Markets   300
15. The Beginnings of Global Economics   319
16. The Art of Selling   345
17. The State takes over Distribution   359

Epilogue   379

Index   383

Illustrations

PLATES IN HALF-TONE
Between pages 96 and 97

The Scribe

King Arcesilaus of Cyrene supervising the Weighing of Silphium

Egyptian Ships being loaded

Roman Money-changers

Querns and Bread-ovens in Pompeii

A Roman Shopping-street in Pompeii

Vendors of Cloth. A Roman Shop-sign

The Forum in Rome about A.D. 310

Mercury, the God of Commerce

Wine-store of a "Caupo" in Pompeii

A Dealer in Cushions demonstrates his Wares

Cracow Merchants inspecting their Bales

An Augsburg Weaver

Arrival of a Caravan at Tuggurt Oasis, Southern Algeria

Advertisement Board of an Egyptian Interpreter of Dreams

Chinese Figure of a Loaded Camel

Herrings being pickled

Map of Africa by Sebastian Münster

Jakob Fugger with his Chief Accountant

Georg Guise, a Hanseatic Merchant at the London Steelyard about 1532

A Large Caravan outside the Great Wall of China

By Waterway to China

Venice in the Fifteenth Century

The Antwerp Stock Exchange in 1531

The Building of the Dutch East India Company in Amsterdam

The *Fondaco dei Tedeschi* in Venice

The Conference Room in the *Fondaco dei Tedeschi*

The London Office of the Dutch East India Company

Between pages 256 and 257

The St Gotthard Pass

Sailors from England and Brittany drying Newfoundland Cod

Broadsheet on the Subject of British Subsidies for Frederick the Great
A Scene in Leipzig at the Time of Napoleon's Continental System
The "Herring-tamer"
The Textile Store of Mr Echigoya in Edo
Batavia (Djakarta)
Novgorod on Lake Ilmen
Canton
The Island Fortress of de Diu
Anamabo
An African Market at Lovangiri, Lovan, about 1670
The Slave House on the Island of Gorée
Inscriptions left by Portuguese Sailors at Ruanda Mutundi
The Cotton Office, 1875. Painting by Edgar Dégas
A Warehouse at Frankfurt-on-Main
Colbert, Louis XIV's Minister of State
Henry Hope
The Three Principals of the Firm of Baring studying the Account of the Firm of Hope
A Girl Assistant in a Paris Hosiery Shop, 1830
Early Nineteenth-century Travelling Textile Salesman
Early Nineteenth-century High Road from Valparaiso to Santiago
The Old Royal Exchange in London
Liverpool Harbour
A Trading Post of the Hudson's Bay Company
A Mechanical Elephant at a Berlin Exhibition, 1891
A Mid-nineteenth-century Shop in a Paris Boulevard
The Famous Rue de Rivoli, an Elegant Shopping Street
Harrods, one of the Big London Department Stores
Gorky Street in Moscow
The New Face of a City; Fifth Avenue, New York
Shops in Kandy (Ceylon)
Shop-window on 42nd Street, New York
Soviet Citizens in the GUM Department Store

IN THE TEXT

1. Columbus's crew bartering with American Indians   *page* 16
2. Cotton Rugs, the Currency of the American Indians   21
3. Paolo Toscanelli's Map of 1474   23
4. Phœnician Settlements   27
5. Sailors on the Nile   33
6. Numerals Throughout Seventy Centuries   38

Illustrations

7. Trade Routes of the Phœnicians   *page* 41
8. A Greek Trireme   47
9. Bronze Tablet with Cypriot Characters   52
10. Etruscan Ship   60
11. Shop-sign of a Coppersmith in Pompeii   71
12. Shop-sign of a Butcher, Pompeii   77
13. Trade Routes of the Roman Empire   80–81
14. An Arabian Caravan   87
15. Trade Routes to the Middle East   88
16. Caravanserai in Cairo   90
17. World Map of the Twelfth Century   111
18. Woman Spinning   116
19. A Groom   120
20. The Merchant   122
21. A Hanseatic Merchant Ship under Construction   132
22. Wool-weaver with a Shuttle, Scissors, and Knife   138
23. Trade Routes to Northern and Southern Europe   141
24. Tilsit, on the Trade Route to Novgorod   143
25. Coat of Arms of the Fuggers "of the Lily"   157
26. Address of a Letter written by Anton Fugger   164
27. The Money-changer   168
28. A Merchant's Premises   172
29. The Yardstick   173
30. The Life of a Sixteenth-century Merchant   176–7
31. The *Santa Maria*, Columbus's Flagship   180
32. Woodcut depicting the Voyage of Balthasar Sprenger   182
33. A Spanish Trading-post off the Central American Coast   186
34. Trading between Spaniards and American Indians   187
35. Genoa about 1493   190
36. Spanish Merchants off the Coast of Haiti   194
37. Lisbon in the Sixteenth Century   196
38. Stone with Viking Runic Inscription   202
39. A Seventeenth-century Ship   211
40. Portuguese Merchants in India   212
41. Mozambique, the Principal Portuguese Base in Africa   219
42. Processing of Silk Fabrics in the Sixteenth Century   227
43. Decorative Vignette from an Eighteenth-century French Atlas   239
44. Loading Plan of a Slave Ship   247
45. A Smoker   253
46. The Settlement of New Amsterdam, now New York   255
47. The Circulation of Trade between Three Continents   272–3

48. King James I's Tract against Tobacco   274
49. Counting-house of a Hamburg Merchant   287
50. Political Cartoon about the Abolition of Protective Tariffs   307
51. New York Stockbrokers   328
52. Morning Scene at Billingsgate Market, London   335
53. Quay and Harbour of Shanghai, 1860   344
54. The Magasin du Printemps Department Store in Paris, 1883   349
55. The First Typewriter   358
56. A Russian Black Marketeer arrested by Red Army Soldiers, 1920   364

MERCHANTS MAKE HISTORY

I

World without Merchants

━━━━∿∿∿∿∿/⊙\∿∿∿∿∿━━━━

ONCE UPON A TIME, when China was again in the grip of a famine, the Emperor sent his wisest official to a stricken province. "It's all the fault of the merchant Wang," the people told him. "He bought up all the grain and kept it in his vast storehouses so that he might sell it at a usurious price." Angrily, the Mandarin ordered the culprit to be brought before him in chains.

"How dare you keep back grain in order to sell it to the hungry people at an outrageous profit! You have been making money out of the misery of the starving!" shouted the Mandarin.

"Allow me to tell you the story of my actions," Wang the merchant replied. "Last year the harvest was exceptionally good. The grain remained in the fields; many would not even cut it because the price was so low that the work was hardly worth their while. The people were squandering their bread, which appeared to have lost all value. It was then that I began to buy grain. True, I paid a low price for it. But at least the peasants garnered it. Ought I to have paid more? Everybody was glad to see me buy grain at all.

"And then the harvest failed. All of a sudden there was no grain to be had. Apart from myself no one had laid in any reserves; everybody had felt sure that there would always be plenty. Then there was famine. People were beginning to come to me, saying, 'Your granaries are full; give us grain.' But they still had enough to eat, they still would not see that only with extremely careful management could disaster be averted. Prices were still not high enough to teach them to bear some measure of hunger. Ought I to have opened all my granaries then? My

13

modest reserves would have been eaten up within a few weeks; the people would have lived again as in the previous year, the year of a good harvest. I therefore held back, no matter how they insulted me, maligned me, and threatened me.

"The famine got worse. Only when the price had risen again did I open my first granary. It was soon emptied—at a good profit, I admit. The people were beginning to get used to the idea that there was always a reserve. 'Wang has plenty of grain,' they would say. But soon the shortage was upon us again, and prices continued to rise. Once again I opened a granary. This time my profit was even greater. But ought I to have kept the price down? The people had to be made to realize that there was not enough grain available; they had to be taught to be even more economical, to restrict themselves even further. This they could learn only if everything was more expensive than it had been in the past.

"Eventually I opened my third and last granary. The price now was enormous. Everybody could see how scarce grain had now become. A lower price would have been self-deception.

"And now I was left without any reserves. But I kept this from the people to prevent panic and despair. Instead I sent out messengers to all provinces, to wherever I had friends. To all of them I wrote: Send grain; I will pay exceedingly high prices—only send grain!

"Everybody thought that I was tremendously rich—that was the only reason why my business friends promised to send grain. No doubt I shall have to sell it at an even higher price than I did my own grain—but the people will pay the price."

The Mandarin was angry. "You have no heart for the hungry," he said. "You have profited from their hunger. You waited for prices to rise merely because you wanted to make greater profits. And now you are trying to tell me that you were serving the people, that you were trying to save them from starvation. You shall die for this!"

The merchant Wang blenched. He bowed down before the Mandarin and said, "My lord! From all the points of the compass the caravans are setting out with the promised grain. When the merchants hear that I am no longer alive they will turn back. There is no grain left in this province. Unless supplies arrive soon all the people here will die."

"I will have it proclaimed on all the roads that I shall accept the grain and pay for it on behalf of the Emperor. What do I need you for?"

"You would have to pay at least the same price as I had to promise—and that was higher than the price I was paid for the last of my own grain. Are you going to sanction the usurious prices which you say it was criminal of me to demand? Besides, how are you going to pay? In this entire province there is not enough ready money available."

"I shall use your fortune for payment!"

"I was not paid in ready cash. I was given land, mortgages on houses, promissory notes. I myself can use these things. The foreign merchants cannot. They trust only my word."

"They will have the same trust in the official of their Emperor."

"When they hear that you had me executed for demanding prices well below those which they must charge you they will take fright and turn back. There is famine in other provinces, too, even though not as great as in ours. They will have no difficulty in selling their grain elsewhere."

"Are you trying to say that you alone can save this province?"

Calmly the merchant regarded the Mandarin. "Yes, that is precisely what I am saying," he said with assurance. "They trust only me, they will send their grain to no one but me. I want to make a profit; I must make a profit. I am a merchant, not an official. If I lose through a miscalculation then I have failed as a merchant and that is the end of me. I want to make money—I must make money—by serving the community."

The Mandarin regarded the merchant in silence for a long time. Then he commanded: "Take off his chains. Let's hope he produces the grain he has promised."

Perhaps this imperial official was the first to understand what it means to be a merchant.

Trade has existed since time immemorial, probably since the earliest Stone Age. Flint tools were manufactured in certain localities in far greater quantities than could possibly be needed in that neighbourhood. And such cudgels and knives have, in fact, been found at great distances from their place of manufacture. How did they get there? Were they taken there by merchants? Probably not.

Trade without merchants exists to this day. The peasant woman who takes her eggs or vegetables to market in the near-by town in order to sell them there is undoubtedly engaged in trade. But that does not make her a merchant; she remains a peasant. In the old days, when a prince or a king sent his messengers abroad with a lump of silver or fine pieces of pottery with orders to buy precious weapons, glittering pieces of jewellery, choice fabrics, or rare animals, then these men were certainly engaged in trade. But that did not make them merchants. Their task performed, they returned to their former avocations: they served their master at his court, in his army, or on his estates.

The merchant, on the other hand, lives by trade, by profiting from wares which others, not he, have produced.

Columbus does not appear to have noticed at all that he found no merchants in America. True, the Indians came to meet him, peacefully,

1. Columbus's crew bartering with American Indians. (From Bernardine de Sahagun, *Historia de las cosas de le Nueva España*, Vol. V)

amicably, prepared to barter the few things they owned against the wonderful, unfamiliar articles which the strangers had with them. They gave of their food, their adornments, even, in so far as they had any, of their gold and silver in exchange for the truly miraculous things owned by the strangers. But when they had satisfied their curiosity and surrendered all the possessions they had brought with them they returned quite happily to their villages. After all, they were no merchants.

The Spaniards disembarked, settled down comfortably in their little fortress, and assumed, as a matter of course, that the Indians would continue to supply them with food until their own crops ripened. After all, did they not still possess a multitude of tempting articles, from bright glass beads to excellent steel tools such as knives, axes, and scissors? Surely all these things were precious in a country which had no iron and whose people were still, as a rule, using stone tools?

No doubt the American Indians would have been only too pleased to acquire these articles—but what were they to use for payment? They had nothing left to offer the strangers. That was due not so much to the poverty of these fishermen, hunters, and collectors of food, as to the fact that there were no merchants to bring in supplies from farther afield.

After a few weeks the Spaniards had eaten all their food and received no fresh supplies. As they could not believe this to be due to perfectly natural and comprehensible causes they suspected ill will, treachery, deliberate tactics. Yet all the time the poor naked Indians were sitting in their huts, scared, among their miserable Stone Age weapons; they were terrified of the invaders with their breastplates, their cross-bows, their swords, and their muskets. What were they to do? The strangers were ever more insistently demanding food and gold.

For a while they succeeded in satisfying the importunate strangers by surrendering their own scarce supplies, until they themselves were starving. But when the enraged Spaniards burst into their villages to take by force whatever they found there, they encountered open resistance, and there was much fighting which, in spite of their splendid equipment, frequently ended with the defeat of the Europeans. On his second voyage to America, Columbus found only the ruins of the settlement of the companions he had left behind. The unfortunate Indians were to be cowed into submission by a frightful retribution. What then was left to them but to flee to the mountains to escape the demands of their terrible enemies?

Columbus never asked himself why he encountered not a single merchant on the "Indian" coast. After all, he knew from the accounts he had studied so thoroughly, above all from Marco Polo's report, that a highly developed trade flourished on the East Asian coast. Thousands of ships of all sizes, the Venetian world traveller had reported, would call year after year at the powerful trading cities of the coast, bringing spices and precious fabrics from India, and loading silk and finely fashioned brass and pottery articles.

Nowhere in the letters of the great discoverer of America is there a single word of complaint about the absence of merchants. He never realized what caused the initial failure of his colonization plans.

Merchants were not known either to the local peoples of the Antilles or to the highly civilized inhabitants of the highlands—the Mexicans in North America, the Mayas in Central America, or the Incas in South America. True, they bartered among themselves a few of the goods in particular demand. The Mexicans went to the south to get the feathers of the quetzal bird for their feather cloaks, to get soconusso cocoa from what to-day is Guatemala, and to get murex, the shellfish yielding purple pigment, from the Gulf of Nicoya; the Chibchas carried the salt from their mines along a special salt route— the same route as that taken by the Spanish *conquistadores* when they marched on Bogotá from the north.

When the Spaniards entered Tenochtitlán for the first time, as the friends and guests of the Aztec Emperor, they marched past countless market stalls piled high with fruit, vegetables, and fish. The market women were offering their wares, calling out to the buyers, eager to sell. "Just like back home in Medina del Campo on a great market-day," is how one of the *conquistadores* described the scene in an account extant to this day. Just as in Spain, the peasants had come to the capital from the neighbouring countryside to sell their produce; they had come as producers.

It is true that in the Aztec Empire there was a class of 'merchants,' but these were highly respected powerful gentlemen, warriors who carried their weapons hidden under their clothes. When they set out beyond their frontiers they did carry some goods with them and offered them for barter, but their real task was to spy out the foreign land. At a favourable moment they would cast off their outer garments, draw their swords, and pounce upon their gullible 'customers.' To regard them as merchants would be setting a very dangerous precedent.

When the proud Spanish hidalgos sailed to the New World in order to make their fortunes without much effort, when daring *conquistadores* acquired entire empires with no more than a handful of soldiers, they did not care much about merchants. But merchants were there, all the same, among that motley crowd.

Most of the ships leaving Sevilla were equipped and manned by Spanish or foreign merchant firms. The Welsers of Augsburg acquired and tried to exploit an entire colony—what is to-day Venezuela. The representative of the great Florentine merchant family of the Medici, Amerigo Vespucci, gave his name to the new continent: America. English merchants, too, took part in the voyages to the New World during the first few decades. But in all the numerous notes made by these merchants we never find the decisive observation: we found no merchants.

Oddly enough, the merchants themselves do not at first seem to have thought of engaging in trade in the new country. Each settlement cultivated whatever it needed for living. Only after the silver-mines had been discovered, first of all high up in the mountains of Peru, at Potosi,[1] and later at Zapatecas, in Mexico, did a trade begin to flourish, supplying the workmen with meat, bread, draught animals, and tools over a distance of hundreds of miles.

How different might have been the opening up and colonization of America if trade by merchants had existed from the beginning. And yet there had been, in North America, long before the Spaniards, a far from inconsiderable barter trade. The Mohave Indians, who lived in the north-western part of the present state of Arizona, made regular journeys across the mountains to the Pacific coast in order to catch fish and collect the shells which they needed as ornaments for their elaborately woven garments. As a rule they brought with them far more shells than they required for themselves, and this surplus they bartered with their neighbours, the Hopi Indians, for fabrics.

These Hopi in turn travelled farther to the east, across high mountains and endless wastes, in order to obtain in what to-day is the state of Colorado the salt they needed. This they acquired in exchange for their woven fabrics. Yet another Indian tribe, the Hopewell, who lived in the basin of the Ohio, travelled as far as Lake Superior in their search for copper, and as far west as the Rocky Mountains in order to obtain obsidian stones for their weapons and bear-teeth for their clothes. The Hopewell Indians were renowned far and wide as skilled artisans; when other tribes needed articles fashioned from shells or copper they brought with them bear-teeth or rare feathers for the medicine-men's ceremonies. As a medium for barter the wampum, a string of shells, gradually gained universal currency instead of money. Even transactions between Indians and Europeans were settled with wampum. But invariably we find the same picture: the producers exchanging their own produce with one another direct.

And in what manner was this done?

Every few years the Indians from the north-western coast of North America, the Kwakiutl, would come in their boats to meet for certain festivals and to boast of their wealth. The initiator of a transaction would offer a copper dish for sale, suitably praising its value. But at

[1] Potosi is now part of Bolivia.

the same time he would not omit to advertise his own wealth. Whenever one of the guests made an offer which did not come up to the value of the copper dish the vendor would jeer, "You haven't got it in you to acquire this copper dish! Its price must correspond to my own dignity!" And the pile of rugs offered in exchange would rise and rise, to some 1600, and still the scoffs would continue: "This mountain of rugs very nearly touches the sky. Yet my name is that of the Kwakiutl, and you cannot measure yourselves with us." Presently a chieftain from the tribe of the vendor would rise and hold forth at length about the glory of his fellow tribesmen and his legendary ancestors. "I know how copper dishes are traded. You keep talking about your wealth, chief. But have you properly considered how much this dish is worth? Come, add another thousand rugs." Up and up went the price of the dish. Already 3200 rugs lay on a pile, and still the buyer had to add the valuable coffers in which the rugs were kept. Finally the vendor demanded, "Increase your own fame, you chiefs, by adding this boat!" And only when this demand too had been met would he declare himself satisfied.

And now the buyer would turn to the vendor. "But why were you so ready to accept my offer, chief? You accepted much too soon. Indeed, you must think me a very poor man. But I am a Kwakiutl, one of those who have given their name to tribes all over the world. You gave up before I had finished bartering. Evidently you are beneath us." And of his own free will the buyer would add a further 200 rugs, merely to demonstrate his pride and wealth.

This kind of grappling for reputation and dignity, this festivity called by the Indians potlatch, could easily lead to open quarrel if one party considered itself humiliated. The desire to impress could take on extreme forms: a chief might throw 400 rugs and seven valuable boats into the fire, merely to show his rivals what kind of a fellow he was. Another might pour oil on his house and burn it to the ground. Only when a further 200 rugs had been consumed by the flames would the contending parties be satisfied.

This desire to impress is found to accompany the business of barter trade also with other primitive peoples. They do not exchange goods but bring presents. The recipient of such a 'present' must then show that he is the nobler and the richer of the two; in other words, his present must be more valuable than the one he has received.

In former times the inhabitants of New Guinea and the near-by islands used to visit their neighbours with a large, carefully assembled fleet of many ships in order to bring them a 'present,' at first perhaps no more than some foodstuffs of no particular value. The recipient replied by a return present, having learned from clever hints, flattery, and praise what his visitor would like to receive from him—maybe a bracelet he himself was wearing. Presently the value of the gifts exchanged would go up: finely polished stone axes or girdles adorned with shells would change ownership. But all this was merely the prelude. The real purpose of the voyage was the valuable kula, chains of small smooth discs made by the women from reddish shells. Ancient custom demanded that one kind of kula chain must pass only in the direction of east to west, whereas another—heavy bangles fashioned from a different kind of shell, and credited with secret masculine powers—must

2. Cotton rugs, the currency of the American Indians. (From A. Peñafiel, *Libro de los Tributos*, Berlin, 1880)

be given as 'presents' only from west to east. As the recipients would soon give away these 'presents' to other parties, they could cover considerable distances.

In the South Seas we find yet another form of this elegant exchange of goods which has nothing to do with trade proper—the wasi. After the harvest the inhabitants of the Trobriand Islands, who practise agriculture, meet together in order to make the fishermen a rich present of root and grain crops, the largest and finest garnered by them. They do not have to wait long for a present in return. A few weeks later, when the catch of fish has been particularly successful, the entire fishing fleet makes for the shore in order to bring fish to the waiting husbandmen. It is a sacred custom that this return present must reach at least the value of the fruits of the harvest; but in any event mere self-respect would prevent the fishermen from giving less. They do not want to be shamed by the farmers or to lower the value of another man's produce. Throughout these transactions there is never any mention of price.

In their outriggers the Polynesians sailed thousands of miles across the limitless vastnesses of the Pacific, from the north-eastern coast of Asia down to Tahiti and Easter Island, perhaps even occasionally to the coast of South America—but they never thought of engaging in trade, of profiting from their knowledge of foreign islands. Certainly they had information about their neighbours, but it did not occur to them to import from them goods in order to sell them at a profit.

In November 1778 Captain Cook landed in the Hawaiian Islands, which had been discovered by the Spaniards two centuries before but had long since been forgotten. He was revered like a god by the people and heaped with presents, so that he was able to replenish his badly depleted supplies. Well provided with all he needed, he set sail again. However, unfavourable winds forced him to return to his former anchoring place. There he had an unpleasant surprise: the shore was deserted. In vain did the English implore their old friends to bring them food. The poor people had nothing left. No offer, however tempting, produced any results. The English thereupon tried to obtain food by force. There were arguments, quarrels, open resistance, and fighting. Cook tried to restore peace—in vain. Fighting, he retreated towards his boat. He was knee-deep in the water when he was struck from behind on the head with a cudgel. The great discoverer suffered the same fate as the first European settlers on the coasts of America— all because no merchants existed.

Traders, on the other hand, had been sailing to the Baltic coast since time immemorial in search of tin and golden amber. In exchange they offered copper vessels which, in the North, must have been as much a cause of wonder as European steel goods were in sixteenth- or seventeenth-century America. Yet the traders of the second millennium B.C., perhaps even of the latter part of the third millenium, had not been invited by anybody; they had not been lured by dazzling promises, but had set out of their own accord in order to seek the rare raw materials which did not exist on the coasts of the Mediterranean.

Why was it that in Central Europe at this very early date there was this extensive commerce to which archaeological finds testify? How was it that trade was known in the Old World so early when, many centuries later, there was still none in the New? And why did the

Spaniards and even the Portuguese fail to notice this peculiarity of America; why did they never complain of it? This question is the more mysterious since, at about the same time, the Portuguese encountered flourishing trade organizations in the East Indies.

Before Vasco da Gama sailed for India, a Portuguese scout had found out that the whole Indian Ocean represented a fully developed trade area. To start with, this scout advised, the explorer should make for the port of Sofala, in the far south of the African east coast. There he would find enough people who knew the entire Indian Ocean,

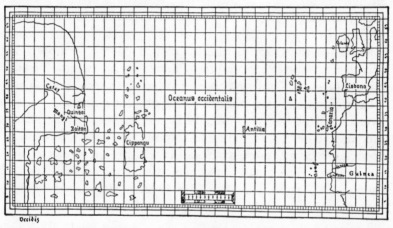

3. Paolo Toscanelli's map of 1474 showing Japan and the East Indian islands, all within reach of Portuguese seafarers. Columbus based his voyage on this map. (Reconstruction by Hermann Wagner, 1894)

since countless ships set out from there towards all the important centres of the Orient. And this proved to be the case.

On the western coast of the East Indies Vasco da Gama found a surprisingly rich world of commerce. In all the ports there were countless traders, mostly Arabs, who at once posed the age-old questions of the merchant: What have you to offer? What are you after? What can we show you? What will you pay?

Whatever the Europeans wanted they could have: jewels and pearls, gold and silver, spices of all kinds, precious silks and skilfully woven cotton goods, and, of course, foodstuffs in unlimited quantities. The only source of annoyance was the price. What the first Portuguese traders had to offer was not very much. Apart from precious metal

there was demand only for linen fabrics, so that the sailors sold even
their shirts at a good profit. The rest was scarcely worth consideration
in the eyes of the experienced Arab traders. Asia was not dependent
on European goods.

This trade area extended from Sofala to the Moluccas, the Spice
Islands, as far as the Chinese coast and the islands of Japan. Only on
the African coast did the world trade of those days cross the equator;
it reached as far as the island of Madagascar. Beyond, the world was
once more dark and unknown. Nowhere did the natives of those areas
attempt to penetrate farther, to open up new countries, or to increase the
supply of merchandise. At the Moluccas the world ended because
beyond there was no trade.

When Marco Polo, the great Venetian traveller, returning home
aboard the proud fleet furnished in China by his imperial friend and
patron the great Kublai Khan, was driven by winds to the island of
Java he enquired what country lay beyond the horizon to the south.
Everybody shrugged their shoulders. True, countless islands were
rumoured to lie beyond; at times a ship might sail there, navigating by
that strange constellation, the Southern Cross—but no one could say
what these explorers had found. Adventurers may well have sailed
the seas of the south, but hardly ever a merchant.

2

First Journeys into the Unknown

━━━━━━━━━◦ᴠᴠᴠᴠᴠᴠ◉ᴠᴠᴠᴠᴠᴠ◦━━━━━━━━━

ON THE EASTERN SHORE of the Mediterranean, immediately north of the spot where Beirut is situated to-day, two rivers run into the sea—the Nahr Ibrahim and the Nahr Feidar, known to the ancient Greeks by the names of Adonis and Phædrus. In winter, when the rains start, roaring torrents of water rush down from the heights of the Lebanon, carrying with them boulders and stones torn from the mountainside.

In summer these rivers dry up almost completely. It is then that men collect from the riverbeds the strange stones and lumps of metal ore washed down by the rivers, pretty chunks of stone in bright colours. The Lebanon contains a great variety of metals, even though not in great quantities.

Thus, 5000 years ago, men may have wandered through this area—shepherds belonging to nomadic Bedouin tribes, farming folk from far-off Mesopotamia who were finding the space too cramped for them between the two rivers, just as some 1500 years later Abraham was to leave Ur of the Chaldees to seek a new home in Palestine.

It was about that time that the inhabitants of Mesopotamia, the Sumerians, made a series of important discoveries. They tamed the wild cattle, they tilled the soil, they planted the first strains of grain. They invented and built the wheel. Their cattle drew their wagons.

Instead of stone they began to use a metal, at first rarely, and then with increasing frequency—copper. Copper was in great demand; it could be melted and fashioned and hammered into weapons. Stone, on the other hand, remained hard and brittle. But in the very areas where the new civilization was springing up, in Mesopotamia and the Nile valley, there were hardly any copper ores.

We know that as early as 5000 years ago the malachite mines of the Sinai peninsula, in the middle of what must even then have been inhospitable desert, were being worked by the Egyptians. They shrank from no sacrifice of men or effort in order to obtain this precious metal.

But copper has one annoying property: though it is easy to shape, it remains soft, far too soft. For axes, hatchets, and weapons of war the hard stone continued to be superior to copper.

The people who picked up the copper ores washed down by the rivers Adonis and Phædrus were particularly favoured by fortune. For upon smelting, these ores yielded a metal which had all the good qualities of copper but, at the same time, was unusually hard. The reason for this remained a mystery for a long time, even to the fortunate discoverers. Much later it was explained: what the waters had washed down from the mountains was not pure copper ore but ores containing a certain proportion of tin—in fact, that very proportion which yields bronze: one part in ten parts of copper. A strange coincidence. As far as we know, tin scarcely exists in the Middle East, in Western Asia, or in North-west Africa. Only here, on the Syrian coast, did a caprice of nature bring tin up to the surface, and, moreover, together with copper.

What the rivers had washed down from the mountains during the winter months was not much, but it was enough to assure the inhabitants of that area of an exceptional technical lead. With the new bronze axes it was possible to cut down the trees which grew on the slopes from the shores of the Mediterranean right up to the heights of the Lebanon: the mighty cedars, whose gigantic trunks had resisted the blunt stone axes and the soft copper tools alike.

Timber was the second source of wealth of the area. In Egypt there were no forests. For the building of houses, for the kilning of pottery, timber had to be brought over great distances, from the middle reaches of the Nile, where vegetation in those early days must have been more plentiful than now, or even across the Mediterranean.

The people of Mesopotamia collected their timber from the near-by mountains, chiefly from the Zagros range in the North-east. But such tremendous trunks as those of the Lebanon cedars did not exist anywhere else. For the great public buildings, for temples and palaces, they were indispensable. Hence emissaries would come to Syria from the East and from the far South, asking for timber. They brought with them presents to gain the goodwill of the population of the Lebanon— jewellery, household goods, and weapons, the precious manufactures of young civilizations.

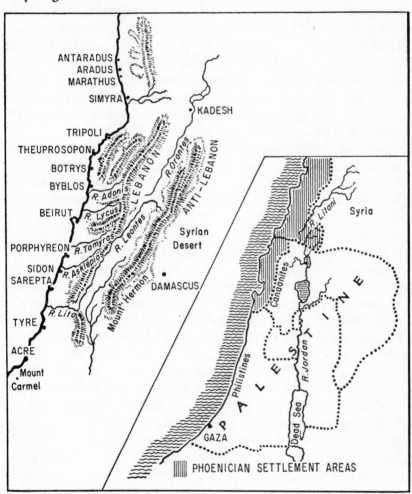

4. Phœnician settlements

Thus, at the estuary of the rivers Adonis and Phædrus, there arose a settlement which soon became renowned and respected even in such highly developed countries as Egypt and Mesopotamia—the city of Byblos. To-day it is difficult to establish who were its inhabitants, since no written records have survived. All we know from very early Egyptian inscriptions is that Byblos heads the list of all Asian principalities.

"Byblos" continued to be an important word for the Egyptians for thousands of years to come. It was from Byblos that those strange ships came which the Pharaohs sent out on the high seas, into the Red Sea, to the legendary countries along the Arabian and East African coasts, and to Punt, the land of frankincense. In old inscriptions these ships are represented by the sign for Byblos, the letters KBN, and the sign for ships. These passages are therefore to be read as "Byblos ships." Without them the Egyptians would not have been able to navigate the stormy Red Sea.

What kind of ships were they? They appear to have been ships with a keel—ships, that is, built upon one huge beam as the keel. Until then only flat-bottomed ships made of planks had been known. On keel ships one could venture out on the high seas. Even much later keel ships are found only where the type of the Byblos ship had been known.

In the north of Europe the Danish coast was inhabited by people living mainly by fishing. They must have sailed out on to the open sea, for their kitchen refuse, which they used to throw upon huge piles, contains the bones of high-sea fish. Moreover, rock-carvings of the early Bronze Age show such craft. But in all probability these were not proper ships but rafts. Several tree-trunks were lashed together— and what a tremendous amount of work the cutting of these huge trunks with miserable stone axes must have involved—and a deckhouse was fitted on top to provide better shelter from the waves.

Most primitive peoples know the dug-out canoe, a boat made by hollowing out a tree-trunk. This is done carefully by fire, and after a great deal of slow and laborious work some real masterpieces of boat-building are produced in the middle of the jungle. The boldest and most skilful navigators of the world, the Polynesians, used such hollowed out tree-trunks, either coupled in pairs for greater safety or fitted with outriggers, for sailing the vastnesses of the Pacific Ocean until the eighteenth century.

Boats were known also to the ancient Egyptians. They had been developed from earlier rafts. Sidewalls were fitted on to a flat bottom made from planks fastened together. These flat-bottomed boats were suitable for the shallow reed-grown waters of the Nile. Indeed they were safe enough on the wide river so long as it flowed quietly. But as soon as a storm sprang up they had to run for the nearest port or else make fast by the river-bank.

A characteristic type of ship was developed by the Chinese, the junk, capable of carrying hundreds of passengers and many tons of cargo. But the Chinese junk was a plank ship, not a keel ship. It had a flat bottom, although braced and reinforced, with the tall deckhouses and superstructures built upon it. For this reason the junks, in spite of their considerable size, had a relatively slight draught. In a gale they were not nearly so safe as the keel ships. No doubt this was the reason why Chinese shipping developed rather late, a long time after the Arabs with their superior keeled vessels had appeared in Chinese waters.

It was thanks to these keel ships and to the favourable position mid-way between Egypt and Mesopotamia that a merchant class arose in Byblos—that class which lives by acquiring merchandise and selling it at a profit. Wherever there are merchants in the world to-day they are the heirs of those who lived on the Syrian coast 5000 years ago.

We know, of course, that tens of thousands of years ago, in the Stone Age, certain objects travelled great distances. During the last glaciation some 20,000 years ago men painted pictures on the wall of a cave at Font de Gaume in Central France, including a huge old bison with enormous withers—a striking and unmistakable picture. Many years after this cave had been discovered, French scholars found a kind of sketch for this picture, a flat stone with an incised drawing, in another glacial cave in the *département* of Ain, approximately 200 miles away from Font de Gaume. How did the sketch get there? Clearly it was treated as a carefully guarded treasure. Had it been stolen? Had it been brought along by nomadic hunters? Or had it been bartered against some other article?

In Southern Russia scholars have found a spot with thousands of stone axes—far more than the few people who travelled past there could possibly use. No doubt the manufacturers exchanged them against other articles, for to this day these axes are found in all parts of Eastern Europe.

But barter is not the same thing as regular trade. Barter was practised also by the American Indians among themselves; barter was practised by the Polynesians and the natives of Australasia. In times of drought messengers or entire tribes travelled great distances in search of food. Joseph's brothers went to Egypt to buy corn. They appealed to the royal governor and "bowed down themselves before him with their faces to the earth," unaware that their own brother stood before them. Clearly Joseph's brethren were not merchants but peasants and herdsmen. When they made purchases they did so for their own consumption.

The inhabitants of Byblos, on the other hand, were neither peasants nor herdsmen, nor yet artisans. They earned their living chiefly through the exchange of merchandise which they had not manufactured themselves. And that is the decisive criterion.

Here we have the fundamental difference between the merchant who does not produce wares himself, and the manufacturer who may distribute his own manufactures, barter them, or sell them to a third party.

Byblos lived by its trade. After all, it was situated at the exact spot where two alien highly developed and mutually complementary civilizations touched—that of Egypt and that of Babylon. As the Egyptians journeyed northward, along the seashore, across the Sinai peninsula, and along the coast of Palestine, they arrived at a point where the dark mountains of the Lebanon descended right down to the Mediterranean. There the comfortable road ended. There lay Byblos.

From that point the travellers had to turn towards the interior of the country and to cross the Lebanon in those parts where to-day the railway runs from Beirut to Damascus or Aleppo, according to whether one wants to continue eastward and cross the Anti-Lebanon, or turn north between the two mountain-ranges.

We cannot tell what gave rise to the construction of the Byblos ships. But we believe we know the technical prerequisites. These were, first of all, the tall cedars of the Lebanon, which were particularly suitable for the building of the powerful new vessels. Some 1500 years later the Pharaoh of Egypt still sent his messenger to Byblos with a request for cedar trunks. In exchange he offered rich presents. We possess the account of an Egyptian who came to Byblos with such instructions. Unless we misinterpret the somewhat obscure text, this cunning Egyptian tried to cheat the ruler of Byblos out of these presents. He claimed that they had been lost en route, but the text does not make it quite clear whether they were supposed to have been lost in a shipwreck or stolen by thieves. He thus expected Byblos to supply the timber without any present in return, out of mere respect for the power of the Pharaoh and from humility towards his great gods. When the ruler of Byblos indignantly rejected such an imposition, the presents which had allegedly vanished suddenly reappeared and the transaction was concluded without further hitch. True, by that time the forests near Byblos had all been cut down, so that the ruler had to send his men up into the mountains. Teams of oxen dragged the long tree-trunks down to the coast.

Without the bronze axes it would hardly have been possible to cut down these powerful trees and fashion the timber adequately. It seems probable that bronze nails were used to fit these massive beams together more firmly than could have been done with the ropes made by the Egyptians from reeds and fibres.

Although the journey from Egypt to Byblos must have been difficult enough, that to the Euphrates offered truly tremendous difficulties. Nevertheless we find in this area routes going back to the earliest times, routes travelled by nomadic Bedouins, by tribes fleeing after defeat, and by great armies. It was along these routes that the merchants began to travel.

Everybody regarded the merchant with great suspicion. What was he up to? Was he trying to spy out the land where an attack could be staged? And even if he pursued peaceful aims, was he not out to cheat? A man who did not produce anything himself but was living from the work of others! Was it not better to kill him straight away?

But as soon as he spread out his treasures all hearts softened—above all, those of the women. There were sweetly smelling resins from the Lebanon which one could rub into one's skin and use for make-up; there were coloured unguents for beautifying one's eyes and cheeks. Modern cosmetics are based partly on alcoholic solutions, but in those days people loved fragrant oil.

The noble Egyptians used the resin and the oil of cedars for embalming their dead, so that their bodies should be preserved after death, because without a body there was no continued life for the soul. Their priests used resins for burning in the temples.

This barter with the produce of the Lebanon rapidly developed into an extensive trade in cosmetics and perfumes. From Asia Minor Syrian traders brought antimony, which was used by the elegant ladies of Egypt as an additive to the red pigment with which they outlined their eyes. Antimony was brought from what to-day is Armenia and was then called Naïri; the Egyptian name for antimony was *naharin*. Another beautifying substance was *haru galban,* which came from Persia.

From the earliest days the Egyptians were acquainted with laudanum, the resin of the cistus plant which grew along the shores of the Mediterranean. Laudanum was the ware sold by the merchants who, according to the Bible-story, bought Joseph as a slave.

The great boom in the perfume trade began when the merchants reached the Red Sea and made the acquaintance of myrrh and frankincense on the south coast of Arabia. The fragrant frankincense was carried by caravans from Hadramut, in Southern Arabia, over the long and tedious land route to Egypt, and across Syria to Mesopotamia. The quantities involved must have been enormous. In the temple of Ammon alone, in the sacred city of Thebes, 2189 jars and 304,093 bushels of incense were burned in the twelfth century B.C. The Chaldeans burned incense to a value of 10,000 talents of silver annually—one talent being 55 lb.—in front of the altar of Baal.

The principal customers were the great ones of the earth—the Pharaohs and princes, who wanted to give precious presents to their womenfolk, and the priests who needed the fragrant perfumes for their rituals.

Since these were articles which did not exist at home, or only in small quantities, this trade did not worry the domestic producer. The stranger arriving with such merchandise was safe against violence and theft since he enjoyed the powerful protection of king and priests. Any act of theft would jeopardize the future journeys of the foreign traders. And what would the priests do in the temples then when there were no clouds of incense rising up during the ritual to glorify the deity? It was easy enough to induce the believers to make donations and pious contributions to be used for the purchase of the valuable incense. But how were the foreign merchants to be encouraged to come again unless they were assured of protection—and appropriate profit? Thus the merchants owed their first regular trade to the priests. Soon demand exceeded supplies from Southern Arabia. Merchants were compelled to travel farther afield and to seek new sources of resin, incense, and oils.

At the same time the demand for metals was growing. Copper was needed for weapons and vessels, gold and silver for ornaments—all of them metals rarely found in Egypt or Mesopotamia. Egypt mined its gold at a few sporadic locations in the desert east of the Nile and in Nubia. (The name of that country was derived from the Egyptian word *nob,* meaning gold.) But these deposits were soon inadequate. Copper supplies must have been more difficult still, until the discovery of the copper island of Cyprus. (*Kupros* is the Greek for copper.)

5. Sailors on the Nile

We know practically nothing about these first merchants; but we see how one island after another, one country after another, was engulfed by the rapidly swelling stream of trade. Byblos rose to power around the year 3000 B.C.; a few centuries later it was the turn of Cyprus. About the middle of the third millennium the Cretan civilization began to unfold; by the turn of the millennium it had spread as far as the Ægean Sea and led to the foundation of Troy in the strait leading to the Black Sea, and of Mycenæ on Greek soil. But the rise of Mycenæ did not begin until Crete had declined from the peak of its power—or should we say, its trade.

Rock-drawings dating back to the third millennium have been found on the island of Malta; these show ships which are quite unmistakably keel craft. All indications again point to the Eastern Mediterranean. About the end of the third millennium traders from the eastern Mediterranean must have discovered the Straits of Gibraltar and hence the exit from their limited sea. In Southern Spain, along the estuary of the Guadalquivir, an empire arose of which we have but vague reports from a much later date—the land of Tartessus. It was probably the rich copper deposits of this region which caused its rise to prosperity.

Not warriors but merchants forged the first trade links between the eastern and western Mediterranean. Besides, the inhabitants of the narrow coastal strip of Syria were not strong enough to maintain a fleet or numerous enough to found colonies—as later the Greeks did. Only when Assyrians and Babylonians, Egyptians and Persians, were pressing upon them did the inhabitants of the Syrian cities leave to settle in foreign lands.

How was it that the merchants could dare to travel to far-off countries inhabited by barbarians, by people who would receive any stranger landing on their coast with distrust, or who might even kill him as an enemy? The warrior relies on the power of his weapons. The shepherd knows how to defend his herd against wild beasts, and he can also defend it against enemies trying to steal the animals from him. When it is a case of gaining control of a watering-place urgently needed by his flock he will not ask whether he is entitled to it. Even the peasant is secure in his tenure not through law, but through custom and tradition, through the power of his village community. But any commercial transaction is first and foremost a legal transaction. There can be no trade without law.

The merchant sets out on his journey to foreign countries with a load of valuable merchandise; frequently others—friends, partners, or relations—may have entrusted to him wares to be sold on their behalf abroad. He has no wish to steal the possessions of others. If he were to resort to violence the inhabitants would instantly flee to their woods, swamps, and mountains, and nothing would induce them to display their own wares, to disclose the secrets of their country, to supply the desired metal ores or the precious amber.

The law is based on the principle that the stranger, too, enjoys protection. He may be of different blood, of different skin-colour, he may worship a different god or speak an unintelligible language.

Property is sacred. Promises must be honoured; obligations under-taken must be kept. If merchandise is accepted then the price asked by the owner must be paid. If no agreement can be reached the transaction cannot take place.

Herodotus, the Greek world traveller, reports at a much later date, the fifth century B.C., on how the "mute" trade on the African west coast was transacted—and no doubt things were similar at an earlier period in the western Mediterranean.

The Phœnicians did not converse with the shy and timid inhabitants of that inhospitable coast. They laid out their wares on the shore and returned on board their ships. Only then did the people come out of hiding; they inspected the goods closely and put down as much gold as they were prepared to give for them. Then they vanished into the bush. The following morning the Phœnicians once more disembarked and went on shore in order to see how much gold had been offered for their merchandise. If it was enough they took the gold and sailed away; if they were not satisfied they left the merchandise and the gold and again withdrew to their ships. During the night the natives came again, either to raise their offer—*i.e.,* to put down some more gold—or to take back the gold they had put down in the first place. It was now up to the strangers either to leave their wares for a little longer, waiting to see whether the people would put down once more the original quantity of gold or else to depart without any business having been transacted. "Never does one party deceive the other and take both gold and merchandise," the Greek historian records with astonishment.

It is interesting to speculate on how long it must have taken for this kind of trade to develop to a point where each party knew approximately what the other expected of him. And, no doubt, another long period of time elapsed before the local people dared to talk to the strangers direct, before they felt reasonably sure that they had indeed come with peaceful intentions, to engage in trade only and not in pillage. It is necessary to have faith in an order, in a law which guarantees advantage to both sides.

Byblos was much too weak to stand up to Egypt or Mesopotamia by force of arms. When its merchants travelled there they put themselves under the protection of these countries. They enjoyed only such protection as was granted to them voluntarily. It was, in fact, in Meso-potamia that the law was developed in a most remarkable way.

We have an inscription from the third millennium B.C.—an inscription by the King of Lagash, by name of Urukagina, which offers us a glimpse of this ancient civilization with its strongly developed sense of law and justice:

> Urukagina built the palace and the temple. Dug the canal, erected the wall. Since olden days the sailors lived on their ships, the herdsmen slept by their asses. The priests measured out the corn. The goodly fields of the gods provided the living and the place of pleasure of the King. The asses and fair cattle were seized by the priests. To the men of the King they distributed the corn, clothes, fabrics, and bronze vessels. In the orchard of the poor the priest seized the trees and took away the fruit. When a dead man was laid in his grave the priest took seven urns of beer for his drink and 420 loaves and 120 measures of corn for his food, a garment, a young kid, and a bed for himself.
>
> Urukagina restored the old rules. From the ships he removed the sailors, from the asses and sheep the herdsmen, from the corn the controllers of the storehouse. The payment of money that was made in the absence of a white sheep or lamb he stopped. Within the frontiers of his realm down to the sea there were no more controllers. When a dead man was laid in his grave the priest now took three urns of beer for his drink, 80 loaves for his food, a bed, and a young kid. In no place did the priest enter the orchard of the poor any longer. If a good ass is born to a subject of the King, and his superior says unto him: "I will buy it from thee," if he do buy, let the other say to him: "Pay thou with good money!" When the house of a great man is situated next to the house of a subject of the King, and the great man says: "I will buy it," if he do buy it, let the other say to him: "Pay thou with good money!"
>
> Urukagina spoke, and the children of Lagash he delivered from drought and theft and murder; he set up freedom for them. Neither to the orphan nor to the widow is any injustice done by the powerful any more.

Clearly and unambiguously the King here formulates the principle: payments and taxes are determined not arbitrarily by power, but by the law, and the protection of that law was undertaken by himself, even against the priests. The law stands above all considerations, social or divine; its order is subject to no other. It reposes on itself.

There are many social systems which do not acknowledge the law. They rest upon other principles: power, for instance. Such a society may be headed by a king, a chieftain, a priest, or a medicine-man. Everything is subject to his will; whatever he commands is supreme law. His arbitrary ruling continually refashions the order of precedence and the distribution of property. He takes whatever he likes for himself: if he wants to show favour to some one he gives him something regardless of whether this article has until then 'belonged' to him or to another—for this 'belonging,' in the sense of possession, does not represent a legal claim or private ownership. And the people silently bow to the command imposed upon them.

Or elsewhere the principle may be that all land is 'common property,' that the tools and means of production belong to the 'community' and that household equipment may be used by everybody. But there is no such thing as 'community'; even within the smallest circle, within the family, a certain order must rule. Hence a council of elders, or a ruler, apportions the land, tells the shepherd boy what task he has to do, and assigns the tools to the artisan. This order thus rests upon the wisdom and sense of justice of him who apportions all possessions, albeit for no more than a day or a few hours. Everybody else is dependent on him.

The right to the ownership of land and working tools, the right to dispose freely of one's own labour and time, is not tied to anybody's caprice but rests upon itself.

Could this 'law' be extended also to those who did not belong to the tribe, to the nation, to the subjects of the king—extended, that is, to men of other faith, to heathens and heretics, to men with different skin-colour and strange language? This was by no means a matter of course. Only slowly did mankind accept this proposition.

"Pay thou with good money!" the Sumerian King urged some 4500 years ago. It was thanks to this attitude that the Syrians were able to develop an extensive trade. The Syrian merchant felt secure even in Mesopotamia; he was protected by a law which applied equally to everybody. He need not fear that anyone, whether king, priest, or footpad, would seize his wares, expel him from the country, or even kill him.

Only gradually did this idea of law and justice gain ground. One and a half millenniums later the savage inhabitants of the Crimea, the Scythians in Tauris, still slaughtered every stranger who was driven by the winds to their inhospitable coast. In the Mediterranean, on the other hand, merchants met with a friendly welcome at a relatively early date. This is attested by finds from excavations in Crete. On this island magnificent palaces existed at a very early date, during the latter half of the third millennium B.C., but they appear to have had no fortified walls whatever. Their occupants clearly did not live in permanent fear of attack by robbers. Nobody attacked them.

The merchants themselves, naturally, had no thought of war. Any hostile action would have immediately scared off the Cretans. And that was not the purpose of their trade voyages. The inhabitants were to be encouraged to produce their wares, above all such eagerly sought-after metals as copper and, at a later date, tin.

Co-operation between Crete and the Asian mainland, in particular the Syrian coast—*i.e.,* Byblos—must have been entirely happy, scarcely interrupted by quarrel or war. A fleet of warships, superior to all others thanks to the keel construction, made the land secure against raids by barbarians. No adversary was a match for this fleet.

6. Numerals through 70 centuries

Sumerian cuneiform script: 1A: The "unit" (but also the symbol for 60). 1B: The "tens."

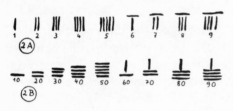

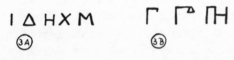

After 600 B.C. the Chinese used vertical and horizontal "bamboo" numerals. 2A: The digits. 2B: The "tens."

In Greece the Herodian numerals were in use after 600 B.C. 3A: The "units." 3B: The "fives."

4: In the sixth century A.D. the Arabs used numerals from which our modern Arabic numerals have evolved.

Gradually, however, the barbarians also learned how to build ships. They, too, had an ample supply of tree-trunks—powerful oaks which might well measure themselves against the cedars of Lebanon. The skill of metal-working, the smelting of copper, and the manufacture of bronze likewise began to spread; indeed, from the moment the barbarians manufactured weapons of iron they gained superiority over the inhabitants of the eastern Mediterranean.

Thus the "maritime people," as the Egyptians and Babylonians called the wild hordes, appeared off the coast—among them we can now identify Sards, the inhabitants of Sardinia, Sekelans, the inhabitants of Sicily, and the earliest Greeks.

The 'golden' age of the merchants was over, and the 'iron' age of the heroes was beginning. All that had been built up by long, laborious, peaceful efforts now collapsed. The barbarians enforced the exchange of goods by the sword. Ships in the Mediterranean were threatened on all sides. Piracy was rife. Massive castles were built on the seashore, made of huge stone blocks, in Greece (Mycenæ) and on the coast of Asia Minor, at Troy at the entrance to the Dardanelles, and on the Bosporus at the entrance to the Black Sea. The centre of gravity of commercial power began to shift towards Mycenæ and Asia Minor about the middle of the second millennium. Crete had to deliver presents or tribute to the King of Egypt, "consisting of bars of gold and silver, silver rings, baskets filled with lapis lazuli, ornamental vessels (including some shaped like the heads of lions, bulls, dogs, griffins, and goats) made of gold, silver, copper, and silver-gilt, chains of red and blue pearls, and daggers." We are then told that the nobles of Retenu (in Syria) and Kefti (in Crete) "carry upon their backs the gifts of wine, garments, cattle, and incense."

If the Pharaoh of Egypt now wanted copper from Cyprus, the country of Alaschia, he no longer sent merchants but his messengers to the local king, his 'brother,' requesting supplies.

No limit was set to the arbitrary power of the great rulers. If it suited them they could reply to a present with other presents, or they could express a wish for rare articles. Since they were not living by commerce they did not have to obey its laws, rules, and usages. Had the legacy of the Syrians thus been frittered away? Was there no one to succeed Crete?

South of Byblos two new cities sprang up—Tyre and Sidon, cities inhabited by a new nation of traders who did not use the sword to enforce tribute but sought, in the spirit of ancient Byblos, to engage in a peaceful exchange of merchandise. Protected by tall walls and by the sea, they were able to resist all passing hostile armies, while Ugarit, also known as Ras Shamra, one of the most important trading cities on the northern coast of Syria, had been pillaged and utterly destroyed by the wild warrior hordes of Phrygians and Mysians from Asia Minor. The trade route from the Mediterranean to the Euphrates thus shifted towards the south: it now led via Tadmor, later known as Palmyra, to the middle Euphrates.

The position of Tyre and Sidon was based on the far-flung network of mercantile bases and trade settlements situated along the shores of the Mediterranean, the Black Sea, and even the Atlantic. To exclude competition the Phœnicians kept their voyages and their knowledge of foreign countries a secret. Whenever they offered their merchandise there were goods from strange, unknown, mysterious countries surrounded by an aura of danger. Fabulous beasts were said to inhabit them, enough to scare off any stranger who might take it into his head to travel to these lands himself. It is therefore not possible to establish with complete certainty to what parts the Phœnician merchants did in fact penetrate.

That they were busy sailing to Tartessus in Southern Spain we know from the Bible. The proud ships of Tarshish were positive symptoms of overweening pride to the ancient Jews. It is almost certain that the Phœnician ships also penetrated to the "tin islands" in the Atlantic; whether these were in fact the British Isles or merely the Channel Islands is unknown.

From the Canary Isles they collected the lichen or the dragon-tree, a pigment vastly superior to the Tyrian purple from the murex shellfish and responsible for the particular brilliance of the Phœnician fabrics. Later the Canary Isles were entirely forgotten, so that the West had to rediscover them in the fourteenth century. The Romans still knew about them, and the Elder Pliny reports a voyage which King Juba of Mauritania organized to them.

The Azores were unknown to Greeks and Romans alike. Yet on one of the smaller islands of this group, the island of Corvo, Carthaginian coins have been found. This means that prior to the destruction of Carthage in the second century B.C. ships from the Mediterranean must have penetrated that far.

If, on the other hand, it was possible to sail from the Mediterranean to the Azores, the question arises of whether ships from the Old World were able at that time to travel right across the Atlantic to America. Many indications seem to point that way, but there is no evidence of any sort.

That the Phœnicians accomplished astonishing feats of navigation we know from casual mention by Greek and Roman authors. Herodotus reports that the Phœnicians had sailed, at the behest of the Pharaoh, through the Red Sea and all around the coast of Africa. But Herodotus refused to believe the account himself, especially as the Egyptians had claimed that during their westward voyage the sun had been on their right. Did this not run counter to all experience? Surely, if you sailed westward the sun would be on your left? But that, of course, is true only of the northern hemisphere. The very reasons which caused Herodotus to doubt the circumnavigation of Africa by the Phœnicians seem to us to confirm it.

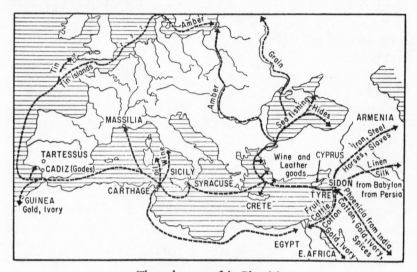

7. The trade routes of the Phœnicians

The extraordinary extent of the Phœnician trade in the first millennium B.C. is witnessed also by the words of the prophet Ezekiel:

O Tyrus, thou hast said, I am of perfect beauty. Thy borders are in the midst of the seas, thy builders have perfected thy beauty. They have made all thy ship boards of fir trees of Senir: they have taken cedars from Lebanon to make masts for thee. Of the oaks of Bashan have they made thine oars; the company of the Ashurites have made thy benches of ivory, brought out of the isles of Chittim. . . . All the ships of the sea with their mariners were in thee to occupy thy merchandise. . . . Tarshish was thy merchant by reason of the multitude of all kind of riches; with silver, iron, tin, and lead, they traded in thy fairs. . . . Syria was thy merchant by reason of the multitude of the wares of thy making: they occupied in thy fairs with emeralds, purple, and broidered work, and fine linen, and coral, and agate. Judah, and the land of Israel, they were thy merchants: they traded in thy market wheat of Minnith, and Pannag, and honey, and oil, and balm. Damascus was thy merchant in the multitude of the wares of thy making, for the multitude of all riches; in the wine of Helbon, and white wool. . . . The merchants of Sheba and Raamah, they were thy merchants: they occupied in thy fairs with chief of all spices, and with all precious stones, and gold. Haran, and Canneh, and Eden, the merchants of Sheba, Asshur, and Chilmad, were thy merchants. These were thy merchants in all sorts of things, in blue clothes, and broidered work, and in chests of rich apparel, bound with cords, and made of cedar, among thy merchandise. The ships of Tarshish did sing of thee in thy market: and thou wast replenished, and made very glorious in the midst of the seas. Thy rowers have brought thee into great waters.

3
Athens lives by its Grain Trade

———∿∿∿∿∿∿⦵∿∿∿∿∿———

AFTER A LONG and terrible war, and a military and political collapse unprecedented in Greece, the harbour of Athens, Piræus, slowly began to regain its former importance. Its external appearance had considerably changed since the days before the Peloponnesian Wars (431–404 B.C.). The famous "long walls," which had linked Athens with Piræus so that supplies for the capital were secure even in times of war, had been razed to the ground under the terms of the peace treaty with Sparta. Athens was not allowed to retain any 'allies.' It had lost its leadership of the Attic League. Since there was no longer an Athenian fleet in existence, pirates were lurking everywhere to capture the cargo of merchant ships and kill their crews or sell them into slavery. Many a respected Athenian met a pitiful end as a servant in a foreign land.

The merchants of Athens, however, sailed out in the face of all these dangers in order to import grain from the coastal cities on the Black Sea. Along the southern coast of what to-day is Russia the cultivation of grain had developed to such an extent during the preceding decades that vast quantities of wheat were exported from these granaries. Not only Greece, but the countries of the eastern Mediterranean lived off this wheat. One of these numerous "Black Sea sailors" was a certain Stratocles. Just before putting to sea he seems to have had doubts about the advisability of taking money across a sea made unsafe by pirates. In return for a suitable payment in Athens, the banker Pasion, who had evidently financed such grain purchases before, offered to give him a letter of credit for the distant land of the Scythians. This is the earliest

record of a banker prepared to finance far-reaching commercial transactions. Unfortunately, we have to confess that he was not a very
attractive character. Pasion was a *metoikos*—which means that he was
neither a slave nor a full citizen, but half-free. As he had risen from
lowly beginnings he possessed no fortune of his own. He depended
therefore on the brokerage of other people's capital. But as he was
scarcely known outside Athens, his name, of course, was not enough
for a letter of credit. Pasion, however, had a client who was pre-
eminently suited for such financial transactions—the son of Sopaios,
then the all-powerful minister of Satyros I, King of the Crimea, from
whose fertile fields the Greeks had been importing grain year after year
to fill the storehouses in the harbour of Piræus and feed the population
of their cities. Stratocles handed his money over to the son of Sopaios,
who was staying in Athens at the time; he, in turn, made out a payment
order to be honoured by Sopaios in Trebizond. Nowadays we would
say that the son had drawn a bill of exchange on his father. Armed
with this paper, Stratocles sailed for the Black Sea. No sooner had he
left Athens than disheartening news arrived at Piræus: Sopaios had
fallen into disgrace with his King. Wicked enemies had denigrated him
to his master, and Satyros had stripped him of all his honours and
offices and cast him into prison. At the same time Satyros had sent
messengers to his Pontine subjects in Athens, ordering them to
confiscate all monies from the son of Sopaios and to compel the young
man himself to return to the Crimea at once. In case the Athenians
should support the young stranger the King threatened diplomatic
measures. That was a tough language. Athens was anxious, following
its crushing defeat in the Peloponnesian War, to build up again the
foreign trade by which it lived. It possessed no fleet of warships which
might have ensured protection and lawful treatment for Athenian
merchants abroad; commerce, in the final analysis, depended on the
goodwill of one's business partners. Was Athens to court diplomatic
difficulties and strained relations for the sake of a young man?

All this caused the son of Sopaios a great deal of worry. But he found
a way out. He made over his money to the banker Pasion, and at the
same time confirmed in writing that he had no claims whatever on him,
and that he, Sopaios's son, was entirely destitute and of no means. At
most Pasion was to pay a trifling sum to the emissaries of the Crimean
King. The scheme appeared to work perfectly. The messengers

from the Pontus declared themselves satisfied with the banker's explanation.

They had hardly departed when the son of Sopaios demanded his money back from Pasion in order to travel hurriedly to Byzantium. It was then that the banker showed his true colours. He flatly denied having any of his money in safe keeping. He simply referred to the declaration which the young man himself had made before the Pontine emissaries in order to protect himself from prosecution. In the midst of the young man's desperate efforts to get his money back from the fraudulent banker glad tidings arrived from the Black Sea: King Satyros I had restored all his honours to his minister, as the accusations against him had proved to be unfounded. Sopaios's influence and power were greater than ever. At last his son was able to take steps against the treacherous Pasion. And the reason why we are so well informed about this lawsuit is that counsel for the plaintiff was none other than the famous orator Demosthenes.

The banker stubbornly refused to pay anything. He arranged for the slave Kittos, the only witness to his conversation with the young man, to disappear. How then was anybody going to prove that he had received any money? However, the skilful advocate succeeded in tracing the slave and making him give evidence. Pasion, cornered, declared himself prepared to repay the embezzled money, but asked to be permitted to do so secretly in Pontus so that nothing should leak out about it in Athens. Naturally he wanted to save his tarnished reputation as a businessman; or maybe his new move was again no more than the plot of a cunning rogue?

Agreement was reached, and King Satyros was appointed adjudicator. Pasion admitted his debt in writing and promised full repayment in the Pontine Kingdom. The document was to have been torn up the moment Pasion had paid up. In the event of his trying to evade payment King Satyros was to confiscate the banker's fortune in the Crimean Kingdom. His minister Sopaios, the creditor's father, was to see to it that Pasion was punished.

This important document was entrusted to a certain Pyron of Pherai, a man enjoying a great reputation as a Black Sea mariner; he was authorized to receive the repayment in the Pontine Kingdom. But even before he set out the document—allegedly so carefully kept—disappeared as if by magic. We do not know how the cunning debtor accomplished his trick; presumably he had hired somebody to steal the document. His subsequent conduct, at any rate, seems to point that way.

Once more Pasion thought he was out of the wood. He denied everything. Indeed he felt so sure of himself that, when the suit was resumed, he hit back vigorously at the plaintiff. He denounced the plaintiff, the son of Sopaios, as having engaged in illegal financial transactions in Athens. It was true that the Pontine citizen had repeatedly advanced money in respect of a shipload of freight and made an excellent profit from this business. Pasion now asserted that this ship had belonged to a man from Delos—and to lend Attic capital on ships from Delos was against the law. The Court had great difficulty in establishing the true state of affairs. When all these moves still proved of no avail the rogue Pasion turned to King Satyros himself— but the King would not hear of helping him. On the contrary, he summoned to himself all the Athenian masters of merchant ships who happened to be in the Crimea, or, as it was then called, the Kimmerian Bosporus, and instructed them to give what help they could to his subject in Athens. Moreover, he gave them a letter to the city of Athens, couched in similar terms. As far as we know, Pasion had to pay up in the end.

Sailing the seas was a great adventure, not only because the voyage was to strange countries but because the sea itself was swarming with pirates. The merchant Lykon, while voyaging from Piræus to Libya, was attacked by pirates at the very gates of Attica and so severely wounded by an arrow that he died in Argos. Another merchant, Nicostatos by name, was taken prisoner by an enemy warship, a trireme, during the same year, 370 B.C., while pursuing escaping slaves, and was himself sold into slavery until his brother Deinon later bought him free.

We also have information about a few particularly feared pirates. One report mentions a certain Alexander of Pheræ, an 'ally' of Thebes, who by a daring coup actually gained possession of the port of Athens, Piræus, even though only for a brief moment—but long enough to snatch up all the cash from the money-changers' tables.

How, then, was Athens to protect its merchants? For a war fleet of its own the city's modest means were insufficient, and allies were unreliable.

8. A Greek trireme

King Philip of Macedon was prepared to join in a struggle against the pirates, but the Athenians feared that the Macedonian officers were merely out to seize the most important islands along the trade route to the Pontus for their own King. After all, Athens lived by its grain trade; without it it would starve. Dare it put itself in the hands of an over-powerful neighbour? How well justified were these misgivings was shown before long when war broke out between Athens and Macedon. Then King Philip himself took part in the raids on the merchant ships. In the year 340 B.C. he succeeded in intercepting a fleet of Athenian merchant ships and warships at the Bosporus. One hundred and eighty vessels—according to other sources, even 230— fell into his hands, as well as 700 talents of silver, worth to-day nearly $1,400,000. The captured warships he had rebuilt as merchant ships, which again brought in good money. As the rapacious pirates were menacing commerce more and more, Athens was compelled to fortify Cape Sunium, on the south-eastern tip of Attica, in order to give some protection at least to ships leaving and arriving and to prevent an attack on the harbour of Piræus itself. There are also frequent references to convoys. In the year 362 B.C., for instance, the triarch (or admiral) Apollodorus was called to the Hellespont to take over a convoy of grain ships from the Black Sea, the Pontus Euxinus, the "hospitable sea." Off the city of Hieron he had to wait 45 days for the stragglers; he then escorted the ships as far as Sestos in the Dardanelles (on the Gallipoli peninsula).

There the fleet found new orders awaiting it: it was to protect the grain ships on their voyage to Maronia, on the southern coast of Thrace. In the Ægean Sea the great convoy from the Black Sea dispersed. New, smaller groups were formed, and these sailed from island to island, always in fear of capture by pirates. Ships from the ports of Asia Minor would find protection all along the coast in friendly cities; the Athenians, on the other hand, had to cross the sea. The real threat to them began at Cape Sunium.

As the coast of Thrace was the most dangerous part of the journey, the triarch Apollodorus ordered a few fast triremes (ships with three banks of oars) to escort the freighters to Styrne with their cargo of grain, and, if necessary, to tow them there. Since Maronia and Thasos had been contesting control of this little harbour for several years, the task was not without danger. The inhabitants of Maronia might only too easily capture the convoy since it must pass close by. And the Athenians, to make matters worse, had in their convoy a few ships from Thasos. Bad weather delayed the voyage; eventually the fleet was forced by gales to drop anchor off Styrne. Officers and sailors began to grumble because they had not been paid punctually. In the end the sailors melted away in order to enter mercenary service on shore or to be hired by the merchant shippers of neighbouring Maronia or Thasos, who were promising them not only high wages but a cash advance. Admiral Apollodorus was unable to do anything as he had no money on board. Moreover, his own appointment as triarch had long expired. About all this he sent an impassioned complaint home, asking help of his friend and lawyer, the well-known Demosthenes.

It is easy to imagine how anxious the merchants in Athens must have been about their freight when unfavourable winds or pirates detained the ships in some foreign port without any news getting through to Athens. And the courage that must have been necessary for a man to entrust his fortune to a captain sailing to uncertain foreign parts! In the year 400 B.C., when a merchant named Eraton died in Athens, his creditor filed an action for repayment of a loan to the sum of two talents, or what to-day would be $4200. True, some property had been mortgaged to him, but after his debtor's death this no longer seemed enough to him. He sued the debtor's heirs, demanding repayment of the debt in full. At great personal sacrifice they had to dispose of their entire remaining possessions.

Of the three sons of Eraton only one was then living in Athens. The other two were away on business voyages at the time of the lawsuit and only returned three years later, safe and well and with substantial sums of money. They now filed a suit for compensation against the over-anxious creditor who, they maintained, had forced their brother into unfavourable panic selling. They made the point that they were *emporoi*—i.e., merchants enjoying a privileged position and specific protection by the law against over-rash suits. The *emporos* was a merchant who carried his wares on board ships owned by others. A merchant who had his own ship and conducted his business by means of that ship, and hence as a rule travelled aboard it in order to buy and sell in foreign ports, was known as a *naukleros*.

In the fifth century B.C. the law used the term *naukleroi* only for the masters of ships. Subsequently the two terms began to be confused. The merchant who owned his ship continued to be referred to as an *emporos* on some occasions, but was always called *naukleros* when the emphasis was not on his trade but on his ownership of the vessel— i.e., his position as captain. The business of the *naukleros*, however, was not confined to the carriage of his own merchandise: he also transported goods belonging to others. According to another interpretation, the *naukleros* need not even be the owner of the ship, or even the captain or helmsman; he merely had to engage in commerce by means of a ship under his command. Such a *naukleros*, therefore, was not so much a merchant as a carrier, or forwarding agent, who might conduct his business also by means of chartered ships. His principal task consisted in taking on himself the very considerable transport risks and getting the ship with its cargo safely to its destination.

The news of King Philip of Macedon's victory over the Greeks in the battle of Chæronea (338 B.C.) caused great excitement in the island of Rhodes. The *emporoi* and *naukleroi*—i.e., merchants as well as ship-owners—hurriedly unloaded the grain they had just loaded for shipment to Athens, because they were afraid of its falling into the hands of the victorious Macedonians. Evidently the *naukleroi*, too, were responsible for the safety of the merchandise entrusted to them.

We have practically no records about the merchant families of Athens. The noble Athenians preferred to take up politics or philo-sophy rather than commerce, which in their hearts they despised. No wonder that the foreign trade was left to the slaves and the half-free. But as soon as these merchants engaged in lawsuits, the great gentlemen, the lawyers or politicians, were only too pleased to act for them, for these suits yielded fat fees for counsel. The law records and sentences which have come down to us represent the merchants less as entrepreneurs in charge of purchase and sale in foreign countries than as captains seeing their vessels with their valuable cargoes safely to their port of destination.

Having spent many years as a merchant on the seas then known, and having accumulated quite a nice fortune in the process, an old, experienced mariner would retire to somewhere near Piræus and decide to let his money work for him; he might lend it to others, maybe to young men whom he himself had trained. One such retired sea captain, Parmenides by name, was visited one day by Aparaturios, who wanted to borrow money from him. Aparaturios was in difficulties, because he had borrowed 40 minæ on his ship, and his impatient creditors were demanding it back at the very moment when he wanted to set sail. A political refugee from Byzantium, Parmenon, was prepared to lend him 10 minæ (about $336) provided the old captain Parmenides could find the balance of 30 minæ. As the ex-captain did not at that moment have this amount in ready money he persuaded the banker Heracleides to lend him the sum; Parmenides undertook to stand surety for it. Rather a complicated financial transaction—and, as we shall see, it came to grief.

First of all, Parmenon and Aparaturios quarrelled. Parmenon seemed to have greatly over-estimated his financial resources; in fact, he had scraped together a mere three minæ (no more than $112) which he was now furiously demanding back. The old captain came to the rescue, buying off the Byzantine and taking upon himself the entire debt of Aparaturios. Pending repayment of his 40 minæ he had the ownership of the vessel transferred to his name by contract. But even before the ship was able to leave harbour Heracleides's bank crashed. The cunning Aparaturios thereupon tried to sneak out of Athens quietly, complete with ship and crew. But Parmenides, the old seadog, had been on the look-out. He knew human nature, and no doubt had been disillusioned before.

He at once obtained a court order to have the fugitive crew arrested and the ship put on a chain. He next handed the vessel over to the creditors of the crashed bank as a lien for his pledge; the entire crew, composed apparently of slaves, were simply confiscated. The sale of the vessel by distraint produced 40 minæ, the exact amount of the captain's debt. Parmenides came off lightly, but the dishonest Aparaturios had lost a ship.

Business transactions in Piræus were at times rather complicated, and a good portion of psychology and shrewdness were necessary if one was not to be cheated by the numerous rogues. We must be careful, however, not to generalize from a few individual cases, or cast aspersions on the probity of the Athenian merchants. Records of lawsuits invariably present a one-sided picture; they do, however, provide an excellent glimpse of the everyday life and anxieties of the merchants of the time—and not only of that time.

Another point that stands out clearly from all these accounts is the tremendous importance which the Black Sea had gained for Greek trade by the fourth century B.C. A hundred years earlier, when the great traveller Herodotus of Halicarnassus visited those areas, the great agricultural transformation was just beginning. Cattle-breeding and fishing were being supplanted by arable farming; thus Herodotus still encountered tribes of horsemen who lived as nomads with their herds. In his day the Greek merchants' main import from the Sea of Azov— the Maiotis, as they called it—was fish. The salt which was obtained in summer by the evaporation of sea-water on the foreshore was used for pickling it on the spot. Indeed it was fishing and the fish trade that gave rise to the first Greek cities in Colchis, the land where Iphigenia was kept a prisoner during the Trojan war, pining away with nostalgia for her native Greece.

Herodotus also reports merchants travelling from the shores of the Black Sea as far as the Baltic in order to buy precious amber on the Samland coast, or eastward to the Altai, passing north of the Caspian, in order to bring back gold. His account is still a colourful mixture of fairy-tales, legends, reports but improperly understood, and factual accounts of travel adventures and trade relations in this strange world. We are told about those fabulous people, the Hyperboreans, who slept throughout six months (an echo, no doubt, of the knowledge that the polar night lasts six months) or about gigantic ants which dug the gold from the ground in Central Asia.

A century later vast areas along the Sea of Azov had been turned by the plough. The Pontus became Greece's granary. To a large extent it offset the grain imports which used to come from Sicily, but had ceased since the Peloponnesian War, in which Athens had tried in vain to capture the city of Syracuse, the centre of the Sicilian grain trade.

Carthage, that ancient Phœnician foundation (reputedly 814 B.C.), gradually became a dangerous rival to the Greeks' trade supremacy. During the war the Carthaginians succeeded in forcing the Greeks back from the western part of the Mediterranean and in blocking their passage through the Straits of Gibraltar, or, in the language of the day, past the Pillars of Hercules. Only the Carthaginians could sail out to the far islands in the Atlantic, to the Isles of the Blessed. Traders from the eastern Mediterranean were no longer able to call there.

9. Bronze tablet with Cypriot characters. Bronze tablet of Idalon
(After M. Schmidt, *Kyprische Inschriften*)

In the eastern Mediterranean the victories of Alexander the Great shifted the centre of gravity of commerce from the Greek mainland to Rhodes and Delos, those important islands in the Ægean, to Alexandria, Alexander's magnificent foundation in Egypt, and to Antioch on the Orontes in Northern Syria, immediately south of to-day's Alexandretta.

During the years after Alexander's death the island of Rhodes experienced an astonishing rise to power; it became the true hub of world trade. Whenever the later Greek geographers drew a world map they began by ruling two lines which intersected in Rhodes. One of them ran from the Pillars of Hercules along the Algerian coast via

Carthage to the southern tip of Sicily, and thence to the southern point
of the Peloponnesus and to Rhodes; from there it followed the southern
coast of Asia Minor and then ran, somewhat fancifully, along what
was said to be a continuation of the Taurus mountains across Mount
Elbrus to the Himalayas. The second line, also a little fancifully, came
up from the south along the course of the Nile—which was considerably stretched for the purpose—and ran via Alexandria to Rhodes and
thence along the Ægean coast of Asia Minor to Byzantium on the
Bosporus, to the Danube estuary, and across Russia to the Baltic—
the Russian rivers being all forced into a north–south direction, with
the Dnieper, then known as the Borysthenes, being made to follow the
meridian of Rhodes. These then were the co-ordinates of the known
world. And at their intersection, right at the centre, lay the port sought
out by heavily laden ships from all parts of the Mediterranean and the
Black Sea. The ships which the Rhodians built in their shipyards,
according to entirely new principles, were objects of amazement and
wonder among all seafarers of the day. But the Rhodians guarded their
secrets jealously; no stranger was allowed into their shipyards.

After Athens, Alexandria, and Pergamon, Rhodes was one of the
most beautiful cities of the Greek world, and moreover a centre of Greek
civilization. Rhodes at that time had three harbours, all of them artificially constructed. From the hills the city descended to the sea in the
shape of a fan, like an amphitheatre. It was girdled by walls on all sides,
even along the sea. From afar sailors would spot the enormous statue
of Helios, the famous Colossus of Rhodes, one of the Seven Wonders
of the World, which was destroyed by an earthquake. In the market,
the *deigma*, merchandise was exhibited from many foreign lands.

The ancient world frequently admired the method by which Rhodes
tried to solve its social problems. "The Rhodians," Strabo recorded,

> look after the *demos*, the people, although they are not ruled by them; they endeavour to
> ensure a livelihood for the masses of the poor. The people are therefore supplied with
> grain, and the prosperous support the needy as their forefathers did before them. Thus
> even the poor have enough to live on, and the city has its own requirements adequately
> satisfied, especially where shipping is concerned.

Rhodes owned considerable territory on the near-by Asian mainland,
and many a Greek city paid a large sum in order to enjoy the protection
of the powerful Rhodian fleet.

This centre of world trade was ruled by a relatively small group of old-established families—wealthy merchants, bankers, landowners, proprietors of shops, and officers of the fleet. The island's most important achievement, without any doubt, was the development of a law of the sea, based on Syrian and Phœnician models. It soon gained acceptance throughout the entire Mediterranean area. Even the Roman emperors still pronounced judgment in accordance with "the law of Rhodes."

Relations between Rhodes and Syria were particularly lively. There were many Syrians living in Rhodes; they played an important part in the island's trade, in the exchange of Eastern for Western merchandise. Amphoræ, those beautifully shaped pottery jugs for wine and oil, have been found in all the major trade-centres of the Hellenistic world—in Greece and in Asia Minor, in Egypt, Syria, and Palestine, as far as Seleucia on the Tigris, in Susa, Carthage, Southern Italy and Sicily, in Southern Russia and the western Black Sea ports, and even on the slopes of the Carpathians. The pattern of this trade and the composition of merchants and sea-captains had changed very little. Piracy, too, was much the same as before, even though the Rhodians maintained a considerable fleet to combat this menace. Besides, conditions were not much better in the western Mediterranean: merchant ships there were terrorized mainly by the Tyrrhenians, by which presumably is meant the Etruscans.

When one of the successors of Alexander the Great, the diadoch Demetrius Poliorcetes, the "destroyer of cities," as he was called by followers and enemies alike, attacked Rhodes he called upon all pirates in the Mediterranean to enter into his services. In return he promised them a considerable share in the loot of the merchant city. However, their hopes of rich booty were disappointed. The beleaguered city gallantly resisted all attacks.

Rhodes owed its rise to the *emporoi,* the import-export merchants of whom we know already from Athens. It was they who took upon themselves the risk of shipping valuable cargoes to all ports of the Mediterranean and the Black Sea; they were entitled to call on the fleet at any time, asking for convoy escort.

During his absence an *emporos* could not be sued in a court of law or sentenced; there were no restrictions on his leaving the country, and even in times of war he was allowed to move freely. An Athenian citizen, Leocrates, was accused of having left Athens secretly during the war against King Philip of Macedon, just before the decisive battle of Chæronea. This, the Public Prosecutor Lycurgus declared, was tantamount to desertion. Leocrates, however, pointed out that he had left the city in his capacity as a merchant, and that this right could not be denied to him. All that Lycurgus could say in reply was that Leocrates's name was not included in the list of merchants regularly using the port of Piræus. The lawsuits of *emporoi* were heard by special courts without delay; indeed, their entire activity was covered by special laws. At the same time, we find, rather surprisingly, that the business of an *emporos*, an import-export merchant, could be discharged by the half-free *metoikoi*, or even by slaves, who, as a result, gained special protection by law, whereas only full Attic citizens were allowed to engage in trade in the Athenian market.

We are faced here with a principle which runs through the whole history of commerce. For the long-distance trade—for the import and export of goods—the merchant, as an independent class, is indispensable. The sale of goods manufactured within the city, on the other hand, is the exclusive right of the manufacturers—*i.e.*, the artisans. Why indeed should a middleman be allowed to step in and profit from such transactions? The simple artisan, the tailor or the shoemaker, was clearly distrustful of the smooth, slick, cunning Syrian, who might lure his customer away from him.

In the import-export trade, on the other hand, the main emphasis is on the risk, on the pleasure of doing business, and on the prospect of fat profits. It needed courage to furnish a ship, load it at great expense, and then wait for months, and sometimes years, until the captain returned with ship and merchandise. Courage, too, to risk an entire fortune in such an enterprise. A merchant needed confidence in himself, in his abilities, and in his knowledge of people. And he had to enjoy the confidence of others to get them to lend him money, and that, moreover, under the restrictive conditions of marine loans.

Wherever these merchants appeared their competitors grumbled. But their customers received them with open arms. They were delighted to be able to buy goods which did not exist in their own country: foodstuffs and indispensable raw materials, jewellery and ornaments, and sweetly smelling perfumes. Moreover, they could get rid of their own surpluses at excellent prices. That was just what annoyed the local consumer, the man in the weekly market, for naturally the prices rose steeply the moment the foreign buyers appeared. Rulers and police viewed every stranger with great distrust, in case he was a spy of a foreign power, a disguised pirate on reconnaissance, the political agent of a neighbour country, or the emissary of a group of discontented exiles engaged in subversive activity against their own city.

The oldest records show us the foreign merchants living in special quarters. The Assyrian merchants in the Hittite Empire had to live outside the city walls, where they were at the mercy of an enemy. Before Alexander the Great conquered Egypt the Greeks there inhabited their own port—Naucratis—where they lived as a self-contained colony. It seems probable that the Syrian merchants had lived abroad under similar conditions for hundreds and perhaps thousands of years. It is even possible that the Jewish *ghetto*, into which the Jews moved voluntarily, goes back to these historical conditions rather than to the religious reasons usually adduced in explanation.

From the Black Sea the Greek merchants advanced across the Danube area as far as Northern Europe; they pushed into Western Asia, along the ancient trade routes and through Persia and the Indus valley into India and Central Asia. Presently they succeeded in finding the way through Egypt to the Red Sea, to the east coast of Africa, and even to India.

Caravans would set out from Antioch on the Orontes: they might not be seen again for months or even years, until one day they reappeared on the eastern frontiers of the immense empire. Until then they were regarded as missing.

As a result of this intensive commerce daily life in the Mediterranean area underwent considerable changes. Sugar from sugar-cane, which grew only in India, was unknown in Hellenistic times. For a sweetening agent honey was used, and for fermentation grape-sugar, palm-juice, or dates. Sugar as a food was hardly known. Even in Roman days sugar was still regarded as a medicine, as we know from Pliny. Yet sugar-cane was being cultivated at that time in Arabia, although it did not reach the Mediterranean zone until the late Middle Ages. From India came spices, in particular cinnamon and pepper, which were then definite luxuries.

In Ptolemaic times trade between the West and India was in the hands of the Arabs who acted as intermediaries; they simply did not allow any rival into the Erythræan Sea, to-day's Indian Ocean. If the Greeks wanted to deal directly with India and to bypass the obtrusive and expensive Arabs, they had to choose the land route from Antioch via Babylon and Persia into the Indus valley.

It was by way of India that two important plants came to the West— rice and cotton. Very ancient Chinese documents report that rice was planted by the emperor in person, so great was its importance as a national food. The Greeks first came to know rice in Alexander's campaigns. Not long afterwards we hear that it was being cultivated also in Mesopotamia and, a little later, in Syria. The historian Strabo saw it in Syria in the days of Augustus, but he knew nothing of it being planted in Egypt; on the other hand he reports it as being grown in the land of the Garamantes—*i.e.,* in Northern Africa, south of Carthage. Could the Phœnician merchants have brought it that far to the West?

The Greeks also made the acquaintance of cotton during the campaigns of Alexander the Great. According to our sources they met it in Bactria, or what to-day is Soviet Turkestan. Cotton used to be cultivated in the upper Indus valley at the time of the most ancient of Indian civilizations, around the third millennium B.C. To the inhabitants of Mesopotamia it remained unknown, although trade relations then existed between these areas. Admittedly, we find occasional mention in cuneiform inscriptions of "wool" growing on "trees," but this "cotton tree" was not related to our modern cotton plant; the fibre it yielded was very inferior. Nor was cotton known in ancient Egypt. At any rate, early Egyptian garments were made not of cotton but of linen.

The Greeks first planted cotton in the island of Tylos in the Persian Gulf; from there it spread rapidly through the greater part of the Hellenistic world. If we interpret Pliny correctly and if we are right in translating his word *byssus* by "cotton," the plant was cultivated even in Greece itself. However, it took several hundred years before the cultivation of cotton in Egypt reached a scale which made that country independent of imports from India.

Many kinds of fruit also came to us from the East in the train of Hellenistic commerce. The name *Citrus medica* shows that the Romans regarded the lemon as a fruit of the Medes—*i.e.,* of Persia. The orange was not introduced into the Mediterranean area until the victorious advance of the Arabs. The cherry had been known in Italy for several centuries, but it was the general Lucullus, a well-known gourmet, who introduced a particularly delicious variety of sweet black-heart cherry from the Pontus, where it was cultivated in orchards (64 B.C.). Many types of fruit which had long been known in their common variety were introduced in cultivated strains from Syria and Persia—the plum, for instance. The Elder Pliny, who lost his life in the eruption of Mount Vesuvius in A.D. 79, reports that the apricot, which came from Armenia, was being introduced into Rome just as he was writing his book. The peach, the *Malum persicum* or "Persian apple," was gaining ground in the Roman Empire at much the same time. Theophrastus made its acquaintance during Alexander's campaigns, but it was only Augustus who brought it back from Persia. It probably came originally from China. Pliny also reports that the Greeks in Alexander's army ate bananas while in India.

The Persians had been visiting the Indus valley long before Alexander; the Arabs had been sailing to India for thousands of years, even to Southern India, although at first only by hugging the coast. Yet neither of them had succeeded in trading the merchandise of those remote countries to any considerable extent; they confined themselves to occasional transactions. The regular movement of merchandise only started with the Greeks.

This Greek trade was no longer confined to luxuries, such as incense for the gods, unguents, perfumes and cosmetics for both men and women, indigo, spices for gourmets, pearls and precious stones, choice fabrics of cotton and, increasingly, silk. It was the Greeks who moulded Alexander's huge empire into one vast economic unit, even while it was falling apart into several separate kingdoms.

Megasthenes, the Greek Ambassador to the Court of King Chandragupta (321–296 B.C.), reports that the Indian customs administration had its headquarters in a special customs house by the great gate of Pataliputra on the Ganges. On the approach of a caravan four or five customs officials would rush out, and then carefully they would write down the quantities and origin of all merchandise, making sure that all articles bore a seal of origin. If these seals were broken, or if a customs official became suspicious for any other reason, a thorough investigation followed, leading frequently to heavy fines. A favourite practice, even at that time, was the confiscation of the articles in favour of the State, followed by their sale by auction to the highest bidder. There were heavy penalties for false customs declarations.

Both exports and imports were subject to heavy duties, designed to protect the domestic producer. Native articles could not be sold by merchants in their place of manufacture, lest the king should lose the revenue from customs duties. This ban applied only to merchants, not to artisans. As a rule, the customs duty was one-fifth of the value of the goods; for fruit, vegetables, seeds, dried fish, and dried meat it was only one-sixth, and for clothes, animals, grain, fats, and salt it was only one-twentieth. Quite apart from customs, the merchant's life was made increasingly difficult by a growing body of bureaucrats who interfered in everything and issued ever-new regulations. Strangers were treated with particular suspicion. They needed not only passports but special permits for every time they entered or left the country.

Yet once these trade relations with India had been well established, they were not swept away even by political troubles. India's wealth continued to attract the Greek merchants; these merchants, however, began to abandon the dangerous overland route which led from Broach, then the chief transhipment centre for merchandise from central Asia, via Pattala in the Indus delta, across the Persian Gulf to the estuary of the Euphrates, and thence upstream to Babylon.

The sea route was gaining in importance; this led from the Malabar Coast in Southern India across the Indian Ocean to the island of Socotra on the African coast, off the Gulf of Aden, and thence on to Aden (whose Greek name was Eudaimon) and Arabia, later to be called Arabia Felix by the Romans. Although there were numerous Indian merchants in the Ganges valley and the North-west, foreign trade in the Indian Ocean appears to have been chiefly in the hands of the Arabs until Roman times. Few Indian merchants seem to have joined the ranks of the bold mariners of those days, and much later still the Indians ventured out on to the sea only with great caution and deliberation. Even the Greek merchants who visited India in Hellenistic times and left us accounts of the land and its people remained exceptions until the Greeks discovered the secret of the monsoon. But this was only achieved by Hippalos about 100 B.C.

Egypt's chief export article in its trade with India continued to be linen, which was the only commodity accepted as payment for spices and cotton. The Arabs in Hadramut and on the northern coast of

Arabia, who acted as middlemen in this entire trade, firmly refused to buy any other articles.

From far distant regions only luxury goods were imported, such as spices, precious stones, delicate cotton fabrics, gold, ivory, and perfume; from the Sudan came frankincense and myrrh. In the Mediterranean, on the other hand, heavy freighters were carrying bulk cargoes—grain from the Crimea and from Egypt, some also from Sicily, copper from Cyprus, the Sinai peninsula, and even Spain, iron from Northern Asia Minor, mercury from Cappadocia, tin from England and Spain, partly by way of Carthage and partly by the land route through France, oil and honey from Syria, figs from Asia Minor, timber and

10. Etruscan ship, found in a tomb of the eighth to seventh century B.C.

pitch from the forests of Thrace, and wool from Lydia, Phrygia, and the western coast of Asia Minor.

We have a report of a merchant named Zenon importing vines from Chidus and Chios into Egypt—we have his receipt for 30,000 seedlings made out to another merchant. He cultivated oil-bearing plants, onions, leeks, lentils, sesame, the castor-oil plant, beans, peas, lupins, and even roses. Herodotus had reported that no vines were grown in Egypt and that all wine drunk on the Nile had to be imported. But now, thanks to this commerce, Egyptian agriculture had undergone considerable changes; the kingdom of the Pharaohs, formerly cut off on all sides, became part of that great economic system which comprised all the Hellenistic states, and indeed the entire Mediterranean and, beyond that, the whole world known to antiquity.

The North African trade was beginning to be transformed by the introduction of the camel, progressing gradually from Egypt towards the west of North Africa and rendering possible journeys by caravan across vast waterless deserts.

Everywhere we see traces of this flourishing trade: wine amphoræ from Rhodes, Cnidus, and Thasos have been found in Southern Russia and on the Nile, among the western Greeks in Sicily, in the South of France, and in Iran. Greece continued to live on grain from the Black Sea area. Whenever there was a hold-up in traffic through the Bosporus, or when Byzantium increased the passage dues for ships, the effects were instantly felt throughout the Greek world.

Ships were increasing in size. On the Nile they soon reached a displacement of 500–600 tons. Ptolemy IV owned a yacht of over 4000 tons, which contained not only vast dining-halls and a library, but even a gymnasium. Journeys were taking less time. From Alexandria to Rhodes a merchant would need only four days now, from there to Southern Russia another ten days, or up the Nile to the Sudan also ten days.

Owing to abundant supplies from all parts of the world the prices of the principal foodstuffs began to drop. Besides, peace had at last been established and piracy suppressed, so that marine transport risks, and hence the excessive freight rates, were greatly reduced. Whereas at the end of the fourth century the carriage of an article from Athens to Delos cost two drachmas, a generation later the same freight cost only half a drachma.

Egypt was supplying grain so cheaply that the small farmer in Greece was ruined. Since on his meagre native soil he could not possibly compete, he emigrated to the countries of Asia and to the Nile valley. Besides, wages went much further there than in Greece, simply because everything was so cheap. A workman on the Nile earned more than a scribe in Delos, and an office employee more than an architect in Athens.

But while Hellenistic commerce was spreading farther and farther, while the wealth and hence also the importance of merchants was increasing in the island of Rhodes and in the great ports of Antioch and Alexandria, a counter-movement designed to throttle trade had come into being.

The Greek conquerors had made the acquaintance of the Oriental

State with its all-powerful and arbitrary control of business and inter-traffic. The State, moreover, wanted the profits for itself. Even the kings who came from Greece, the successors of Alexander the Great, as well as their ministers and senior officials, presently began to partici-pate in commerce; they drew it into their sphere of influence, and eventually got it entirely under their control. Apollonius, for instance, a minister in Alexandria, dealt in iron, wool, oil, horses, and—needless to say—slaves. We know about this 'sideline' of the great gentleman because an employee of his—we might say his right-hand man—one Zenon, made use of his official journeys for engaging, alongside his official duties, in various private transactions, including quite a few on his own account—transactions of a similar variety to those of his minis-terial master.

Free trade was a thorn in the side of officialdom. Everywhere State monopolies were being set up—for the cultivation of oil-bearing plants, for the extraction of oil, and for its sale. Private trade was stifled by high taxes. There were taxes on slaves, on buildings, on turnover, and on inheritance. Duty had to be paid on the keeping of cattle, poultry, and even bees. To meet the requirements of the army free deliveries had to be made of cattle for slaughter, skins, and honey. Even urban crafts were taxed. Special licences were necessary for weaving, fishing, selling groceries, and making pottery; naturally, all these cost money. Manufacture and sale of oil, salt, flax, the fulling and dyeing of cloth, the kilning of bricks, the manufacture of glass and papyrus were all State monopolies, as was also trade in jewels, wine, lentils, cheese, spices, and sodium.

Local potentates and high officials moreover issued additional arbitrary ordinances which assured them of unlimited power in the economic sphere. Soldiers and officials acted on innumerable instances as entrepreneurs and merchants. They confiscated land and property, expropriated the workshops of artisans, accumulated large sums of money on their military campaigns or by shady deals, and took bribes. True, they lacked specialized knowledge, but for that they had highly qualified slaves to whom the management of their businesses could be entrusted.

Their only danger was free competition—but then what were laws and prohibitions for? The State regulated everything—the areas to be planted under oil-bearing crops and the size of fields; the State issued the seed-stock, and in the textile industry fixed all prices from the raw material to the finished article, limiting the profit margin of the middle-man. Without official permission the few free workers were not allowed to leave the place of work assigned to them. For an officially fixed wage they had to work in that place and nowhere else.

Foreign competition was kept out by high tariff walls. Even more effective were arbitrarily fixed prices for imported articles, which caused the merchants to lose all interest in such business.

Yet it was the Greek merchants who, in the first place, had welded the separate parts of the vast empire conquered by Alexander into one economic unit and who subsequently had held them together when Alexander's successors, the *diadochi,* tore the separate provinces apart and transformed them into independent kingdoms.

It was due to the merchants that everywhere the most favourable conditions of soil and climate were being utilized for the growing of grain, flax, and oil crops. They brought these crops to where they were wanted and were able to offer them anywhere at a reasonable price. Throughout the entire Hellenistic sphere the peasants were moving their homesteads to wherever they found more favourable living conditions. The Greeks were leaving their hard and stony soil and emigrating to the fertile Nile valley, to Syria, and to Mesopotamia.

Mysians and Phrygians in Asia Minor, Jews and Arabs, Iranians and Libyans, were likewise seized by this urge to travel. Countless foreign colonies arose in the Egyptian cities; we have knowledge of Bithynian and Cilician groups. There is occasional reference to the great wealth of the Jewish colony in Alexandria; at the beginning of our era the Jews there spoke Greek among themselves. The Syrian colonies, presumably, were no less rich and respected. The great majority of them were merchants who preferred to stay in the background lest they should arouse the envy of officials.

By then the states of the Hellenistic world were ruled by the soldiers, by the successors of the generals who, together with Alexander the Great, had conquered these rich lands of the Persian Empire and were now demanding their share in the huge booty. What did they know of the peaceful, unobtrusive work of free merchants? Accustomed to command, they believed that they could prescribe to the subjected nations their way of life and work. Free trade seemed unnecessary to them; they tried to supplant it by their bureaucratic apparatus. They did not notice that life was slowly grinding to a standstill, and that all enterprise was disappearing, and that the people were doing but reluctantly what they were ordered to do.

The frontiers of the individual states were closing, traffic across them ceased, the exchange of merchandise came to an end. True, riches continued to accumulate at the courts of the kings who, though of Greek origin, had become Orientals in their mode of living, but the broad masses of the population stood apart and aloof from political life. Rome met very little resistance.

4

The Fall of Rome

————~wwwwl/(O)/wwww————

IT WAS ANOTHER red-letter day in the island of Delos. Ships were arriving in endless succession, heavily laden with an unhappy cargo: human beings, slaves. Crowded together in a narrow space were thousands and tens of thousands, and still the sailing-boats and galleys were bringing further masses of humanity. Rome had won another victory.

Even to-day, after the horrors of the Second World War, when millions of people spent years in captivity or forced labour, we find it difficult to picture just what a Roman victory meant. In the train of the victorious Roman legions a wave of misery and human grief swept the land.

Prisoners of war had always gone into slavery. Whoever surrendered in battle forfeited his life. And slavery, at any rate, seemed preferable to death. Hannibal sold the Romans he had captured at the battle of Cannæ in the slave markets of the East. After Rome had won the Second Punic War most of them were bought back by their relations.

Rome had sold entire cities and nations into slavery. The whole population of the Greek trading city of Tarentum, some 30,000 human beings, were sold in the slave market in 209 B.C. When the renowned and wealthy trading cities of Capua and Syracuse were captured all the inhabitants were made slaves.

During the Second Macedonian War any leading figures not readily submitting themselves to the service of Rome were dispatched into slavery by the caravan load. Not only the Greek intelligentsia but the entire Macedonian nobility were thus sold into slavery. Rome condemned the whole nation of the Molossians in Epirus to slavery because they had dared to offer resistance. The inhabitants of 70 cities had to take the sad road to the slave markets. Twenty-two years later, when the Romans conquered Corinth, they destroyed the city and deprived all its inhabitants, some 140,000 people, of their freedom. In the same year, 146 B.C., Carthage fell; once again the victors sold the surviving population.

In his *Gallic War* Caesar reports that one-third of the young men of military age in Gaul lost their lives to the Roman sword and that a further third were sold into slavery. A large proportion of these slaves were bought and sold in Delos. For some time this island was dependent on Rhodes. But as the inhabitants had supplied food to the Macedonians, the enemies of Rome, the victors simply decided that the entire population must quit the island. Under Roman protection Delos thus became a free port, eminently suitable for this most pitiful of all forms of commerce. Revolting as this trade may seem to us, we must nevertheless take a closer look at the organization which made it possible to sell and ship such vast numbers of slaves in so short a time.

Clearly such large numbers of people could not possibly be kept on the island for any length of time without grave risk of famine and epidemics, which would be most detrimental to business. The ships which brought the unfortunates from the theatre of war to Delos thus had to leave port again as soon as possible, taking their human cargo to its destination.

Every Roman army was accompanied by several wholesale merchants, the *mangones*, who would buy up the booty of the soldiers, sort it, and dispatch it to Delos. To make the enterprise worth while the average price realized by a slave had to be the equivalent of $56 to $84; particularly valuable slaves, however, had to be picked out first and advertised separately. The greatest demand was for good cooks and—significantly—experienced merchants, who realized correspondingly high figures. The price paid for a beautiful young female slave could be as much as $672. 'Worthless' slaves had to be sold at a cut price of no more than $8.40.

From these figures it is easy to calculate that the capture of a city of 10,000—quite apart from the treasures seized during the looting and from the land and property distributed among the soldiers or sold by auction—would yield something like $280,000 from the sale of human beings alone. No wonder that the Roman wars began to assume the character of vast slave hunts. No general would set out without surrounding himself first with slave merchants who made him firm offers for the booty to be expected. Each victory meant great sums of money with which all the debts incurred earlier could easily be redeemed. Thus the impoverished Roman landed gentry, who until recently had tilled their own fields, became a wealthy class within a few decades.

The Romans did not suspect at that time that this disastrous slave policy would do them a great deal of harm in the future. Their entire politics came to be dependent, to a certain extent, on the slave traders. It was they who advanced money for expensive wars and who insisted on the wars being waged ruthlessly, in a way that would break the will of the enemy nation to resist. After all, they could make profits only if the generals mercilessly turned the vanquished into slaves. The great gentlemen, who did not look beyond their attractive profits, evidently did not realize this at first.

The slave trade was only able to achieve such huge profits because its 'merchandise' was available at such incomparably low prices. So long as Rome waged its wars as definite wars of conquest and depredation, so long as it burst into wealthy and flourishing kingdoms and seized their treasures to finance its own war effort, the campaigns yielded a good profit. The prisoners taken in open battle were not nearly numerous enough to meet the costs of the extensive organization connected with the slave trade in Delos. Entire nations had to be enslaved to assure the soldiers of sufficient revenue.

At first glance the enslavement of a whole nation or even a major city might seem impossible. Of course, the vigorous young men, the women, and the girls were sold easily enough; but who wanted to acquire the aged and the infirm, the sick and the children? They represented a great financial burden which, in normal times, would be borne by the community. For the slave trader who acquired an entire population wholesale, there was only one possibility—ruthlessly to pick out from the multitude of human beings those who would achieve a price above average. The remaining population had to be discarded before new expenses were incurred.

After the destruction of Corinth in 146 B.C. its territory was given away as presents or declared *ager publicus*—*i.e.,* property of the Roman State. How, then, were the unfortunate people who had been released again as unsuitable by the slave traders to make a living?

Even more frightful was the fate of the slaves. Manacled and branded, they were shipped from Delos to Italy, to the great estates with their appalling slave barracks, the *ergastula.*

Not all slaves had to do hard physical work; not all of them died miserably in the slave barracks. A proportion of them, no doubt numerically small but none the less of great importance, were made to take up responsible managerial posts on estates, in enterprises, and in offices—activities for which their masters lacked the time or perhaps even the ability.

Roman senators and generals acquired huge fortunes within a short span of time. Caesar became one of the richest men in Rome as a result of his victories in Gaul; his officers and officials acquired enormous fortunes, and even his soldiers returned with very considerable treasure. The looting of Celtic temples caused Rome to be so flooded with gold that a pound of it with a currency value of $504 was offered for sale for 3000 sestertii ($22.40). The rich booty made by the soldiers in Asia Minor brought them even greater profit. What could they do with all that money?

They looked for suitable bailiffs or men of business. That was why slave traders had a standing order to discover experienced and clever merchants who might be entrusted with the management of these enormous fortunes. Naturally, this wrought a complete change in the whole merchant class, not only in Italy but throughout the Mediterranean area. As all money, all power, and all trade was accumulating in the hands of a few Roman magnates, people as a rule with no commercial experience and but indifferent education, all business came to be in the hands of slaves.

The Roman master would give his slaves his instructions, threatening severe punishment for any mistake or failure. He himself had no understanding of business matters—but had he not purchased an expensive slave who had been recommended to him as an experienced merchant from Corinth, Athens, Rhodes, or Tyre? If anything went wrong it could only be because of the carelessness, laziness, negligence, or malice of his slave. A Roman citizen was free to have an insubordinate or incapable slave flogged or even killed. And under such constant threats the unfortunate slave was expected to conduct complicated business!

Many of them, a great many, failed. They had never been consulted; they had had no say when they had been sold at a high price as possessing heaven-knew-what qualifications. They were faced with insoluble problems. In the end they would be banished to some estate in the country to end their days pitifully in the *ergastula*. Others succeeded them, and others still, until at last a man would be found who measured up to his master's requirements. Frequently, no doubt, this was due not so much to his business ability as to his skill in making himself indispensable to his master.

Such a slave would then propose risky transactions, promising great profit—such as exports to some new province—which would depend entirely on his own specialized knowledge. Once the proprietor had committed himself to such business he was to a large extent dependent on his slave. Naturally, he could have him flogged or even killed, but that would not get him anywhere. On the other hand, if everything went well, the slave's master could earn a multiple of what the slave had originally cost him in Delos. Presently he would wish to engage in further, even more extensive transactions. He would offer the slave his freedom, or he would make over to him part of his own huge fortune on credit or for administration. Thus began the rise of the disenfranchised towards freedom, social standing, wealth, and, ultimately, unlimited power. And these were by no means isolated instances.

Anyone who knew his way about Rome tried first of all to gain the favour of the imperial chancellery—staffed entirely by slaves—by means of presents, flattery, or the right go-betweens. Whatever was suppressed in the chancellery would not come to the Emperor's ears. This was well known even to otherwise powerful and influential senators and officers. And what applied to the imperial chancellery applied in many another case. After all, what was a simple soldier, or even a cunning politician, to do with the fortune which fell to him unexpectedly when his army had won a victory, when his party had come to power, when a profitable governor's post was offered to him? He simply bought a slave who was used to handling large fortunes; to him he left the management of his affairs, possibly with the threat of having him crucified if there was the slightest embezzlement.

In the first century A.D., when Augustus came to the throne, Rome was practically ruled by slaves. Everywhere slaves sat in influential posts, naturally not in their own names but on behalf of their masters, who neither wished nor knew how to discharge these functions themselves. Maybe the ultimate decisions were still those of their masters who may have insisted on having the last word. But in fact business had become far too involved for any individual to gain an intelligent grasp of it at a single quick glance.

Why did not the Roman magnates choose their collaborators from among the free citizens of Rome? Until the end of the third century Rome was a purely agrarian country, with trade playing but a subordinate part. When wealth began to flow in it was far simpler to buy a good, experienced slave to manage the troublesome business of finance. Moreover, senators were precluded by law from engaging in any form of trade or commerce. Men who did not wish to stay on their country estates but wanted to make a career in the State would choose the way through the army, through politics, or through the senior civil service.

Small farmsteads began to be supplanted by enormous estates worked by slaves. These, very sensibly, made no attempt to compete with the great grain-producing areas of Sicily, Egypt, or the Black Sea zone. Instead they went in for oil and wine—export articles in great demand. Campania, in particular, soon became the main supplier of these goods, which were exported to the conquered provinces of Spain and Gaul. Slaves were also engaged in crafts on a considerable scale, mainly in building, pottery, tailoring, and various luxury trades.

The entrepreneurs, the employers of these artisans, bore Roman names; mostly they were senators of ancient line. But in their households they employed thousands of slaves. The pottery manufactories of Arretium, present-day Arezzo, employed sometimes as many as 40 slaves—craftsmen who had brought this art, native in Greece and Asia Minor, with them to the West. One of these artists was a slave from Asia Minor, Brygus, who had taken his name from his people, the Brygians. Nowadays a vase signed by Brygus fetches a very high price.

The ultimate aim in a slave's life, no doubt, was to be set free. The most capable and intelligent achieved this aim, and so, frequently, did the most ruthless and the most cunning. We have a *stele*, a gravestone, from Capua from the first century B.C. It shows a naked man standing on a stone base. From the left a man in Greek clothes approaches, clearly pointing to him. On the right, in dignified attitude, stands a Roman in his toga, calmly extending his right arm towards him. On this *stele* Publilius Satur had perpetuated the darkest hour of his life, when, stripped to the skin, he was sold as a slave. He was later set free, as emerges from the inscription, by his master, Publilius Stephanus; from modest beginnings in Capua the enfranchised slave had risen to wealth and great renown. Where had he come from originally? Clearly he owed his first name to his former master; his second name, Satur, might easily have been assumed later. How many such freedmen, enfranchised slaves, were living in rich Campania at the beginning of our era? How great was their influence? To what extent did they

11. Shop-sign of a coppersmith in Pompeii

develop the new agriculture, the urban crafts, or the trade in choice export articles?

An example of this type of man is Trimalchio, the character described by the wealthy and witty Petronius in his *Satyricon*. Petronius, the sybaritic friend of Nero, the "arbiter of elegance," or fashion-king of the capital, certainly knew more than just one man of this type. This is how Trimalchio boasts to his dinner guests about his experiences in the port of Puteoli, the import harbour of Rome:

I was once just what you are, but by my own merits I have come to this. A bit of sound sense is what makes men; the rest is all rubbish. I buy well and sell well: some people will tell you differently. I am bursting with happiness. . . . As I was just saying, self-denial has brought me into this fortune. When I came from Asia I was about as tall as this candle-stick. In fact I used to measure myself by it every day. . . . Still, I was my

master's favourite for 14 years. . . . Then, as the gods willed, I became the real master of
the house, and simply had his brains in my pocket. I need only add that I was joint
residuary legatee with Caesar, and came into an estate fit for a senator. But no one is
satisfied with nothing. I conceived a passion for business. I will not keep you a moment
—I built five ships, got a cargo of wine—which was worth its weight in gold at the time
—and sent them to Rome. You may think it was a put-up job; every one was wrecked,
truth and no fairy-tales. Neptune gulped down thirty million in one day. Do you
think I lost heart? Lord no, I no more tasted my loss than if nothing had happened. I
built some more, bigger, better, and more expensive, so that no one could say I was not a
brave man. You know, a huge ship has a certain security about her. I got another cargo
of wine, bacon, beans, perfumes, and slaves. My wife did a noble thing at that time; she
sold all her jewellery and all her clothes, and put a hundred gold pieces into my hand.
They were the leaven of my fortune. What the gods wish soon happens. I made a
clear ten million on one voyage. I at once bought up all the estates which had belonged
to my patron. I built a house and bought slaves and cattle; whatever I touched grew
like a honey-comb. When I came to have more than the whole revenues of my own
country, I threw up the game: I retired from active work and began to finance freedmen. . . . Meanwhile I built this house. . . . As you know, it was a tiny place; now it
is a palace. It has four dining-rooms, 20 bedrooms, two marble colonnades, an upstairs
dining-room, a bedroom where I sleep myself, an excellent room for the porter; there is
plenty of spare room for guests. . . . Take my word for it; if you have a penny, that is
what you are worth; by what a man hath shall he be reckoned. So your friend who was
once a worm is now a king.

Trimalchio was not an isolated case either in Rome or in the western
Mediterranean area as a whole. Among the proud Romans who would
not lower themselves to engage in trade, the smooth, quick-witted,
experienced, and daring Orientals were bound to rise to the top. And
were things different in the East?

Rome had granted full Roman citizens' rights to many Greek cities,
even if their inhabitants were not Greeks but Orientals. The best-
known instance is that of the Apostle Paul, the son of a citizen of
Tarsus, on the south-east coast of Asia Minor, who was a devout Jew
and a Roman citizen.

There were large Jewish communities in nearly all the trading cities
of the Mediterranean area, particularly in Alexandria and Antioch.
These people were by no means all descended from the Jewish people,
but included many who had adopted the Jewish faith.

Thus we see a strange stratum of people, former slaves and the sub-
jugated inhabitants of Rome's Asian provinces, controlling the trade
and presently the entire economic life of the Roman Empire. The Elder
Pliny complains that the *latifundia,* the vast estates, had ruined Italy.

But he overlooks the great social strains and stresses between the new class and the Roman State which had practically surrendered to it the nation's economic life.

The whole pattern of the Mediterranean area had been extensively changed by the new businessmen. The great estates switched over to the production of oil and wine, exported at first to the conquered provinces in the West. Presently, the olive and the vine were being planted also in Spain and Southern France—here and there even in Northern Gaul and Germany. The Elder Pliny reports that olive-oil had become the principal export of the Iberian peninsula. In his day the oil from Venafrum, in Italy, was still regarded as the best in the entire Mediterranean area, but soon it was excelled by that from Bætica —what is now Andalusia. On the fragments of clay vessels, which to this day form an entire mountain in Rome, the Monte Testaccio, we find innumerable Spanish seals. A considerable part of them come from the imperial vineyards of Tarraco, present-day Tarragona.

This trade with Spain, and later also with Southern Gaul, eventually ruined the Roman peasants just as it did the big Roman estates. People in the provinces just worked harder and for less money than those in the neighbourhood of the capital, where huge food subsidies encouraged idleness. Before long, however, a shortage of bread grain was beginning to make itself felt; Southern Russia, one of the principal granaries of the Old World, had been lost to it when hosts of Asian horsemen pushed the Scythians back from the eastern steppe.

In the first century A.D. grain exports from Sicily and Egypt declined considerably and eventually ceased altogether. Yet at the same time, the population of the Roman Empire had greatly increased, especially in the western provinces; that of Spain had doubled between 50 B.C. and A.D. 150, and much the same was true of Gaul. Italy, in the meantime, was being depopulated.

The Roman peasants had simply begun to emigrate to the conquered provinces where they could occupy a privileged position, acquire land cheaply, and get rich quickly, thanks to their experience in the cultivation of the vine and the olive—always on condition that their produce could be exported. And that depended on transport. In Spain Gades, present-day Cadiz, on the Atlantic coast, became the biggest, and no doubt also the richest, city.

Money now became the decisive key to a social career. Membership in the Senate, previously confined to the Roman aristocracy, became subject to a 'census,' a kind of means test, in the amount of 250,000 denarii. If a person became poor he was eliminated. On the other hand, new men rose to membership; before long even the sons of freed slaves were permitted to become senators provided they owned the necessary fortune. Admittedly, this kind of rise was rare; it was still apt to arouse public disapproval, and, what was more important, membership in the Senate would cut off the upstart from the sources of his wealth since senators were precluded from engaging in trade. On the one hand, money was everything and its influence unlimited; on the other, the acquisition of money by way of commerce, indeed by any business activity, was forbidden to senators and generally looked down upon. Thus Roman society was divided into two sections—on the one side were the officials, senators, and soldiers, on the other stood the merchants, the bankers, and the industrialists. A dangerous split of society! Moreover, the days when only soldiers could rise to wealth were beginning to come to an end.

Since the period of great conquests had ended, soldiers were no longer able to acquire rich booty of gold, silver, and slaves; hence they could not easily accumulate a big fortune. Instead, trade began to develop. First it transformed Campania, and then Spain, Gaul, and Africa, into flourishing provinces. It brought wealth to Egypt. But soon the picture began to change.

The decline did not start in the East, nor at the threatened frontiers on Rhine and Danube, but in Spain, in the very province which had suffered least under big landowners or under incursions by barbarians. Yet from the middle of the second century onward complaints became more and more frequent about the decline first of the Spanish cities and later of the countryside. What was happening?

Unfortunately, the Roman historians have left us far more information about conditions in Egypt and in Asia than about those in Spain, Gaul, or even Britain, although surely the western provinces were among the most important at the time. Indeed, the Emperor Hadrian (117–138), under whom the Roman Empire attained its greatest territorial extent, was a native of Spain.

In order to provide a reliable administration for this vast Empire Hadrian built up an apparatus of officials drawn, significantly enough, from the class of freedmen, or emancipated slaves. Not the representative of the Emperor or the Roman Governor, but officials employed by the State now tried lawsuits, managed the great estates, and controlled public life. In effect, this reorganization marked the final victory of the freedmen—*i.e.*, the former slaves.

Without over-exaggeration this social transformation might be formulated as follows: anyone wishing to make a career for himself in the Roman Empire had to have a slave among his ancestors. This meant that he could scarcely have been a genuine Roman any longer. In our histories of the Roman Empire we read a lot about the infiltration of Rome by nations from the East, about the influence of Eastern religions even among the Roman legions on the Rhine and the Danube, and about the key rôle played in Rome's economic life by Syrians, Egyptians, and above all Jews; all this can be explained quite simply by the positions held in the administrative apparatus by emancipated former slaves.

Hadrian's reforms meant the victory of the merchants over the soldiers and landowners. Naturally, the Emperor and the public were unaware of this aspect; to them the reorganization was merely the codification of a state of affairs already existing. For a couple of centuries the great gentlemen in Rome had been content to have their business affairs run by their slaves or manumitted slaves. They themselves knew nothing of trade or commerce, or money matters generally; they had no wish to understand these matters nor were they allowed to. But of course they wanted to make money, to get rich, and to get rich quickly. That was what they had their slaves for—the slaves they had bought with their newly gained money.

The old word for merchant, 'chapman,' is derived from Latin *caupo*—the proprietor of a wine tavern, who also traded in the local produce. In the eyes of Roman law this *caupo* was invariably a cheat, a man out to fleece his guests, especially when the tavern comprised an inn or a hostel. The *caupo* was liable for all losses; if anything disappeared it was assumed—in the eyes of Roman justice—that it must be the doing of the fraudulent *caupo*. Even if he was innocent it would not hurt him to have to pay up for the lost article. Let him be more watchful next time!

Ranking high above this despised merchant were the soldier, the landowner, the politician, the senior official. They ruled in Rome, they were responsible for the welfare of the Empire, yet they did not suspect that its prosperity depended on trade. On the contrary. They merely saw the free interchange of merchandise within the huge Empire as an economic threat to Italy herself. Italian agriculture and Italian artisans could not compete with the cheap products from the provinces. To eliminate this competition Rome made special laws.

As early as the first century, the Emperor Domitian (81–96) had tried to cut down on wine and oil production in Spain and Southern France. Trajan (98–117) decreed that all senators must invest money in Italian agriculture. This did not help much; even in Italy the cultivation of the vine and the olive had to be reduced. Growing of wheat was encouraged instead. Imports from the provinces were quite simply cut by law. Inevitably, prices rose as a result. And, as the cultivation of wheat required fewer people than the tending of vineyards and olive-groves, the unemployed countrymen began to flock to the big cities in the hope of finding work—unless, as in Rome, they could be fed generously by the emperors without doing any work at all. The free peasants were now in the majority, and even the great estates could no longer manage without free agricultural workers.

The emperors viewed this drift from the country with displeasure and anxiety. They saw the rural areas getting depopulated and the cities getting crowded; they saw the lengthening queues in front of the *annona*, the State food-issuing office for the unemployed. Who was responsible for this unfortunate state of affairs? The merchants, of course! They imported cheap goods from the provinces in order to make profits. They were underbidding the hard-working peasants, merely because somewhere else the sun shone longer, the fields yielded more generously, or the people lived more modestly.

Agriculture was declining from bad to worse while the merchants were getting richer. The reforms of the Emperor Hadrian, the last great "augmentor of the empire," marked the beginning of the disastrous trend which led eventually to the total suppression of the independent merchant. Hadrian wanted to eliminate the middleman wherever possible and to bring together the consumer with the producer. The imperial officials were to see to it that property was distributed 'justly' within the Empire.

At first these imperial decrees were not too stringent. The Empire was still prosperous; everywhere the exchange of goods between the provinces had created new wealth. The State was still in a position to pay out the sums it was exacting from the merchants, but nevertheless the road to disaster had been embarked upon. Once the barbarians' assaults on the frontiers of the Empire became more violent, once incapable emperors such as Commodus and Caracalla started to wreck the internal structure of the State by their extravagance and their ruthless persecution of political opponents, the merchants had to bear the entire burden of the wars.

The Emperor ordered them to be organized in compulsory guilds; precise lists of obligatory deliveries, to be made without payment, were drawn up and imposed on them. Let those hard-boiled rogues—Syrians, Aramæans, and Jews—see how they got their money; let them

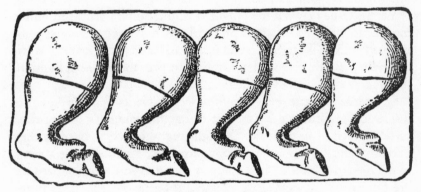

12. Shop-sign of a butcher, Pompeii

squeeze it out of their customers just as the Emperor was squeezing it out of them!

When the Romans were engaged in war on the lower Danube the local prefect simply summoned the merchants of the neighbouring province and issued the following order: "By a certain date so many thousand bushels of wheat, so many thousand horses, and so many carts must be available in Thrace." Complaints and lamentations were of no avail. Soldiers do not recognize the word "impossible." Unless the merchants made their deliveries punctually, not only would their entire fortunes be forfeit to the State, but the indignant Emperor would have them all crucified! And the miracle happened. On the appointed date the supplies necessary for the campaign were duly delivered.

Once or twice the merchants stood for this, biting back their anger.

Then they concluded that they were in the wrong business. They urgently advised their sons to choose a different livelihood. They would try to buy them a nice estate, as far away from their old place of residence as possible, far from the extortions of imperial officials. The merchant class began to melt away.

The emperors tried to check this trend by holding the merchant guilds responsible. The merchant's occupation, as all other professions, was declared hereditary. A son was compelled to succeed to his father's business, whether he wished to or not. But this did not stop the rot. Nobody wanted to take on any office; the rich people fled; the merchant class broke up. Its place was being taken by State officials or unscrupulous speculators.

Yet the trade between the provinces of the Empire depended on the merchants. Italy had risen to prosperity by exporting wine and oil—primarily olive-oil—to Spain and Gaul, and even to the Eastern Mediterranean. But this required a merchant to plan the business, build up the organization, and carry the risk.

So long as the State received compulsory deliveries from the provinces it was able to distribute free food in Rome; for doing that it needed no merchants. But the agricultural producing units which lived by their overseas trade, by exporting to other provinces, declined in the absence of the merchant class. Their output was not even enough to feed the great cities in their immediate vicinity. As a result, these cities began to be depopulated about the end of the second century, even in such provinces as Spain and Southern Gaul, which did not suffer from barbarian invasions. The State began to notice a drop in tax revenue.

Taxes in the Roman Empire were collected not from the taxpayers—for that the State lacked the necessary machinery—but by tax farmers who, in return, enjoyed certain privileges. In the case of conquered and subjected provinces this system might have been justifiable; but once all provinces had been given Roman citizenship rights the method of tax collection had to be reorganized. The emperors therefore decreed that henceforth the municipalities were to be responsible for the payment of taxes—in other words, the rich people, who had accepted honorary office, were made liable, with their own fortune and even their lives, for the payment of all taxes.

After all, it was argued, the merchants were merely advancing the money which they could always recover subsequently from the peasants in their capacity of tax farmers. Besides they were making such vast profits from deliveries and commerce! Let them collect the taxes throughout the land! When in fact their servants appeared on the farmsteads to drive off the livestock or impound the crops needed for the imperial armies or for supplying the cities, the oppressed began to resist. There were peasant revolts, such as the one in Egypt in A.D. 172, when Alexandria was very nearly looted, or one in Gaul, when the city of Alesia was burnt to the ground. The rich people—*i.e.*, mainly the merchants in the cities—were finding it more and more difficult to pass on to the countryside the tax expenditure incurred by them. In the end they had to dip into their own pockets.

Soon there were scarcely any merchants left. True, small merchants, the *caupones*, would still travel from place to place, or even settle down to open an inn. But they lacked the decisive prerequisites of the wholesale merchants: knowledge of a wide range of merchandise, a grasp of the market situation, extensive organization, and, above all, capital.

More and more frequently do we encounter complaints that there are no public-spirited people left. Nobody was prepared to take on honorary posts in municipal administration. Compulsion had to be used to find men for civil office.

The change was clearly felt in the cities. The urban artisans lacked a sufficient market because exports to distant provinces were declining, and simultaneously imports from farther afield were arriving less frequently. Admittedly, supplies were still coming in from the surrounding countryside, but no foodstuffs or raw materials from more distant sources. Goods were becoming shorter and prices were rising. By the end of the second century famine was threatening even those provinces which only a few centuries before had been so rich—Egypt, Sicily, and North Africa. To some extent the higher prices were due to a devaluation of the currency. While Marcus Aurelius had adulterated his silver coinage by a 30 per cent. addition of base metal, under Septimius Severus (193–211) this admixture rose to 50 per cent. The nations north of the *limes* no longer accepted silver coins, but demanded gold. The one class which could have reunited the severed ties between the separate provinces, and between town and countryside, no longer existed.

"Nobody shall have any money except myself and my soldiers," the Emperor Caracalla (211–217) is reported to have said. While an

13. Trade routes of the Roman Empire

enormous fortune accumulated in his hands Rome's currency collapsed.

No man was permitted to choose his career freely; a son had to succeed his father. Above all, the sons of the *curiales*, the city fathers, were not allowed to seek safety elsewhere. They had to be responsible, as their fathers had been before them, for the extortionate taxes. And still the taxes rose.

Without commerce the entire Empire crumbled. It was easy enough for the soldiers to confiscate the property of political opponents or to

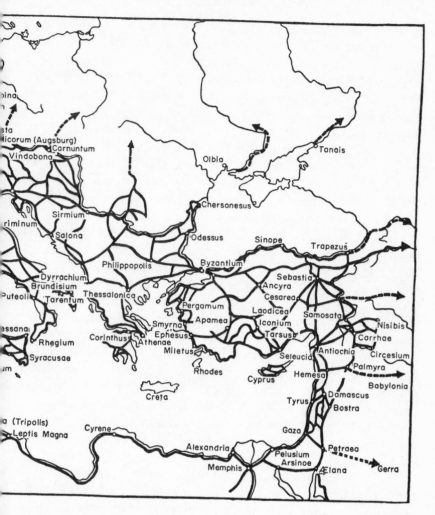

gain exemption from taxes in recognition of their military exploits. But who was to buy the surpluses? Who was to supply the goods the public wanted? Who was to organize the exchange of commodities between different provinces?

Since the Greek helmsman Hippalos had discovered the monsoon, the regular wind which reliably drove the ships before it, the Greeks had been sailing from Africa to India year after year between the months of June and September, and returning from India to Africa between December and March. The main entrepôt in the northern part of the west coast of India was Baryzaga, which we met in Hellenistic days under the name of Broach (south of present-day Baroda); farther south on the Malabar coast was Muziris, the pepper port, which had a numerous Roman colony—presumably mainly Greeks, Arabs, and Egyptians. They made their livelihood from commerce which was gaining in importance all the time. The newly rich Romans would insist on having Indian merchandise, while the moralists of Rome angrily condemned such luxuries. These complaints have given rise to the theory, supported by many historians, that the Roman Empire collapsed because of its trade with the East—*i.e.*, because of its trade deficit. But this view is no more tenable than the theory that Rome declined because of its great estates.

There is, of course, no doubt that to begin with the exchange of goods between the Mediterranean area and India led to a trade gap. For the luxury articles they imported, the Romans had to pay with precious metals—gold and silver, coined and in bullion—since they hardly had any merchandise to offer of interest to the East. According to Pliny, some 25,000,000 denarii flowed from the Roman Empire to India every year. This is confirmed by the numerous Roman gold and silver coins that have been found in India. Soon, however, the balance shifted, first because the emphasis of Roman imports from India switched from luxury articles and spices to bulk commodities such as cotton, and secondly because the Mediterranean area was presently in a position to supply goods which were in demand even in India: linen from Egypt, fabrics and fine glass from Syria, bronze from Italy, tin from Spain, and oil and wine from Asia Minor.

The cotton imports caused a boom in the textile industry of Egypt and Syria, and Roman arts and crafts were making considerable profits from exports to India. The Indians even bought Syrian horses. After the beginning of the second century the quantities of Roman gold and silver coins found in India showed a marked decline. Trade was balanced by them.

The Indian trade cannot therefore be blamed for the economic difficulties of the Roman Empire. What Rome lacked was the pulse-beat of economic life. River ports like Xanten on the Rhine, and sea-ports like Aquileia on the Adriatic were silting up. Since merchandise was no longer delivered voluntarily, the state itself had to turn manufacturer. In Gaul, Britain, and Italy State-owned arms factories,

State-owned weaving-mills, dyeing plants, and tanneries were set up. All in the hope that the State might take the place of the now defunct trade.

Exchange of commodities and specialization of labour were supplanted by the self-sufficiency of the big estates. Every one produced only what he consumed himself. The coinage was losing its importance as nobody any longer had any wares to sell. The only trade that still flourished was that in luxuries, because the imperial court itself acted as the buyer. But payment had to be made in gold.

The end was at hand. In vain did the Emperor Diocletian issue price regulations, market ordinances, and currency reforms. They were of no avail. Without the merchant class the Empire, internally weakened and undermined financially, collapsed under the assault of the barbarians.

5

The Man from the East

IBRAHIM IBN YAACUB, a much-travelled Arab merchant, was greatly astonished at what he found between the Rhine and the Elbe. The people were uncouth and lived, like a big family, on extensive estates. Everything they needed they produced themselves; they grew their grain and sheared their own sheep; their women and girls spun, wove, and sewed throughout the long winter. The cattle supplied not only meat but also hides, which were tanned and made into shoes, breeches, and jerkins. There was little there for a merchant. Even the King had no permanent place of residence, but would set up his *palatum* first in one place and then in another, staying until the food supplies of the immediate vicinity were exhausted. Princes and peasants were satisfied if, beyond meeting their own requirements, they were able to support the King's armed retainers.

That at least was the impression of the Arab traveller who had journeyed from the Volga across Poland into the land of "King Huto" —the Emperor Otto the Great (936–973). To his surprise, however, the picture suddenly changed when, having crossed the Rhine from the east, he entered the city of Magandscha, the city we know now as Mayence or Mainz. There he found coins from Samarkand! Spices were on sale in amazing quantities—pepper, ginger, cloves, and galingale—a root related to the ginger-plant. Undoubtedly these goods had been brought by merchants along the land route via Central Asia and Eastern Europe.

It seems, therefore, that, alongside a subsistence economy, an extensive trade network had survived, with Mainz as its final outpost. The

84

Arabs had preserved something of the trade which the Roman emperors had throttled within their Empire, by their compulsory measures. So long as the Romans wanted merchandise from countries beyond their frontiers, from the remote and unknown East, they had to protect the merchants. Otherwise they simply would not come. That was why the merchants survived in the east of the Empire even after the west had sunk back into a primitive subsistence economy. They continued to exchange the goods of the Mediterranean area against those of India; indeed, they further extended their relations when the Chinese, advancing across Central Asia to the Pamirs, penetrated into Turkestan. Under the protection of Chinese troops the China trade now began to develop, over a well-nigh endless road stretching across the whole of Central Asia. Only valuable merchandise was carried along this lengthy and hazardous route, for only it could bear the exceedingly high transport costs. Among these goods, silk was the most important. At the time of the Roman emperors we know that it was literally worth its weight in gold.

Between the empires of Rome and China there lived the Parthians, who were not slow to exploit the advantages of their geographical situation. Greeks and Romans were dependent upon the costly mediation of Parthian agents. For that reason they tried to bypass the Parthians by finding a sea route to India and thence to China.

We possess two Greek records describing this trade: a *periplous* of the Erythræan Sea, the Indian Ocean—*i.e.*, one of the many sailing directions which used to be drawn up by the masters of Greek vessels on the strength of their own observations to make the journey to unknown seas easier for their colleagues—and an account of the journey made by the merchant Alexander to the trading centre of Kattigara in Eastern Asia, presumably in the neighbourhood of what to-day is Saigon.

Arabia Felix, "happy Arabia," was the Roman name for the province on the south-eastern coast of the Arabian peninsula. From here Egyptian linen, Syrian glass, and various arts and crafts were exchanged against Indian cotton, Chinese silk, and, above all, Indonesian spices. A large proportion of these goods were taken by the land route from the south coast of Arabia, in earlier days even from Hadramut, via Petra (south of the Dead Sea) to the Sinai peninsula and to the Mediterranean. From Petra the trade routes ran to Damascus in the north, to Basra in the north-east, to Gaza in the west, to Elath on the Red Sea, and across the Arabian desert to the Persian Gulf. The real peak of Petra's commercial importance was at the beginning of the third century; after that its wealth slowly declined, presumably because of heavy attacks by Arab desert tribes. In those days a rectangular black stone was revered in Petra as a divine symbol—a model for the Caaba in Mecca. Numerous Greeks participated in this extensive trade, but its hub was undoubtedly with the Arabs. Even Jews, Syrians, and Egyptians had to bow to their superior commercial ability. Politically, however, the Arabs seem to have been incapable of forming a powerful community—until the son of a merchant, Mohammed the Prophet, brought about a change. As a young man he had travelled on his father's business to Mecca and the great markets of Syria, where the Arabs had been selling their wares for centuries. There he made the acquaintance of Christianity and Judaism. Driven by inner voices, the Prophet preached to his heathen fellow tribesmen the faith in one god—Allah.

After the death of Mohammed in 632 his successors, the caliphs, within a few decades had conquered nearly the whole Middle East. Boundless wealth fell into their hands, wealth largely produced by trade. When the Muslim General Amru captured Alexandria eight years after the death of the Prophet, he reported to the Caliph Omar:

> The great city of the west has fallen. Its riches and beauty cannot be put into words; it comprises 4000 palaces, as many bath-houses, four theatres and places of entertainment, and 12,000 provision stores. Forty thousand Jews are paying taxes; 200,000 Copts and Greeks will likewise be taxed in future.

In 642 the Arabs conquered Persia; in 698 they conquered Carthage and the whole of western North Africa; between 710 and 714 the Iberian peninsula fell to them, and in 719 they even penetrated into Southern France. Would this enormous powerful empire last? Their military successes the sons of the desert owed mainly to their boldness and their unshakeable faith. After the capture of Alexandria, when General Amru wanted to save the world-famous library, the Caliph Omar said contemptuously: "If the writings agree with the Koran they are superfluous. If they disagree they must not be tolerated." Thus, during the next six months, the priceless papyri were used to heat the many bath-houses of Alexandria.

Soon the merchants came to the fore again. For centuries Arab merchants had been maintaining business relations with the countries of the Middle East and India. In countless caravans they had crossed the desert from oasis to oasis; they had sailed the seas; they had organized the exchange of merchandise between Greeks, Romans, and Indians. It was in this spirit that the new Arab Empire was built up.

Along its frontiers the fanatic horsemen galloped across the country-side, breaking enemy resistance, burning, killing, and destroying. But

14. An Arabian caravan (Arabian miniature)

inside the Empire there arose the magnificent residences of the caliphs; trading centres began to flourish. The arts and sciences had found a home.

Probably one of the main reasons why the Arab world developed so successfully was the fact that the State did not concern itself with economic affairs. The new rulers had no intention of regulating everything or of collecting all the profits themselves; they left to the private entrepreneur, to the merchant and the farmer, both risk and gain. At the court of the caliph it was the merchants, not the officials, who were in the majority. Once more, as many centuries earlier, they crossed the desert with their caravans of camels or sailed away in their ships to return with choice fabrics, precious weapons, spices, and jewellery for their ruler. Admittedly, the merchant had to pay high taxes to the caliph, but these he simply added to the price. Naturally, this kind of trade was not suitable for bulk commodities. Foodstuffs, grain, oil, and wine, and industrial raw materials such as copper and tin, played a subordinate part. Goods which did not yield a high profit were of no interest to the Arab merchant. What he liked best were out-of-the-way and rare articles. Arab merchants now sailed to East Asia, to the Spice Islands, and even to China—well beyond the limits reached by the Greeks. They probed down the east coast of Africa and got as far

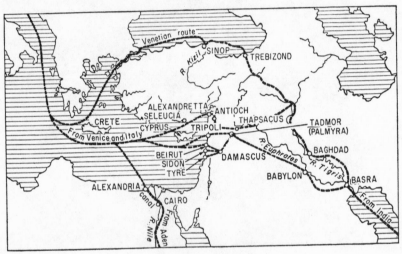

15. Trade routes to the Middle East

as the island of Madagascar, which had remained unknown to classical antiquity.

Merchandise from China, from India, from the countries south of the Sahara, or from the distant land of the Franks could bear surcharges of 100, 200, or more per cent. The dangers alone which threatened the merchant while he was away—terrible sandstorms, thirst, Bedouin bandits, and greedy customs officials on the frontiers—made all business a venture and an adventure.

From the seventh to the ninth century the Arabs controlled the great islands of the Mediterranean, from the Balearics across Sardinia and Corsica to Sicily, Malta, Crete, and Cyprus. There was no naval power that could oppose them. The turning-point came only when the Normans snatched Sicily from the grasp of the Saracens, as the Arabs were called at that time.

However, the focus of the Islamic world and of Arab trade was not in the Mediterranean but in the Indian Ocean. True, even in Roman days commerce had been extended as far as the Erythræan Sea, from the estuary of Tigris and Euphrates to Northern and Southern India, as far as the island of Taprobane, present-day Ceylon, and even to Kattigara in East India, but it had always been conducted through intermediaries.

It was left to the Arab merchants to develop a prosperous flow of trade reaching from Mesopotamia, from the new capital of Baghdad and the port of Basra, to India, Madagascar, Indonesia, and even China.

From the Pillars of Hercules, now called Gibraltar in honour of the Arab general Al-Tarik, right into the heart of China and India, Muslim rulers were in power, accepting for many centuries to come the centralized leadership of the caliph. Under Arab rule the ancient Bactria, now also known as Balkh, and Chowaresmia (also known as Chorasmia or Khwarizm), with the oasis cities of Bukhara and Samarkand, the area south of the Sea of Aral, flourished. From here caravans set forth along the silk route to China.

In earliest times, those referred to by Herodotus, the trade route did not follow the silk route, but led from the northern coast of the Black Sea, bypassing the Caspian Sea in the north, across Kazakhstan, where to-day unending wheatfields have forced back the steppe, to the Altai mountains, which were rich in gold. There the road ended; not even the most adventurous of the men who had set out from the north coast of the Black Sea to reach the heart of Asia would venture across the towering mountains and the endless Gobi desert. That, at least, is what Herodotus says.

Or is it possible that the distrustful merchants withheld their real knowledge from the stranger who questioned them so closely about all matters pertaining to trade and foreign countries? The fact remains that not until two centuries later, when Alexander advanced as far as the Oxus and the Pamirs, do we have news of a road that reached as far as Cathay, the land of silk. Later, when the Chinese had extended their power across Central Asia to the edge of the great Takla Makan desert, to the slopes of the Pamirs, commerce between the Middle Kingdom and Europe began to flourish under the protection of Chinese garrisons and guard-towers. The chief beneficiaries were the Parthians, who made the most of their geographical position. They barred the Romans and Greeks—and this, to them, included the Aramæans of Syria—from crossing their kingdom. The Western merchants took their merchandise only as far as the frontier of the Empire, the Euphrates. From there, Parthian caravans undertook the further transportation.

16. Caravanserai in Cairo. (Engraved by E. Ollivier from a drawing by P. Coste, 1890)

Slowly the camels would move over the Zagros mountains and across the deserts of Iran, across the Elburz mountains, and the Kara Kum desert in Southern Turkestan, to the city of Balkh. This part of the journey took several months, even though the ancient Persians had built fairly good roads in these areas.

The real hardships did not begin until the caravans had climbed the slopes of the Pamirs and reached the "Stone Tower," the fortified out-post of the Chinese frontier guards, which for many centuries remained a landmark for the China traders.

Between one caravanserai and the next the travellers had to cover hundreds of miles; there were only few water-holes in between. Tents were pitched night after night and guards mounted, and the travellers, exhausted from the day's exertions, the heat, the searing sun, and the fierce sandstorms, sank into deep sleep. Now was the chance for the thieves to pounce on the rich caravan and plunder it. Even powerful emperors, even the energetic Mongol rulers, frequently preferred to conclude treaties with the tribes of horsemen along the edge of the desert and to make them generous presents so that they should leave the passing merchants in peace. It was cheaper to pay a kind of road toll in advance than time and again to send armies into the desert. In good days, when the power of the Chinese emperors was great and much feared, merchants could travel confidently and safely from one stop to another, from one caravanserai to the next, always certain of a friendly welcome. But woe betide them when internal disputes were tearing the Empire asunder, when the steppe people were in revolt, or when daring gangs of robbers threatened the land! How could forces of any size be supplied for any length of time, on the edge of the desert, among the few oases? The fast-moving thieves would vanish into the infinity of the sea of sand and emerge once more the moment another caravan approached.

To reach the next oasis with its caravanserai was a happy occasion for the merchants. The solid wall offered adequate protection against both sandstorms and raids. Here the bales of merchandise could be re-sorted, the camels fed and attended to, and invalids cared for. In the wide open courtyards the travellers pitched their tents just as they would in the desert. There was an abundant supply of foodstuffs for sale. But no sooner had the travellers recovered a little from the exertions of the preceding days than they would be urged on by the leader of the caravan. On no account must any time be lost. Even under the most favourable conditions the journey from the Stone Tower to the Great Wall of China, the proper frontier of the Chinese Empire, took three whole months of hardships, privations, perils, and adventure.

"The peril of the west," a traveller of that date complains about a journey through the basin of the Tarim,

is the flowing sand, the thousand-mile-sand. Like a whirlwind it rushes into the thundering gorge, sweeping you along, crushing and shattering—there is no foothold for you. And if you succeed in escaping there is nothing beyond but infinite emptiness. . . . The land scorches its people; if you look for water you will not find it anywhere.

Forsaken and hopeless you stand, and nowhere is there any help. Far and wide, nowhere is an end to be discerned. And so the caravan merchants wend their way through the night, like mariners upon the seas, steering by the stars.

Foreign merchants were not allowed to enter the Chinese Empire itself—at least not when the emperor of China was powerful enough for his command to be obeyed. In times of political unrest, no doubt, the Chinese officials and frontier guards would accept bribes to improve their meagre pay. There were hardly any free merchants leaving China during the first few centuries—only caravans headed by imperial officials, taking the silk route to the West. In addition to their merchandise they took with them weapons and supplies for the frontier garrisons.

Before the impenetrable sandy desert of Takla Makan the silk route divided into two roads, both of them clinging nervously to the slopes of the mountains surrounding the Tarim basin, since it was down these mountain slopes that the little water came which fed not only the oases but also the wells and water-holes where stops had to be made *en route*. Admittedly, the area must have been more humid then than it is now: trees must have grown there then, though they have long since been covered by sand. Nevertheless it must often have been a case of pressing on, thirsty and exhausted, until the next oasis was reached.

Upon their backs the camels had to carry water, tents, weapons, and even a large part of the food. Hence it was not possible to carry large quantities of merchandise. And yet, while trade flourished along the silk route, every one grew rich—the merchants, the oases and cities in the Tarim basin, Khotan, Tashkent, Kashgar. Great prosperity also came to Bukhara and Samarkand. Kashmir, the gateway to India, and the countries of Bactria and Chorasmia lived by this trade. Even when silk began to be cultivated in the West, silk from China continued to be an article in enormous demand, an article for which fabulous prices were paid.

The Arab merchants were attracted by the valuable wares of East Asia and India. Leave the cheap rubbish for the common hawkers, the little men who had never tasted the gale on the high seas or the storm in the desert, who had never known the bliss of roaming the infinite world!

Before long East Asian and Indian crops were cultivated in the West: sugar-cane was grown not only in Egypt and Cyprus, but also in North Africa and Spain; cotton, India's principal export during the era of the Roman emperors, was cultivated in what to-day is Algeria; indigo in North Africa; mulberry-trees for the cultivation of silkworms at Gabes, south of Tunis.

The Indian trade did not develop without some temporary setbacks. In 740 the Arab merchants had to leave the trading city of Broach because the local traders' opposition to Islam had turned into a hatred of all foreigners. Before long, however, the Arabs returned because they had found a powerful supporter in the ruler of Hyderabad.

This mighty Indian ruler, who was so favourably disposed to the Arabs, earned the special praises of the Arab merchant Suleiman, who visited his country about the middle of the ninth century. They brought with them a multitude of magnificent merchandise: pearls and precious stones, steel blades from Damascus, fiery Arab stallions, fine muslin, pepper, cinnamon and cloves, silk from China. In the evenings, moreover, they would recount wonderful tales from all parts of the world. They would speak of their caravan journeys across deserts and steppes, of hunger and thirst, of hardships and sufferings, but also of the far island of Madagascar and of slit-eyed Chinese. They would describe their voyages in small ships tossed by storms and gales, they would tell of shipwreck on unfamiliar coasts, of touching hospitality, and of the merciless avarice of foreign princes. And into their accounts they would weave many strange tales, of the giant bird, the roc, which could pick up an entire ship in its talons to let it drop back into the sea, of desert spirits who lured the traveller from his route, and of powerful sorcerers who put charms on entire cities, turned human beings into animals, and dissolved palaces into thin air.

These were the colourful stories told and retold in the bazaars, interwoven with new accounts and real-life experiences of merchants and mariners, and linked to historical personages and events. Thus the Caliph Harun al-Rashid would walk night after night through the streets of his sleeping city to see that justice was done and injustice punished; a beautiful princess would sigh in her sleep; a daring young man would slip into the palace; a bold prince and a fearless navigator would survive hare-brained adventures. These were the fairy-tales the merchants told one another as they journeyed from the Atlantic coast of Morocco to China, from Madagascar to Samarkand, along the endless routes of slow-moving caravans and in sleepless nights at caravanserais while the jackals howled outside and the guards nearly dropped with fatigue.

And what a multitude of things these merchants had to talk about and to marvel at! To the east of India lay the empire of Ruhni, present-day Bengal, where rhinoceroses lived and where a woollen fabric was manufactured so delicate and gossamer-like that an entire garment could be pulled through a ring. There were miraculous dreaming gardens and white palaces in Chorasmia (Khwarizm), south of the Sea of Aral. In Zanzibar there were offered for sale the ivory tusks of elephants; from Arabia came splendid horses, of a beauty and fire unmatched anywhere in the world. Long stories could be told of the jewels of powerful princes—their origin, how they had come down to them, and what curses and what blessings they carried. This was no world for cool, sober calculation. Calculation and accountancy had no place in Arabic civilization: there a strange magic surrounded all everyday occurrences, and even trade was steeped in its aura.

The merchant took his valuable wares to the powerful princes, the caliphs, the emperors and kings; he entered the royal residence as a great gentleman in his own right. There he would present his most beautiful and most valuable article to his host—not from fear, but because he knew the noble mind of the ruler. And, sure enough, he was not disappointed. The prince's gift to the strange visitor, who had entered his residence with such a generous gesture, was worth a multiple of what he had received. Only after such an exchange of presents, which was determined by the person and position of prince and merchant, would the remaining goods go to the bazaars. Here again there were no fixed prices. When a caravan had only just arrived even the most beautiful articles were sold cheaply; but if a caravan had not come in for months, or if rumour reported it to have been looted by thieves, or when news had arrived of severe gales in the Indian Ocean, prices would rise to vertiginous heights.

In a bazaar wares were not 'retailed' or 'distributed.' What took place here was business—and that, to the Eastern mind, meant haggling. Wrestling for a price, getting the feel of the market, fencing with one's business opponent—all these were not tedious labours but sheer delight, an exercise of the intellect and of psychology, a duel in which the customer had to be vanquished and yet won over.

The indispensable features of the bazaar were the semi-darkness of vaulted arches in narrow streets, the zealous traders standing in their doorways, the market crier inviting passers-by to enter, the dignified ceremonial which preceded business transactions: a non-committal conversation over a cup of coffee, enquiries about the health and prosperity of one's partner, and accounts of one's latest journey. The bazaar, above all, meant the display of an exceptional range of merchandise.

No ordinary commodities, however, were bought and sold in the bazaar—no commodities, that is, for which a market price could be calculated and fixed—but only precious things, jewels, choice fabrics, silks and the finest cotton goods, colourful carpets, rare weapons and tools. But there were also various odds and ends—second-hand articles such as might have been made by a craftsman for a wealthy customer at one time, junk bought by the poorest of the poor, spices and medicinal herbs, and mysterious articles such as tiger hairs or huge human teeth credited with magic powers—with powers to cure diseases and make wishes come true.

The bazaar was a place of unending surprises: insignificant things would reveal themselves as unique objects of wonder. A young man would buy an oil lamp, a worthless lamp, scarcely fit for further use; yet anyone rubbing it would suddenly have a powerful genie obeying his commands. Who would have said, just looking at the carpet, that it could carry its purchaser through the air? Even the powerful caliph himself would be well advised now and then to stroll through the bazaars, looking at things, examining, and seizing his opportunity.

Arab trade was predominantly conducted in these bazaars. In Anhilvada, the capital of Gujarat in India, there were eighty-four bazaars alone, organized according to different trades and crafts. Who knows how many there were in Baghdad? Or in Basra, on the Persian Gulf?

We are familiar with this world from *The Arabian Nights*. In the semi-darkness of the bazaar the sharp dividing-line between truth and fiction, between reality and fairy-tale, was blurred. The Arab merchant was no hero or pirate, as were the earlier Greeks. Nor was he a big businessman who let his money and his slaves work for him, as did the Roman senators or their freedmen. The Arab was an adventurer, gambling rather than calculating. Placing his firm trust in Allah, and in Kismet, he sailed forth into the unknown; if it was written that he should drown in the waves of the sea or fall into the hands of pirates, he could not escape his fate anyway. But his sleek dhow, the Arab sailing-ship, would surely take him to some shore where he would find brethren in the faith. Thus, trusting in Oriental hospitality, he travelled on the back of his camel from Morocco to the Chinese frontier. Months, perhaps years, would pass before he returned. Whether rich or poor—it was all in Allah's hand. Terrifying were the storms, terrifying the depths of the sea and the reefs of unknown coasts. If a caravan lost its way, if an exceptional heat-wave dried up the wells, the animals would be the first to die of thirst and then the men. Bleached bones along the trade routes testify to countless tragedies.

As late as 1674, when the routes were very much safer, robbers ambushed and looted a caravan consisting of 2000 merchants and 500 armed men between Persia and India, and made off with jewellery and fabrics worth at least $4,900,000.

Clearly this kind of trade was possible only if profits were correspondingly great. For the merchandise they had brought from Turkestan, merchants in Kabul used to achieve a price which was roughly five times what they themselves had paid; thus, even after deducting their high transport costs, they were left with a net profit of 300 to 400 per cent. It seems probable that during the first few centuries of the Caliphate profits were, if anything, even higher.

The arrival of a caravan was always a great event; emerging from the desert and slowly advancing towards the city, the camels with their dignified gait, each of them carrying the 450-pound loads customary for long distances, the bearded men's faces burned black by the sun of the desert against which even the white burnous provided but insufficient protection—all of them exhausted and emaciated, half-parched with thirst, frequently sick or wounded by robbers.

The same was true for ships returning to their home ports after an eventful voyage. As the broad hulls were more suitable for shallow water, the ships preferred to hug the coasts; but suppose they were to run aground on a sandbank or to strike a reef? The planks, lashed to the keel with ropes of palm bark and pinned with treenails, were but inadequately covered with the grease of a sea fish or with a very thin layer of pitch. And yet these pitiful vessels ventured out over tremendous distances—to Zalla or to Mombasa and Malindi on the east coast of Africa. Perhaps the busiest port at the time was Sofala, in the much-

The scribe. Egyptian limestone statue, about
2650 B.C., in the Louvre

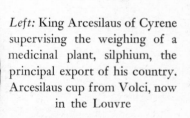

Left: King Arcesilaus of Cyrene
supervising the weighing of a
medicinal plant, silphium, the
principal export of his country.
Arcesilaus cup from Volci, now
in the Louvre

Egyptian ships being loaded:
Queen Hatshepsut traded suc-
cessfully with the "Land of
Punt"; seventeenth century B.C.

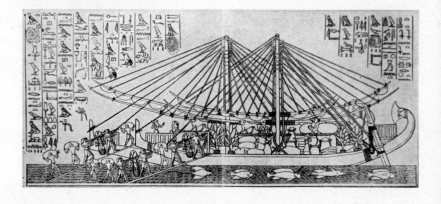

Roman money-changers

PLATE II

Querns and bread-ovens in Pompeii

A Roman shopping-street in Pompeii

PLATE III

Vendors of cloth. A Roman shop-sign found at St Wendel

PLATE IV

The Forum in Rome about A.D. 310. Attempted reconstruction by
Lessi and Gattesi, 1902

PLATE V

Mercury, the god of commerce; Pompeii

Wine-store of a "caupo" in Pompeii

A dealer in cushions demonstrates his wares

PLATE VI

Cracow merchants inspecting their bales. From a fifteenth-century Cracow illuminated manuscript

An Augsburg weaver: the great Augsburg merchant houses had their beginnings in trade in linen and later fustian

Arrival of a carav
Until recently a co
mon scene in the E
Tuggurt Oasis, Sou
ern Algeria. Frer
wood engraving ab
1850

PLATE VII

Advertisement board of an Egyptian
interpreter of dreams

Below: Chinese figure of a loaded
camel and camel-driver of the T'ang
period, A.D. 618–960. Silk, tea, and
spices used to cross the deserts of
Asia on the backs of camels. Off-
white glazed clay

Herrings being pickled. Wherever Hanseatic merchants were established there was a smell of fish and brine. Anonymous copper
engraving of the seventeenth century

PLATE VIII

Map of Africa by Sebastian Münster, Basle, 1489–1552

PLATE IX

Jakob Fugger with his chief accountant Matthäus Schwarz
(*From the costume biography of M. Schwarz*)

Georg Giese, a Hanseatic merchant at the London Steelyard about 1532.
Painting by Hans Holbein the Younger, 1497/98–1543

A large caravan outside the Great Wall of China: an embassy from the Tzar of Russia on its way to the Emperor of China in 1692. From an account by Evert Ysbrant Ides, Amsterdam

PLATE XI

By waterway to China: an expedition of the Tzar Ivan V made use of the Siberian rivers in 1692. An account of this successful journey to Peking was published in Amsterdam in 1710 by the Dutchman Evert Ysbrant Ides

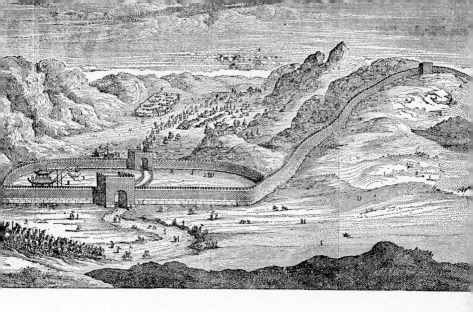

nice in the fifteenth cen-
y. Woodcut by Erhart
vwich from Bernhard von
eydenbach's *Wallfahrts-
buch zum Hl. Grabe*

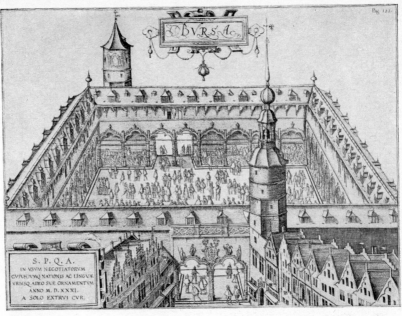

The Antwerp Stock Exchange in 1531, the chief centre of dealings in merchandise and money in the sixteenth century. The destruction of the city by Spanish mercenaries meant the end of the Fuggers' grand projects for trade with America

PLATE XII

The building of the Dutch East India Company in Amsterdam. For more than a century it was the hub of the East Indies trade

The *Fondaco dei Tedeschi* in Venice, since the thirteenth century the seat of German merchants in the city. After a fire in 1505 the palace was rebuilt at state expense, and its external walls decorated with frescoes by Titian and Giorgione. Engraving by R. Custos, 1651

PLATE XIII

The conference room in the *Fondaco dei Tedeschi*. Engraving by R. Custos, 1651

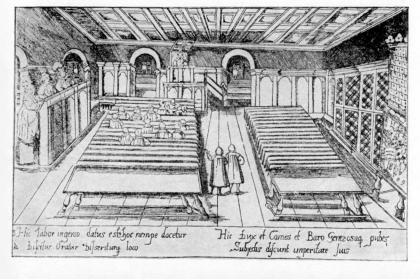

PLATE XIV

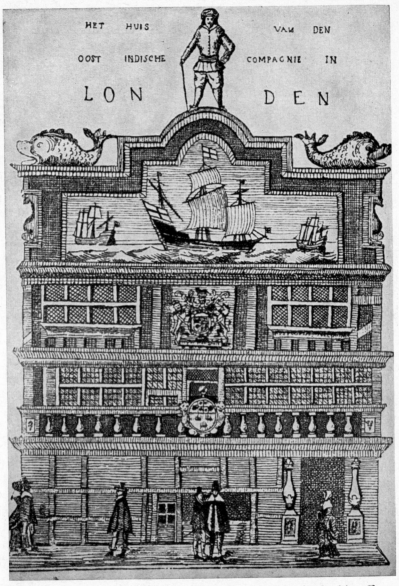

The powerful Dutch East India Company also maintained a big office in London. London wanted to become the centre of the European spice trade, but beginnings were discouraging

renowned gold country of Monomatapata. Africa supplied ivory, tortoiseshell, and ambergris, an excretion of the sperm whale used for perfume.

Arab merchants were established everywhere. Their ships sailed from Siraf and Ormuz on the Persian Gulf, and from Katif and Muscat to the Indian ports of Sendapur, Mangalore, Fandarina, and Cranga-nore, to buy there the "Indian cane" (*i.e.,* sugar cane), cinnamon, pearls, perfumes, and pepper—the last mainly in Kaukamali on the Malabar coast. Kaukamali was, at the same time, the principal port of call for all ships bound for Ceylon, East India, and China.

From the Maldive Islands, west of Ceylon, came the gossamer-thin clothes woven from tree-bark; from there also came ambergris, and, for the sailors, fresh milk, oil, honey, and salted fish. In Aghena, the capital of Ceylon, the Indians, Muslims, Jews, and Christians had their own representatives at the law courts. Pilgrims from all over the world travelled there to venerate the imprint of Adam's foot; no one hoping to impress his listeners in the bazaars back home could afford to miss the famous footprint.

Ceylon was the terminal point of the great overland trade route which led from Samarkand via Balkh, Kabul, Multan, and the Indian peninsula down to its southern tip. Merchants were prepared to endure the appalling hardships and the high costs of the overland route in order to avoid the dangers of the sea voyage. But it was beyond Ceylon that the real adventure began: the crossing of the stormy eastern sea to the "land of the Rami," where camphor, coconuts, and muslin were traded. From there the pilgrims arriving in Ceylon brought gold, furs, and aloe wood. We cannot be sure what the Arabs meant by this mysterious land of *al Rami*; maybe the Coromandel coast on the eastern side of Southern India. Or possibly Sumatra. From Ceylon the ships went to the Nicobar Islands, to Sumatra, Java, and Borneo, and beyond. Of Siam and Cochin-China the Arabs knew only the coastal settlements.

Some time around A.D. 787 the first Arab ship called at the Chinese port of "Kanfu"—probably not Canton but Hangchow, the capital of Chekiang, south of the Yangtze river. An Arab merchant reports from that period:

When merchants arrive in China by sea, the Chinese first take over all their merchandise and store it in warehouses. Throughout six months it is kept there, until the very last merchant ship has arrived. Then they take 30 per cent. of everything and return the rest to the merchants.

Even with this exorbitant tax the merchants still made fabulous profits. Simultaneously they stocked up cheaply with silk, since here "even the lowest man goes about dressed in silken clothes both summer and winter." Moreover, they bought the delicate porcelain which was in such demand in the West but was unsuitable for overland transport on the backs of camels.

Thanks to the Arab merchants political relations between the Middle Kingdom and the Caliphate in Turkestan were close and amicable, especially as both empires saw a common enemy in the fierce desert tribes of Central Asia who, time and again, would take a fancy to the rich cities of China or to the flourishing trade centres along the north-eastern frontier of the Islamic empire.

In the tenth century the town of Mazadachan, in Chorasmia, south of the Sea of Aral, was ringed by 12,000 forts. There was an abundance of foodstuffs and fruit in the town; the only thing the Arab visitor missed was nuts. Woollen and cotton fabrics were woven in the city, for export to Eastern Turkestan and China. The Chorasmians must have enjoyed travelling; they were found in large numbers in all the major cities of Western Asia. Their wealth was founded entirely on trade. The Arab Al-Maqdici lists a large range of goods which were traded in Chorasmia—pelts of marten, grey squirrel, sable, desert fox, beaver, and hare, as well as wax, arrows, swords, cork, ambergris, a type of leather called *kimucht,* honey, rams, cattle, and, somewhat surprisingly, Slav slaves. All these goods came from the Volga. The Chorasmians themselves cultivated grapes, which they dried and sold as raisins; they baked cakes, extracted oil of sesame, made clothes, carpets, rugs, precious brocades, veils, locks, bows which only the strongest men could draw, and a particularly tasty cheese called *ruchdin.* On the Sea of Aral they built ships.

Another Arab reports:

Kyat is the principal city of Chorasmia, the gateway of Turkestan, the principal market for the wares of Turkomans and Chasars; it is the place where all wares flow together. The city possesses great wealth.

The starting-point for the caravans to Persia and India was Urgench.

There the trade routes from the south intersected with those leading from the Volga to Central Asia.

The great market of Itil, on the Volga estuary, presented a strange picture. Sitting on wooden forms specially knocked together for the purpose, surrounded by the pretty Slav girls they were offering for sale, were the Russian merchants. On the river-bank they had put up a circle of lesser idols surrounding a large idol to which they would pray: "Oh, lord, I have come a long way with my sable skins and my pretty wenches. Graciously accept these my offerings, the foodstuffs, and the alcoholic beverages, and send me a merchant whose purse is filled with dinars and dirhemes [Arabic gold and silver coins] and who will buy from me all that I wish to sell, without arguing and haggling!" Not always were these Germanic Russians patient enough to wait for a merchant; besides, they were probably less good at haggling than at swordplay. When opportunity offered they would loot the rich ports in the area of present-day Baku. Later these savage raids ceased, and Russian merchants brought their beaver pelts and black-fox skins, and, above all, their slaves, to Baghdad.

This trade in Russian girl-slaves flourished for many centuries. The road which these unfortunate victims took was either through Thuringia and Mainz, across France, down the Saône and the Rhône to the Mediterranean and to Moorish Spain, or via the Black Sea to the Middle East.

As the intermediaries between the Greek, Indian, and Chinese civilizations, the Arabs transmitted much valuable knowledge both to Western Europe and to China. To this day we use Arabic numerals, which represented a tremendous advance on those used by the Romans. Indeed, it was only the symbol for zero which made possible our modern way of decimal arithmetic. It might almost be said that all modern bookkeeping and business accountancy would be impossible without it.

At the beginning of the ninth century a man from Chorasmia, named Mohammed, son of Moses, but called by the Arabs quite simply al-Khowarizmi—*i.e.,* the man from Khwarizm—published the mathematical textbook which became known by the name of "Algebra."

In China the Arab merchants made the acquaintance of gunpowder, of saltpetre, the "Chinese snow." At the end of the eleventh century we find the first reference to the compass needle which was to become

so exceedingly important for all high-sea navigation. Paper, invented
in China about A.D. 105, was brought to Samarkand by Chinese
prisoners of war in 751, and was from then onward manufactured there
and exported to the entire world as a highly prized merchandise.

The population of China is reported nearly to have doubled between
A.D. 652 and A.D. 733. During the following twenty years it continued
to rise from 45 to 52 million. China's own agriculture was in no
position to meet the growing demand for rice and grain. In seasons
when the monsoons and rains failed, disastrous famines swept the
country. Whereas in A.D. 630 one bushel of grain cost only 10 copper
pennies, by A.D. 765 the price had risen to 1400 copper pennies; during
the political unrest of the succeeding years the price in besieged cities
rose as high as 70,000 copper pennies. Who was to blame? Naturally
the foreign merchants!

Significantly enough, it was a Chinese merchant who led the revolt
of 878. The Arabs called him Bantchoa, the Chinese Hwang Tchao.
Countless foreigners were killed. But the popular indignation also
turned against those Chinese who had embraced Buddhism, Islam,
or Christianity. Chinese sources put the dead at 26,000, some as high
as 200,000. From then onward the Arabs sailed only as far as India,
to Calicut, the Malabar coast, or, at the most, to Ceylon. There they
met the Chinese merchants.

Only few Eastern merchants travelled to Christian Western Europe
north of the Alps. These merchants came from the vast, colourful, exciting world of the East, like the Ibrahim Ibn Yaacub who visited
Mainz. They found unassuming people living in poor villages. Whatever they needed they themselves produced. If a merchant bought up
merchandise anywhere this immediately resulted in shortage and hardship for the regular consumers; apart from modest reserves for emer-
gencies there simply was no merchandise. But on the great Christian
holidays, when the peasants from the surrounding countryside streamed
into the cities, when the nobility assembled in order to engage in
knightly sports, the foreign merchant, the "man from the East," was
there with a staggering display of goods. In the square outside the
church, by the gateway to the episcopal palace, or under the protection
of a powerful castle he put up his stall, simply and crudely knocked
together, but piled high with dazzling things such as the people of those
days could scarcely even dream about: valuable fabrics, magnificent

weapons, and rare spices. Here we have the tentative beginnings of a market—at first only at "fairs," a word derived from Latin *feria,* meaning a Church feast, and reflecting the close connexion between religious observances and worldly trade. In order to be prepared for these great occasions, some of the merchants began to place orders. Thus they provided a livelihood for the local artisans.

This was by no means an easy task: opposition to the merchants appeared at times to be insuperable. The artisans wanted to deal direct with the consumers; they wanted, as in the past, to produce their goods to the order of the lord of the manor, the clergy, or the peasants of the neighbourhood.

Amid these inhospitable surroundings the unarmed strangers enjoyed the protection of the great lords, for they knew how to gain their favour. From far afield they would bring them choice fabrics, precious weapons, hunting falcons, or thoroughbred horses. Animals were always in great demand. The Caliph Harun al-Rashid sent Charlemagne silken garments, perfumes, tents, a live elephant, and an intricate water-clock wrought from brass. An Indian Embassy presented the Emperor Augustus with a tiger and a python. A live rhinoceros was brought by merchants to China from the land of Huantchi, presumably Sumatra. It caused a tremendous sensation.

6

The Italian Cities:
Trade becomes Business

The grape and olive harvest in Istria has been plentiful: a command has been received for the surplus to be shipped to Ravenna. You have numerous vessels: see to it that this transport is carried out. You will not find it difficult, experienced as you are in long-distance freightage. The sea is your home: you are familiar with its perils. If the winds prevent you from gaining the high seas, your ships are yet able to defy the gales by sailing along the coast or making for the estuaries. When the wind drops your sailors disembark so that from the shore they might haul their ships along. I myself have seen this and I gladly confess that I was much struck by the appearance of your dwellings. . . . Like waterfowl you live in dwellings scattered over the surface of the sea. You have united severed tracts of land; against the fury of the waves have you built your dykes. The fish you catch are sufficient to nourish your entire population. Among you there are no distinctions, hence there is no envy among the citizens. This equality guards you against vice. Your salt-pans have taken the place of fields. They are the foundation of your wealth and the guarantee of your livelihood. Men can live without gold, but not without salt. Hold therefore your ships in readiness to bring wine and oil from Istria as soon as word is sent to you.

The author of this letter, written at the beginning of the sixth century, was Cassiodorus, the Roman Minister of Theodoric the Great, King of the Ostrogoths. It is addressed to the inhabitants of that coastal area which nowadays includes the city of Venice.

The storm of the great migration of peoples had swept over Italy; the Roman Empire had been smashed. Even in Rome itself the barbarians were established; but their seat of residence was Ravenna. They had conquered the Empire as warriors, but their King, determined to administer it in the manner of a Roman Emperor, surrounded himself with Roman officials. His orders to them, particularly on the perennial problem of the food supply, met with success. Wine and oil from Istria had to be delivered: it was to be shipped to Ravenna. The man responsible for the implementation of these orders—a Roman in Theodoric's service—knew only too well that there were ways and means far more effective and much cheaper than imperious commands. He paid money to gain the co-operation of the most capable and energetic. Not for nothing was Cassiodorus descended from a Syrian family which had lived for some time in Southern Italy. He also knew why he addressed himself to the Venetians.

About the middle of the fifth century a few families had fled to the islands from the ancient cities of the Venetian plain, Aquileia and Patavium (present-day Padua), to escape the headlong advance of the Huns. But it was not until half a century after Cassiodorus's letter had been written to the Venetians, when the Lombards had burst into Italy and were roaming the mainland, killing and sacking, that Venice began to rise to importance. Again the inhabitants of Aquileia and the rich families from Friuli and Verona sought safety on the islands lying in the lagoons off the Adriatic coast.

From the beginning the Venetians took upon themselves most of the goods traffic between Byzantium, the capital of the East Roman Empire, and Ravenna, where the highest Greek official in Italy, the Exarch, had his residence. Venetian sailors thus brought to Italy the goods traded at the Golden Horn—silk from China, blades from Damascus, fabrics from Mossul (the famous muslin), and spices from India. But for these close relations with Byzantium, Venice would certainly not have grown so rapidly. By then, the Byzantines had learned to grow mulberry-trees and to breed silkworms, so that silk fabric for the precious garments of the clergy, the princes, and the nobles was now also beginning to come from Byzantium.

From Egypt the merchants brought back flax and fine linen; there, too, it was possible to buy those Indian spices which the medieval cooks considered indispensable. There was a great demand for cloves from the Moluccas. Compared with these articles, precious stones and pearls now played a subordinate part. On the other hand, a new food-stuff was beginning to gain ground—sugar. Nearly everything that was sold from the eastern Mediterranean to the Western world passed through Venice. With great skill the clever Venetians not only gained

political independence as a Republic, but also obtained from Charlemagne a trade privilege which was endorsed by the Greek Emperor in
Byzantium. East and West alike used Venetian merchants whenever
they wanted to exchange their wares. Along the boundary between
the East Roman Empire and the West Roman Empire now resurrected
under the Franks, the Venetians established their commercial power.
They possessed no political hinterland, nor, to begin with, any industry.
All they had was their ships. What protected them against attack was,
on the one hand, the jealousy of the great Powers and, on the other,
their unique situation in the sea. "The Venetians are born of the
sea," a Greek author of the day wrote. "They are rogues like the
Phœnicians, but of great cunning." Above all, they were real merchants. In Byzantium, by way of contrast, all-powerful officials still
believed that they could guide and control the economic life of their
people by means of decrees, monopolies, privileges, licences, and
maximum prices.

When the East Roman Empire, threatened by the Muslims, was no
longer able to defend its possessions on the Adriatic, the Duke Pietro
Orseolo subjected the coastal cities of Istria and Dalmatia, mainly
because they supplied the timber needed by the Venetians for building
their ships.

In the Christian West a trade centre owed its reputation to the great
Church feasts, whose splendour was heightened by the relics of saints
which would be exhibited on these occasions. Princes, nobles, and
above all the high clergy, would come from all over the world—in
short, customers would congregate. Such commercial considerations
played a considerable part when, in the ninth century, the relics of
St Mark were transferred to Venice from Egypt.

The mere fact that the Venetians succeeded in acquiring these greatly
revered relics in a country ruled by Islam reflects their considerable
diplomatic skill. But for their close trade relations with the Arab
peoples this success would not have been possible. At the time of the
negotiations ten Venetian galleons lay at anchor in Alexandria.

In the course of their trading with the East the Venetians came to
know many a process upon which they themselves founded important
industries. The secret of weaving and finishing silk fabrics came from
Byzantium; from Egypt they learned the skill of glass manufacture,
which was soon to spread the fame of Murano throughout Western

Europe. In Venice textiles were dyed and oil pressed. But the main industry remained shipbuilding—the basis of the city's dominion of the sea.

There was one dangerous rival on the west coast of Italy—Amalfi. Favourably situated on a spit of land in the Gulf of Salerno, Amalfi grew into an important trade city which successfully defended its independence both against Byzantium and against the Lombards. Its position, like that of Venice, was based exclusively on trade and shipping. Ships from Amalfi called at Alexandria and Beirut, partly to take pilgrims to the Holy Land, partly to purchase merchandise which was readily saleable in Italy. Before long the merchants of Amalfi had founded trading-posts in Palermo, Syracuse, and Messina—*i.e.,* in cities held by the Muslims. The Muslims welcomed this trade which brought them considerable gain. They generously granted the strangers their own settlements, the so-called *fonduks,* where the foreign merchants could live among themselves; similar *fondaci* existed for foreigners in Venice.

History appeared to be repeating itself. The Assyrian merchants in the Hittite Empire lived in similar quarters; the Greeks had their own self-contained settlements in Egypt; and before long the German Hanseatic cities would repeat the pattern by setting up their agencies at the Steelyard in London, the 'counter' in Novgorod, and at the Rialto in Venice. In the Islamic view the law of the Koran applied only to believers; hence the Christians were allowed their own jurisdiction, an early example of that consular jurisdiction which many countries enjoyed in Asia down to our century.

Amalfi made the most of its advantages. At the peak of its prosperity the small town had a population of 50,000—a quite astonishing figure for those days. It is probable that it was then by far the most populous city of the entire Christian West. Its currency enjoyed high regard throughout Italy and even in the Levant. Its laws were respected everywhere and frequently taken over by other cities. The institution of a special court of law to deal with cases of maritime trade, the *Consolato del mare,* became a model for the entire law of the sea of the West.

A citizen of Amalfi, Flavio Gioja, has been credited with inventing the compass. This is not strictly correct, as the compass-needle had been known to the Chinese, though in the shape of a fish. Certainly Amalfi may claim to have been the first to use the invention for navigation on the seas by combining the magnetic needle with the compass chart.

Amalfi's rôle came to an end when the Normans seized Sicily and, in 1131, captured the city itself. No sooner had Amalfi recovered from this blow when the Pisans conquered and sacked the city, destroying it for good. To-day only ruins survive to mark its ancient position and size.

Genoa's rise to power began with the Crusades. Situated between France and Italy, Genoa was easy to reach also for the Germans. It was there that the Crusaders took ship for the Holy Land, and the major part of their supplies passed through Genoa. As early as 1097 the city, at the suggestion of Pope Urban II, dispatched a fleet to Syria; two years later a far greater Genoese fleet secured the supply of food and weapons to Antioch, where the Crusaders were being hard pressed by the armies of the Emir of Mossul. This well-organized flow of supplies was an important factor in the successful resistance of the beleaguered garrison and the ultimate repulse of the besieging army.

During the following years Genoese naval transports helped in the capture of Cæsarea and other Syrian trading cities, where Genoa succeeded in ensuring for herself a predominant position with numerous privileges. Genoese consuls represented their merchants in Tyre and Sidon.

In accordance with its geographical position the City-state preferred to concentrate on the western Mediterranean, leaving the eastern part to its great rival, Venice. In 1138 a Genoese fleet conquered the island of Minorca, in the Balearics, and freed the Christians held prisoner there by the Moors. Eight years later the Genoese, in close alliance with Count Raymond Berenguer IV of Barcelona, captured the cities of Almeria and Tortosa on the east coast of Spain. This did not, however, cause them to rupture their commercial relations with Moorish Spain; on the contrary, they concluded a treaty of trade and friendship with the Muslim King Abdullah Mohammed of Valencia, who gave them permission to found their own factories in Valencia and Denia.

Genoa was altogether anxious to buttress her commercial position in the western Mediterranean by diplomatic agreements. She concluded trade treaties with the rulers of Majorca, North-western Africa, and Egypt. The most favourable, no doubt, was the agreement of 1156 with Sicily, under which the King of Sicily was expressly bound to protect

Genoese trade and to push out the French and Provençal merchants. Genoa was also linked by close friendship with the Popes, who were looking for a counterpoise against Venice. Pope Alexander IV exempted them from all trade taxes in his temporal domains. In Southern France, too, there were countless Genoese merchants, especially in Narbonne and Arles, where they likewise enjoyed considerable privileges.

Venice meanwhile was further developing her position in the eastern Mediterranean and in the Black Sea. Fortunately, the Crusades did not interfere with the entire Eastern trade, but only with that to Syria. Relations with Central Asia remained unaffected. In spite of their consideration for their Muslim trade partners, the Venetians permitted their fleets to intervene in the military decisions of the Crusades. They tipped the scales in the naval battle of Joppa and made possible the capture of Tyre in 1124. In return Venice was granted, in all cities that were captured, the privilege of her own jurisdiction, her own churches, and her own weights and measures.

The growing power of the city in the lagoon was viewed with serious misgivings by Byzantium. Venice had long ceased to be a mere trading city; she now had extensive territories in Istria and Dalmatia, she possessed Croatia, and was trying to block the land route—or more properly, the river route—down the Danube. In the war between Byzantium and Sicily Venice sided with the latter. The East Roman Emperor thereupon forbade entry to his country to all Venetians. When the Emperor Manuel lifted the ban, some 20,000 Venetians once more set out for the East Roman Empire with large sums of money; however, in 1171 they were arrested without warning and all their merchandise confiscated. Neither protests nor threats were of any avail. Byzantium, however, had under-estimated the proud merchants of Venice; they now blockaded the Byzantine Empire, cutting off all trade. Within a few years the Emperor had to yield and even promise compensation for the losses suffered by Venice. Once more Italian merchants, including many from the city in the lagoon, settled in Byzantium. To all appearances peace and friendship had been restored. But the Venetians were merely awaiting their chance of revenge. That chance was to come soon.

The meeting-place of the knights gathering for the Third Crusade— which was aimed not at Syria but Egypt—was Venice. But where were the knights to find the large sums which Venice demanded for ferrying them across? The aged Duke Dandolo made them a curious proposition: they could work their passage by temporarily entering the services of the city of Venice.

Thus the Crusaders, working their passage, first conquered Dalmatia and then Constantinople. Mercilessly the Lombards and the French, who had set forth to perform a pious deed, sacked the Christian city. Venice had her revenge.

She now occupied the most important islands and capitals in the eastern Mediterranean—Corfu, Crete, Eubœa, Adrianople, and the countries of Epirus and Ætolia. She founded several colonies on the Black Sea coast: from Sudak, on the southern coast of the Crimea, merchants travelled to Moscow and even as far as Novgorod, where they encountered traders from the Baltic.

Even more important was the fact that, from the Black Sea, the Venetians were able to deal directly with the countries of Central and East Asia; this trade yielded good profits. That was why great importance was attached to the friendship of the emperor in Trebizond and the kings of Armenia, through whose territories the trade route to Turkestan lay. No longer were the Venetians to be dependent on those overbearing Crusaders in Palestine or on the Muslim Sultan in Syria.

Nevertheless, to ensure good relations even with him, the Venetians paid the Sultan a voluntary 10 per cent. tax on all their turnover in return for permission to buy and sell goods without let or hindrance throughout his empire. The treaty concluded with the Sultan of Aleppo was even more favourable: he demanded a tax of only 6 per cent., and, in return, permitted the Venetian merchants to equip their own quarter in Aleppo, where they could enjoy their own jurisdiction, not only in civil cases but also for criminal law. Similar favourable trade agreements were concluded with Egypt in 1238 and with Tunis in 1251.

Unparalleled wealth accumulated in Venice. Merchandise arrived from Northern and from Eastern Europe, from the Mediterranean area, from the Middle East, and even from Africa and the Far East; and on every consignment the Venetians made a profit. They enjoyed a monopoly, based partly on their business relations, partly on their wealth, which enabled them to grant credits and undertake great risks, and finally also on their military and political superiority. A shrewd commercial policy was combined with an ever-watchful determination to tolerate no rivals. Military power went hand in hand with political friendship; this, in turn, was frequently buttressed by financial assistance and strengthened by occasional presents.

Secure on her islands, Venice could afford to wait calmly. Her adversaries she played off one against another, using every opportunity of acquiring privileges cheaply. Lombards, East Rome, the Saracens, Normans, Crusaders, and the Sultans of Egypt, Iconium, Syria, and Tunis—all these were mere pawns on the chessboard of Venice's politics. By making use of the one, who often did not even know what the game was, the others could be made pliable and ready to negotiate; frequently one opponent was won over in order to subject another. Eventually the Venetians were firmly established along all the important trade routes of the eastern Mediterranean. Along her canals Venice shipped a truly inexhaustible stream of merchandise from Asia to Central Europe.

About the year 1260 the brothers Niccolo and Maffeo Polo visited their trading-station in Constantinople to look around for more beautiful and cheaper precious stones. On the Bosporus the Venetians enjoyed such a degree of protection that it was safe for Niccolo to take his young wife with him. Later, however, the two merchants conceived the idea of visiting their business connexions in Sudak, in the Crimea, who bought for them the precious stones from the caravans arriving from the Far East. To see for themselves what this trade was like, to talk to the people who brought the valuable wares from far-off countries, to see if it was possible to buy even more favourably—these were the considerations which induced them to leave the young wife behind in Constantinople and to cross the Black Sea to the Crimea.

What they heard in Sudak gave them no comfort. In Southern Russia a new, huge empire had arisen whose ruler controlled all trade. The caravans from the interior of Asia now travelled only as far as his residence on the Volga; there they turned back. Ought they not to pay a visit to this powerful prince?

The merchants in Sudak urgently advised them against such a dangerous enterprise. They were afraid of the Mongols, those wild horsemen who had swept through the whole of Asia as far as Central Europe, carrying with them murder, arson, and pillage, sparing no one, neither man nor woman, neither the aged nor the children. Hair-raising stories were being told about those ruthless campaigns half-way across the world. Only five years previously the Mongols had once again fallen upon Poland, laid waste the land, and destroyed Cracow. How could one do business with them? But the Polos were prepared to risk it. Surely there were some monks who had already visited the Mongols? And what a missionary could do surely an experienced merchant, used to negotiation, should be able to do as well.

At the court of the Mongol ruler they subjected themselves to the ancient Oriental customs: they surrendered all their precious jewels to the ruler as a gift. They were not deceived in their expectations; the Mongol prince received them hospitably and returned their presents generously. They were free to move through his territory, and to buy and sell whatever they wished. As they had no serious competitor business was most profitable. Their daring had paid dividends. But how were they to return to their country?

In the meantime the victorious Greeks had driven the Venetians from Constantinople. This way home, therefore, was barred. In Armenia war was raging between the Mongols and the Muslims. On the advice of their host, the Venetians decided to travel in a wide arc around the Caspian Sea, through the West Siberian steppe and the western provinces of the gigantic Mongol empire, into Persia. But in Samarkand they were halted again.

Luck, however, was with them. They met an imperial envoy returning from Persia to the court of Kublai Khan, the great Khan of Mongolia. The envoy took a liking to the clever men from the West. Would they like to accompany him to the great Khan? The temptation was irresistible. What had begun as a brief visit to business connexions in the Crimea became a journey whose end was nowhere in sight. Back home a young wife and a newly born son were waiting. Nevertheless, this unique opportunity of seeing the land from where all the rare merchandise came could not be allowed to pass unused. They accepted the invitation.

The journey took many months: from Samarkand over the icy heights of the Pamirs, along the silk route through the Tarim basin in Central Asia, across the deserts of Mongolia to Karakorum, the seat of the Mongol emperor. Slowly, very slowly, the caravan crept forward. True, the imperial envoy received every help from the Mongol authorities: horses and foodstuffs were provided free of charge, the roads were

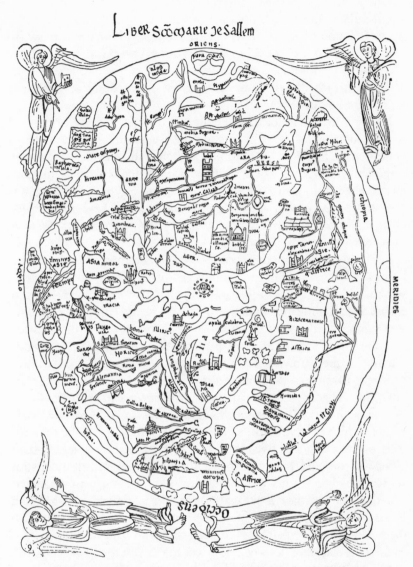

17. World map of the twelfth century, drawn by Canon Heinrich of Mainz

protected by garrisons and guard-posts, but the rigours of the unending journey were appalling—scorching heat by day, icy cold at night, and also the high passes, and the long distances which demanded forced marches so that the next water-hole was reached in time, the howling storm which cut through even the thickest sheepskins, the rarefied air up in the mountain passes, which were blocked by ice and snow, so that the caravan was forced to wait for several weeks. The hardships were too much for the Mongol envoy; he died on the journey. But the Venetians reached their destination and were most amicably received by the great Khan.

Kublai liked them for their intelligence and for their integrity; soon he treated them as friends. Eagerly he listened to their accounts of conditions in the West. At last he dispatched them to Europe with an important message: he offered to fight side by side with the Christians against the Muslims in Asia Minor, Syria, and Egypt. Indeed, he was prepared to become a Christian himself and to have his subjects converted provided learned monks could convince him of the truth of their religion.

With this truly revolutionary offer the Polo brothers set forth on their homeward journey. The great Khan had given them golden tablets on which he had engraved his name with his own hand; these were to ensure that all along their route the merchants would enjoy the Emperor's protection. They were to receive free of charge whatever they desired, and they were entitled to issue orders to the troops in the garrisons. Thanks to these powers the long journey was accomplished without incident. But when the Polos returned home in 1269 everything had changed. The Pope was dead, and no successor had yet been elected. Nor was there an Emperor left. There was nobody to whom the Venetians could have delivered the magnanimous offer of the powerful ruler of the East. For two years the Polos stayed in Venice, in vain. Then, as they did not wish to keep their exalted friend and patron waiting any longer, they decided to return to East Asia empty-handed. On this journey they took with them Niccolo's son, young Marco Polo. At the last minute the new Pope sent a few monks to accompany them, but when the party had reached the mountains of Armenia and learned the alarming news of a new war in the East the Papal emissaries lost heart. The Polos continued on their journey alone, trusting in the protection of the imperial seal. The hardships of the journey proved too much for young Marco. For several months the caravan had to halt in the foothills of the Pamirs until he recovered from his sickness. After what must have seemed an eternity the Venetians arrived at the great Khan's court in Peking.

Kublai no longer had his residence in the inhospitable steppe but in the middle of prosperous China with its flourishing trading cities, thronged with hundreds of thousands of inhabitants. From the Spice Islands, from Indonesia, from India, from the interior of Asia, and from far-off Siberia—from all corners of the earth came merchandise and tribute, sent to the great Khan by the nations he had subjected: magnificent horses, tigers, and rhinoceroses for the imperial big-game pits, rare weapons, and precious jewellery. With amazement the Venetians watched countless ships arriving in the great ports day after day, laden with pepper and cloves, with Indian fabrics, with gold and silver. Vast wealth flowed into the court from customs revenue and from the tax on salt sold by the Chinese to foreigners, from silk and from Chinese ceramics. Kublai Khan appointed young Marco Polo, to whom he had taken a particular liking, to be overseer of State revenues. Marco did not deceive his master's trust; he served him loyally. From his journeys across the length and breadth of the Empire he sent the Khan rare hunting animals, panthers, and falcons, knowing how these gifts would delight the mighty ruler. There was only one drawback: the Emperor would not let him return home. He had got too used to the company of the lively young man.

Not until many years later did an unusual opportunity enable the Polos to return home: they were permitted to accompany a Mongol princess who was to be married to the ruler of Persia. In order to spare the noble lady the rigours of the overland route it was decided to go by sea, via Indonesia to the Persian Gulf. The voyage took eighteen months; it was so strenuous that most of the party died on the way. The princess and her entourage of women, however, thanks to the Polos' solicitude, survived all hardships and privations. Marco Polo reports that when the moment of parting came the princess wept bitterly.

The Venetians were astonished by three ragged figures turning up one day at the Polos' house in Venice, demanding admittance and claiming to be the rightful owners who had left for the Far East twenty-six years before. They had long been declared dead. In the evening a banquet was given for all relations and for the leading citizens of Venice. The travellers made their first appearance in clothes of precious crimson brocade; before the guests sat down to dinner the hosts withdrew and presently returned in clothes of crimson damask; the brocade clothes were instantly cut up, in accordance with Mongol custom, and distributed among the servants. Half-way through the meal the three men changed into crimson velvet, and the damask clothes were now cut up and given away. After the meal the clothes were changed once more.

But the real surprise came at a late hour when the servants had been dismissed. Young Marco cut open the seams of the shabby garments in which the three travellers had arrived; and from the seams of the ragged clothes tumbled out quantities of pearls, diamonds, rubies, emeralds, and sapphires. No one could doubt any longer that these men were indeed the Polos who had returned at long last. But the strange stories the travellers told of the land of the great Khan were nevertheless disbelieved by their fellow countrymen. They sounded so implausible, so boundlessly exaggerated, that young Marco was nicknamed in Venice "Messer Miglione"—"Master Million." This was also the name given to the book which he wrote about his experiences in Asia—that is, as soon as he found leisure to write it: in Genoese captivity.

During the time that Polo was in Asia Genoa had become the leading naval power in the Mediterranean, despite the fact that it lay wedged between the mountains and the sea, without hinterland. "A sea without fish, mountains without forests, men without faith, women without modesty—that's Genoa for you!" the Venetians used to scoff. But they underrated the sheer determination of their rivals. Genoese merchants also wanted to enter Constantinople and sail through the Bosporus. So long as the protégés of Venice, the 'Latin' emperors, were established at the Golden Horn, the overwhelming part of the Asian trade belonged to Venice. And this the proud lords of Genoa would not accept.

They helped the Greek Emperor Michael Palæologus of Nicæa to reconquer Byzantium in 1261. As a token of gratitude the Emperor ceded to Genoa the suburbs of Pera and Galata on the Bosporus, both of which have remained Christian quarters to this day. In the Black Sea, apart from the Genoese only the Pisans were allowed to trade; to everybody else, but in particular the Venetians, the harbours were now closed.

Supported by this alliance, Genoa became the predominant commercial power not only in the Black Sea but in the entire Eastern trade. For two centuries Genoa retained possession of Kaffa, the most important transhipment centre in the Crimea, to-day's Feodosia. Genoa had settlements in Soldaia (present-day Sudak), Cembalo, Tamono, and Cerco. Genoa concluded trade treaties with the Sultans of Armenia, Egypt, and Syria, with the Berber princes of Africa, and with the Moorish kingdoms. Even when the Christian possessions in Syria were lost again, the Genoese maintained their privileged trade position. A Genoese, Benedetto Zaccaria, married the sister of the Emperor; he commanded the Genoese fleet in the battle of Curzola in which Marco Polo was taken prisoner. In the end this dominant position was undermined by internal quarrels, which led to protracted civil wars and to Genoa's political and economic decline. Even so, the city was to remain for a long time to come the richest trading-port in the western Mediterranean.

Crafts and manufactures at first played only a subordinate part in Venice and Genoa. The merchants of these cities were great gentlemen, city nobility grown rich over the centuries, at least as familiar with military matters as with profitable business. Thanks to their close relations with the East, however, the arts and crafts began to flourish. Frequently foreign artisans were invited from abroad, so that their manufactures could be acquired and sold more cheaply. Thus the famous glass factories were set up on the island of Murano, which supplied glass buttons even to the mandarins of China. In Venice itself lace-making and silk-weaving developed. Before long the Italians were able to supply to the East their own manufactures—woollen and cotton fabrics, weapons and ornaments, skilfully fashioned vessels, and leather goods. They found a ready market on the Red Sea, in Abyssinia, in Tartary, in the islands of the Indian Ocean, and on the coasts of India and Africa.

The principal profit from this development, however, was derived not by the great merchant cities of Venice and Genoa, but by Florence. Situated on the Arno, away from the sea, Florence could not hope to play an important part in commerce. Its inhabitants therefore concentrated on arts and crafts. The rise of Florence began when the monks of the Order of Humble Brethren, previously established in Tyre, transferred to Florence in the face of the advancing Muslims and were received there with open arms. They had learned the art of weaving from the Orientals, and had further developed it; in particular they had evolved a method of dyeing wool, called *calimala,* the secret of which was closely guarded. The Florentines presently succeeded in further improving the finishing of these textiles by imparting to them a beautiful sheen, so that their products soon gained a high reputation in the European markets.

As there was not sufficient wool in Tuscany, this had to be imported from France and Flanders, and even from England. Huge covered wagons travelled from Ghent via Brussels, Paris, Avignon, to Marseille or Aigues-Mortes—then still on the Mediterranean—and across the Apennines to Florence. Aigues-Mortes was also the destination of the consignments of wool shipped from London via Bordeaux, to be transported thence through Gascony and Languedoc. All freightage in the western Mediterranean, however, was controlled by Genoa. This trading city, still powerful, undertook the protection of

18. Woman spinning

these transports. The result was a lower rate of maritime insurance than before. The rate rarely exceeded 15 per cent. and frequently stood at 12 per cent. These are not high figures considering the dangers from wind and waves to which those early awkward vessels were exposed.

Frequently the Florentine merchants had their wool woven for them in Flanders or France; the dyeing, however, was invariably done in Florence itself, chiefly with indigo imported from the East. About 1338 Florence had more than 200 workshops which processed between 70,000 and 80,000 pieces annually. Customers far and wide demanded Florentine cloth; no other material in Europe could match it for perfection.

For a while Florentine exports passed through neighbouring Pisa, which did exceedingly well out of this brokerage. The Pisans, however, were not satisfied, and in 1356, in order to extort from the Florentines a greater share in their profits, they revoked the freedom of trade which Florence had enjoyed. No doubt the powerful sea lords thought that the poor artisans on the Arno ought to be grateful to them for allowing them to find a customer for their wares at all. But they were mistaken. In spite of increased overheads, the Florentines now channelled their merchandise through the port of Talamone, which, though inadequate, belonged to Siena. Pisa had to yield; it could not afford to lose its trade with its rich hinterland. In 1370 it once more exempted all Florentine merchandise from customs duties.

Fifty years later, in order to become independent of Pisa, Florence acquired the harbour of Leghorn for 100,000 gold ducats. It set up its own fleet of warships and a special office for maritime affairs. In the very next year the Florentines obtained permission from the Sultan of Egypt to import and export their merchandise on entirely equal terms with the Venetians. Agencies were set up in the Egyptian cities, and consuls appointed. Soon the first galleon flying the Florentine flag arrived in Egypt; it was followed by ships sailing to Kaffa and Trebizond, Tripolis and Tunis, the Balearic Islands and Catalonia, and even Flanders and England.

On their eastward voyages the ships carried industrial manufactures, which were traded for valuable Oriental goods. When the galleons sailed to the West they did so to purchase raw materials—fine wool from Spain or coarse wool from England. Since the Portuguese had seized Tangier from the Muslims the sea route had become cheaper than the overland route from Bordeaux to Aigues-Mortes. However, it still remained the more dangerous of the two, if only because of the pirates off the North African coast.

In order to purchase wool at such great distances and to bring it to Florence, considerable capital had to be tied up for a long time, and, what was more, not in an occasional transaction of great risk and correspondingly great profit, but currently at low rates of interest, so that the domestic textile industry should remain competitive. To this end Florence developed an elaborate banking system.

The Venetian and Genoese merchants were themselves rich enough to equip their ships. If a ship returned it brought great gain; if it was lost the loss was so great that no insurer or banker would be prepared to underwrite it at a low premium. Only a regular, steady business made it possible to spread the risks evenly and to make capital a calculable factor in the total production costs of an industry. At the peak of its prosperity Florence had eighty banking-houses, with branches throughout Italy—the Bardi, Pazzi, Villani, Capponi, Buondelmonti, Corsini, Falconieri, Portonari, and, more powerful than all others, the Medici. About the middle of the fourteenth century the Pazzi alone had sixteen branch offices—in Avignon, Paris, Bruges, London, Majorca, Morea, Rhodes, Cyprus, and Tunis.

The vast capital of the Florentine banking-houses came from their highly profitable money transactions. Emperors, kings and princes, and above all the Church, had the taxes paid by their subjects and believers, as well as the sums sent by them to their allies, remitted through the banks. This was done for two reasons. First, there was but little precious metal about in the Middle Ages; if all payments from one country to another had been made in cash all economic life would soon have come to a halt. Charlemagne was unable to levy a monetary tax because there were not enough coins in his realm. His empire was still too deeply rooted in an economy based on payment in kind. Such a market economy as was able to develop slowly in a few cities depended entirely on the small quantities of coin current in the Christian West.

Year after year large sums of money flowed into Rome from all parts of Christian Europe: indulgence money, Peter's Pence, the taxes levied from believers for the maintenance of the Papal See and for its great ecclesiastical and political purposes, contributions to the Crusades —in all, very considerable sums collected as money or precious metal and now to be transported to Italy over great distances and along hazardous routes.

The Florentine banks simplified the procedure. They accepted the monies in the countries of payment, used them to pay for the wool bought locally, and then paid the Vatican out of the proceeds of the cloth sales. Moreover, they collected from the Popes a considerable transfer charge. The firms authorized by the Pope to collect money for him in foreign countries all made excellent profits. It was to this close connexion of banking and the Holy See that the Medici owed their rise to the position of the richest family in Florence.

In this way the Florentines paid for their wool without any great capital of their own. The Florentine banking-houses, moreover, used the Church monies for granting credits, often to very considerable amounts. The Bardi, for instance, made enormous loans to the King of England, at times a multiple of their own capital. When Edward III stopped all payments in 1339 his bankers, the Bardi and the Pazzi, went bankrupt. King Philip VI of France decreed autocratically that the Florentine merchants and bankers must pay large fines for their 'usury'—fines which, needless to say, went into the King's pocket. Without powerful political backing the Florentines were practically helpless against such arbitrariness.

Around the middle of the fourteenth century the city on the Arno had about 100,000 inhabitants, 110 churches, and 39 monasteries and convents; it was the biggest city of the Christian West. Arts and crafts were flourishing; within a single year the textile industry produced cloth valued at 1,200,000 gold ducats. Science and the arts rose to new heights.

Florence had gained this position not with the aid of powerful armies or mighty fleets of warships, but solely through the hard work of its artisans and the shrewdness of its merchants.

What the Florentines looked for was a regular, sound business. The city's entire way of living bore a middle-class stamp. Even the richest families fell in with the simple usages of their fellow citizens. The tone was set by the artisans, by the guilds—in particular by the fourteen so-called lower guilds, whose number was subsequently enlarged by those of the workers in the cloth-mills and by the tailors and barbers. Among the seven upper guilds the clothmakers ranked first, followed immediately by the money-changers, or, as we would say, the bankers.

To the Florentines the customer was a 'business friend,' who was offered, in free competition, the best merchandise at the lowest possible price. The customer should feel satisfied with his purchase. Only on that basis could a durable business be built up. That was why Florence was most careful to see that all obligations were met, that the terms agreed were observed, that the quality of the merchandise was up to the vendor's promises, that delivery dates were punctually kept, and that the coinage remained genuine and unadulterated.

Every country, indeed most cities, struck their own coins, whose gold or silver content fluctuated, and which might be accepted in one country and refused in another. A money-changer had to know countless different coins and examine every one for its real value. Against this background the Florentine florin—the name itself is derived from the city—remained stable. When Abu Abdullah, the Sultan of Tunis, saw his first gold florin in 1252 he was amazed by the superb finish and the purity of its gold. He asked the Pisan merchants what the inscription "Florence" meant.

"Oh, that's nothing special," the Pisans replied. "It is a region where our hill tribes come from—like your Arabs."

"This coin is not the work of any hill tribes," the Sultan replied.

The Florentines were solid, reputable merchants. "You must deal with your business friend fairly and squarely. You yourself must remain absolutely reliable: the kind of emotion which a nobleman or a farmer, a peasant or a landowner, a warrior or even a beggar can afford, has no place in commerce. The merchant must never forget that he is merely the trustee of the possessions of others and that he

19. A groom (from Herrad von Landsperg's *Hortus Deliciarum*)

lives by the trust of others." These remarks by a Florentine schoolmaster are vastly different from the principles which governed trade in Venice or Genoa.

For the merchandise traded by the Venetians the 'prime cost'—*i.e.*, their price at their place of origin on the Black Sea, the Syrian coast, or in far-off Asia—played but an insignificant part. After all, high or low purchase prices depended on so many things: in times of war, or of fierce storms, or when princes arbitrarily blocked the roads, prices would soar. But if several caravans arrived at the same time they had to sell their wares cheaply because they were neither willing nor able to wait long. But even these 'low' prices still ensured a considerable gain for the caravan traders.

Commercial calculation, on the other hand, presupposes that purchasing prices remain more or less stable so that a definite figure can be computed for them. Next, the costs and risks of transportation have to be not only assessed but also covered by insurance or by the setting aside of reserves. This, in turn, presupposes a continuous, steady exchange of goods, such as would enable the merchant to spread an occasional loss over several successful transactions. He must know what percentage of his ships will be sunk on an average; the limits between which his costs will fluctuate; and at what times, and where, goods will be offered in quantities sufficient to enable him to stock up again. Above all, he must be able to count on a reasonably steady market for his merchandise.

A merchant dealing in such articles as wool and woollen fabrics—goods constantly in demand—would soon be able to estimate fairly accurately the average magnitude of his risk, and what would be a reasonable price. In short, he would know what figures to put down in his balance sheet. That was something entirely unknown in the Eastern trade as practised by Venetians and Genoese. The great merchant princes of those cities never calculated; calculation to them seemed pointless from the start. If in a foreign port they found ample supplies and low prices they stocked up on favourable terms. After all, things might be quite different on their next visit. In those circumstances, how could they calculate 'prime costs'? If their ship and merchandise were swallowed up by the sea or seized by pirates they would lose their money at a single stroke—a fate which very nearly befell Shakespeare's Merchant of Venice.

The Florentine merchant, by way of contrast, demanded security. He wanted to be in a position to see at any moment exactly how much he was worth: not in nebulous outline, as the Venetians might have been content with—"two or three ships fully laden with precious merchandise from the East"—but in precise figures: so and so many thousand florins.

For this purpose he had to write everything down; he had to keep accounts, to enter in his balance sheet the size of his stock, the goods he had dispatched, the monies due to him from his customers, and the sums owed by himself. He then had to assess conscientiously the risks of his transactions and set aside appropriate sums. If he had been excessively cautious, if he had overrated the perils of a journey, then his profit at the end of the year would be greater than expected. If, on the other hand, more ships had been lost, or if his customers would not pay as promptly as he had assumed, or if his goods did not achieve the prices envisaged, then his balance sheet would show a smaller profit, or possibly even a loss. The mere idea that a fortune could be computed,

20. The merchant (woodcut by Hans Weiditz)

that a variety of factors could be expressed in figures, had seemed unthinkable to the Venetian or Genoese merchant adventurers of the early Middle Ages. What was the use of figures? Did they provide any security? Why write things down laboriously, day after day, when a single gale at sea could make nonsense of all calculations, and when a single successful transaction could make up for all losses?

A man who can obtain credit at any time at the mere mention of his name naturally needs no balance sheet. But the small artisan in

Florence, the merchant who dispatched his woollen fabrics, had to prove his financial position to the banks. And they would investigate him very thoroughly. The first question, invariably, was about his 'capital.' That was the reliable basis of all credit. Whether a man had a lucky touch in business, whether he came from a famous family which, in case of need, could be relied upon to help—all that was not so important as the reserves behind a man: his merchandise, his workshops, his buildings. Credit depended no longer on the person, but on a man's financial standing expressed in precise figures.

In the ledgers of the merchants the vast quantities of merchandise were reduced to a few dry figures. Commerce lost its colourful variety, the charm of adventure, and became a sober, one might almost say a petty, act of calculation. Human beings with all their hopes, their courage, their anxieties and their weaknesses were now supplanted by accurately computed 'fortunes.' The merchant now was "worth so and so much." We have become familiar with this way of thinking since the days of the Florentine merchants, but we should not forget how utterly new and revolutionary this idea was in the thirteenth century. The transition from merchant adventure to sober calculation became possible only because Florentine trade was based on the sale of its arts and crafts in accordance with solid middle-class principles.

At the time when Venice built up her industries no accurate calculation was needed. Manufacturing secrets were carefully guarded, and the Venetian warships saw to it that no rival infringed the monopoly of the city's artisans or merchants. The Florentines, on the other hand, were engaged in fierce competition with the artisans of other cities. Price and commercial efficiency alone were decisive. The Florentines were forced to calculate accurately and shrewdly.

But was it possible to make a fortune with prices calculated to such a nicety? Indeed, was it worth while to have to borrow money from the banks in order to bring wool home from far afield and then sell the dyed fabrics to foreign customers on credit? With amazement the great merchant princes of Venice and Genoa watched the Florentine merchants, those petty penny-pinchers, grow rich. Accustomed to profits of 100 per cent. and more, they could not imagine that it was possible to build up fortunes by operating with a very modest profit margin. Naturally, a big turnover was necessary, and this could be achieved only by selling cheaply. The Venetians and Genoese did not notice that part of their high profits were swallowed up by their heavy losses, whereas the Florentines had reduced risk to a minimum and would sooner decline an uncertain business deal than get involved in a doubtful adventure.

Carefully they would examine the 'credit standing' of their customer; neither personal connexions, nor respect for a great noble name, nor yet the non-committal recommendation of some exalted person, would induce them to give money or merchandise on credit to an adventurer. Bitter experience had taught them not to trust the dazzling glitter of high office; the memory of the English and French kings who had defaulted on their payments was an ever-present warning to the once-bitten Florentines.

The people who got rich in Florence were not so much the artisans as the bankers, but in their business it was almost impossible to separate commercial from purely banking transactions. The banking-houses granted credits to the artisans to enable them to order English wool from the merchants without having to pay for it until delivery had been made in Florence and found to be in good order. The merchants who purchased the wool could draw the money they needed from the banks in London, Bruges, or Barcelona.

Thanks to this enormous financial power the Florentines could always purchase their raw materials where they were cheapest. If a transport was sunk or robbed, the banks would come to the help of the merchants. They would spread the cost as evenly as possible among all their customers. At first they merely 'assessed' the risk. Presently, however, their accountants worked out, on a mathematical basis, precise rates of probability for their insurance business. Even accidents were calculable.

To ensure a smooth and safe way of remitting money the Florentines invented the 'bill of exchange.' Unlike the payment order instructing a business partner to pay the bearer the sum specified, the bill of exchange represented the drawer's obligation to meet the sum himself at any time in the event of the bearer not having been paid by the recipient. The bill thus became a regular debt of the drawer. As a result, a bill of exchange, when transferred, became ready money: the Florentine banking-house stood surety for it. It was upon this voluntary liability that its superiority was based.

By way of contrast, the Venetian banks, which were mostly in

Jewish hands, were not permitted to conduct any commerce in goods but only financial business, while the Christians were altogether forbidden to charge interest. Venice lived by its commerce and shipping. Three thousand merchant ships and 45 war galleons with a crew of 25,000 soldiers and 11,000 sailors were at her service. Sixteen thousand people were employed in her arsenal. Florence had no military strength, yet the payments entrusted to her banks passed safely through the length and breadth of Europe.

Florentine merchants carried with them, wherever they went, their sober business sense, precise commercial calculation, and reliability. Above all, they planted these ideas in the countries from which they bought their wool—Flanders and England.

7

Strength through Unity:
the Hanseatic League

WHAT SHREWD MERCHANTS had for long been fearing at last happened: King Valdemar IV of Denmark, called Atterdag, struck. Without any declaration of war his navy captured the Baltic island of Gothland. Visby, the powerful trading centre on the Baltic, then perhaps the biggest and richest city in all Northern Europe, now belonged to Denmark.

For a long time past not only Danes but the entire greater and lesser nobility of the Baltic had been looking in envy at the powerful cities which so prided themselves on their freedom, and at the "pepper-bags," as they called the merchants who sat securely behind their high walls, getting richer all the time. After all, who were these peddlers in the eyes of the kings of Denmark, Sweden, and Norway, the Dukes of Holstein, Mecklenburg, and Brandenburg, or the Grand Master of the German Order in Prussia? Not one of the merchants could compare in splendour or importance, in power or fame, with the great lords who sat in their vast estates, deriving enormous incomes from levies and rents. But the citizens just sat in their towns and, banded together in their "Hanseatic League," defied kings and princes.

The war had been triggered off by the rights and privileges enjoyed by the German Baltic towns at the great fair which was held every year at Falsterbo and Skanör in south-western Sweden between St Bartholomew's Day (August 24) and St Denis' Day (October 9). Merchants came from all countries to buy fish, principally herring, which was caught in large quantities along the near-by coast of Schonen. Fish was a favourite food, especially during the long winter and for Lent, which was strictly observed. Falsterbo and Skanör may not have smelt very pleasant during those weeks, but a great deal of money changed hands.

From this trade the kings of Denmark derived handsome profits, since they charged the merchants high fees for admission to the market. Whenever a king found himself short of money he would assign these privileges for a long time ahead. Or he might grant to a few cities the exclusive right of fishing for herring or selling the catch—in return, needless to say, for an appropriate fee.

With their money the clever merchants of the Hanseatic cities on the Baltic, the so-called Wendish towns, had acquired a trade monopoly for herring in the province of Schonen, in Southern Sweden. And that was worth a good deal. The herring fleet comprised 40,000 boats and employed 300,000 fishermen. The salt for pickling the herring came from Northern Germany, chiefly from Lüneburg. The profits from this trade went not only to the Lüneburg merchants but also to the great nobles from whose land the salt was obtained. They were among the richest men in Northern Germany.

It was to break this trade monopoly and to strip these rich pepper-bags of their privileges that King Valdemar seized Visby in 1361. True, this capture did not mean the end of the war, but the Danish King already regarded himself as the victor; after all, he was in alliance with the most powerful rulers of Northern Germany. The Margrave Ludwig of Brandenburg was his brother-in-law; the entire levy paid by the free city of Lübeck, a sum of 16,000 silver marks, had been mortgaged to Ludwig by the Emperor Charles IV. Would they not all stand together to put those impertinent hucksters in their place?

The Hanseatic cities replied by a trade embargo. However, in this predominantly agricultural area this had little effect. The first attempts by the Hansa towns to resort to arms were dismal failures. The unfortunate leader of the Hanseatic war fleet, Johann Wittenburg, burgomaster of Lübeck, was executed by his fellow-countrymen after suffering a crushing defeat in the Sound. But the war went on. The Wendish towns concluded an alliance with those in the West, as well as with Sweden and Mecklenburg, with Holstein, and with many Jutland nobles, so that the Danish King's war effort soon collapsed. Valdemar fled his country. In the Peace of Stralsund (1370) his subjects confirmed the ancient privileges of the Hanseatic towns: freedom in trade in the kingdom of Denmark, Hanseatic jurisdiction in Schonen, and the monopoly of fish exports from Falsterbo and Skanör, as well as from Bergen in Norway. Hanseatic ships were again allowed to sail through the Sound unmolested. The Hansa merchants had won their victory and had gained self-confidence and world-wide respect. It had been a long and difficult road.

Under the assault of the wild hosts from the East—Germans, Huns, Avars, and finally Magyars—even the modest village-to-village trade which had developed in Roman times came to an end. First to recover was the long-distance trade. On the feast-days of the Church, which provided the only diversion in a dreary day-to-day existence, the great nobles as well as the general population of the countryside made their way to the fairs and to the markets. And indeed these occasions were a popular fête. All around the church and along the roads leading to it, the itinerant merchants would erect their tents or market-stalls. Time and again we find references to Jews, Arabs, and Wends visiting these fairs.

Only slowly and tentatively did people begin to settle in these cathedral cities or in the neighbourhood of powerful and influential monasteries, in order to manufacture merchandise predominantly for these markets—tailors making clothes, wheelwrights repairing wagons, armourers forging weapons. The artisans in the city processed the raw materials which they obtained from outside, from the surrounding countryside—wool and flax for clothes, hides for leather and shoes, timber for furniture and vehicles, iron for weapons and implements. From the earliest times, however, we find a curious inconsistency in the attitude of these artisans. For their own purchases they usually needed the merchants who supplied their raw materials; but when it came to selling their own products they wanted to deal with the consumer direct.

The countless guild regulations and market ordinances of medieval cities which have come down to us reflect all the producer's hostility to the middleman. Merchants were forbidden to offer in the market wares manufactured locally; these could be sold only by the artisans, by the members of the guild. Trade by middlemen within the city walls was a criminal offence. These rules thus barred both the small local merchant and the itinerant merchant from farther afield. The latter was only allowed to supply merchandise from far-off countries.

It is impossible to over-emphasize the distinction which the ancient city laws made between external trade and local trade, by opposing the local dealer—*i.e.,* the small shopkeeper—to the merchant proper. Not until the artisans in a town produced more than they could sell in the local market did they begin to show interest in the merchant. It was then that they needed an intermediary who would gain for them a wider market.

It is, of course, an open question whether, in the restricted conditions of the early Middle Ages, the artisans would have even thought of manufacturing more than was required by their local customers, if it had not been for an external stimulus. The foreign merchant who attended the great Church feasts and fairs naturally looked around in the city for any merchandise he might take home with him or sell elsewhere *en route*. If he saw a well-made piece of work he would buy it; he might even order more articles for the next fair. He merely had to be careful not to offer his newly acquired goods in a town where the same articles were manufactured. Otherwise the local artisans, fearful of their livelihood, would have demanded a sales ban to be imposed on his goods; these might even be confiscated or, at least, declared subject to high customs duty.

The merchant clearly had to show a great measure of consideration for the manufacturer. He was welcome only when he brought the artisan orders from far afield. As early as the tenth century the weavers of Ghent, Ypres, and Bruges organized annual fairs to sell their cloth to long-distance merchants who would carry it away "over sea and sand." Before long, Flanders cloth enjoyed an outstanding reputation throughout Northern Europe, in England—which at the time had practically no textiles industry of her own—in France, Holland, and Germany. Since local sources of raw materials were nowhere near sufficient, Bruges bought up almost the entire English wool clip.

Bruges was originally the terminal-point of a long trade route leading from the Mediterranean through the Rhône and Saône valleys via Dijon and the plateau of Langres into Champagne. Presently a new market developed—the lower Rhine valley, with the ancient trading city of Cologne, the starting-point of the route to the Baltic region ever since Roman days. Urban crafts were beginning to flourish also in

Westphalia, but unlike the Low Countries, where wool-processing was the main trade, the Westphalians developed linen-weaving, which is centred on Bielefeld to this day. These textiles were taken by merchants to the Baltic.

There had been extensive trade in the Baltic basin even before the Germans. The Normans had for long sailed down the Russian rivers and, after a not inconsiderable "towing stretch," when their ships were hauled overland, down to the Black Sea and even to Byzantium. The great geographical extent of this trade, however, should not deceive us about the fact that Scandinavia at that time had scarcely any merchandise to offer. The Normans mainly took along with them loot extorted from the inhabitants of Russia—honey and wax, and above all the slaves with whom they flooded the markets of the eastern Mediterranean. In exchange they bought jewellery and silk. Naturally, this was no basis for any regular or reliable trade. Not until the Germans introduced their merchandise from Western Europe did intensive commerce begin to develop on the Baltic.

Two economic zones were now in contact, zones fundamentally different but almost ideally complementary—the industrial West with its centre in Flanders and the undeveloped wide-open spaces of Eastern Europe, an ideal source of raw materials. The Baltic trade zone consisted of three areas: North-western Russia, with Novgorod as its capital, Lithuania between Memel and Dvina, and Poland on both sides of the Vistula. The most important of these was Novgorod, on Lake Ilmen.

Before the foundation of Lübeck the occasional merchants from the West had travelled across the ancient Haithabu and later through Schleswig along the Schlei to the Baltic. These men from the lower Rhine, from Franconia, Frisia, Saxony, and Westphalia were united in a 'brotherhood'; our records also speak of a similar "Schleswig brotherhood" in the Westphalian city of Soest in the twelfth century. In Birka, on Lake Mälar, not far from where to-day is Stockholm, the Frisians were established.

After the adoption of Christianity the hub of the Swedish trade shifted to Sigtuna, near Uppsala, then both the centre of Christianization and trade, while Visby on the island of Gothland became the new centre of the Russian trade. From the very beginnings we find references to German merchants there. Indeed, they were so numerous that in

1190 a German Church was built there—St Maria Teutonicorum. By 1280 there were more Germans than Gothlanders in Visby, so that the town became a mixed community run according to German law. Visby was in complete control of the Russian trade. This superiority the German merchants owed to their bigger and stronger ships, the *Kogge* and later the *Holk*; they were the first ships suitable for the carriage of bulk cargoes—wax for the churches, honey, tar and pitch from the boundless forests, charcoal and potash. But the real profits came from the trade in furs, which were brought all the way from the White Sea and Siberia. The decisive point was that Western Europe was able to offer in exchange goods which were almost indispensable to the Russians—salt from Lüneburg, and cloth from Flanders, and later from England. Herring, now that the process of pickling was known, could be sent over great distances.

From Poland came the grain for the large population of Flanders, from Mecklenburg and Brandenburg the timber for shipbuilding, and from Prussia the yew wood for the much-feared weapons of the English bowmen who had tipped the scales in the battles of Crécy and Agincourt. Brewers' malt, on which the brewing industry of the Wendish towns depended, was produced in Holstein, Altmark, Brandenburg, Mecklenburg, and Pomerania. Thanks to this brewing barley Hamburg became the leading brewing city throughout Northern Europe, and was to supply the areas along the North Sea coast with beer for the next few centuries. Several hundred brewers made beer for Amsterdam alone. Wismar was second to Hamburg only in the quantity but not the quality of the beer it brewed; it supplied mainly the Scandinavian market. The home of hop beer was the small town of Einbeck, west of the Harz mountains; there was an Einbeck beer-tavern in Hamburg as early as the middle of the thirteenth century. The *Bock* beer, popular to this day, owes its name to Einbeck.

Wherever Hanseatic merchants were established there was a smell of brine, of herring in little wooden barrels, of resin, of beer, and of dried skins. There was continuous coming and going in the ports: day after day ships were unloaded and reloaded, barrels rolled into cellars and warehouses, and huge wagons with woollen cloths and linen fabrics manhandled into position. No sooner had a ship arrived than it was hurriedly re-equipped for the next journey. Every shipload meant a profit. Perhaps some customer was already waiting somewhere for cloth or herrings. Ships were always scarce; no one knew when one of them might not be uselessly detained for weeks or months by gales at sea or political unrest. The head of a Lübeck merchant-house did not speculate: his transactions were sound and judicious, his prices fluctuated but little. It was inconceivable that the demand for herring should suddenly stop, or that timber should no longer be needed, or that the thirsty sailors would not demand beer.

Besides, what were the producer countries to do with their surpluses? The taxpaying peasants and backwoodsmen, the fur-traders and the great estates supplied grain, honey, cattle, timber, and valuable furs for

21. A Hanseatic merchant ship under construction (from Bernhard von Breyden-bach's *Wallfahrtsbuch zum Hl. Grabe,* Mainz, 1486)

which there was no market in the immediate neighbourhood and which, in fact, acquired their value only if traded far afield in exchange for other merchandise.

The Hanseatic merchant knew that he was indispensable: from this knowledge he derived his dignity, his pride, his security. The aristocratic gentlemen of the German Order might grumble at times about the stuck-up pepper-bags and secretly despise them as peddlers and "herring-tamers." But they knew very well that without the Hansa merchants their ambitious colonization and settlement drive could not survive. From Lübeck ships carrying wine, beer, cloth, salt, and fish sailed through the whole of the Baltic. Everywhere the merchants found business partners—Germans who had settled permanently, or at least for a number of years, and were familiar with local conditions, who would buy up the harvest at the right time of the year, who would have the timber cut down and would collect the furs from the trappers. Even in distant Novgorod the Germans had a colony, a trading-post known as the Court of St Peter, a large 'counter' where the merchandise was stored and the merchants accommodated, both those locally resident and the voyagers from back home.

Such a 'counter,' or trading factory, existed also in Bergen on the Norwegian coast. Discipline there was almost as strict as in a monastery, especially for the younger merchants. They were instructed to lead a God-fearing, well-conducted life, always to be conscious of the value of their good name, and of their duty to do honour to their mercantile calling. The experienced merchants knew only too well that a great deal of annoyance could be caused by some young buck kicking over the traces. The merchants were tolerated in the foreign country only because they were needed. They were there only on sufferance. It was only natural for the inhabitants to envy the successful foreigners who kept a firm hold on all commerce, autocratically fixed all prices, and were getting richer all the time. Sometimes an unimportant, trifling incident would be enough to spark off a wave of xenophobia which could lead to persecution, expulsion, heavy losses, and possibly serious clashes. All that was bad for commerce. It might cause a protracted trade war, as in Novgorod in 1388, when three years passed before the Russians yielded.

The big Hanseatic ships also sailed to England to buy wool. For some considerable time past Flanders had been unable to manage without English supplies. The English monasteries with their vast estates intensified their sheepbreeding when they discovered how profitable an occupation it was. After the bankruptcy of the English crown the Florentines angrily withdrew from all trade with England, so that the Germans soon had the field to themselves. Their counter in London was the famous Steelyard; it was from there that English commerce was controlled until the sixteenth century. Whenever the Germans bought wool English agriculture profited; when they did not buy heavy losses were suffered.

This unparalleled commercial power of the German merchants was viewed with jealousy by the English. Admittedly, they could no longer do without these important purchases, but at least they were hoping to gain for themselves greater advantages, higher duties, and above all credits. But their representations were turned down by the Germans. Whenever the Hansa merchants lent money to the King they insisted on securities, to make sure they would remain unaffected even by national bankruptcy. Advances were granted only in respect of future wool clips. Even this respectable steady trade in mass consumption goods still carried a considerable degree of risk. During the war with France, English ships fell upon the Germans lying off Sluys, the port of Bruges. The King flatly refused to return the looted ships or to pay compensation. The Hanseatic merchants thereupon imposed a complete trade embargo on England. Three years passed before the proud King yielded and made full restitution.

Yet the German merchants attached great importance to being able to sail through the Channel and along the west coast of France, peacefully and unthreatened, down to the Bay of Biscay. Once or twice a year the merchants would make the voyage in close convoy, escorted by well-equipped warships, to bring back French and Spanish red wine—in great demand by the Church, which needed it for sacramental purposes, and by wealthy customers in the bleak North and East. Red wine was the favourite beverage along the western and northern coasts of Europe. The "Biscay sailors" considered themselves a cut or two above the merchants trading with Russia and, even more so, above the herring-traders. They did not have the support of an English counter, but they knew that they would be welcome anywhere if they purchased wine and in exchange offered furs from Russia. Moreover, trading in open port the Germans were not subjected to those pinpricks which made life so difficult at times at the Novgorod counter whenever the Russian nobles thought those foreigners should be taught another lesson.

Without the furs from Eastern Europe the Hanseatic merchants would have been in a difficult position in many markets, especially in France and Spain, as the bulk cargoes like timber, wax, and grain were, as a rule, shipped only as far as Bruges. In the far North the Germans needed to have no fear of rivals; in Western Europe, on the other hand, several nations were only too anxious to break into the envied trade of the Hanseatics.

On the whole the Hanseatic towns succeeded in holding their own without resorting to arms. Only as a last resort would they declare war, and they had every reason to avoid this ultimate step—trade would be at a standstill, the merchants would be losing money, and no victory, however impressive, could make up for the losses suffered during the war years. As a rule the Hanseatic towns confined themselves to breaking off commercial relations and imposing a boycott; in this way they demonstrated to the enemy that he was also a customer at the same time and was only damaging himself by expelling the merchants. But woe to a rival who would use dissension or war in order to break into the profitable business laboriously built up by the Hansa. At once the gates of the principal German cities would be closed against him; he would lose his old customers as well as the new business. Unity, a common front—this was the whole meaning and purpose of the Hanseatic League.

It is impossible to state definitely whether the Hanseatic League was a confederation of cities or an association of merchants. Certainly it never was a clearly defined unified organization with a federal head or a precisely laid down number of members, with a clearly formulated statute and well-defined obligations. At first the merchants of a town would group themselves together—as in Soest or Cologne. The next stage, presumably, was a guild of merchants who would visit certain markets and support each other as fellow countrymen, such as the United Gothland Traders of the Roman Empire, who were established in Visby. King Henry II of England granted permission to the traders from the Rhineland and Westphalia to form an association. The merchants from Lübeck, then still a young town, strove hard to obtain equal status with those of Cologne; eventually Hamburg, too, received royal permission to set up its Hansa in London, an association with special privileges. In 1281 these German associations coalesced—not without some lively opposition from Cologne—into the London Hansa of Germans.

This association was confined exclusively to merchants; the towns themselves were not involved. The patrician merchants felt powerful enough to stand on their own feet in a foreign country provided they fell in with the foreign laws and provided also they offered sufficiently large advantages to their customers. But as their business became more extensive and their profits bigger, so also grew the number of their opponents and rivals. True, the merchants had insured themselves by promises and letters patent against all misuse of power—but what use were parchment and seals against arbitrariness and caprice, and, above all, against the avarice of princes?

When France was at war with England the Count of Flanders swept away all privileges with a stroke of the pen and flatly prohibited the importation of English wool. Thereupon the Germans cut off all supplies from the East, mainly of grain. Also, they no longer bought any Flanders cloth. That was a heavy blow to the thickly populated area which was unable to feed itself, and for the weavers who were now cut off from their market.

There were, of course, many merchants who participated but unwillingly in these embargoes because they themselves were not interested in the English wool trade. But the point was to stand together so as to show the powerful Count that a privilege guaranteed by letters patent could not be infringed at will. Only if all German trading-houses refused to supply merchandise to Flanders and to buy goods in Flanders could the Hanseatic League prevail. And they succeeded: for eighteen months Flanders was as though dead, then the Count yielded. It was then that the German towns were first given the name by which they were to become famous: *Die Stede van der dudischen Hanse*—the towns of the German Hansa.

Who belonged to that League? Even this question cannot always be answered for certain. The most important towns, of course, were regular members. They sent their delegates to the "Diet meetings," where they would vote in the consultations and, in times of military conflict, undertake the obligation to supply so and so many warships and meet a definite part of the war expenditure. But many a smaller town would hang back in times of emergency without necessarily leaving the League; it would not, however, go as far as to act in defiance of a decision taken by the important members of the Hansa, such as having commercial relations with a town on which a trade embargo had been imposed. At the peak of its power the Hanseatic League had seventy-two members.

The German towns, however, were so variously organized and governed by such a variety of laws that it was not easy to lay down uniform principles. Some towns belonged to a bishop, others to a territorial ruler, or perhaps to the German Order in Prussia, while others yet might have to consider a powerful neighbour when formulating their policy. There were also towns which had been mortgaged by the emperor to some powerful prince. But the patrician merchants of even these towns would regard themselves as belonging to the Hansa. They would act as though they were free members of the great League. And the territorial rulers, who depended on their merchants, respected this wish. The Prussian towns were regarded by law as 'corporations' in their own right, entitled to deal independently with the German Order even though they recognized the Order's sovereignty over them. Berlin was not a free imperial city but a Hansa town with definite rights and duties.

There were no regular financial contributions to the Hanseatic League. As the need arose, especially in times of war, contributions were exacted and voluntarily paid by the merchants—such as poundage dues on all Hansa merchandise. For that reason the League was unable to maintain a fleet of warships; it remained dependent on those ships, the so-called "peace ships," which the individual towns made available. Not even the cost of important embassies and congresses could be passed on to the members in accordance with any regular system. In fact, the League was no more than an association of merchants.

In the West German cities the artisans predominated; in the harbour towns on the North Sea and the Baltic, on the other hand, it was the merchants and sailors, frequently also the shipbuilders, and occasionally the brewers. As a rule the brewers themselves undertook the transportation of their beer, mostly in large barrels loaded on wagons and ships, not only within the immediate neighbourhood but also to distant destinations. In fact, the brewers practised the business of the import-export merchant more than any other manufacturers. It was this import and export business that determined the policy of a Hansa town. It was concentrated in the hands of a few merchant families, the wealthiest and most highly respected of whom would sit on the City Council. The law of Lübeck stipulated as late as the end of the thirteenth century: "Only a man whose livelihood does not spring from a craft may be a member of the Council." The Council members decided on whom to admit whenever a vacancy arose through sickness or death.

In the inland towns, on the other hand, the more numerous artisans gained greater influence on the management of local affairs. But frequently the patrician merchants, backed by the harbour towns, retaliated brutally. Squeamishness was unknown. In 1301 ten master craftsmen who had started a rebellion in Magdeburg were publicly burned in the market-place. The weavers of Cologne fared no better. "And wherever the weavers were caught, they killed them in the street. They searched them out in the houses, in the churches and in the monasteries, and none of them was spared, neither old nor young. Their womenfolk were expelled and their fortunes seized."

The merchants learned their business during long, hard, and frequently troublesome years of apprenticeship. The young men would

22. Wool-weaver with shuttle, scissors, and knife (woodcut from Stephanus's *Boek van dem Schakspel*, Lübeck, fifteenth century)

sail away in the big ships, and stay for a year or two—and sometimes quite a number of years—in a foreign counter to gain experience of the country and its people, and of the merchandise handled. For months on end they would accompany the heavy covered wagons on their overland journeys. They knew most of the Hanseatic towns; everywhere they had friends who would give them advice and information, and who would probably help them out of difficulties, even without any binding legal obligation. A far-flung fraternity of German merchants, ruled not by statutes but based on mutual respect and joint work—that was the essence of the Hanseatic League. The merchants were able to trust one another, for they had all been through the same school. Few stood out above the average, but that average was fairly high. Reckless or dishonest traders, with too much of an eye to the main chance, speculators who would corner all goods in order to force up prices, or fraudulent dealers who thought little of the good name of their vocation, had no place in a Hansa town. To be respectable, to subordinate one's own ambition to the common weal, to be as mindful of the interest of one's town as of one's personal advantage, to help a fellow citizen whenever he was in difficulties and not exalt oneself above him—these were the qualities esteemed in Hanseatic society.

The Hanseatic merchants dealt in bulk commodities for the general public—fish, grain, and beer, salt, timber, and cloth. These goods could not be sold with the high profit margins possible with spices or silk. The moment prices began to rise the consumers would start complaining, artisans would grumble, and the poorest in the town would become rebellious. The words 'usurers' and 'cheats' would be on everybody's lips. People would gather in the streets and angrily urge the town council to take steps against this unheard-of price increase. There would be indignation also among foreign customers. Time and again there was trouble with the Russians in Novgorod, with the Swedes in Stockholm, with the Norwegians in Bergen, and with the English in London—whenever the customers thought the Hansa merchants were all too ruthlessly exploiting their privileged position. At once the cry went up that the Germans should be stripped of their privileges, and that local traders should sail out to market the domestic manufactures and purchase the necessary foreign commodities. Why should the Hanseatic League make such enormous profits? The League would be on the watch against strangers breaking into its jealously guarded markets—but at the same time it had to remember the reactions of its customers and their powerful princes.

The Frisians, who did not belong to the Hanseatic League, were quick to use a famine in Flanders for collecting grain from the Baltic coast in their own ships. Once in Danzig, they decided they might as well continue to participate in this profitable commerce. But Lübeck was not prepared to permit this at any price: the merchants from Kampen and Zwolle, on the Zuider Zee, were allowed to sail only as far as the Sound or, at the most, to buy fish at Schonen. Not a mile farther. In retaliation the Frisians tried, though in vain, to stop the Wendish Hansa merchants from sailing down towards the Channel.

This did not worry the Hanseatic towns unduly, since fish, beer, and above all Russian furs, were in any case transported along the safe land route from Lübeck over the Trave to the Elbe and thence by wagon to the West. Only such bulk cargoes as timber and grain were shipped by sea around the Jutland peninsula towards Norway and Flanders. The difficulty was finding homeward freight for these ships. Flanders cloth or Indian spices bought in Bruges were too valuable commodities to be exposed to the stormy sea. On their return voyage, therefore, the ships chiefly carried wine from France and salt from Portugal or even Spain. Lüneburg had long been unable to supply the large quantities of salt now demanded at Schonen.

The voyage to the Bay of Biscay, to the isle of Oleron off the Loire estuary, was a joint enterprise of Germans and Dutch; this unity was promoted by the large numbers of pirates and sea-rovers lurking off the Channel coast, eager to seize valuable ships. Nevertheless, relations between the Hanseatic and the Dutch towns, which felt excluded from the Baltic trade, remained tense. Holland's subsequent secession from the German Empire was, to some extent at least, due to these commercial antagonisms.

The merchants of Lübeck viewed the Portuguese salt with misgivings; they feared its competition with Lüneburg salt. Altogether, the interests of the individual Hanseatic towns clashed often enough. When Eric of Pomerania imposed a universal Sound toll, Lübeck declared war. The Wendish and Pomeranian towns sided with Lübeck, but not so the Prussian ones, whose military zeal was dampened by the German Order. Under the terms of the peace treaty the victorious towns were subsequently exempted from the Sound toll, whereas the Prussian towns had to continue paying. In 1471 King Christian I of Denmark barred the Sound to Dutch ships trading from the Bay of Biscay, but when Lübeck failed to make adequate payments to him he lifted the prohibition again.

Lemberg (nowadays Lvov) was the meeting-place for Russians from Kiev and Moscow, for merchants from Hungary and Prague, for Italians from the Black Sea and Constantinople, and for the Central German traders from Nürnberg and Ulm. There was much dealing in Hungarian copper, in Oriental merchandise like silk and spices, in woollen cloth from Flanders, Westphalian linen, and iron articles from Nürnberg. The Poles, in order to oust the Hanseatic towns of

Thorn and Danzig, endeavoured to channel the Lemberg trade to Cracow. Casimir the Great granted staple rights to this town: all merchandise had first to be exhibited for sale there. Only then could it be transported farther, along the Warthe river, avoiding the territory of the hated German Order. But the Order hit back: it granted to the town of Thorn staple rights for all Polish goods passing through its territory.

23. Trade routes to Northern and Southern Europe

Such squabbles were a considerable hindrance to commerce. The towns had to try to appease the quarrelsome princes, promise them advantages, lend them money, and, if all else failed, resort to arms. Their principal aim was peaceful commerce. They did not want to see the vast area from Novgorod to Bruges and down to the French Atlantic coast, and from Bergen to Lemberg, split up by customs barriers. They wanted it as a vast, unified market for the German merchant.

Throughout nearly three centuries the Hanseatic towns were able to accomplish just that—a remarkable achievement. Especially if one considers the small size of the German towns. Of the twelve million inhabitants of the Holy Roman Empire of the German Nation barely more than 300,000 were living in towns during the first half of the fourteenth century. The biggest city was Cologne, the only one numbering more than 20,000 inhabitants. Lübeck had rather less at that time; Hamburg in 1275 had only about 5000, and a whole century later the figure still did not exceed 8000. Bruges, meanwhile, had a population of 50,000 and Prague of 40,000. Then came the Black Death with its fearful ravages among the narrow streets.

With these small numbers the merchants nevertheless compelled the powerful territorial rulers to keep the peace, punished them for illegal seizure and looting, and made them honour their promises and treaties. They were able to do this only because time and again they found new allies and because their customers realized the advantages offered them by commerce. Force would have got them nowhere.

When a wedding took place at the court of the wealthy Duke of Burgundy the nobles required so many furs that prices soared steeply. Stocks had to be hurriedly replenished by fresh supplies from Russia. The princes of the Church depended on wax, incense, and wine. The population of Flanders suffered famine when the harvest failed and the German merchants were unable to supply enough grain.

The North European trade was exceptionally extensive for those days. On the other hand, over the St Gotthard Pass, the most important Alpine road in the late Middle Ages, no more than 1200 tons of freight would be carried, even in a good year. To transport this quantity of merchandise 600 freight wagons were needed on the level stretches of road and 2000 to 3000 carts in the mountains. As the pass was open only during the summer months this meant that about twenty carts would laboriously make their way up the mountain every day. These are very small quantities indeed compared with the 1000 Hanseatic ships which plied between the Gulf of Finland and the Schelde. Each ship carried between 30,000 and 40,000 'loads'— i.e., 60 to 80 tons. Apart from the voyage to the Bay of Biscay, which took a whole year, the ships did their round trips several times. The annual turnover of the Hanseatic merchants was something like 200,000 tons, and rather more in good years. To this must be added the considerable overland trade.

Dependence on the two counters in Bruges and Novgorod, however, eventually led the Hanseatic towns to lose all spirit of enterprise and to confine themselves to brokerage between these two markets—in other words, to content themselves, without any risk, with a safe though limited profit. "Safety first" was the slogan governing the activities of the German merchants in the fifteenth century. And that in spite of the fact that the Hanseatic League owed its spectacular rise to the daring of the merchant adventurer. This was an alarming trend,

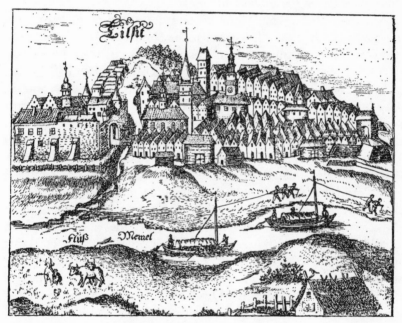

24. Tilsit, on the trade route to Novgorod

the more so as conditions in Northern Europe had meantime greatly changed. The most important of these changes was the collapse of the Russian Empire in Novgorod.

The eclipse of the Hanseatic League during the subsequent centuries was due to the fact that the two cornerstones of its commerce, Flanders and Russia, had lost their importance because of political influences in the face of which the merchants were powerless. The Germans had based their wealth on the exchange between two areas far removed from each other. Now they lost their unique position as intermediaries.

In 1487 the Tsar Ivan III captured the town of Novgorod. A large part of the population, including the German merchants, were forcibly transferred to Moscow. Many of them died during this compulsory resettlement. In 1494 this displacement was repeated. Twenty years later, when the Tsar returned to the Germans their old counter in the Court of St Peter, the Baltic trade had come to an end. As many centuries earlier, the valuable furs once more travelled to the South. They were lost to the Flanders trade.

Although cloth manufacture continued to flourish in Flanders it was no longer the controlling factor in the North European market as it had been during the thirteenth and fourteenth centuries. Gone were the days when the town of Ypres could afford to build a cloth-hall 433 feet in length, or when the weavers, fullers, and shearers, the dyers and the soap-boilers, and all the other ancillary trades of cloth manufacture accounted for 60 per cent. of Bruges's population of 50,000, then the biggest town in Europe. During the Hundred Years War with France (1337–1453) the English had marketed their wool in Holland. As a result, cloth manufacture in the towns of Middleburg, Zieriksee, and Dordrecht grew in volume. From 1384 to 1388 the staple—i.e., the compulsory market—for English wool was in Middelburg; after that it was shifted to Calais. After 1400 Leyden moved into first place. But the Dutch cloth continued to be sold via Bruges because the Hansa merchants refused to buy cloth anywhere except in Flanders; they stuck firmly to their old business partners. Needless to say, this was not greatly to the liking of the Dutch, especially as east of the Zuider Zee their own towns belonged to the Hanseatic League and wanted to break into the Eastern market on their own account. They were, moreover, enjoying a greater share of the herring fisheries, as the herring had by then disappeared from the Swedish coast and were found in the North Sea instead. The Dutch were now in a position to make good use of the Biscay salt which the Hanseatic ships were bringing from Portugal. Amsterdam, it has been said, was founded upon herring-heads. Why, one feels tempted to ask, did the Hanseatic towns not break with Bruges and deal directly with the Dutch producers? After all, there was frequent opportunity for such a rupture.

Piracy off the Flanders coast increased considerably after the Hundred Years War. In 1447 five Prussian ships had to fight three engagements with powerful pirate vessels before gaining entry to the harbour of

Bruges. As Burgundy, which owned not only ancient Flanders but also the county of Holland, did nothing to protect the merchants against the pirates, the Hansa Diet decided on a compulsory staple for Bruges: all merchandise taken to Bruges or acquired there became subject to duty. From the proceeds of this the merchants robbed at sea were to be compensated. In other words, the merchants passed on their losses to the Flemish producers.

The Hanseatic League would probably have got away with this project if it had had to deal merely with the three towns of Bruges, Ghent, and Ypres, and the rural district of Bruges. But the proud Duke of Burgundy prohibited the levying of the duty. His noble counsellors had long been nursing a silent dislike of the overbearing and bumptious pepper-bags—and now was their opportunity. When the negotiations with the Burgundians dragged on indefinitely with no prospect of agreement, the Hanseatic League in 1450 moved the staple from Bruges to Deventer.

Now it was the Prussians who protested—not only the Grand Master of the German Order but also the towns—because Deventer also belonged to Burgundy. The East German merchants moved to Amsterdam and Middelburg, and the West German ones to Mechelen (Malines) and Antwerp. In order to unite the two groups the Hanseatic League decided in 1453 to move the staple to Utrecht.

In vain did the Italians from Florence, Lucca, and Genoa, the Spaniards from Catalonia and the Basque towns, the Portuguese and the Bretons implore their Hanseatic business friends to return to Bruges. The Duke of Burgundy remained indifferent to the fact that the cloth-makers of Flanders could now find no market, that neither English nor Spanish wool was being imported, and that the towns were slowly starving. He remained hard, invoking his prerogatives as the territorial ruler, prerogatives which some unknown upstart merchants had dared infringe. When the unemployed weavers of Ghent revolted in despair, the ducal troops crushed the rebellion.

Eventually the League made a concession on the issue of jurisdiction: it acknowledged the sovereignty of the Duke, who in turn recognized all their Hanseatic rights and privileges. Bruges undertook to compensate any German merchant who might suffer loss by piracy, ducal officials, or any other cause.

Thenceforward the Hanseatic League unshakeably maintained the staple in Bruges, even after England had long ceased to send its wool there because of its own textile industry. The British had long been envious of the huge profits made by the Germans in their commerce. As early as the fourteenth century a saying was current in England: "The Hanseatic merchant buys a fox-skin from an Englishman for a penny in order to sell back to him the tail for a florin." At first the English merchants, whose appearances in the Baltic became increasingly frequent, applied for admission to the Hanseatic League, but their application was turned down in 1379. They thereupon formed their own association which received a royal charter in 1491 under the name of Merchant Adventurers. They followed in the footsteps of the Hanseatic merchants and visited Antwerp, Norway, Sweden, and Denmark, and also Bordeaux. Every one was delighted that the Hanseatic towns at last had a rival who offered better prices and sold more cheaply in order to break into the business.

The English demanded the same rights as they had granted the Germans in London—*i.e.*, free access to the Hanseatic towns. The League, however, was not at any price prepared to admit its English rivals. In 1446 the English Parliament therefore decided to withdraw the Hanseatic privileges. Again a trade war broke out. The English fleet raided a group of merchant ships sailing to the Bay of Biscay; the Dutch ships, about fifty in number, were released again, but the Hanseatic ships, of about the same number, were simply incorporated in the English fleet. For the sake of the Steelyard in London, upon which the laboriously built-up wool trade depended, the Hanseatic League did not want an open rupture. Negotiations were started.

The merchants, however, decided to take their revenge. Lübeck merchants, sailing to Bergen, captured an English ship off Skagen. In 1458 the English once more attacked a Biscay convoy. Lübeck thereupon sent its trading ships to the West, but England was not prepared to give in. In 1468 the Steelyard was closed, the merchants resident in England were arrested and their merchandise confiscated. Open warfare had begun.

The Hanseatic League's next step was to put an embargo upon the trade in English cloth throughout its entire sphere of influence. It barred the Elbe–Trave route and induced Denmark to close the Sound. Only small quantities of English cloth reached Breslau and Cracow by the tedious overland route via Cologne. England had to give in.

In 1473 the Hanseatic League not only had all its privileges restored but moreover received a payment in compensation. The buildings in London and Boston, hitherto leased to the Steelyard, became Hansa property.

The area around the Baltic had become a pacified safe-trading zone. Between the Sound and the Gulf of Finland, where merchants "carrying salt, hops, cloth, and other needful things were formerly robbed of ship and merchandise, and the sailors thrown overboard and drowned like dogs," now reigned law and order, as King Gustavus Vasa of Sweden acknowledged. It was this peaceful commerce which enabled Sweden to rise to prosperity. Germans had long been in charge of the copper- and iron-ore mines in Norberg; in the fifteenth century these ores were the principal export of the country, ranking even above timber.

The Hanseatic League could exist only as long as the separate towns were able to pursue a policy of their own, dispose freely over their finances, wage war even against an ally of their own territorial overlord, or else stand aloof from wars involving their country. No sharp dividing-line existed between domestic and foreign policy. Thus the counts of Holstein were able, throughout several centuries, to be liegemen of the King of Denmark and, at the same time, allies of the city of Lübeck against Denmark. More than once a 'governor' of Sweden rose against the King in Denmark; to do so he needed the support of the German towns.

In strongly centralized states the territorial rulers concentrated in their own hands all rights and duties, and compelled their 'subjects' to serve their political aims. This was as true of Burgundy as it was of Tudor England, of Scandinavia, and of the new Muscovite Empire. In the end it came to apply to Germany too. In its endeavours to maintain its privileges the Hansa was not supported by any German state. In a strong state, on the other hand, neither the Hanseatic League nor a German Baltic trade could have developed. Power politics would only have impeded peaceful commerce.

Free from political alliances and antagonisms, the Hanseatic League was able to pursue economic aims, conclude treaties, enter into obligations, or remain neutral. Hansa merchants were established in specially privileged counters—in London, Bruges, Bergen, and Novgorod, in Copenhagen and in Stockholm, in Cracow and in Lemberg. No outside support could have given the Hansa merchant the same degree of protection as the medieval system which raised him out of the national sphere and recognized him as an 'estate.' We have heard of the impassioned protests made by the English merchants against such privileges. But the King of England listened to those protests only when the concept of the national state had prevailed. In 1471 the Stockholm city by-law, under which half the City Councillors were to be Germans, was rescinded. The Council of the Realm decreed that "every town shall be governed exclusively by Swedish men born in the country." No foreigner was permitted to hold office as mayor or alderman.

'National rights' were triumphant. Yet fundamentally it was no more than mere envy: the local merchants saw only the monopoly of the Hanseatic merchants and the numerous privileges which they themselves had been refused in the Hanseatic towns.

The Hansa merchants were said to have earned fabulous wealth thanks to their monopoly. But was this really the case? As a rule they contented themselves with a small profit margin. They could remain competitive only if their charges were moderate. No doubt a large fortune was occasionally accumulated, but this was the exception rather than the rule. Only rarely would a fortune exceed 10,000 florins. Heinrich Castorp, Mayor of Lübeck during the second half of the fifteenth century, certainly owned more, but we do not know any details.

The commerce of the Hanseatic League was based on a limited but sound gain. Security, especially during the later centuries, was more important than uncertain profit. The Baltic commerce lacked the dazzle of the trade with the Orient, the glitter of gold, the rustle of silk, the sparkle of precious stones. Certainly the German merchants of Bruges dealt in these articles also, receiving them across the Mediterranean area, but their main business was in unassuming everyday commodities—in barrels of herring, cargoes of grain, tuns of beer. In the early sixteenth century there was not a single merchant house in any of the Hanseatic towns that could have compared with the Fuggers and Welsers of Augsburg; indeed, even the lesser firms in Southern Germany surpassed the Hansa merchants in wealth.

Great fortunes are not so easily acquired from herrings and timber, Flanders cloth, or even Russian furs. There were no serious risks and no great fluctuations of prices—and only these could yield great profits. Any usury, any sharp dealing would at once jeopardize the good name of the 'reputable' merchant and possibly mean the loss of irreplaceable business partners. The reliability, not the size of a business house was the decisive factor in the North.

We are familiar with the faces of many important merchants. Hans Holbein drew or painted the portrait of many a Steelyard merchant— Hillebrant Wedigh of Cologne, Georg Giese of Danzig, Dirk Tybis of Duisburg, or Cyriakus Kahle of Brunswick. Calmly, with clear-eyed confidence they regard us, secure in their sense of independence. These men were neither speculators nor reckless gamblers. They conducted their business in accordance with sound principles; they turned their money over and made good sound profits. Their real capital was trust— the trust of business partners in even the remotest countries, trust not so much in their financial power and commercial ability as in their business probity. They did not wish to outsmart anybody or court risky enterprises. The favour of princes neither dazzled nor tempted them. They were, in short, respectable merchants.

8

The Fuggers, Kings and Slaves of Credit

━━━◢◣◥◤◢◣◉◢◣◥◤◢◣━━━

IN RESPONSE to the Emperor's urgent call for help, Anton Fugger, the great merchant from Augsburg, was hurrying to Innsbruck. He was travelling in spite of the bitter cold, stopping neither by day nor by night; yet he was a reluctant and dispirited traveller, for he guessed what lay ahead of him. Once again—as so often before—he would be required to come to the rescue. But this time he would remain firm. He would have to refuse. His partners had exacted his solemn promise that he would not lend the Emperor any more money. There had to be a limit; the credit of even this greatest of merchant houses was extended to the utmost.

So then, on April 3, 1552, the great merchant sat face to face with his Emperor. Though no more than fifty-two, the monarch was an old, tired, spent man. He was tortured by gout. Upon his shoulders rested a responsibility he was no longer able to bear. His features reflected boundless disillusionment; his eyes were desperately imploring.

"I need money," he said. "You must help me, Anton Fugger."

"Impossible," the merchant replied. "I have no ready money left; everything is tied up. In these difficult times not even I can lay hands on any more. My credit, too, is exhausted."

The Emperor Charles V was silent for a while. Then he said in his soft, almost toneless voice, "You've got to find a way. I must have the money." This then was the man reputed to be the most powerful Emperor that ever ruled Europe, who owned half the globe, whose possessions extended to the newly discovered Americas and to vast territories in the Far East, who was at the same time Roman Emperor, King of Spain, Duke of Burgundy, Archduke of Austria, King of Naples and Sicily, the renowned victor over Moors and Turks. And this man had no money; he was reduced to begging and pleading.

In his quiet, dignified way he explained to his friend the desperate, almost hopeless position: his former ally, Maurice of Saxony, who owed to the Emperor his Elector's Hat, had gone over to the enemy, to the Protestants. His army, the only one north of the Alps, was moving in forced marches towards Southern Germany. Soon he would reach the Alps, perhaps even Innsbruck. Unless a force were raised in a hurry Habsburg would collapse. But troops cost money, a lot of money, and the imperial coffers were empty. All attempts to raise funds elsewhere—in Augsburg, in Ulm, in Nürnberg, in Strasbourg, in Venice, or in Genoa—had failed. All purses had been firmly closed or else had been empty. The head of the house of Fugger was the only one who could help.

The Emperor recalled the many decades throughout which the two houses of Habsburg and Fugger had co-operated. Together they had risen to power in the preceding century. Must they not stand shoulder to shoulder in this last, supreme effort?

Anton Fugger was deeply moved; but he could not help. Clearly and in detail he explained to his sovereign what his accountant had set out for him in plain figures in his famous "Golden Counting-house."

Six years before the Emperor had owed the house of Fugger about 2,000,000 florins; from his brother, King Ferdinand, a debt of 443,000 florins was still outstanding. A further 1,500,000 florins were invested in Spain, in its landed estates and mercury-mines—in other words, the money had been advanced to the Spanish State; 1,250,000 florins were invested in Hungary's commerce, and a further 250,000 florins in Naples. To that had to be added warehouse stocks in Antwerp, Augsburg, and other German cities.

Nevertheless, Fugger had then decided to make available once more a very large sum of money in order to finance the war against the Protestant League of Schmalkalden—even though this action had done him a lot of harm with his Augsburg fellow citizens, the town government, and with business connexions in Southern Germany, most of whom sided with the Protestants. Only with Fugger's help, they were saying, could the Emperor defeat the Protestants.

In 1547 the Emperor had called Fugger to his headquarters camp near Wittenberg, in order to demand from him more money. Anton Fugger regretted; he wished to withdraw from all business, to give up everything, to get out of all obligations. The Emperor, intoxicated by victory, was threatening terrible punishment to the Protestant towns. To avert the worst, Fugger went down on his knees to pacify the Emperor. Again he had to pay. More and more the firm of Fugger came to depend on the House of Habsburg.

Every one had been stripped and squeezed dry by the Emperor, friends and foes alike—the latter by high levies and the former by excessive credits. Now the Emperor was poor and forsaken, and Southern Germany was in the hands of the enemy. This meant that the former sources of money had dried up, since anyone trying to transfer funds to the Emperor was risking vicious reprisals on the part of the incensed Protestants. To make matters worse, France was openly siding with the enemy. She threatened to confiscate the capital or merchandise of any merchant lending money to the Emperor. She also guarded the sea route from Spain to the Netherlands. What was Fugger to do? The Emperor kept pressing him. Just once more, just this once; this was the last time he would ever want money! If he refused not only would Southern Germany be lost, but also upper Italy, Hungary, and the Netherlands—and that would strike the Fuggers in their vital spot. It was even doubtful whether the Emperor would be able to hold out in Spain.

While the two men—the Emperor and the merchant, the inflexible statesman and the coolly calculating businessman—were in interminable negotiation without coming to any conclusions, news arrived that enemy troops were approaching Innsbruck. To avoid surprise and capture by a fast raiding party the Emperor had to flee to the mountains during that same night. Everything seemed lost.

What would his great uncle, Jakob Fugger, have done? Would he have yielded? Anton well remembered the incisive firmness with which that great merchant had answered the same Charles V when, under all kinds of pretexts, he had not punctually redeemed his debts. No insolent imperial counsellors would get out of their obligations towards Jakob Fugger with impunity. After all, to whom did Charles V owe his imperial crown? Yet even Jakob "the Rich" had always emphasized that it was in the interest of his house to co-operate closely with the Habsburgs, never to abandon them, and to face, side by side with them, all troubles and difficulties. Anton Fugger yielded. He could not and would not betray the tradition which had marked the rise of his house. And a spectacular rise it had been; a rise watched by contemporaries with amazement and admiration, but also with indignation and envy. Even the Emperor depended on the Fuggers; it was their money that decided his war.

The merchandise sold in Southern Germany was imported from Italy. Laboriously it had to be brought across the Alps on large covered wagons. In consequence, only valuable, expensive articles could be marketed in Southern Germany, which in turn meant that the customers were the great nobles who alone could find the money for such costly goods. The knights wanted magnificent swords with damascene blades, counts and dukes sought precious clothes of velvet and silk, the churches needed frankincense—all of them articles from the East.

These goods reached Southern Germany by three routes: the Rhône valley and Alsace; over the Alpine passes; and across the Black Sea and up the Danube. Along these routes prosperous towns sprang up, only to decline at once when war or unrest interrupted commerce. From the products of the artisans alone the merchants could not have lived, since every town was anxious to keep out foreign competition. Everywhere the masters of the guilds were on the Council; jealously they guarded the livelihood of the honest artisan. As for Oriental merchandise, the merchants were welcome to make on it what profits they wished! And the princes of the Church and the knights seemed prepared to pay the most fantastic prices for such fripperies!

The longest, but for some time the most favourable, route was up the Danube; it was more convenient than the difficult Alpine passes. From Constantinople the route went via Belgrade, Budapest, and Vienna to Passau, Regensburg, and Nürnberg, or via Prague to Leipzig. These German cities were also the starting-points for the trade routes to Eastern Europe—Cracow and Lemberg, and thence into the boundless steppe of Southern Russia, the countries whence came the wax for innumerable candles and the honey then so important for sweetening food and drink. Sugar still hardly existed at that time.

When the Mongols captured Southern Russia and the Turks settled in the Balkan peninsula this trade came to an end. Instead, in the fifteenth century, a trade developed from South-west Germany to the Rhône valley; cities such as Basle, Strasbourg, and Constance grew rich. Now the Swabian merchants themselves ventured abroad. Across France they extended their trade relations to Spain.

What attracted them there more than anything was the saffron cultivated in the fields of Catalonia. Saffron was indispensable for apothecaries, for culinary purposes, and even for the dyeing of textiles. The Ravensburg trading company enjoyed what was almost a monopoly in Spain in the fourteenth century. It bought up the entire saffron harvest. It maintained trading-posts in the French towns along the route—in Avignon and Marseille, in Barcelona, Saragossa, and in Genoa. The sons of the great merchants of Ravensburg—the Muntprat family, for instance—used to be sent abroad to acquire a thorough grasp of this trade; on one occasion they were captured by Corsican pirates. From the rich French provinces, from Burgundy and Champagne, the Swabian merchants exported such luxury articles as fabrics and lace into far parts of the East.

In the south the Alps barred the road. True, a great many armies marched through Augsburg into Italy, but the merchants were discouraged by the high costs of transport. Trade across the Alps only got going properly when the Swiss started to build bridges over their turbulent mountain torrents and made the St Gotthard Pass negotiable, and when the Tyrolese improved the road over the Brenner Pass. Venice, naturally enough, endeavoured to channel all commerce over the near-by Brenner, while Genoa championed the route via Milan and the St Gotthard, or occasionally that up the Rhône valley.

Passau, Regensburg, and Nürnberg, Basle, Strasbourg, and Ravensburg were well-known trading cities at a time when Augsburg was known merely as a bishopric. To begin with, Augsburg owed its prosperity not to its trade but to its artisans. All around the town, mile after mile, the fields were blue with the blossoms of flax as far as the eye could see. All the villages in the vicinity were working for the merchants in the town, who were prepared to accept any quantity of linen. At last they were able to sell to the Venetians something that could bear the costs of transport over the Alps. What else was there to offer the Italians in exchange for their valuable Oriental merchandise?

In one of these villages outside the gates of Augsburg, in a place called Graben, lived the Fuggers, a peasant family weaving linen on a fairly considerable scale. By their hard work they soon rose to a position when they took the linen woven by other families to town to sell it there. In 1367 Hans Fugger decided to give up weaving and to become a merchant. With the then considerable capital of $61.60 he began to market his father's linen. He married twice, first the daughter of the Master of the Weavers' Guild, and after her death another weaver's daughter, Elisabeth Gefattermann.

It was a turbulent epoch. The guilds were forcing the old-established noble families to accept them into the town councils as equal members. Moreover, an important change took place in the weaving trade itself. Pure linen fabric, such as was manufactured also in Northern Germany, particularly in Bielefeld, was being supplanted by fustian, a roughened material whose warp consisted of linen but its weft of cotton. Hans Fugger's fustian soon earned an outstanding reputation in the great Southern German markets of Ulm, Nürnberg, and Frankfurt. His business progressed so well that in 1397 he bought a house in the best business quarter and opened a large vaulted hall for his wholesale business. When he died in 1408 he left a fortune of 3000 florins —in terms of purchasing power about the equivalent of $56,000 today.

The demand for fustian grew yearly. But where was all the cotton to come from that was needed for its manufacture? Linen production had posed no raw material problems since the immediate vicinity supplied the necessary flax. Cotton, however, which mostly came from Egypt, had to be imported via Venice. The few cotton-fields of Spain only met domestic requirements. The Venetians were making sure that cotton was not traded anywhere else. They defended their monopoly with an iron hand. Florence and Genoa might control the North European wool trade, but the cotton belonged to Venice.

The German merchants who maintained their own house on the Rialto were strictly forbidden to travel beyond Venice lest they should deal directly with the merchants from the East. Anyone trying to evade the law risked severe penalties. But the very connexion with the city in the lagoon yielded a handsome profit to any enterprising merchant.

During the first half of the fifteenth century the artisans of Augsburg rapidly rose to prosperity. The new fustian was highly esteemed everywhere because of its durability and low price—in France, England, and even in Spain. In exchange, silks, spices, and Mediterranean fruit entered the country. Southern Germany became an industrial area not yielding in importance even to the much older Flanders. Among the heavy covered wagons which made their way from Augsburg to all corners of the globe were also those of Fugger's widow and her two sons, Andreas and Jakob. From Venice they imported more and more cotton for their own weaving shops. Needless to say, they had their share of trouble with the greedy territorial rulers who, in order to muscle in on this new wealth, exacted high customs duties. In 1442 Duke Otto of Bavaria complained that the Fuggers—like other merchants and long-distance hauliers—were bypassing the road over the Hüchelberg in order to save on customs duties.

In 1452 the two brothers, who had gradually come to direct the business, separated. Four years later Andreas, whom the people of Augsburg even then called "rich Andreas," died. His son, Lukas, who sat on the Grand Council of Augsburg as representative of the weavers, held a number of honorary offices: Inspector of Wool, Inspector of Herrings, and Taxmaster. He was, above all, the trusted representative of the guilds; at the same time he was a merchant. On behalf of his native town he went to Frankfurt to negotiate guarantees for travelling merchants. His goods went to Milan, Venice, Nürnberg, Frankfurt, Antwerp, and London. We can follow his traces everywhere. To the later Emperor Maximilian, who was for ever in financial straits, Fugger conveyed a commercial bill from Innsbruck to Antwerp. This money was to pacify his restive soldiery.

This was the beginning of the great credit business of the house of Fugger. Lukas developed a liking for easily earned interest and charges; he permitted himself to be tempted into lending out his money to the great lords who were for ever spending more than was in their coffers. Frequently there were disputes when their debts were due for repayment. The town of Louvain, for instance, could not be made to redeem its huge debt of 10,000 florins either by court judgment or by proscription. To make matters worse, some of Lukas's customers, whom he had trusted too far, went bankrupt, so that even the rich Fugger eventually had to suspend payments. The house of the Fuggers "of the doe," as this branch of the family was known after its coat of arms, declined into poverty.

Jakob Fugger, on the other hand, remained on the solid ground of the weaving trade and of commerce. He sold the cloth from his own and other Augsburg workshops, himself purchased the cotton and dyestuffs, and began dealing in silks and woollens, in clothes, spices, and perfumes. When he died in 1469 he was reputed to be one of the richest citizens of Augsburg, even though the tax books list him only in the seventh place. Lukas Welser, who had made a rich marriage, is shown as owning twice as much as he—14,000 florins.

But it was under the sons of Jakob that the house of the Fuggers "of the lily" reached the peak of its power and prosperity. It enjoyed such a reputation that the Emperor Frederick III bought from it large quantities of gold and silver brocade, silk, and woollen materials for the marriage

25. Coat of arms of the Fuggers, of the "line of the lily." (From a book of antiquities by P. Apian and B. Amatius, 1534)

of his son Maximilian to Margaret of Burgundy. The Fuggers sold the output of 3500 looms; in their warehouses were bales of red and black material for dress trains, and fabrics in parrot green, sulphur yellow, golden yellow, and rose pink. Textiles from all over the world were kept in stock: arras from the Netherlands and Frankfurt, white cloth from Friedberg, red cloth from Kromburg, grey cloth from England, black cloth from Lemberg, coarse woollen cloth from Nördlingen, velvet from Venice, Carcassonne, and Lyons, satin, damask, and taffeta, bombazine, silks, and cottons. In order to cultivate their business connexions, only Ulrich, the eldest of the Fuggers, remained at home; his brothers, Andreas and Hans, went to Venice, while Georg went to Nürnberg to conduct the trade with the East. Markus, Jakob's third son, was a priest in Rome, and the youngest son, also called Jakob, was likewise intended for the priesthood. However, when Andreas and Hans died unexpectedly at an early age, the family asked him to give up his idea of becoming a priest and to become a merchant instead. At the age of eight the highly gifted Jakob was sent to Venice in order to learn the business during a three years' stay at the *Fondaco dei Tedeschi,* the traditional trading and living quarters of the Germans. Nowhere else could a merchant gain such an insight into world trade as in Venice, where Oriental spices, Greek wines, Venetian lace, glass, and silks were traded in exchange for metal, timber, grain, leather, woollens, and linens, and furs from the North. There, moreover, young Jakob learned double-entry accountancy, then called *à la Veneziana,* and learned to understand the interplay of business and politics. He made the acquaintance of the Florentine banking-houses, like that of the Medici; he saw what money and credit could achieve; but he also realized the dangers accompanying such business, dangers to which his rich cousin Lukas had fallen victim. To begin with, the elder Ulrich ruled in the Golden Counting-house in Augsburg while Jakob was employed in the 'foreign service.'

During the war of 1487–88 the Archduke Sigismund of the Tyrol had seized the mines owned by Venice; the Venetians, however, defeated the reckless Archduke and forced him to pay some 85,000 florins in compensation. As he could supply no more than 60,000 florins' worth of copper he obtained a credit from Jakob Fugger; as security for his loan Fugger demanded and received the assignment of the rich Schwaz mining company which had begun to work the recently opened silver-mines, the most productive in the Tyrol.

The agreement was a masterly stroke by young Fugger. The mines in Schwaz were to supply the silver to Fugger at the same price at which they used to deliver it to the Archduke—five florins for each mark (equal to 280 grammes or about ten ounces). On each mark of silver Fugger had to pay the Archduke three florins in taxes, so that the silver cost him eight florins per mark in all. His problem, therefore, was to take the silver, received at a fixed price, to wherever it would fetch a good price in the market—and as a rule, this would be in Venice. It is probable that the Fuggers made a profit of at least four florins on each mark of silver.

The Tyrolean business had thus proved profitable, and before long Fugger was able to extend it considerably. The spendthrift Archduke had been reckless enough to get involved in financial complications with his neighbour, the ruler of Bavaria, and had glibly assigned to him Freundsberg and the Schwaz mines to a total amount of 100,000 florins. But the Habsburgs in Vienna were hostile to Bavaria; they therefore induced their cousin to break with the Bavarian merchant, Baumgartner, and to hand over the entire silver business to the Fuggers.

In 1488 alone the Fuggers advanced to the Tyrolean Archduke the unprecedented sum of 150,000 florins—30,000 florins payable immediately in cash, and the rest in monthly instalments of 10,000 florins. From the business records of the Augsburg firm we know the profit which this transaction yielded. On the 40,000 marks of silver (about 24,500 lb.) which they received in respect of their loan, the Fuggers, after deduction of their overheads, made a profit of about 55,000 florins, or something like 40 per cent. of the sum advanced.

The Tyroleans, horrified by their ruler's disastrous financial transactions, heaved a sigh of relief when his nephew Maximilian took over the county of Tyrol and the Vorarlberg territories against payment of an annuity of 52,000 florins as well as the residual debt with the house of Fugger, in an amount of 46,000 florins, which he redeemed with 5750 marks of silver paid in 42 weekly instalments. Thus began the close co-operation of the Fuggers with the Vienna Habsburgs in the person of Maximilian, who was shortly afterwards elected Emperor of the Holy Roman Empire. Known as "the last knight," Maximilian had far-reaching, indeed boundless plans. He wanted to secure for his house the neighbouring kingdoms of Bohemia and Hungary and to drive the Turks out of Europe. He dreamed of adventures and great chivalrous tasks without giving a thought to the vast sums of money which would be necessary for his projects. This money was to be found for him by the Fuggers.

Jakob Fugger first of all developed the silver-mines of the Tyrol until they were working to capacity. In 1491 he once more made a loan to his sovereign—120,000 florins, advanced on the security of increased silver deliveries. This advance was nowhere near being repaid when Fugger had to grant further credit to the Emperor—this time to the tune of 10,000 florins a month.

In 1494 Maximilian suddenly tried to sever his relations with the Fuggers and to mortgage the silver-mines to a Nürnberg syndicate in order, by this questionable procedure, to obtain further sums of money. The Augsburg merchant, however, intervened energetically. He insisted on his mortgage, and compelled the Emperor to break off negotiations with the Nürnberg group. In 1494 the trading company of the Fuggers was transformed into an open company, probably the first in Germany, under the name of "Ulrich Fugger and Brothers, of Augsburg." A 'firm'—the term came from Italy—is more than a loose association of partners; it is a corporation in law, with its own capital. The three brothers, Ulrich, Georg, and Jakob, undertook, for a period of six years, to leave their 'capital plus gain' in the business on a basis of an equal share in the profits. The company's sign was a trident, based on a misinterpretation of the name of Fugger; in fact, it comes from the old German word for dyeing.

Having derived such benefit from the silver trade, the enterprising Fugger now turned his attention to copper, a metal in great demand not only in Europe but even more so in the East and in India, where mineral raw materials were scarce. Eastern merchants were increasingly asking for copper in exchange for their spices and jewels. With the copper trade Jakob Fugger assumed the management of his company. The decisive point was co-operation with the Hungarian copper-mine owners, the Thurzos, who lacked the capital to get the neglected copper-mines of Hungary into profitable working condition again. Hans and Georg Fugger concluded leases with the Augsburg Thurzos; the Fuggers undertook to market the copper and in exchange advance the sums necessary for improving the technical equipment of the mines, in particular the liquation plant where the silver was separated from the copper ores. This process required large quantities of timber and a considerable amount of water-power.

The next problem was to overcome the difficulty of transport. First of all, the Hungarian King's permission to export the copper was needed, and then permission from the neighbouring territorial rulers to allow its transit. Everywhere the powerful nobles and influential towns wanted to profit from customs duties or at least from their right of staple. The Hungarian copper used to travel from the mines at Neusohl (now Baňska Bystrica, in Eastern Czechoslovakia) via Teschen (now Těšín or Cieszyn on the Czechoslovak–Polish frontier) to Breslau (now Wróclaw) and thence to Danzig. In difficult—and costly—negotiations with Maximilian, Jakob Fugger bought exemption for himself from the Vienna staple and the Danube tolls, so that his copper could be shipped up the Danube through Vienna to Regensburg. Being no longer dependent on Antwerp, he marketed the copper where the merchants most urgently needed this commodity for export to the East—in Venice.

This kind of business policy was possible only by firmly relying on the Habsburgs; they were the masters of the Danube traffic on which, in the last resort, everything depended. The most powerful competitor of Hungarian copper, however, was the Tyrol. If the Fuggers wanted to control Europe's entire copper trade they had to get a footing in Tyrolean copper as well. Already the Tyrol's silver was very largely under their control. As the Medici had done on wool, so the Fuggers based their banking business on silver and copper.

In 1498 Ulrich Fugger had tried, in conjunction with other merchants, to form a syndicate—probably the first in Germany—to regulate the copper market and fix the price of copper. At that time, this meant saving the copper price from collapse. Copper sales had come to a standstill because the war with the Turks had barred the way into Asia. In a letter to the Emperor Maximilian the Augsburg merchant explained that hardly any copper had been sold in Venice during the preceding nine months because the Venetians, from fear of the Turks, were refusing to ship valuable cargoes by sea. The routes to Milan and to France, as well as that to the Low Countries, were blocked. If he, Fugger, had not then bought copper no one else on earth would have undertaken such a risky business. The mines would have stopped producing and would have failed miserably.

As so often happens with this kind of agreement, the partners quarrelled because the allegedly 'independent' Thurzo trading company had thrown large quantities of Hungarian copper on the market. The cartel broke up.

Jakob Fugger now offered four florins per quintal of Tyrolean copper, arguing that he paid no more for it in Hungary. He got his way, and in 1506 Maximilian prohibited the export of Tyrolean copper by anybody else. In return for a new loan of 60,000 florins the Fuggers were also assigned the copper and silver output of the mines and smelting works of Rattenberg. Before long they were reaching out for the former Bavarian mines of Hausham. They even wanted to lease some Swedish mines and the Bohemian mine of Joachimsthal.

When in 1496 the Emperor mounted a campaign into Italy, his treasury was once more at a low ebb. The imperial cities refused to advance any money on account of the 'common penny,' which had been floated, since nobody trusted the Habsburg Emperor. It was then that Jakob Fugger generously offered him the sum of 121,600 florins against the mortgage of the Tyrolean copper-mines. This agreement successfully concluded, the Augsburg merchant first of all kept back the still outstanding balance of the earlier silver loans; he next paid out in cash to the Tyrolean Government the full sum owed to it by its Habsburg sovereign. After deduction of all these items there was a mere 13,000 florins left for Maximilian. With a great deal of difficulty he persuaded Jakob Fugger to grant him further advances to a total of 27,000 florins, in respect of future silver deliveries, so that a sum of 40,000 florins eventually flowed into the imperial coffers.

Over the next few years the Fuggers invested the enormous sum of 1,064,499 florins into the Hungarian copper-mining business, by way of modernizing the mines, building roads, setting up smelting works, and redeeming privileges. Admittedly they did not find these sums single-handed. The balance sheet for the year 1511—*i.e.*, fully 15 years later—still shows a business capital of only 245,463 florins, of which no more than 81,000 florins belonged to Jakob Fugger and 87,853 florins to the heirs of his brother Ulrich; the rest belonged to the heirs of his brother Georg.

Even at the time of his first great loan to the Archduke Sigismund of the Tyrol, Jakob Fugger had been able to find the money only with the help of Antonio de Cavallis of Genoa. The wealthy Prince-Bishop of Brixen, Melchior von Meckau, had so much money invested with the Fuggers that they found themselves seriously embarrassed when, after the Prince-Bishop's death, his heirs immediately demanded the withdrawal of their share. Undoubtedly, it was dangerous to get involved in such risky financial transactions with the Crown. But what was the alternative for the Fuggers? Maximilian's financial position was getting steadily worse. Even the imperial taxes did not help—for if they were paid at all they arrived only after a long delay. The nobles of the Empire, in the face of this situation, proposed that compulsory loans should be imposed upon the great merchant-houses in Augsburg, Ravensburg, and the Hanseatic towns. But the merchants remained inflexible. Once again the Fuggers had to come to the rescue. As security for a sum of 50,000 florins they had extensive domains assigned to them—the lands of the county of Kirchberg and the manor of Weissenhorn. Since the loan was never repaid these lands became

Fugger property; they belong to the family to this day. But even this 50,000 florins was not nearly enough.

At last, in 1509, the League of Cambrai promised the Emperor substantial sums of money, to be paid out in instalments in Rome, Florence, and Antwerp. Jakob Fugger undertook the transmission of this money. After having the accounts assigned to him he paid out part of the sum within a fortnight and the balance within six weeks in bills of exchange drawn on Augsburg. That was a remarkable banking transaction for those days. The costs and dangers of transport, whether of precious metals or merchandise, justified what was then called an 'arbitrage' or *cambio arbitrio,* a differential computation of the amount paid in at one place and paid out at another. With such large sums this produced a considerable profit.

To transmit money from Rome to Augsburg was comparatively easy, because it had only to be offset against the payments which were made regularly in Germany to the Holy See. This alone represented a very considerable financial deal for those days. Conditions were then particularly favourable because since 1494 Florence had been a democracy under French protection. The Medici had been expelled and the other banking-houses, like the Strozzi and Salviati, were relying largely upon France. Germany had a free hand.

There was no end in sight to the Emperor's financial difficulties, nor to his fantastic plans. In order to become Pope he wanted to bribe the Roman cardinals. Once again the Fuggers were to have advanced enormous sums on the security of future Papal revenues. Already they owned the entire silver output of the Tyrol for eight years ahead, and the copper output for the next four. Pressed by the Emperor, Fugger replied cautiously that he did not know how many more years he could expect to live or how the fortunes of war would go in the near future. Moreover, he explained, he had "much other great business, and more coming in every day"; business was "coming into his house such as, a few years before, he would gladly have ridden a long way to pursue." Nevertheless, he was turning it all down because he had reached a ripe old age and had no children; he would content himself with his existing business and not seek any new.

What sort of business was it that came "into the house" of the Augsburg merchants? Since the Portuguese had discovered the sea route to India the spices no longer came to Europe by the laborious route via

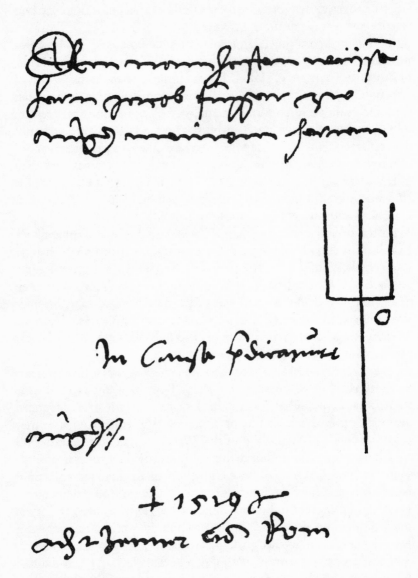

26. Address of a letter written by Anton Fugger from Rome in 1519 to Jakob Fugger, with the latter's receipt note and the firm's trademark

Egypt or Syria, but along the Atlantic coast of Africa to Lisbon. Venice lost its predominant importance. The marketing of the spices which now came in via Western Europe had to be organized anew; moreover, a way of equalizing the payment balance with Portugal had to be found.

After all, the spices were not captured booty but had been purchased for a considerable price. Indeed, a good deal of haggling was usually necessary with the local rulers, the proud maharajahs, the powerful Moguls. For payment they demanded precious metal and then still more precious metal, as well as copper in unlimited quantities, and finally linen and linen clothes. All these commodities were traded in Antwerp. Until then the English had been the only ones to sell their cloth there in competition with that from Flanders; the Italians and the Hanseatic merchants had remained faithful to Bruges even though the Swin had become so silted up that sea-going ships were no longer able to enter.

The South German merchants realized the importance of Antwerp when the King of Portugal established his 'factor' or business agent there in order to market the Indian spices, mostly by the entire shipload. In 1484 the Bruges counter of the Hanseatic League complained that the staple was being held in Antwerp all the time, and not merely for the great fairs at Whitsuntide and in the autumn, on the Feast of St Bavo. Unlike Bruges, which was hamstrung by guild regulations, Antwerp granted the merchants full "fair privileges," above all exemption from customs duty and protection by law during the whole year.

Antwerp opened for the Fuggers the door to the Asian business. In 1505, in conjunction with other German and Italian merchants, they equipped a fleet to bring merchandise back from the East Indies. They were not allowed to make this voyage a second time: the Portuguese wanted to pocket the profits themselves. From then onward an Augsburg factor was established in Lisbon who would regularly send large quantities of pepper to Antwerp, where the Fuggers maintained a house of their own and further consolidated their leading position in the pepper market. At the same time they increasingly channelled their silver and copper to Antwerp. Before long they also transacted major financial business from Antwerp.

When the Emperor Maximilian relinquished his guardianship in

Burgundy of his grandson Charles, later to become the Emperor Charles V, upon his coming of age, he received a sum of 100,000 florins as compensation. And who but the Fuggers accepted this money for transmission to Vienna? The Augsburg firm was even doing business with England. At first it had confined itself to transmitting England's financial contributions to the Emperor, since the real bankers of England were still the Italian firm of Frescobaldi. This banking-house, however, was not in a position to hold such a large sum in ready money; very soon they had to borrow 60,000 florins from the Fuggers in order to be able to pay out the sum in Germany at all. Without the help of the Augsburg merchant-house Maximilian would probably not have been able to pay his German mercenaries. Before long a request came in also from the Netherlands Court, from the young Duke Charles. Bernhard Stecher, the Fuggers' factor in Antwerp, had to advance him 27,000 pounds at 40 pfennigs of Flemish money at a rate of interest of 11 per cent., on the surety of the town of Antwerp. A year later, with this loan still not repaid, new requests for money were already coming in, as Charles had to travel to Spain to assume the crown. Yet the coffers of rich Burgundy were still hopelessly empty.

The principal business of the Fuggers consisted not in granting credit and profiting from interest, but in the transmission charges, the 'arbitrage.' They undertook to transmit monies not only for the German clergy, but also for that of Poland, Scandinavia, and Hungary— in particular the service fees which became due when a bishop succeeded another. The Pope deposited all incoming monies, especially those of the Jubilee Year of 1509, with the Fugger bank, which already handled a large part of the transmissions from Germany. New business came along. When the 24-year-old Albrecht of Brandenburg, of the house of Hohenzollern, though already Archbishop of Magdeburg and Administrator of the Bishopric of Halberstadt, wished in addition to become Archbishop of Mainz, he required a Papal dispensation— and this cost a good deal of money. Moreover, he had to pay 42,000 Rhenish florins to the Cathedral Chapter of Mainz in order to redeem Gernsheim, which had been pawned to Hesse.

Behind these financial transactions were aligned big political moves. The Hohenzollerns, supported by the March of Brandenburg, by the German Order in Prussia, and by the biggest and most influential

Archbishopric, wanted to become the leading power in the Holy Roman Empire. They undertook to pay the sum of 21,000 ducats in Rome against Albrecht's promissory note. The Fuggers' factor in Rome, Johannes Zink, succeeded in getting the Pope to grant to Albrecht, in exchange for a further 10,000 ducats, an indulgence for the Cathedral of Mainz. At first the Hohenzollern emissary had a bad fright; where on earth were they to find the new sum, considering that their credit was exhausted with 20,000 ducats? The Elector Joachim of Brandenburg advised his brother Albrecht to make arrangements with the Fuggers. The 10,000 ducats which Albrecht was to pay to the Pope were intended for the construction of St Peter's; for this purpose the Pope had indulgences issued throughout Germany.

To each indulgence box the representative of the house of Fugger held a key. The boxes could be opened only in the presence of witnesses and of a notary; half the sum in the box was transferred to the Pope—through the Fugger bank—the other half went to the Fuggers in part redemption of their advances to the Archbishop. The coins, we read in the records, "rang merrily in the boxes." In 1517 the Archbishop Albrecht owed the Fuggers only a little over 6000 Rhenish florins, or one-sixth of his original credit; the balance sheet of 1527 no longer lists him as a debtor at all. The business had been smoothly completed, but the unity of the Church was finally broken. The indulgence, however, proved a bitter disappointment to the Pope; according to the Vatican accounts it yielded only 5149 florins. From this total had to be deducted the commission for the Fuggers, so that the Holy See, which in any case was entitled only to half of the balance, received a mere 2466 florins. The Archbishop collected altogether 8436 florins, of which he had to surrender 3000 to the Emperor, so that he was left with only 5436 florins. The violent recriminations which followed were addressed chiefly against the "indulgence traders," in particular the Dominican Tetzel, who had shown himself a little too smart at business.

The reverse came from an unexpected quarter. After the death of King Ladislaus of Hungary in 1516, the young King Louis allowed himself to be persuaded into a dangerous adventure. His baptized Court Jew Szerenzich convinced him that the one way of getting rich quickly and easily would be to admixture to the silver coinage not a quarter but half its weight in copper. The Diet agreed, and the country was flooded with money. Soon, however, it was discovered that this bad money would not buy any merchandise abroad. Even the workmen of the Thurzo copper-mines resolutely demanded to be paid in old coinage or else to be given double wages, considering that everything had become more expensive. The factor had to give in. The general indignation turned against the foreign merchants, chiefly against the Fuggers, whom Szerenzich, now deposed and under arrest, blamed for the national misfortune. With a great deal of difficulty the Fuggers'

27. The money-changer. All money-changers and moneylenders at that time were Jews because Christians were forbidden to charge interest. (Woodcut from Mainz, 1486)

representative at Neusohl moved all valuables to Cracow for safety. Angrily the King of Hungary demanded from the Fuggers a sum of 604,105 florins for the mint's "lost profit" and for other losses allegedly caused by them. He declared magnanimously that he would settle for 200,000 florins and, moreover, would regard the 125,000 florins already confiscated by him as part payment towards that sum. He would then "forgive them" the remainder of the fine. Jakob Fugger now mobilized his influential connexions. He addressed himself to the imperial chancellory, to the King of Poland, the Emperor himself, the Archduke Ferdinand, and the Dukes Wilhelm and Ludwig of

Bavaria. In support of Jakob Fugger's complaint, the Emperor was to "set the whole empire in motion against Hungary." An even weightier step was the threat by the Augsburg merchant that he would make sure that "in no place in Germany would Hungarian copper be accepted for buying or selling unless King Louis relented, compensated the Fuggers, and immediately reinstated them in their commerce."

These were weighty words. Fugger's nephew, Georg Thurzo, advised him to give up the Hungarian business altogether, but the proud merchant replied that he would not be driven out of his realm by anybody and that he "would make profit while he could." Jakob Fugger was sixty-six at the time. Only on his deathbed, in 1525, did he have the satisfaction of hearing that the King of Hungary was again offering him the lease of the copper-mines.

Between 1526 and 1539 the Fuggers sold 267,000 quintals of copper from Hungary, most of it via the Baltic to Antwerp, as well as 112,000 marks of silver, most of which they supplied to the Hungarian mint. However, when the Turks occupied Buda in 1541 Anton Fugger thought it wiser to withdraw from the now hazardous Hungarian business.

In view of the success of his close co-operation with Maximilian, Jakob Fugger was vitally interested in the election of his successor. He had to prevent Francis I of France from becoming German Emperor. The scales would be tipped by money. The Electors insisted on cash payment or promissory notes from the great South German merchant-houses, chiefly the Fuggers. But were the merchants to have more confidence in imperial promises than in those of the princes?

Francis I was steadily driving up the demands of the Electors. Whereas at the beginning of March the imperial crown could have been had for 500,000 florins, a few weeks later the price had gone up by another 200,000 florins. At last, when the time for the election came, the Elector of Brandenburg unexpectedly went over to the French side. Charles V had to spend 850,000 florins to make sure of the votes he needed. Of that total the Fuggers alone advanced 543,000 florins; the Welsers, the second richest firm in Augsburg, contributed 143,000 florins, and the Genoese and Florentines between them raised approximately 165,000 florins. Not all this money went into the Electors' pockets; the Spanish agents had to be paid, and the Swabian League and the imperial knights under Franz von Sickingen received 171,000 florins. A further 29,000 florins had to be paid to the Swiss mercenaries—and thus the list continued interminably.

Jakob Fugger, the great "Governor," never accounted for his decisions to his partners, the sons of his brothers. His hand alone was firmly on the helm of his business. According to the property registers for 1511 and 1527 the business assets of the Fuggers (not counting their private property) increased from 245,463 florins to 2,021,202 florins, although a sum of 48,672 florins was withdrawn from the business in 1511 for payments to various members of the family. Altogether a profit of 1,824,411 florins was made over a period of 17 years, or on average 54½ per cent. per annum. Never before had a private person accumulated such a fortune. The Fuggers then owned five times as much as the Medici had done in their heyday. In terms of present-day money their fortune would have to be estimated at about $28,000,000 with a real purchasing power about five times that figure.

Jakob's successor, his nephew Anton, was careful during the first few years of his management not to get involved in any more credits to the Habsburgs. He gladly left this business to the Genoese, who rose to the leading place in European finance during the next few decades. Later records enable us to trace clearly the gradual shift of the Fugger trade away from ore-mining and the metal business towards the Indian commerce handled at Antwerp.

In 1546 the mines and the entire Hungarian trade accounted for no more than 368,000 florins on the profit side of the Fuggers' business, whereas a sum of 1,066,000 florins was outstanding from Spain where their investments in 1527 (after deduction of liabilities) had been no more than 170,000 florins.

The Spanish business had been started by Jakob Fugger. When the Emperor Charles V had proved tardy in repaying the debts he had incurred in connexion with his election, the far-sighted Augsburg merchant had made sure of a valuable collateral: he had 'leased' the revenue of the great religious Orders of chivalry in Spain, whose enormous landed property came under the sovereign's ownership upon their sequestration. The estates of the Orders, the so-called *maestrazgos,* supplied agricultural produce—mainly grain. This was sold in Lisbon, and exchanged there at favourable prices for East Indian spices which were then shipped to Antwerp. The Fuggers were thus able to do magnificent business in Spain with their money without any serious transmission problems.

Between 1538 and 1542 the Fuggers, at an increased lease fee of 152,000 ducats, had an annual revenue of 224,000 ducats, which means a profit of 50 per cent. During 1551 and 1554 they even operated with a profit of 85 per cent. on the invested capital. To this must be added the mercury-mines of Almaden, which had first been worked in Roman times. Until the days of the Fuggers, however, the mercury in Spain had been used almost exclusively for the manufacture of cinnabar pigment; the Fuggers, experienced mine-owners that they were, knew of course how important mercury was in silver production whenever the necessary wood was not available for ordinary smelting. The mercury evaporates, and this vapour combines with silver to form silver amalgam from which the mercury can be recovered. The mines of Almaden acquired tremendous importance for the Peruvian silver production, since the extraction of silver at Potosi at an altitude of over 12,000 feet was possible only with the help of mercury. As no timber was available at that altitude the ores could not be smelted in the ordinary way. Year after year the Spanish mercury went to America, and year after year the Fuggers made their profit.

The American trade! The Fuggers and their business partners, the Welsers, knew only too well what was at stake. Would Southern Germany succeed in maintaining its predominant position or would it decline into a remote corner bypassed by the great stream of world commerce? Venice was an example of a leading trading city utterly declining within a few decades.

Spices no longer came to Europe via the Red Sea and the Mediterranean, but by the sea route around Africa to Lisbon. The Turks, moreover, blocked the export of cotton from Egypt. Augsburg thus lost its most important source of raw materials. Moreover, its staple article, fustian, was not selling any longer. It was being supplanted by pure cotton materials from India. Was the fate of Southern Germany inextricably tied up with that of Venice?

With its 15,000,000 inhabitants Germany represented a large and receptive market during the first half of the sixteenth century. Economically it controlled the entire Scandinavian and East European areas, as well as the Danube basin. The position of the Hanseatic traders and of the great Southern German merchants was still unshaken in Poland

and Hungary. Besides, there was a justifiable hope that it would be possible to extend the commercial network over England and the Low Countries. The confident Hanseatic merchants were still established at the Steelyard in London. The English, as yet, did not enjoy among the Iberian nations, who had a firm hold on the Eastern as well as the American trade, the same degree of confidence and friendship as the

28. A merchant's premises. (Woodcut by the "Petrarch artist," *fl.* 1514–36, from *Der Teutsch Cicero, Augsburg,* H. Steiner, 1534)

great German merchant houses. It should, therefore, be possible to build up anew an overseas business from Antwerp. This great plan had first been conceived by Jakob Fugger "the Rich." The great advantage which the Fuggers had over all their competitors was that they controlled the merchandise which alone was in demand in the East—silver and copper. Moreover, they had the necessary capital at their disposal for buying entire shiploads from the King of Portugal and paying for them in cash. Who could compete with them in this respect?

Antwerp accepted any quantity of silver and copper. There was no need for worry on that score, as there had been some years earlier in Venice when Hungarian copper had to be marketed at bargain prices because the Turks had cut the sea routes. Cotton would sell readily in any quantity; perhaps linen fabrics might be exported to the East

29. The yardstick. The customs posts on the Rhine—there were over forty of them in the fourteenth century—measured the capacity of every single barrel. In addition to barrel duty there was also sack duty. (Title-page of Kern's *Visierbuch*, Strasbourg, 1531)

Indies in exchange? In Antwerp, moreover, there was no need to consider the local artisans and merchants, as the Hanseatic League was obliged to do in Bruges. Already the Fuggers were establishing trading-posts in the principal Hanseatic towns; already they were taking a share in the Baltic trade; already their messengers were being dispatched to Scandinavia and Poland. They even wanted to break into the Italian business by supplying Venice and Milan from the North. Only

France had to be excluded so long as the quarrel between Francis I and the Emperor continued. But perhaps that would be settled one day.

The Fuggers sought and found support from other Southern German merchants. This is clearly revealed by the balance sheet for 1539; as partners in the firm we find Hans Welser and his brothers with a share of 29,000,000 maravedi, equal to 80,000 ducats, and Sebastian Neidhard with the huge sum of 39,400,000 maravedi.

What, then, caused these schemes to fail? They were wrecked not by any natural or inevitable difficulties, but by the friend of the Fuggers, the Emperor Charles V.

We are familiar with the personality of the man on whose realm the sun never set, the last sovereign to embody the entire majesty and dignity of imperial power as understood by the Middle Ages, the victor of the battles of Pavia and Mühlberg, the conqueror of Tunis. The painters have given us his portrait—dignified, august, truly imperial. The historians commend his clear reason, his balanced judgment, his grasp of the great questions of politics. But we also know him as the leading merchants of his day saw him—Jakob Fugger the Rich and his nephew Anton. They saw a very different person.

The Emperor suffered from one positively fatal weakness: he was no good at arithmetic. The costs of waging a war had increased out of recognition since the armies of knights and their retainers had been supplanted by mercenaries who had to be paid by the sovereign. A Milan *condottiere* once told King Louis XII of France that wars needed money, more money, and still more money. A normal levy of mercenaries would cost, according to a calculation made in 1532, roughly 560,000 florins for six months' pay and equipment, but not taking into account supplies of food, baggage train, and various sundries. A Spanish corps kept in Southern Italy for about six months cost 1,250,000 ducats.

Against all warnings by his Ministers the Emperor time and again got involved in major campaigns. He enlisted large numbers of mercenaries, made far-reaching promises which could never be kept—and was invariably surprised to find his coffers empty. Disaster was only just averted in 1525, during the war against Francis I of France, when the two armies were menacingly facing each other at Pavia and no money available. How were the muttering mercenaries to be paid? Fortunately the Emperor was victorious. For the moment his financial worries were at an end since the French had to pay an enormous ransom (1,250,000 ducats) for their King, who had been taken prisoner. Within two years, however, the same situation arose again. Again there was no money to pay the discontented troops. Thereupon the imperial army, incensed, marched upon Rome and mercilessly sacked it. It was a long time before the Eternal City recovered from this *sacco di Roma*. Its riches had been plundered and its artistic life ruined. Half a century later a similar catastrophe took place in Antwerp under Philip II. Again there was no money to pay the troops; again the troops mutinied. For three days the mutinous troops looted the city, killing 8000 burghers and accumulating a booty of 15,000,000 florins. More than 500 of the finest buildings went up in flames. Antwerp was reduced to poverty.

Whenever he was in bad financial straits the Emperor expected the great merchant-houses to come to the rescue. Without giving it a second thought he would mortgage the future and make countless promises. If the merchants held back he simply extorted the money from them by threats. This is what Lucas Rem of Augsburg wrote about the Emperor Maximilian, the grandfather of Charles V:

> He was pious, not of high intelligence, and always poor. He pawned so many towns and castles, revenues, and estates in his country that little was left to him. He always wanted to wage war and yet lacked the money for it. At times when he wanted to make war his servants were so poor that (like the Emperor himself) they could not pay the hostelry bill for the night.

To get funds for his war against the League of Schmalkalden the Emperor Charles V ruthlessly put the screw on his friends, the Fuggers in Augsburg (now a Protestant town), on the Genoese, and on the merchants of Antwerp. No sooner had he won a victory than he summoned the Fuggers to his headquarters near Wittenberg in order to borrow more money. It was then that Anton Fugger, weary of Habsburg cunning and brutality, wished to withdraw from business altogether. But that was no longer possible. He who sups with the Devil needs a long spoon. The millions invested in the Spanish business held Fugger firmly chained to the services of the house of Habsburg. The entire business capital of the Fuggers, some 5,000,000 florins, the largest sum ever owned by them and probably by any single firm at any time, was fully tied up in extensive dealings with the Habsburgs. And even this enormous fortune had not been enough;

30. The life of a sixteenth-century merchant. The print shows a Nürnberg merchant's house. (Woodcut "An Allegory of Trade" by Jost Amman, 1539–91)

Anton Fugger had had to obtain credit. Could he afford to let the Emperor fall? In an anxious letter to his faithful factor, Oertel, in Antwerp, a man only too ready to grant credit, Fugger said, "It is indeed His Imperial Majesty's great weakness that he wants to wage war and borrow the money for financing it; I wish these great gentlemen ceased delighting so in wars."

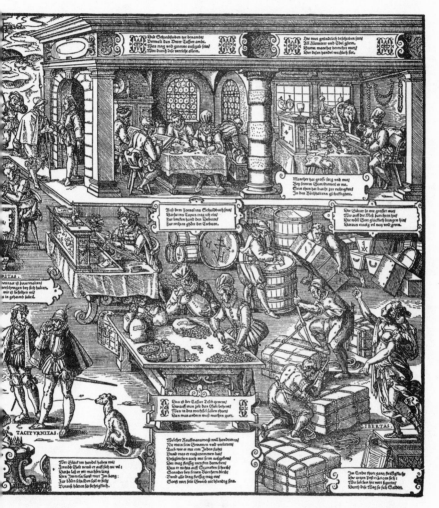

Nevertheless he gave in. At Villach, to where the Emperor had fled from Innsbruck, he granted him the enormous credit of 100,000 ducats cash and 300,000 scudi in bills of exchange on Venice—an unparalleled sum for those days. But he did not have the courage to chalk up his loan to his firm: he made it on his own private account. No doubt he knew why.

9

The Elusive Treasure of El Dorado

QUEEN ISABELLA OF CASTILLE wanted to meet the man who had for several years been pestering her Government for support for his revolutionary plans. Christopher Columbus proposed to sail across the ocean to the West—instead of circumnavigating Africa to the East—in order to get to India. According to his calculations, this route would be very much shorter; moreover, it would lead straight to the heartland of the rich Asian trade. A mere 60 degrees of longitude west of the Canary Islands, which belonged to Spain—*i.e.*, after no more than one-sixth of the circumference of the earth—his ships must invariably encounter the first islands off the Asian mainland. The Crown of Spain would gain the commerce with India and win dominion over the richest lands on earth.

But the verdict of the experts who had carefully examined the proposals of the Genoese had been unfavourable and often positively damning. To begin with, all his calculations were wrong or at least totally unsupported by fact. It was indeed possible that the Asian continent extended very much farther to the East than had hitherto been assumed. But as far as the Eastern trade was concerned, what mattered was neither the east coast of Asia nor any islands off it, but only India itself, above all its western coast and Ceylon. On this point all the old authors were agreed, as were also the Arabs through whose hands the spice and jewel trade had been going for centuries.

India, however, was situated only 35 degrees longitude East of the entrance to the Red Sea, and only 45 degrees East of Egypt. Even if the route round the tip of Africa was very much longer than was in fact assumed in Portugal, was a crossing of the boundless ocean to India not a piece of utter folly? And even if this westward route did lead to India, would Spain be in a position to maintain commerce with those distant lands?

But the strongest argument against Columbus's plans was the man himself. True, he called himself a merchant, but did he possess any of the qualities which marked a good merchant? In earlier years he had worked for the Genoese merchant house of the Centurione, who had sent him first to Chios and later to London. While sailing to England an attack by French pirates drove the young merchant to Lisbon. Subsequently he represented the house of Centurione in Madeira, then an important producer of sugar-cane, a valuable and, at that time, rare sweetening agent. This then was the sum total of his commercial experience. He had married the daughter of a senior Portuguese official.

What turned the learned Spanish counsellors more than anything against the adventurer was the frivolous manner in which he seemed to be planning his voyage and his boundless, positively fantastic demands. The first voyage, he explained, was to cost practically nothing; he would take with him no military force of any size nor any merchandise for barter. Instead the Genoese stubbornly demanded the title of Admiral and the rank of supreme official in the territories to be discovered, as well as a major share in all treasures. What for? Merely as a reward for the discovery? And who was to conquer the country subsequently, who was to colonize it, who was to build up its commerce? To none of these plain questions did Columbus have an answer.

Strangely enough, the very thing that set officials and scholars against Columbus attracted the Queen. To sail to the West across the sea! To preach the word of God to the heathens! To break the power of the infidels who had been barring the West's trade with the wonderland of India and profiting hugely from their part of intermediary! Perhaps even to break the power of Islam altogether by attacking it from the rear! All these were ideas which the stranger developed with great passion and almost religious fervour, imbued with the faith that God had chosen him as His instrument.

At the time, in Córdoba in 1486, the Queen did not see her way to approving the funds for the bold enterprise: her hands were as yet tied by the war against the Moors in Granada. But six years later, in 1492, a small fleet of three caravels set out towards the West—five years before Vasco da Gama discovered for the Portuguese the route to India around Africa.

How different were the preparations for these two voyages! Columbus was content with a few glass beads and other trash, such as in his youth he had fobbed off on the inhabitants of the west coast of Africa.

Oceanica Classis

31. The *Santa Maria*, Columbus's flagship; a fifteenth-century caravel. (From Columbus's report to Santangel, 1493)

The Portuguese, on the other hand, carefully furnished their fleet with gold and silver, presents of goodwill, and bales of woollen fabrics. But when the ships reached their respective destinations the Spaniards encountered naked savages who eagerly accepted anything the Europeans offered to them, whereas the Portuguese found the pampered Arab merchants of the Indian coast unimpressed by their offerings. Even merchandise in demand in the Mediterranean was in their eyes worthless. They advised the Portuguese on future occasions to bring only precious metals, possibly some copper, and above all hempen ropes. Anything else that the Europeans had to offer they turned down with disdain.

The Portuguese returned—not to trade merchandise, however, but with their powerful warships in order to snatch from the Arabs their dominant position in the Pacific Ocean. Within a few decades the picture had changed completely. The Spaniards allowed the great merchants of Western Europe to take part in their voyages to the Americas. In Portugal, on the other hand, the Crown alone controlled all commerce; the independent merchant was excluded.

Yet the wealthy merchant-houses of Southern Germany were trying hard to gain a foothold in the Indian trade. The fleet which in 1504 again set out from Lisbon to make for India round Africa included some ships equipped by the Welsers of Augsburg and laden with valuable German merchandise. In subsequent years the foreign merchants were reduced to purchasing their Indian merchandise in Lisbon and reselling it in Central Europe. The Portuguese, who at first organized their voyages of discovery as commercial enterprises, intent on peaceful trade rather than military conquest, were now flaunting their military power.

The Spaniards, on the other hand, gratefully accepted the help of foreign merchants, even on a considerable scale. When it was found that the newly discovered islands were not part of Asia, the merchant Amerigo Vespucci, the Sevillan representative of the Medici, attempted to penetrate even farther to the West, right round the American continent, if possible as far as the Spice Islands. However, south of the Equator the coast of the new continent was found to project so far to the east as to reach into the half of the world assigned to Portugal. Vespucci thereupon gave up his project: all he did, in fact, was visit Brazil. The Portuguese Cristobal de Haro, the proprietor of one of the most important merchant-houses in Lisbon, who was in conflict with his King, financed Magellan's voyage under the Spanish flag—the first circumnavigation of the globe.

Even though only one ship returned to Spain and even though Magellan himself had been killed in South-east Asia, the voyage yielded financial profit. The great merchant-houses of Western Europe were encouraged, as a result, to repeat the attempt on their own account. Sebastian Cabot, the son of an Italian and the chief pilot of Spain, who had reconnoitred the Atlantic coast of North America on behalf of the English, was commissioned to equip a new fleet in order to repeat Magellan's voyage and find a route to the Spice Islands, or even to the legendary lands of Ophir and Tharsis.

In this expedition the Germans again participated—the Fuggers and, even more so, the Welsers, probably because on the only voyage to the East Indies in which they had previously taken part, in 1504, they had made a net profit of 175 per cent. on their invested capital of 20,000 florins. The Fuggers at that time had contributed only 4000 florins,

32. Balthasar Sprenger's voyage to the East Indies on behalf of the Fuggers, the Welsers, the Höchstetters, and other great merchants, 1505-6. (Woodcut by Jörg Glockendon after Hans Burkmair the Elder)

whereas the Italians (the Genoese and the Medici of Florence) had raised between them 29,400 florins.

Meanwhile, Jakob Fugger, thanks to his influence with Charles V, achieved the repeal of the prohibition which until then had barred all non-Spaniards from the spice trade with the Moluccas. He had an ambitious plan for shifting the spice trade from Lisbon to Seville, from under the wing of a State monopoly to a free trading city. In exchange for 10,000 ducats Fugger was granted the right of having his own plenipotentiary or agent to accompany the fleet.

The vast machinery built up by the Augsburg merchant was now set in motion. The ships were built in Danzig, where there were enough experienced workmen and where timber, tar, and pitch were very much cheaper. Laden with cheap grain, building timber, and copper (from the Fugger mines in Hungary) the new ships sailed to Lisbon and Seville to be used on the India route.

For the fleet which once more sailed forth along Magellan's route in March 1523, under the command of Garcia de Loaysa, Jakob Fugger, in conjunction with his business friend Cristobal de Haro, supplied, at the Emperor's expense, eight entire shiploads of copper, mast timber, tar, pitch, oakum, and other materials from the Hanseatic towns to Corunna, the base of the new trade. A factor of the Fuggers, Georg Wandler, was on board. The fleet sank miserably in the Pacific Ocean. Nothing was ever heard of it again.

Another factor of the Fuggers, Hans Prunbacher, accompanied the next fleet which sailed three years later under Cabot's command. This fleet, too, never reached the East Indies—but this time the reason was that in South America the Admiral was too dazzled by the rumours he heard of the legendary silver mountains. He searched for them in vain, quite forgetting the original purpose of his voyage. Even though only a single ship returned to Seville four years later, it yielded such a large profit that the Fuggers suffered a loss of only thirty-eight ducats. For many years the Fuggers sued in the Spanish courts for reimbursement of their investments lost in the two Molucca fleets.

For a while the Fuggers toyed with the thought of participating in the colonization of America. But their plans for acquiring land in what to-day is Chile came to nothing. The Welsers participated—temporarily—in Venezuela in the conquest and opening up of South America, but without success. Alongside the *conquistadores,* those men of the sword, the merchants were powerless. Besides, they did not find any merchants in the New World with whom they could have collaborated.

The Portuguese, by way of contrast, encountered in Asia a highly developed Arab merchant class whose commercial sphere extended beyond India, to the Moluccas, and even to China. The Portuguese now likewise extended their huge commercial empire to these remote points. Yet there was a very striking difference between the Arab and the Portuguese methods of trading. The Arabs were pure merchants. They offered their wares to the local princes, and would not dream of promoting commerce by brute force. They were gladly and amicably received wherever they went. In addition, the Arab merchants were far too weak to stand up to the local rulers and, instead of waiting for help from their caliph or sultan, they preferred to act abroad as independent free men. Even where energetic entrepreneurs or a family like the Enosaid on the east coast of Africa founded their own sultanates, they managed without support from their native country.

The Portuguese, on the other hand, would never have gained control of the Indian trade by peaceful means. They simply lacked the merchandise to oust their Arab competitors. Admittedly, the precious metal from Central Europe and (since the middle of the sixteenth century) from the legendary silver mountain of Potosi in Peru and the Mexican silver-mines of Guanajuato somewhat restored the balance of payments between Europe and Asia, so that the exchange of goods was once more on a commercial basis, but this was not enough in the long run. An attempt had to be made to bring European merchandise to India. The country best suited to do this was probably Germany, with its flourishing manufactures and mines. Yet the German merchants had been trying in vain to get a foothold in the Indian trade. They were not admitted. Why should those foreign pepper-bags make money from the international trade which the Portuguese had so laboriously built up? As it was, Portuguese officials and courtiers were annoyed at the tremendous difference between the purchasing price in Southern Asia and the resale price in the Antwerp market. They saw neither the costs nor the risks of the traders, nor did they understand the difficult task of equalizing the balance of payments and of supplying other merchandise in exchange for that received.

Things were different in Spain. Year after year the silver fleet arrived from the West Indies, laden with fabulous, untold treasures of silver. Was the King of Spain, on whose realm the sun never set, really the richest monarch on earth? We have the admiring reports of diplomats, including such experienced merchants as the Venetians. They saw with their own eyes the heavy silver ingots which were carried into the royal treasury. The monarch surely must have fabulous revenues. But was it so in fact?

Was it really such a profitable business to transport the silver from an altitude of over 12,000 feet first down to the Pacific coast, then by sea to the isthmus of Panama, then across the narrow neck of land to the Caribbean coast and thence—by no means the easiest of tasks—past the notorious pirates to Spain? No Spaniard ever performed this calculation, nor, for that matter, any of the impressed diplomats. And yet it would have been easy enough to show that the King was losing quite appreciably on every pound of silver that reached his treasury.

Prospecting for the fabulous silver-mines and their working was done by private entrepreneurs. Only one-fifth of the silver went to the King, the remaining four-fifths had to be paid for in the ordinary way. The new town of Potosi had to be built; there were no roads, there was no livestock, the mercury had to be brought all the way from Almaden in Spain, there was no grain and not even fuel. Up there in the mountains there was nothing but bare bleak rock.

Everybody was getting rich: the mine-owners, the farmers, even the workers—all except the King of Spain. Out of his taxes, consisting principally of the 'royal fifth,' he had to maintain his officials, proud and grand gentlemen like the viceroys in Lima and Mexico; he had to support the Church and the sciences, and above all he had to foot the bill for the military protection of his silver shipments. And that was very expensive, for in the Caribbean Sea and on the Atlantic, and indeed in Spanish waters, there was a permanent state of war. Everybody was out to capture those rich silver ships.

The shippers of Rouen, Dieppe, and St Malo turned the hostilities between France and Spain to their own account by sending out their ships on raiding sorties. Similar operations were later also launched from Le Havre. Thus, in 1523 the sea captains of the shipper Jean Ango, captured two of the three ships carrying tremendously valuable Mexican treasure off the Azores. Convoys alone were no protection. Along the coast of the Caribbean numerous fortresses had to be built, and entire fleets of warships had the single task of keeping off the bold corsairs and later also the English.

If we add up all this expenditure we find that it is considerably greater than the revenue from the silver business. The senior officials and the foreign diplomats did not see this; but the merchants were aware of it, and the ordinary people, caught between the millstones of taxes and devaluation, felt it only too clearly.

The Emperor Charles V spent these huge 'revenues' on paying for his election or for his everlasting wars. He did not see that by far the greatest part of his money had already been spent in advance. Generously he gave the Fuggers vouchers for Spanish money or silver, on which they could not in fact lay their hands. The Spanish population desperately tried to keep the silver in Spain. Throughout the Emperor's reign, and also during that of his son Philip II, we frequently find merchants complaining that it was impossible to get any money out of Spain. The merchants of Antwerp even equipped some ships to collect the silver, but at the last moment some authority or other would invariably intervene and prohibit the export of silver in the face of express imperial orders. It was a hopeless situation.

America's silver undermined and ruined first the Spanish colonial empire, then the finances of the Spanish state, and eventually the entire

33. A Spanish trading-post off the Central American coast, the *Isla de sacrificias*. Sixteenth-century sketch-map. (Cf. José Gorbea Trueba, *La fortaleza de San Juan de Ulva*, Mexico, 1952)

economy of Spain. To have realized this, a man had to have some arithmetic at his command—and neither the bold adventurers nor the Emperor possessed that skill. All the captured treasure was spent on equipping new expeditions and new campaigns. Almagro, Pizarro's partner in the conquest of Mexico, lost the greater part of his enormous fortune on his unsuccessful expedition to Chile. The fortune of Jimenez de Quesada, the conqueror of Bogotá, was frittered away in his search for the land of El Dorado, that phantom which receded more and more the longer the Spaniards pursued it. The boundless revenue derived from the conquest of Mexico was wasted by the conquerors on their fruitless journeys of exploration through North America.

The profits of the rich silver-mines were eaten up by inflation. True, much more silver was mined during the second half of the sixteenth century than before, but the devaluation of the currency had so increased the production costs that the real gain melted away. Even the discovery of mercury-mines in South America (at Huancavelica) meant only a slight saving. At the end of the century the same quantity of silver bought only half the goods it had bought fifty years before. Prices, in terms of silver, had doubled.

The Spanish treasury saw only the absolute increase in State revenue. Between 1523 and 1525—*i.e.*, during the last years of Jakob Fugger's life—it amounted to approximately 400,000 ducats annually. By the middle of the century, between 1554 and 1560, the revenue had risen to 3,500,000 ducats—largely owing to the silver-mines of Potosi. During the reign of King Philip III (1598–1621) it was estimated at 24,000,000

34. Trading between Spaniards and American Indians. (Cf. A. Chavero, *Codex Baranda*, Mexico, 1952)

ducats a year. But what about expenditure? Invariably it exceeded the revenue.

In 1543 alone Spain had to contribute 1,000,000 ducats towards the war against France. The result was a national deficit of 700,000 ducats. The Spanish parliament, the Cortes, resolutely demanded in 1548 that all exports of precious metal and money should be prohibited; this was in fact done in 1552. At the same time the Emperor Charles V mortgaged 600,000 ducats of Spanish silver to the Netherlands Government as an advance towards the costs of the new war against France.

The Netherlanders sent one Balthasar Schetz to Spain, but, typically, he received less than 59,000 ducats in cash and a voucher for 400,000 ducats in respect of the next silver shipment from America, a further voucher for 122,000 ducats to be met by the lease fees of the *maestrazgos*

for six years ahead, plus 200,000 ducats on account of the papal indulgence for the next three to five years. Against these enormous sums
credits were then taken up with the Fuggers and the Genoese—Agostini
Gentili and Silvestro Cattaneo. Of the huge quantities of silver which
arrived in Seville during the next few years no more than 40,000 ducats
went to the Netherlands in part payment of official liabilities. And
what about the remaining silver? It vanished mysteriously; it just ran
through the Spaniards' fingers and prices continued to rise.

Philip II suspended all payments. He simply scrapped the vouchers
given to creditors in respect of Crown revenue and instead gave them
five per cent. State bonds. Nowadays we might have called them compulsory war loans. These loans, however, had no negotiable value
outside Spain. Even the silver which the Fuggers had confiscated was
rerouted to Antwerp aboard Spanish ships. It was the beginning of
the end.

Two years before his death the elderly King Philip II speaks in a
letter of his fear that he might go hungry in his old age. This, then, was
the richest monarch on earth, whose revenue at the time of his death was
roughly thirty times as much as that of his father at the time of his birth.

Yet the men in power failed to diagnose the cause. They simply
blamed the speculators, the usurers, the foreigners, the Germans and
Italians—in short, the merchants. The merchants as a class were the
villains of the piece. If only the State were to control all commerce,
limit and regulate it, eliminate the merchants, and expel the foreigners
all troubles would soon be over.

At the beginning of his reign the Emperor Charles V still spared the
merchants. But as his debts increased beyond all bounds he yielded to
his advisers. His evil genius was his secretary, Francisco Erasso, who
was firmly convinced that the German traders were at the root of the
fiscal disaster. At the same time he was himself surrounded by unscrupulous speculators and usurers who were profiting from the general
difficulties. In the end this honourable official was deposed by King
Philip II and sentenced for gross malversation. To Erasso and the
likes of him the moratorium was a welcome opportunity for squaring
accounts with the hated merchants and creditors.

At the beginning of the reign of Charles V there had been practically
no taxes on commerce with America. Soon, however, an import duty
of $7\frac{1}{2}$ per cent. was levied in Spain, known as *almojarifazgo*; to this was

added an export duty of 5 per cent. and a turnover tax (*alcabala*) of 10 per cent. When the merchandise arrived in America another 6 per cent. had to be paid on it. But all this was not enough. New taxes were imposed, forcing up prices: the *averia*, a levy in respect of the escorting warships; the *almirantazgo*, an impost to remunerate the admiral in America and his war fleet; and the *tonelada*, which was to benefit the shippers of Seville. During their first year of office officials had to surrender half their income, the *media anata*. To this were added frequent 'non-recurring' levies such as the *cruzada* (for a crusade) or the *armada de barlovento* for fighting piracy in the Caribbean.

In 1563 the Cortes complained that, weighed down by taxes, many people were going out of business in order to live on their capital. The Spanish fairs and markets declined. From a letter of the Fuggers we learn that in 1571 the merchants left the fair of Medina del Campo before its conclusion, because of excessive duties, even though the settling of fair accounts had not yet been completed. Everything depended on the silver from America. When greater quantities of silver began to arrive from the newly opened mines of Mexico Seville experienced a veritable intoxication. And yet the 600,000 ducats were but a drop in the ocean of the standing debt of several millions, repayment of which was due but had to be postponed again. Nevertheless the King's Secretary of the Treasury, Juan de Curiel, was already arranging for new credits to a total of 500,000 ducats; but these did not materialize because, as the Fuggers' factor reported back home, "he sought all too cunning advantages: the Treasury Councillors found greater readiness and advantage on the part of the Genoese who have a reputation for squeezing blood out of stones."

The May fair in Medina del Campo, where the banking-houses used to settle their transactions by accountancy, without any cash payments, was prorogued until 1575. By that time only few merchants turned up —mainly those connected with the Court, but none from Burgos and other towns, "and business was slow and reluctant."

The Secretary of the Treasury wanted to close the poorly attended fair after less than a month, but the bankers were unable to settle; no precious metal had arrived for a long time and no cash was therefore available. At last the impatiently expected silver fleet arrived with 3,500,000 ducats on board. Of this total, 2,500,000 belonged to private individuals and 1,000,000 to the King—so that even with this shipment he was not able to redeem all the payment promises made by him on account of it.

Before long the total debt had reached a fantastic figure. The list of creditors was headed by Nicolo de Grimaldi of Genoa with 5,000,000 ducats; then followed the two Genoese, Lomellino and Agostino Spinola, with 1,500,000 ducats each. Lorenzo Spinola and the Fuggers were owed between 3,000,000 and 4,000,000 by the Spanish

35. Genoa about 1493. (From Hartmann Schedel's *Nuremberg Chronicle*)

Crown. Then there were Spanish creditors such as the Secretary of the Treasury, Espinosa, with 2,000,000 ducats, and Juan de Curiel de la Torre with 1,500,000.

The result was national bankruptcy. The decree announcing suspension of payments blames, on the one hand, the usury which runs counter to divine and temporal law, and, on the other, the ceaseless drain of money across the frontier, a drain infringing Spain's vital interests. How, one wonders, did the Spanish officials imagine that the war in the Netherlands and in France would be paid for except by the export of money? The decree also laments, in moving language, the decline of the Castilian fairs. Small wonder in view of the Crown's economic policy.

Earnestly the merchants reminded the King that only credit based on trust could save Spain. If the merchants were ruined the King would have no one to help him. Not until the following year was the principal creditor received by the King—Nicolo de Grimaldi of Genoa, Prince of Salerno. He was owed the round sum of 5,000,000 ducats by the Crown of Spain. The merchant implored his royal debtor at least to take over the obligations which he, Grimaldi, had taken upon himself. He would content himself with a shirt to his back provided his good name was saved. His pleading was in vain.

After some sort of agreement with his creditors, based on more promises for the future, which again led to bankruptcy, the borrowing of money cheerfully continued. The Genoese were still not scared off; once more they advanced to the King 5,000,000 ducats. The Fuggers' factor in Spain merely shook his head; it seems, he writes, that "the Genoese have more paper than cash." To begin with, it really seemed as though Genoa was making a profit from these dubious transactions. Agostino Spinola again lent the Spanish Government 1,000,000 scudi; later we hear that the Genoese were paying out 2,000,000 scudi in monthly instalments of 150,000 crowns in the Netherlands. In the following year another Spinola, Ambrosio, undertook to pay out 2,500,000 crowns, and eventually we even have a contract with Ottavio Centurioni for a sum of 10,000,000 scudi. When Spain, exhausted by the naval war against England, proclaimed its third national bankruptcy half of Genoa went bankrupt as well.

But surely Spain was a rich country even without American silver? Why did her commerce decline? Why did prices keep rising? The man in the street blamed the merchants; he did not see how grain production was shrinking. In December 1566 the Cortes complained that cultivation of wheat had diminished to such an extent that Spain, at one time the producer of an exportable surplus, was no longer able to meet its own requirements. Since the wool prices had risen out of all proportion, because of 'speculation,' the landowners preferred to go over to sheep-breeding. It was the sheep that transformed Castile, formerly covered with forests, into the treeless sun-baked plateau it is to-day.

During the second half of the sixteenth century cloth-weaving was still flourishing everywhere. Before long, however, we find complaints about excessive prices and the destitution of the population. As Spanish wool could no longer be processed at home it had to be marketed at the international fairs, mainly in Antwerp. But it was too expensive. Yet it was these Spanish supplies, more than anything else, that so overloaded the market that the international wool price collapsed. The sheep-breeders lost their money. Sheep-breeding in Castile, the so-called Mesta, which totalled some 14,000,000 sheep about the turn of the century, declined to half that number within a few decades.

Were the prices alone to blame? The prices reached their peak around the year 1601; subsequently they declined, but Spain continued to get poorer all the time. The reason why prices were dropping was not an increased supply of merchandise but the progressive impoverishment of the people who were consuming less and less. Was it surprising that the Spaniards should place all the blame for their decline on the usurers and "blood-suckers," on the merchants who were skimming off the profits of the extensive Indian trade, who were sending all ready money out of the country, who were acquiring tax farming rights at low rates, and squeezing the country dry?

About the middle of the sixteenth century the State intervened. Officials were to straighten things out again. What a misjudgment of the functions and possibilities of the bureaucratic apparatus! The first thing was the fixing of maximum prices. The result was that even less grain was being grown and the peasants drifted into the towns. The same applied to wool. But what suffered most was the foreign trade because this could not be hamstrung by maximum prices. At the time of the national bankruptcy of 1576 even the two biggest banks in Seville, those of the Espinosa and the Morgas, had to suspend payments. Liabilities reached the staggering figure of 2,500,000 ducats. Thomas Müller, the factor of the Fuggers, realized what this meant. "As a result, the commerce with the [West] Indies, which had hitherto supported all other, has been totally ruined." The general lack of confidence was spreading. The fleet which was due to sail to New Spain in May could not be loaded because "the Cargadores have neither money nor credit; the merchandise supplied them on credit they can no longer assign to the banks." Instead of the privately owned banking-houses a public or State Bank was now to be set up. After all, the King should have sufficient cash at his disposal, since he confiscated the entire silver fleet and refused to pay his debts. But how was he to transmit money to Antwerp? In Spain no one was prepared to undertake any payment obligations. Only the daring Jewish bankers in Lisbon, who urgently needed silver themselves for the Portuguese East Indies shippers, would issue bills of exchange on Antwerp. Against ready payment in silver and an official export permit to Lisbon the factor of the Fuggers eventually risked issuing a bill of exchange for 230,000 escudos. The delay in the transmission of money, however, had disastrous consequences: the Spanish soldiery mutinied and sacked the flourishing city of Antwerp.

Neither Spain nor the merchants trading with her ever recovered from this blow. With Antwerp there collapsed the trade which until then had distributed Indian merchandise throughout Central and Eastern Europe. Likewise no more goods—such as copper, high-quality textiles, blades, weapons, or armour were sent to Antwerp for marketing in America or India, or even in Spain.

As they could no longer sell any merchandise to Central Europe, the Spaniards had to pay in precious metals for all imports. To their horror they saw their silver running through their fingers. Desperately they tried to keep it in their country. Even America felt the consequences. In 1577, when at long last another silver shipment of 5,000,000 ducats arrived in Spain, the King immediately issued a ban on the exportation of any money. Yet only 1,750,000 ducats actually belonged to the King; the remainder belonged to the *conquistadores* and the great gentlemen in America who wanted merchandise in exchange for their good money. What was more, they wanted merchandise not available in Spain but only in the Netherlands and in Germany. However, all payments to these countries had been prohibited.

It was decreed instead that Spain should re-establish the great fairs, and that this should be done by the State. In this project it was to be assisted by the great Spanish merchant houses, Juan Ortega de la Torre and the brothers Vittoria, who were represented on a semi-official organization, the *casa de contratacion*, in Seville. This *casa de contratacion* was granted a monopoly; private commerce with America ceased entirely. The 'fabulous' profits were to be cut down to a 'fair scale.' This, at any rate, was the idea of the all-powerful bureaucrats to whom a merchant meant a man with a thorough legal and possibly also theological training, with some understanding of the canonic prohibition of receiving interest, and with the ideal of the ascetic life, but who had never spent a sleepless night tormented by anxiety over a ship long overdue. Such were the men to be charged with the development of commerce with America!

Until then the Spanish administration in America had been trying to encourage agricultural production and urban crafts. Rice, silk, hemp, flax, wine, sugar, and cotton were being produced in increasing

36. Spanish merchants off the coast of Haiti (from Columbus' report to Santangel, 1493)
This woodcut was made very shortly after the discovery of America

quantities. Mexican shipyards were building the great galleons which sailed as far as Manila. How, then, was Spain to sell any merchandise in America when the inhabitants there were producing everything themselves? Gradually, therefore, the Government curbed the enterprise of the American settlers: in 1595 they were even forbidden to cultivate the vine. In future, every drop of wine was to be imported from Spain, and on every drop the State would make its profit. Commerce was being strangled increasingly. Ships were allowed to sail only to America from Seville. Sailings could no longer be made according to requirements but only at fixed dates and in large convoys —at first twice a year, later less frequently. Whereas originally sailing in convoy had been for the sake of protection, between 1575 and 1582 it became the normal mode of shipping to the Americas. Two fleets, one from Santo Domingo and the other from Cartagena, carried the whole yield of precious metal and all other merchandise to Europe in order to return with goods in demand in the New World: velvet, silk, lace—in fact, everything which the high officials and *conquistadores* required, including weapons, ammunition, and tools.

Commerce with the Plate estuary came to a complete standstill; the customs barrier at Cordoba cut the American continent in two. The great development plans for the eastern half of South America were thus doomed to failure. Were the Spanish people to be blamed for this? The English used to despise the Spaniards for their lack of enterprise, for allowing themselves to be tied to the apron-strings of bureaucracy. But was this contempt justified? What could the individual achieve against a State which crushed everything? When the plague of piracy became increasingly serious, the merchants of the Northern Spanish provinces, Basques and Galicians, approached King Philip II with a tempting offer: they were prepared, at their own expense, to equip a powerful fleet in order to drive the French and English from the high seas, on condition of trade being freed.

King Philip II declined the offer. He feared that a free, untrammelled merchant class would soon shake off all State control and even avoid paying taxes. And who then would raise the large sums which the Crown owed all the world over? Would the Spanish economy survive in free competition, when merchants were at liberty to deal in Spanish, Netherlands, English, and French merchandise? Instead the King equipped the "Invincible Armada" at State expense; it failed dismally. What was left of commerce about the end of the seventeenth century scarcely deserved the name.

Conditions were not much better in Portugal. The Portuguese colonial empire had likewise become the domain of bureaucrats, courtiers, and favourites, of the higher and middle nobility, of profiteers, and of men looking for easy money.

In all the important Asian ports, which alone were permitted by the Portuguese to engage in commerce, official representatives purchased the merchandise at fixed prices. Fraud and malversation were a daily occurrence. Ships belonging to the Crown carried the goods to Europe where the royal factor tried to market them among the merchants. Although the volume of trade increased considerably profits shrank in the most startling manner. The terms of trade had changed completely; that was the whole secret. As the demand for spices continued to increase, it naturally caused the price to rise; at the same time the supply of precious metal which Europe used for payment of its purchases became more plentiful. In other words, the purchasing power of silver steadily declined. The Portuguese officials had to pay

37. Lisbon in the sixteenth century (a contemporary Dutch engraving)

ever higher prices, in terms of silver, while at the same time encountering ever greater difficulties in finding solvent customers in Europe, now that the great merchant-houses were bankrupt and Antwerp no longer the important entrepôt that it used to be. The distributive apparatus in Europe became more and more expensive.

The bureaucrats in Lisbon were unable to explain this economic process; they put all the blame at the door of their competitors, who were piercing their monopoly and paying higher prices in Asia in order to break into Portugal's sacred purchasing areas. The French were blamed, and the English, and most of all, the Dutch. The spice trade, moreover, had long ceased to be a purely commercial affair; it had become a predominantly financial transaction, since a complete shipload was only allotted to a merchant who paid in advance. And these advances became bigger and bigger. Even after the Spanish bankruptcy the merchants paid advances totalling 900,000 crowns in respect of promised deliveries of spices. A year later, in 1560, the Portuguese Crown suspended payments. The business accounts of the Fuggers and the Maug family alone showed demands totalling 15,000,000 reis. These debts were never paid.

Only the city of Genoa appeared to be an exception to this rule. How could that have been? Davanzati, a citizen of Florence, wrote in 1581 with a mixture of mockery, admiration, and envy:

> The Genoese have invented a new kind of paper business which they call "Besançon fairs" because that was their place of origin. But to-day they are held in Savoy, in Piedmont, in Lombardy, and in the province of Trento, outside the gates of Genoa, or indeed in any other place, so that a better name would be 'Utopia,' that is to say, fairs without locality. In contrast to the Lyons fair no merchandise is bought or sold; all that happens is that 50 or 60 bankers meet together, each with a little paper book, in order to regulate the banking business of nearly the whole of Europe and to renew it by re-exchange at a rate of interest agreed among them, their main purpose apparently being to protract this game indefinitely. In this way they gain 250,000 scudi a year in commission alone.

In view of the then usual commission rate of one-third per cent. from both parties, this suggests an annual turnover of 37,500,000 scudi.

Another observer writes a little later:

> The fairs are the crossroads where the highways of the diverse and separate nations meet. They are the ocean whence all waters of commercial life originate and whither they all return. At these fairs nearly all the merchants of Europe meet together, either in person or through their representatives.

It was at these Genoese fairs that the European merchants, threatened and oppressed by the State and fleeced by countless national bankruptcies, attempted to keep world trade going.

To this end they created a currency that would be independent of governments—the *scudo di marchi*, a unit not represented by any coin but by a definite quantity of gold. The bankers also tried to define the *scudo di marchi* in terms of silver and, in this way, to introduce a double currency. But this part of the project failed. As the large quantities of silver arriving from Peru and Mexico were ruining the silver price, the merchants decided to keep to gold. One hundred of these *scudi di marchi* were worth as much as ninety-nine real gold pieces of best mint quality from Spain, Naples, Venice, Genoa, or Florence. It was now possible to make payments even without gold and yet at the full rate—in any event, gold was in short supply and insufficient for the volume of trade transacted. Payments were made by means of a clearing account, without any money changing hands. But if a merchant insisted on paying cash he was able to do so against a discount of one per cent.

The *scudo di marchi* was thus a hard currency. An Italian contemporary observes: "The clever bankers have achieved what no prince ever succeeded in achieving: they have made possible what had always seemed impossible." Cash was now flowing like water to the most favourable spots, even if the transport of money was still tremendously difficult. The Genoese bankers accepted the silver in Spain and paid out the equivalent, sometimes even in advance, at whichever fair their customer chose. Thus, they might set off a consignment of spices to Antwerp, or later Amsterdam, against a payment of ecclesiastical dues or indulgences from Germany to Rome, or a consignment from Italy to France against an order for luxury goods from Northern France placed in Seville—all by means of their little paper books.

The Genoese fairs survived even the profound crises of the sixteenth century, when, following the Spanish national bankruptcy, most of the banking-houses of Genoa went out of business. Only in the seventeenth century did they too begin to decline, probably because world trade had shifted to Holland and England, where they had little influence.

After the first Spanish national bankruptcy of 1557 the Southern German merchant-houses also went into eclipse—not only the Fuggers and Welsers, but also the smaller ones, like the Kraffts, the Manlichs, the Schorers, and the Maugs of Augsburg, the Ingolds of Strasbourg, all of them respected and prosperous firms trading with the Levant and with England. The decline was universal. "The way our business is nowadays," one of the Fuggers wrote at that time, "100,000 crowns means as much to us as 1,000,000 did some years ago"—even though the value of money had greatly shrunk since. During the last two decades of the sixteenth century and the first two of the seventeenth, bankruptcies among Southern German merchant houses increased at such a rate that only a very few firms were left. For a while Frankfurt on Main, always a focus of commerce, experienced a certain prosperity when the merchants from Antwerp settled there. Johann von Bodeck, the grandson of a nobleman from Thorn, in Prussia, built up a considerable business in the old imperial city. During the last decades of the sixteenth century he imported silk, rice, and drugs from Venice, spices from Amsterdam, mercury from Nürnberg, indigo and wool from Spain. These he then resold—the mercury to Amsterdam, Antwerp, and Hamburg, the indigo, rice, cinnamon, and ginger to Hamburg, and the wool to Amsterdam. He also had a share in the great shipments of rye to Genoa from Amsterdam and Emden. On his instructions Hamburg sent iron and wax to Bilbao. He had money invested in the Dutch East India Company.

In the end he, too, was ruined by credits to princes and cities. He resisted as best he could—but it was of no avail. The Imperial Counsellor Dr Gumpeltzhamer, as the emissary of the Emperor Ferdinand, called on him with strict instructions to obtain a loan of 50,000 taler. Von Bodeck, "more than a little alarmed," tried to point to the poor state of business, but the imperial official threatened that he would block all monies due to von Bodeck from princes and cities of the Empire. He also warned him that criminal proceedings might be taken against him for charging throughout many years six or even seven per cent. interest and lending money to merchants from one fair to another. Under compulsion he eventually invested money in the Mansfeld copper-mines. The city of Leipzig, which already owed him money, was in such straits that it could not install even the most indispensable equipment. The Thirty Years War and the turmoils which followed it finally ruined the old man, who must have possessed a fortune of 500,000 taler about the year 1630.

Small traders continued to exist as before—the huckstress who carried her wares from town to town, the itinerant vendor who turned up at village fairs with his cart. But the international merchant, who had brought prosperity to the Hanseatic towns and to Northern Germany, to Nürnberg and Augsburg and Constance, remained ruined for a long time to come. Emperors, kings, and princes had killed the goose that laid the golden egg.

10

War, Commerce, and Piracy

THE ARRIVAL of English ships in the port of Vera Cruz on the Mexican coast was an occasion for universal rejoicing. They brought a cargo of Negro slaves, tall, powerful creatures, but also good, durable English woollen cloth, keen blades, knives, axes, and shears. And everything was so cheap! The British, moreover, paid excellent prices for the foodstuffs they loaded, and for the Spanish planters' sugar and tobacco for which a ready market had developed in England. Last but not least, the sailors spent their money freely ashore.

Only the Spanish Viceroy of Mexico, in his mountain home, was worried. For several weeks two strongly worded letters had been lying on his desk. The India Council in Seville had sharply complained to him about his subordinates. Why were they tolerating the illicit trade with the English, a trade which was bound eventually to undermine the carefully built-up economy of Spanish America? To break into some one else's business with low prices was not difficult if one had no customs duties or taxes to pay. But where was the money to come from for the salaries of the officials? Between the lines the Viceroy could all too clearly read the charge that, in order to please the settlers, his officials had turned a blind eye—or indeed a pair of blind eyes—on the existing state of affairs, unless in fact they had been accepting bribes from the unscrupulous smugglers. Severe penalties were to be imposed in future on any official who did not take the strongest possible measures against all forms of illicit trade.

The second letter contained a curt order from the King to attack any English ship which entered an American port without special permission with a view to engaging in trade. The crews of such ships were to be prosecuted for smuggling.

John Hawkins, the commander of a small English fleet, suspected nothing of the disaster that was about to befall him. In the past, whenever he had brought slaves from Africa, he had been received amicably, and indeed cordially, by both settlers and officials. Time and again the Spaniards had assured him how delighted they were to have at last some one to supply those indispensable black slaves. Their own officials and the monopolists back home in Seville seemed unable to supply sufficient Negroes—and only they could do the work in the hot plantations of the tropics. How was the young colony to survive if a convoy arrived only once or twice a year? That was not nearly often enough. No wonder prices were rising steeply.

Here, then, was an opening for the English sailors and shipowners. With a cargo of cheap glass beads, a few knives and axes, or a few coloured textiles, they would sail to the Guinea coast to trade this trash with the African chiefs for slaves. This 'merchandise' was always available. Adequate supplies could always be obtained from the hinterland. A single raid on some neighbouring villages was enough to meet all the requirements of the strangers and to purchase, in exchange, those delightful trinkets. True, the Portuguese had complained bitterly about the English engaging in commerce on the African coast which belonged to their King, but the English merchants had pointed out that along the entire length of the African coast the Portuguese had but a handful of bases. There could be no question, therefore, of Africa being a Portuguese possession; anyone was entitled to treat freely with the true rulers of the country, the Negro chieftains.

The Spaniards, of course, were not concerned with Africa at all, that part of the world having been allotted to Portugal. But they did care about America. Hawkins was flabbergasted when the Spanish Governor of Vera Cruz informed him that much to his regret he would have to arrest him and confiscate all his ships. But an English sea-captain was not to be trifled with in this manner. His ships were well armed and his sailors feared neither the Devil nor the French pirates. Were they to haul down their flag before those Spanish dons?

Before the Governor could take any action the English had occupied the commanding harbour-mouth of Fort San Juan de Ulua. The Spaniards counter-attacked vigorously; they stormed the fortifications and barred the exit to the English ships. Only two escaped—Hawkins's ship and a small one under the command of Francis Drake, a young man who had risen from ordinary seaman to sea-captain in the Guinea trade. The infuriated Spaniards sentenced the crews of the other ships to severe penalties for illicit trade, and eventually handed them over to the Inquisition as heretics.

On the high seas, meanwhile, the two escaped captains swore vengeance. They were hard men. They had gained their experience not as peaceful merchants anxious to remain on good terms with their customers, prepared to accept humiliations for the sake of a good profit, but as tough seamen.

38. Stone with Viking runic inscription (1135) from the North American coast, found on Kingiktorsoak Island

It is astonishing to reflect how late the English found their way back to seafaring. After all, did not their ancestors include the Anglo-Saxons and the wild Vikings, who, throughout many centuries, had sailed and plundered the coasts of Western and Southern Europe, who had penetrated to Iceland and Greenland, and even to the American continent? Later, however, England's trade and shipping had got into the hands of foreigners—first the Italians and then the Hanseatic merchants. Even the English war fleet had declined to a pitiful condition towards the beginning of the sixteenth century. But now the trend was being reversed.

When the first reports about the discovery of America arrived in England from Spain, King Henry VII equipped a small fleet which was to seek a northern passage to the real India, the route which Columbus had failed to discover. But since the English lacked extensive knowledge and experience of navigation they invited as their captain an Italian who had traded in spices in Mecca in earlier years,

and who had been established in London as a merchant since 1484—
John Cabot. Although his first voyage in 1496 did not open up the
route to the "Great Khan," as Cabot had thought in his first flush of
enthusiasm when he made a landfall west of the Atlantic, he discovered
something else—the most prolific fishing-grounds in the world. The
coast was bleak and deserted, covered with ice and snow for months
on end. But the sea was alive! Millions and millions of fish crowded
the water—and not the little herrings of the eastern Atlantic, but large
cod.

To the kings of England, Portugal, and Spain, and also to the
wealthy merchants of London, Lisbon, Seville, and Antwerp this
meant nothing; their dreams were of gold and silver, of spices and silks.
But the lesser people, the fishermen along the European coasts, at once
realized what to do when the news reached them. In their solid, seaworthy fishing-boats they set sail for the north-eastern coast of America
to catch the cod in their trawl nets by the ton. Before long, fish from
the Newfoundland bank swamped the European markets. Even
though the Reformation had relaxed the strict fasting rules of the
Church of Rome, the European consumers readily accepted the cheap,
nutritious fish.

Most of the fishermen did not even go ashore—there was very little
to tempt them. Only the English landed to dry their catch during the
summer months, because they had to be economical with the precious
salt which still came largely from Portugal and Northern Germany.
This dried fish they supplied even to the plantations in the West Indies.
It was up to the slaves to manage as best they could with the rock-hard
dried cod in the heat and humidity of the tropics. At least it remained
edible.

It may well be that the fishermen of the sixteenth century made more
money out of their Newfoundland fish than the Spanish did with all
their magnificent discoveries including the fabulous silver-mines. The
demand for fish was tremendous everywhere—in Europe, in Africa,
and in the West Indies. Fishery meant a livelihood. Fish could be
traded for the spices of India, for the sugar from the West Indian
plantations, or for silver from Peru and Mexico.

These fishermen knew nothing of the difficulties of the royal officials
or of the anxieties of the independent merchants. Indeed, they did not
understand why they were being continually harassed by customs

duties, taxes, prohibitions, price regulations, and compulsory monopolies. They hardly believed their ears when they discovered how vastly prices differed on the two sides of the Atlantic. When they sold their fish in Africa Negro slaves were offered to them quite cheaply; upon arrival in the West Indies these Negroes were very nearly worth their weight in gold. What could be simpler than, on their next voyage, to take a few slaves along with them and sell them in America at a tremendous profit?

The men who had served their apprenticeship in the Newfoundland fisheries were accustomed to roughing it at sea. Sometimes they would be fog-bound for weeks, hearing nothing but the faint creaking of the rigging and the lapping of the waves against the hull; all else was swallowed up by the impenetrable fog-bank. On their homeward voyage past Iceland they might be caught in a gale and many a small sailing-boat lost. These conditions produced a hardy breed of sailors who subsequently, during the long wars between France and Spain, would sail forth under some intrepid captain and seize a richly laden merchant ship. The right to engage in armed piracy had been granted them by royal charter. This document could turn a peaceful trading ship into a dangerous sea-raider—provided she carried enough cannon behind the portholes and an audacious band of men. And there was no shortage of sailors, French or British, in the fishing-ports in Dieppe, St Malo, and Dunkirk, or in Bristol, Falmouth, or Plymouth. Whenever news reached the Newfoundland fishermen of some particularly successful capture—such as the feat of Jean Ango of Dieppe who, in 1523 when every one was at peace, captured the Mexican treasures which Cortez had taken from the Emperor Montezuma—the young men could barely be restrained in their eagerness to sail forth and raid merchant ships.

To begin with, the fishermen of St Malo had placed cannon on their ships so that no Spaniard should intercept them. Needless to say, if they should have encountered a ship inferior to them in armament they would not have missed such a favourable opportunity of earning a little "on the side" without asking too many questions about international law. They knew that their King would back them up, even though the countries might be at peace. "There is no law beyond the line," was an old saying. No one could say for certain where that legendary "line" ran beyond which it was permissible to attack, loot, and kill. For the pirates, at any rate, it ran fairly close to the European coast. In their ports, however, the sailors were secure; the well-fortified harbours of Dieppe, St Malo, La Rochelle, and Dunkirk need have no fear of anyone, not even of their own King.

Enviously the English watched the naval exploits of their French fellow-fishermen of the Newfoundland grounds. They themselves were obliged to hold back while their King Henry VIII was allied with Spain. Besides, his daughter, Queen Mary I, known as Bloody Mary, was married to King Philip II. But her sister and successor, Elizabeth, had a soft spot for the British sailors.

There was a fresh wind blowing through the whole of England—a wind both blowing off the sea and blowing towards the sea. Just before Queen Elizabeth's succession in 1557 the privileges of the Hanseatic merchants had been scrapped and the Steelyard had finally closed its doors. The religious Orders, which until then had sold their wool to the foreigners without worrying overmuch about its further processing, were dissolved after the Reformation. Ever since, English wool was processed by English artisans. We hear of one William Stumpe, who acquired the abbeys of Osney and Malmesbury and filled every corner of them with looms. Artisans from Flanders, who had emigrated to England during the religious disturbances, soon helped the local textile industry to reach a high level. But who was to buy the fabrics? English merchants equipped large ships, amply armed them with cannon so they should not be seized *en route*, and loaded them with their cloth.

The natural market was Central Europe, because only there was the winter cold enough for warm woollen materials. But perhaps it might even prove possible to break into the Baltic and the Russian markets?

England's foreign trade was built up by two guilds of merchants—the Merchant Adventurers and the Staplers (or Merchants of the Staple). Both originated in the Middle Ages. In 1379 the Hanseatic League refused to accept the English merchants as members; twelve years later they formed their own guild, which received formal recognition by royal charter. To the great indignation of the Hanseatic League they concluded treaties with the German Order and the Prussian towns; but since at first the English had only cheap cloth to offer, which could not compete with that from Flanders, the German merchants contented themselves with a protest. For the sake of this insignificant cloth trade they certainly did not wish to quarrel with England, which was the supplier of their wool. After all, they enjoyed the backing of the abbeys and big landowners against all attempts by the English merchants to break the irksome monopoly of the foreigners. The English merchant guilds conducted their modest business as best they could: they exported the still rather mediocre English cloth to the Continent where, as a rule, it was bought and resold by their great Hanseatic competitors.

But some audacious men wanted to do more. There were two Englishmen in Seville, Roger Barlow and Robert Thorne, importing spices from India. In 1526 Barlow accompanied Sebastian Cabot on the voyage which was to have gone to China, Ophir, and Tharsis but which unfortunately ended in South America because the master captain decided to go against his instructions and seek the land of silver. Cabot fell into disgrace with the Spaniards.

Barlow at once seized on this opportunity; he prevailed upon his fellow countrymen to invite the famous man to England and to put him in charge of an English fleet with the grand title of Governor of Mariner Adventurers for the Discovery of Unknown Regions, Dominions, Islands, and Places. What his father John had attempted in vain, Sebastian was to achieve—to make England into a colonial power.

In 1553 the small fleet of three ships set sail: not, however, towards the West but to the East, past Norway, to sail around Asia to China. The English did not get far: two ships were wrecked off the Lapland coast, and the third reached the area where to-day stands Archangel. From the coast of the Arctic Sea the master-mariner Chancellor travelled 1500 miles overland to Moscow, where he was cordially received by the Tsar Ivan the Terrible. That alone made the voyage worth while. His visit suddenly made the Russians realize that they might enter into commercial relations with Western Europe without being dependent on the Baltic countries, on Lithuania, Poland, or Sweden, with whom they were at war. The English, for their part, were hoping to obtain more directly—and more cheaply—the valuable furs which they had been buying from the Hanseatic merchants at high prices. At the same time, Russia with its cold climate would make the ideal market for their warm woollens.

Encouraged by these prospects the English merchants founded the Muscovy Company, the first great shareholders' company, which received a royal charter in 1555. Until the eighteenth century it played an important part in the Russian trade, at times controlling it exclusively. But so long as it depended on the White Sea route it had to face the almost insuperable difficulties resulting from vast distances.

But the English had found in themselves a new courage and a new confidence. They now set themselves up on the continent. They established their staple in Emden, which had not been accepted into the Hanseatic League: all English textiles and wool had to be offered in Emden first. Emden quickly rose to prosperity. "Wealth! Why, the signiory of Emden shall be mine!" Christopher Marlowe's Faustus exclaims as he sells his soul to the Devil. Flanders was ravaged by religious wars; the artisans were escaping to England and the merchants to Emden. England benefited from both moves.

Hamburg was delighted when the Merchant Adventurers founded a trading-post within its walls, mainly because this strengthened its hand against Lübeck. Why should the Hamburg merchants worry about the closing down of the Steelyard? With the Hanseatic League in general decline each town had to look after itself. It was due to the English that during the next few centuries Hamburg rose to be the biggest trading city on the German coast; it was in Hamburg that the English purchased the merchandise of the Baltic basin—salt, pitch, wax, and honey—and it was to Hamburg that they shipped their wool cloth.

Much bigger, if perhaps less certain, profits came from the slave trade. The Merchant Adventurers bought Negroes in Africa in exchange for glass beads and knives, and sold them in America for sugar, rum, and silver. Admittedly the legitimate West Indies trade came to a sudden end after the clash at Vera Cruz, but the illicit trade only flourished the more.

To smuggling was added piracy. Francis Drake, thirsting for revenge, looted Panama; he then sailed through the Strait of Magellan into the Pacific, that well-guarded Spanish sea. Although he returned home with only one of his three ships, the loot he made on his voyage was colossal. But this also meant the end of England's trade in Spain.

King Philip II ordered all the properties of English merchants within his kingdom to be confiscated until such time as compensation had been paid and the insolent pirate punished. Queen Elizabeth wavered. Then she decided for the pirate. This meant war against the great sea power of Spain, but it also meant that at last there was a chance of participating in world commerce, above all in the spice trade with Asia.

The Merchant Adventurers viewed the impending war with mixed feelings. True, their sympathies were all with the bold sailors thirsting to be revenged on the haughty Spaniards—and impatient to raid their merchant ships. Was there really no alternative to open warfare? And would England be strong enough on the seas to stand up to Spain?

The less excitable merchants were still seeking some alternative: they wanted to engage in commerce, not in piracy. There were still so many unused opportunities. About the year 1546 Anthony Jenkinson went to the Mediterranean area and for seven years travelled through the East, visiting Algeria, Tunisia, Syria, and Turkey. In Aleppo he met the Turkish Sultan, Suleiman the Magnificent, who was just preparing his campaign against Persia. Jenkinson must have impressed him favourably, because the Grand Turk generously granted the English merchants permission to trade freely throughout his empire. Doubtless he was hoping to revive the old land route with English assistance, and to make the Black Sea once more the great hub of world commerce. Jenkinson returned to London just as the Muscovy Company was equipping four ships with woollen fabrics and pewter vessels for Moscow via the northern route and the White Sea. Here was his chance to join the expedition. The Tsar graciously permitted him to travel through Russia and even gave him letters of recommendation to the Shah of Persia.

Together with two other Englishmen Jenkinson travelled down the Volga to the Caspian Sea, and thence with a large caravan of 1000 camels through the Turkmenian Steppe to Bukhara, on the ancient silk route. As in Marco Polo's day, the Chinese were still bringing nutmeg, rhubarb (then a highly prized medicine), corals, and, needless to say, silken fabrics, in order to trade them for cotton from India, and for sheepskins and furs from Russia. To the great disappointment of the English merchants, however, the Indians in Bukhara had no spices to offer, and showed little interest in the English woollen cloth. They were still receiving sufficient quantities of cloth of superior quality via Syria from Italy and Flanders.

Bukhara, therefore, was not the place for making contact with the Indian trade. The centre of the Eastern trade was in Persia; that was where one would have to station one's agents. Jenkinson convinced the London merchants of this, and, more important still, Queen Elizabeth. The return trip from the Caspian Sea to Moscow alone took him six months. On his next voyage Jenkinson visited Shah Tahmasp at his residence of Khasvin, but the Shah received him rather ungraciously and instantly ordered him to be imprisoned. He feared that the Englishman might be a Portuguese spy. With some difficulty this mistake was finally cleared up. But now the Turks demanded Jenkinson's extradition: they were not going to watch the Eastern trade being rerouted through Persia to Russia, at the expense of their own province of Syria. But his friends foiled the plot against Jenkinson. The Indian merchants in Khasvin welcomed the idea of selling spices to the North; they declared themselves ready to supply any desired quantity provided they received a firm assurance of sale.

Even more favourable was the offer of the King of Georgia: he would supply to the English any quantity of silk they wished. The Tsar of Russia was satisfied; he could see the beginnings of a most promising commerce with Asia. The Muscovy Company did in fact attract a considerable volume of commerce to Russia, which flourished particularly when Persia was at war with Turkey and traffic through the Mediterranean was barred. However, when the Turks captured the province of Shirvan, on the western shore of the Caspian, they cut off the trade route so painstakingly established.

That was the end of a promising business. In 1581 the Company distributed a dividend of 106 per cent. At the same time, the losses in that strange, wild land were not inconsiderable. Looting had to be expected constantly; on one occasion Cossack pirates in the Caspian Sea captured ships carrying merchandise worth between £30,000 and £40,000. Whenever a foreign traveller died the local ruler at once confiscated his property. What purpose was served by endless lawsuits? Even with the Tsar himself there was serious trouble. On one occasion, indignant at the bad treatment meted out to his Ambassador in London, he simply confiscated all English property in his empire.

Perhaps it might be possible to reach Asia by a north-west passage. At first fortune appeared—quite unexpectedly—to favour the voyagers to North America: the third expedition undertaken by Frobisher on behalf of the Muscovy Company returned in 1578 with large quantities of glittering ore which the optimistic finders believed was pure gold.

Unfortunately it was only cat-gold, a variety of mica. Nor did the English find the north-west passage. This was situated much farther to the North among the eternal ice. Another failure. There was no way through to Asia on that side either.

The sailors were right: only by force could the Spanish blockade be broken. That was also Francis Drake's opinion. His programme was clear-cut and plausible: first smash the Spanish war fleet, then sail to India to buy cheaply—spices, silk, cotton, and—in Africa—ivory. There would be no difficulties; on the African coast the ships would load slaves, take them to America, and trade them for gold and silver. That alone would yield fabulous profits. And he ought to know.

Aboard his *Golden Hind* he had seen the greater part of the Pacific coast of America, looted whole towns and richly laden galleons, and crossed the Pacific Ocean to the Spice Islands, where he was offered such quantities of cloves, pepper, musk, and cinnamon that he could not carry it all in a single ship. It was this overwhelming success that decided the issue; Queen Elizabeth knighted Francis Drake on the deck of his famous ship, and openly supported the man whom the King of Spain wanted extradited as a pirate. War was unavoidable. England was risking a high stake—her Indian trade through Seville and Lisbon, her trade through Antwerp, and her trade with the Mediterranean.

It was in the Mediterranean that the English had great expectations. A few years previously the Levant Company had received a royal charter for trading with Turkey; this gave it a monopoly for seven years for an annual duty of at least £500. Clearly, to make this payment an economical proposition there had to be an enormous turnover of merchandise. Valuable presents had helped to buttress this privilege: a great number of silver vessels, thirteen English dogs, and a silver clock, a veritable masterpiece with delicately wrought hunting scenes, mounted huntsmen and running dogs in a forest. In vain did the French Ambassador in Constantinople try to eliminate English influence; he was unable to prevent the establishment of English consulates in Egypt and Syria, and of trading-posts in Constantinople, Aleppo, Scanderoon, Tripoli, Cairo, and Alexandria.

The English supplied woollen cloth, rabbit-skins, tin, mercury, and amber, and in exchange bought spices, pepper, indigo, silk, cotton, and linen in vast quantities. A single ship, the *Hercules*, carried a cargo worth £70,000 in 1587.

Yet there was also a good deal of annoyance with the Eastern potentates. The Turkish Pasha in Cairo exacted his customs duties not in cash but in merchandise, which he himself offered at inflated prices in the local market. Naturally, nobody would buy it. He thereupon simply prohibited the sale of all Oriental merchandise until his own warehouses were empty. On another occasion the Pasha demanded a 10 per cent. duty on silk fabrics; hitherto the tariff had been one-third

39. A seventeenth-century ship (from Joseph Furttenbach's *Architectura Navalis*, 1629)

of that sum. He reduced this duty again only when a propitiatory present had been given him. It would have been pointless for the merchants to complain to the Sultan in far-off Constantinople. They would have had to wait for months for a reply, and during that time their business would have been at a standstill.

All this chicanery might be tolerated and good profits made nevertheless. Was it likely that war would bring the same gains? It was the bold seafarers who tipped the scales: they had served their apprenticeship in the fishing fleets and were now engaged in piracy. They were returning from their voyages with fabulous, dazzling treasure.

To everybody's surprise the powerful Spanish fleet, the Invincible

Armada, was defeated by the English, who at once counter-attacked, penetrating into the Spanish ports, capturing the unsuspecting ships and seizing tremendous riches. Soon no Spanish ship on the high seas was safe from them—but lawful commerce with Spain, Portugal, America, and Africa came to an end. The audacious sailors, the sea-dogs, as they proudly called themselves, could not understand why. Surely they controlled the seas.

In London the experienced merchants put their heads together. To rule the seas by armed force was not enough; it was necessary to revive commerce, and this commerce must be in their hands. Admittedly,

40. Portuguese merchants in India (contemporary woodcut)

the Iberian and American coasts were barred to them; they could do nothing about that. Voyages to Africa were useless if the Negro slaves could not be resold. The Mediterranean, too, had to be written off since no English ship could slip through the Spanish-controlled Strait of Gibraltar. There was only one thing left: to open up the sea route to India round Africa and the Cape, past a hostile Spain, straight towards the centre of world trade.

The two leading lights of the Levant Company, Osborn and Staper, were listening attentively to the project of a young man, a project which at last held out promise of breaking into the legendary Indian trade of the Portuguese.

As a young merchant, John Newbury had repeatedly sailed the Mediterranean. Disguised as a Muslim merchant he had travelled to Baghdad and Basra in order to reach India via the Persian Gulf. There he had fallen into the hands of robbers. His entire party was about to be sold into slavery, but when Newbury revealed himself as a Christian the corsairs took fright. They feared the vengeance of the all-powerful Portuguese. To escape reprisals they simply put him ashore at Ormuz, the trading centre on the Persian Gulf.

The Portuguese Governor had an unpleasant shock when he discovered an Englishman in the well-guarded port; the Venetian Consul also was highly suspicious. The last thing they wanted was a commercial rival. Unconcerned by the upheaval he had caused, Newbury purchased spices, silk fabrics, and indigo. Via Persia he returned to Constantinople safe and sound. Because the Mediterranean was barred he had to take the long, tedious route up the Danube, through Poland, to Lemberg and Danzig. Once home, he sold his merchandise easily and with profit. He was now urging the Levant Company to send him out once more, so he could open up the Eastern trade for England.

The Company readily agreed to his tempting proposition. The voyage was carefully planned. John Dee, the geographer, was consulted, and so was the scholar Hakluyt, who produced a letter written by an English Jesuit in Goa. Queen Elizabeth gave Newbury a letter of recommendation to the Mogul Emperor Akbar the Great and to the "King of China." Hopes, clearly, had been pinned high.

Newbury set out with five companions. Two of them were to stay behind in Baghdad and set up an English trading-post there, two more were to stay in Basra or, if the Portuguese permitted, in Ormuz. He himself would penetrate to India, to Goa.

But his rivals were not caught napping. By the time the English left the port of Tripoli a secret report was already on its way from the Venetians resident in Syria to their representative in Ormuz, who delivered the news post-haste to the Portuguese Governor. Thus, when Newbury arrived there, all unsuspecting, he found himself arrested as a spy. Small wonder. Drake had loaded a cargo of spices in the Moluccas in spite of the Portuguese prohibition, and had moreover ransacked the Spanish possessions. And since 1580 Portugal belonged to King Philip II.

The four prisoners were taken to Goa for their faith to be put to the test. That was fortunate for them. One of them happened to be a painter: he decorated the Jesuit Church there so splendidly that the others were set free. Friends secretly warned them to make their departure as quickly as possible to escape further charges. Only the painter stayed with his Jesuits. This time he was unlucky. King Philip sent urgent orders to have the impudent intruders sent to Lisbon at once for punishment. The ship sank with all hands.

But the remaining three were able to take a good look at the wonderland of India. They visited the rich diamond city of Golconda in the south and the capital of Agra in the north. Solemnly they presented to the Great Mogul the letter from their Queen. The Emperor at once took one of them into his service—the jeweller Leeds. Newbury's other companion, Fitch, was to travel down the Ganges to Bengal and there to wait for Newbury, who would pick him up with an English ship in two years' time. Newbury himself returned to Constantinople by the caravan route through Persia.

But Fitch waited in vain. Eventually he departed, travelling farther to the east, to Burma and Malacca. There he spoke to Chinese merchants who had come over the mountains from the North. All of them were prepared to sell merchandise to the English. After eight years Fitch decided he had had enough; he returned to Basra—luckily unrecognized—via Ceylon, Goa, and Ormuz. On the Syrian coast he embarked on an English ship.

Why had his fellow countrymen let him down? The gentlemen of the Levant Company had studied Newbury's reports very carefully. There was no market for woollen cloth. Neither pepper nor cinnamon could be purchased freely because the Portuguese had the monopoly and were defending it stubbornly. To market cotton goods in Europe seemed difficult; after all, raw cotton was cheaper on the Syrian coast than in India, and to establish costly plantations seemed inadvisable so long as political tension continued. The Indian trade did not seem profitable. The Levant Company gave up.

That was the state of affairs until the Dutch began to make their fat profits. Since Charles V the Low Countries were part of the Spanish Crown, but not of the kingdom of Spain. The Castilians did not even admit the inhabitants of Aragon to the American trade, let alone their King's subjects in the Netherlands. Let them do their buying in Seville. They allowed them to sell the fish which they caught off the American coast, also their luxury goods, such as Brabant lace and Flanders cloth—but even there the local producers grumbled about competition. Neither Charles V nor Philip II could overcome the opposition of their Castilian subjects. The great merchants of Andalusia wanted to enjoy for themselves the fruits of the voyages of discovery, which had, after all, been financed by Castile alone. Nothing annoyed the Netherlanders more than this discrimination. For centuries they had been experienced sailors; about the end of the sixteenth century between 25,000 and 30,000 Dutch sailors were making a living from the sea traffic with Spain and Portugal. Why then should the oceans be denied them? King Philip II believed that he could force all his rebellious subjects to their knees by ordering the seizure of any Dutch ships found in Spanish or Portuguese waters. In 1594 the Dutch merchants were even forbidden to visit Lisbon, no matter whether they belonged to the rebels or not. He was going to show those 'water beggars,' those Geuses, what it meant to cross swords with the great naval power that was Spain. But he made a bad mistake. Although the English had tried in vain to capture the Indian commerce for themselves, the Dutch succeeded in doing just that within a few years.

At the time when the Dutch trade with Spain was still flourishing young Jan Huyghen van Linschoten settled in Seville as a merchant. He later accompanied the Bishop on a journey to Goa and stayed there for five years. On his return voyage he stopped for two years in the Azores, arriving back in his native country at the very moment (in 1592) when the trade war between Spain and the Low Countries broke out in earnest. His travel account, printed in 1595, was based on his own observations and on unimpeachable eye-witnesses. It encouraged the Dutch to risk the voyage to the East Indies. No Dutch ship sailing to Asia was without Linschoten's book; every sea-captain studied it thoroughly during the long voyage.

The basic idea which the Dutch took over from Linschoten was well conceived, sound, and reasonable, in line with the Dutch temperament. There was nothing in it about piracy, force, or war. The coasts of India, he argued, were firmly held by the Portuguese; it would have been lunacy to attack them, especially as the Dutch possessed not a single base between home and the far-off unknown waters, while Portugal had established a succession of safe ports all along the African and Asian coasts. The island of Java, however, and the Malayan archipelago were almost undefended, although Malacca, in Linschoten's words, represented "the staple for the whole of India, China, the Molucca Islands, and all the other isles; there is much selling there, and all the ships call there when sailing to and from China, the Molucca Islands, and Banda, from Java, Sumatra, and the other neighbouring islands."

That was where Cornelius Houtman made for with his four ships in 1595. Houtman was an experienced merchant, acquainted with Portugal and knowledgeable about the East India trade. "Excessive curiosity" had landed him in prison in Portugal, but his fellow countrymen had bailed him out and placed him at the head of their little fleet. When he arrived at Bantam after many months the local inhabitants arrested him. The Portuguese had gone to work surely and swiftly in order to rid themselves of this irksome intruder. However, Houtman was released for a considerable ransom, and sailed on to the Moluccas. Tropical diseases took a fearful toll of his crew, especially as the Dutch did not dare enter ports where the Portuguese were established. When Houtman returned home after 28 months only 89 of his original crew of 249 were alive. But he had succeeded in breaking through the Spanish-Portuguese blockade. Even though the commercial results of the first voyage were not great, they were sufficient to cover the costs, and moreover yielded valuable experience.

Holland now went in a headlong rush into the East India business. Companies sprang up like mushrooms after the rain—in Amsterdam, Rotterdam, and Zeeland. If the Spaniards thought they could close the Asian and American markets to outsiders they made a big mistake. Before the end of the century sixty-five ships were leaving Dutch ports every year for Asia, Africa, and America. That was a bold venture. Frequently only half the ships of a small fleet would return; some would have been swallowed up by the enraged sea with all their crew and cargo, others might have been captured by the Spaniards, or wrecked upon some unknown reef.

It was obviously necessary to choose routes which were unguarded, and to look for new routes away from the old well-known ports and bases. Thus a fleet of four ships under Olivier van Noort sailed through the notorious Strait of Magellan, while another circumnavigated the Cape which they named Horn after their home port. Returning from Indonesia, the Dutch dared not follow the much-frequented route via Ceylon; instead, they described a wide arc to the south, towards the Cape of Good Hope—and *en route* discovered Australia! For months on end the ships, which were still rather small vessels, would sail without sighting land, in an ocean which, in the imagination of the sailors of the day, was inhabited by fearful monsters, by huge sea-serpents and giant swordfish which, according to current legends, would furiously pierce the hull of any ship. Every voyage was a heroic achievement of seamanship.

Indignantly Philip II, King of Spain and Portugal, watched the impertinent intruders, those rebels from his own Low Countries, break into the carefully guarded Asian sphere which by time-hallowed right was the preserve of the Crown and a few monopoly companies. At first he thought he could scare those daredevil seamen out of the Asian trade by making it difficult for them to sell their unlawfully acquired merchandise in Europe. He strictly forbade his Spanish and Portuguese subjects to conclude any treaties with the Dutch; he even forbade them to settle debts they had made with them. Surely, with the few ships which managed to slip through, the Dutch would not be able to build up a permanent business. Sooner or later the consumers in Central Europe would have to return to the true masters of America and Asia. Ports like Antwerp or Amsterdam could not last, the King of Spain thought, if their merchants were barred from Lisbon and Seville. All he was doing, in effect, however, was to seal off his own kingdom from trade with Central and Northern Europe.

Amsterdam gained a firm hold on commerce; every year 640 ships left the port for the Baltic, laden with Flanders and English cloth, iron goods, fish, lace, and linen, as well as with overseas merchandise—spices, indigo, cotton, and sugar. Another eighty large ships set sail for the high seas.

This dramatic upsurge of commerce is easily explained. The States General of the Netherlands exempted the seafarers from all duties; indeed, they made a certain payment to sea-captains sailing to Asia. In order to reduce the rivalry between the five existing companies, they were amalgamated in the United East India Company, which, in 1602, was granted by charter the express right of entering into treaties with Indian princes, building fortifications, appointing governors and judges, and levying troops.

This was rather more than a commercial company; it was a semi-official organization, a political power headed by regular merchants.

The young States General contributed a mere 25,000 florins to the share capital, but in time of war they granted the company military protection. When it came to the test the State would also undertake to stand surety for major loans. During the first few decades this support was of only limited value; sailors and merchants in Asian and African waters still had to be self-reliant. They had to use care in sounding the local inhabitants—whether they were overstocked with supplies they would part with eagerly, or whether their excessive prices would leave no margin for profit. The merchants had to know what goods were needed in a specific place, so that their purchases there could, if necessary, be paid for in merchandise if sufficient precious metal was not available. Here was no government claiming for itself the profit of audacious voyages in order to maintain fortresses, organize patrols by warships, or pay the salaries of viceroys. The dangers were enormous, but then the gain that beckoned was commensurate. The merchants bore all the risk, but they also pocketed all of the profits.

No sooner had the Dutch East India Company been founded than its directors, the *bewindhebbers,* dispatched a large fleet of fourteen sailing-ships to Asia under Wybrand van Waerwyck. From the local ruler the Admiral received permission to build a stone trading-post in Bantam. From this firmly established base his ships sailed out in all directions—to Banda, Achin, and Borneo, to Siam, and eventually even to China. Admittedly, the Dutch were not permitted to enter the Chinese harbours, but since many Chinese merchants called at neighbouring places profitable business connexions with them were easily entered into.

Meanwhile another Dutch fleet of thirteen ships under van der Hagen had set out to strike at the Portuguese wherever they could. Thanks to the ships' numerous and powerful guns the Dutch succeeded in concluding treaties of friendship with the Indian rulers of the Malabar coast, of Calicut and Cochin. In Amboyna, one of the Spice Islands, van der Hagen occupied the Portuguese fort and established a firm Dutch trading-post. At the same time his vice-admiral, Cornelis Bastianenzoon, stormed the Portuguese fort in Tidore, but omitted to set up a trading-station. On his return voyage in 1606 van der Hagen encountered the third fleet dispatched by the Dutch East India Company off the island of Mauritius—eleven ships under Cornelius Matelief. There they established a firm base for the East India merchant mariners.

Although this island had been discovered a long time before by the Portuguese it had since been disregarded. A short while later a fourth Dutch fleet followed, consisting of eight ships and carrying troops to man the newly established bases. It was certainly high time to think of military protection, for the Spanish and Portuguese had united in order to drive the intruders out of their hitherto unquestioned sphere of interest. Regular warfare broke out in Asia. At first everything went wrong for the Dutch. Their attack on the fortress of Malacca was a failure; the Spaniards expelled the Dutch merchants from the Philippines. Soon

41. Mozambique, the principal Portuguese base in Africa (from an account by de Bry, about 1600)

however, the picture changed. Matelief, who was continually receiving supplies and reinforcements from home, first defeated the Portuguese fleet off Malacca and then completely blockaded Goa, the principal Portuguese port. In the Bay of Gibraltar a Spanish fleet was defeated by the Dutch, whose superiority at sea was no longer in question. At last the King of Spain yielded; in 1609 he concluded a twelve years' armistice which provided for full freedom of trade in Asia. In Europe, however, commerce was still subject to permission from the King of Spain. It was a remarkable success.

Two totally different economic systems were opposing each other. The Portuguese—officials, not merchants—stubbornly defended their monopoly; they prescribed to their customers in Europe prices and terms of payment. The Dutch, experienced merchants that they were, knew that gain depended primarily on favourable purchase. While the officials in the Portuguese settlements, acting as their King's representatives, were calmly and patiently waiting for any foreign merchants to offer them merchandise, the Dutch sought out the source of their commodities, trying to get into direct contact with the producers and collectors of the spices. They bought from the planters in the Moluccas, not from Arab intermediaries. This may have involved more effort, but it was worth while. By 1610, one year after the con- clusion of the armistice, the Dutch had forts in Amboyna, Ternate, Matchian, and Batchian, right in the heart of the Spice Islands. They had their own trading-posts in Bantam and Jakarta (later Batavia). The Spanish and Portuguese officials believed that any merchandise exported from Asia to Europe permitted of a net profit. But that was an illusion; even if it had been looted by force of arms in the first place its price was inflated by the considerable expenditure for the maintenance of the colony and the war fleet.

What was needed was sound business. Pillage and loot in the long run did not ensure profits. The idea of loot, therefore, had to be given up. Nor did little Holland even try to manufacture the merchandise needed in Asia. It confined itself to acting as carrier and middleman. Not even in ship-building was it able to compete with those who possessed much more timber—such as Danzig on the Baltic. The Dutch had for a long time been renowned as carriers, as shipping agents, perhaps even as far back as Roman times; since the heyday of the Hanseatic League they had been unrivalled in this field. Vast sums were earned by the Netherlands through their shipping business alone. Even the Portuguese merchants on the Malabar coast were compelled to import merchandise from the far-off Spice Islands and Java on board Dutch ships. And since the Dutch were shipping the East Indian spices to all parts of the world, aboard their own vessels, the marketing of it almost automatic- ally became concentrated in their hands. Even Spanish and Portuguese merchandise went through Dutch hands in the Channel, the North Sea, and the Baltic.

The Dutch were the first to realize that world commerce was a unity. Only he who led in all fields could stand up to foreign competition. Because the Dutch controlled the world freight market they were also in a position to supply Negro slaves to America more cheaply; because they marketed the Negroes in America they received enough precious metal to engage in their Eastern trade. Because they were able to offer merchandise in East Asia, and because they also had enough silver for their purchases, they succeeded in attracting the customers of the Portuguese over to themselves. And because, finally, they offered the Asian merchandise on more favourable terms they displaced the Iberian nations from the European markets. One wheel engaged in another, one link of the chain interlocked with the next.

In the opinion of the Portuguese and Spanish officials there was therefore only one way left to fend off the superior competition of the Dutch—force, war. Spain did not renew the armistice. That was a bad mistake. If the commercial superiority of the Dutch had already been demonstrated beyond any doubt, their sea power exceeded that of Spain and Portugal even more—not least because of the economic power behind the East India Company. True enough, the Netherlands possessed no land forces of any size either in Europe or in Asia. Even in the eighteenth century, when the Dutch East India Company was firmly established in the Insulinde Islands—in the Malay archipelago— their soldiers never numbered more than 10,000 men, most of whom were local inhabitants of little fighting value. But their naval power was outstanding.

Once more Portugal and Spain closed their harbours to the Dutch merchants. At once the Dutch blockaded the Portuguese ports of Goa and Malacca. They destroyed the enemy fleet and any merchant ship which showed itself. Hopefully, Lisbon sent out a new fleet and a new Viceroy. But the Dutch destroyed three of his ships even before they got to the East. Their naval superiority so depressed the Viceroy that he urgently advised his King to make peace instantly and at any price with the superior enemy, even if it meant granting the Dutch full freedom of trade.

In vain. Lisbon could not and would not give in. The Dutch thereupon attacked the Portuguese fortress of Ormuz in the Persian Gulf, and a year later Bombay. On the mainland the Portuguese held out. Dutch attempts at overpowering the lightly held bases along the African coast were likewise unsuccessful. But what use were these fortresses if they were cut off from their home country and from all commerce? And the Dutch did not let a single ship through.

After ten years of blockade the Dutch stormed Malacca in 1641. Tropical diseases and famine had reduced the white garrison to 100 men. Yet the military effort of the Dutch was quite modest; they had only 1500 men under arms, and the same number was provided by their ally, the King of Johore. The blockade of Goa continued. When peace was at last concluded in 1645, Lisbon's commerce, together with that of Goa, was ruined. Amsterdam and London had meanwhile risen to power.

The English had been rather hesitant about venturing to the East Indies around the Cape of Good Hope. They had had too much bad luck along that route. In their first attempt, undertaken by Captain Lancaster in 1592 with a small fleet, all ships were lost. Lancaster himself returned to England on board a French ship, destitute. Surely piracy in Atlantic waters was a more profitable business!

In 1592 British sea raiders captured a large Portuguese East Indiaman, the *Madre de Dios,* off the Azores. Aboard this ship alone they seized £140,000, corresponding to roughly $8,400,000 in present-day prices. On board the Portuguese ship the English found a Latin account of the "Kingdom of China," carefully wrapped in calico and locked in a sandalwood box, as though it were the greatest possible treasure. The English also admired the construction of the East Indiaman, a type of ship developed from the galleon and called a carrack, and possessing the remarkable cargo capacity of 1600 tons. Perhaps it would be worth while after all to sail to the East Indies? Queen Elizabeth entrusted a personal letter for the Great Emperor of China to the ships equipped for the next voyage under Sir Robert Dudley. The letter never reached its destination. All ships were wrecked in a storm.

But the tough British did not give up. The Lord Mayor of London, Sir Stephen Soame, and a number of Aldermen together subscribed over £30,000 for a commercial venture to the East Indies. One out of every three of the subscribers already was a shareholder in the Levant Company; Soame himself and fifteen directors likewise belonged to it. Without their experience of trade in the Mediterranean the British could not have embarked on the East India venture.

Eventually, on December 31, 1600, they received their charter: the Levant merchant Thomas Smythe was appointed Governor of the "Company of London Merchants Trading into the East Indies." This was not a business firm with a fixed capital, but an association of several merchants who had been granted a monopoly of the East India trade. Each member was free to decide what shares he wished to subscribe to in any particular voyage. Each voyage was accounted separately. There was, however, an obligation to take part in the expedition together with other partners.

The need for this arrangement is clear from the balance sheet for the very first voyage. The capital raised was approximately £68,000, of which nearly £40,000 went on equipping the ships. They took with them £21,000 in cash and £6860 worth of merchandise. But they had no profit to show for all this. On the contrary. The deficit of £4000 to £5000 had subsequently to be met by the subscribers to the voyage. They even had difficulties in paying off their crews. Yet all four ships returned home, though badly battered—even the impressive 900-ton *Red Dragon,* which her sailors at one stage had been ready to abandon. The fact was that London was no European entrepôt for spices. The home market alone was unable to absorb them in large quantities, so that they could be sold only at reduced prices. Whereas a few years earlier the Dutch had been selling pepper at eight shillings a pound, the price now dropped to two shillings. But even at this price there were not enough buyers. We do not know what total quantities these ships brought back home; the *Ascension* alone carried 210,000 pounds of pepper, 1100 pounds of cloves, and 6030 pounds of cinnamon.

Far more disappointing was another fact which had emerged on this voyage. The East declined British manufactures. In the hot countries there was hardly any market for the woollen materials which still represented the principal English staple commodity.

The main reason why the London merchants nevertheless decided to equip a second fleet was that they wanted to save the supplies which were still warehoused in Bantam in Java. Again, over £60,000 was subscribed. The equipment of the ships consumed £48,000; £10,000 in cash and £1000 worth of merchandise were taken on board. As the commander of the fleet, Middleton, had been instructed to look around not so much for pepper as for the rarer spices—cloves, cinnamon, and musk—he went on from Bantam to Amboyna in the Moluccas. At first business with the Portuguese seemed to go smoothly; suddenly, however, a Dutch fleet appeared on the scene, forcing the surrender of the Portuguese Governor and emphatically forbidding the English to engage in any commerce.

In Tidore and Ternate the British were likewise able to do business only until a Dutch fleet arrived and compelled them to move. Moreover the Dutch so intimidated the islanders that they hardly dared to supply the English with spices in spite of the handsome prices paid by them. Nevertheless, the three ships returned with so much merchandise from their two years' voyage that taking the two expeditions together the shareholders made a profit of 95 per cent. on their invested capital. And that in spite of the fact that the fourth ship had been lost. Clearly the risk had paid off after all.

London was now trying hard to become the European entrepôt for tropical spices. Their export was permitted without the restrictive conditions of payment in silver which had until then paralysed business. Even so the shareholders of the East India Company were not yet satisfied. Although the two voyages undertaken since the grant of the charter had yielded an appreciable financial gain, English trade with the East was still utterly inadequate. Surely India would offer far greater possibilities?

The Levant merchant Midnall was just then giving a thrilling account of his adventurous journey which had taken him to Agra via Kandahar and Lahore. In Agra he had made a present of a quantity of jewels and twenty-nine thoroughbred horses—which he had specially brought with him from Persia for that purpose—to the Mogul Emperor Akbar the Great. As the emissary of the Queen of England, he demanded for his fellow countrymen freedom of commerce. Moreover, he expressly asked for the right to attack Portuguese ships and harbours whenever they wished to do so, without intervention by the Indians. It was this dangerous demand which threatened to lead to the breakdown of negotiations, since the officials of the Great Mogul were reluctant to annoy the all-powerful Portuguese who ruled the seas.

Midnall, however, persisted. In a personal interview with the Great Mogul—the Englishman spoke Persian fluently—he was in fact granted a treaty which met his requests. No amount of intriguing by the Portuguese at Akbar's Court could prevent this success. The gentlemen of the East India Company carefully examined Midnall's reports and his bold idea of organizing an extensive trade with India herself—not confining themselves to offering English woollen cloth for sale, but buying and selling Indian merchandise or exchanging it for spices in Java. The prospect was certainly tempting, but since Midnall made excessive demands for himself, the Company did not employ him.

Another English fleet set out for Asia to follow up and develop the commercial contacts made on the earlier voyages. It carried a considerable supply of merchandise, worth £7280, as well as £17,600 in cash. After a twelve months' voyage the two biggest ships reached first the island of Sokotra, just outside the Red Sea; thence one of them, the *Red Dragon* mentioned earlier, set a course for Bantam in Java, while the *Hector*, under Hawkins, made for Surat, north of Bombay, then the principal port of the Mogul Empire.

It was difficult enough to navigate across the shallow sand-bar—but these technical difficulties were as nothing compared with the political obstacles which the Portuguese tried to erect against them with the Indian authorities. There could be no question, they argued, of a British settlement at the very centre of Portuguese commerce, between their two bases of Diu and Goa. Reluctantly the Indian Governor allowed the English to sell their merchandise, but he strictly forbade them to set up a permanent trading-post; his rather lame excuse was that only the Mogul Emperor himself could give permission for that.

Hawkins promptly set out for Agra himself. He left William Finch in Surat as his representative, and ordered his ship, the *Hector*, to sail to Bantam in the meantime. In Agra Hawkins was first regarded as the ambassador whose arrival had been promised by Midnall. Hawkins spoke Turkish fluently; his confident manner soon overcame the resistance of the Court, and he succeeded in establishing friendly terms with the Emperor Jahangir, the son of Akbar, who had died in the meantime. The Emperor solemnly granted the British all the rights they could have wished.

Less pleased by all this were the Indian officials along the coast who had been partly bribed and partly intimidated by the still powerful Portuguese, and were desperately anxious not to provoke them. When one day the commander of the English fleet was flatly told that he would have to leave port without doing any business, he lost his temper; off Aden he captured every Indian ship he could intercept. This in turn annoyed the Turks, who were established in Egypt and Syria and derived considerable customs revenue from this position of middlemen in the Mediterranean. The East India Company was just then negotiating with them about a favourable trade treaty which was to open to them the ports on the Red Sea, especially the harbour of Mokha.

In Indonesia the former comradeship-in-arms between Dutch and British was breaking up. The Dutch were beginning to realize what dangerous rivals the British were; besides, since the armistice they no longer needed them as allies against the Portuguese. On pain of severe penalties the Indonesians were forbidden to engage in any trade with other European nations. All protests by the British Ambassador to the Dutch Government in The Hague were fruitless; besides, the Dutch East India Company would not even allow its own Government to interfere in its business. But the determined English would not give up and kept on trying.

In Ayuthia, the capital of Siam, the English were allocated a house of their own, immediately next door to that of the rather distrustful Dutch. Siam's trade in China and Japan was suffering considerably from the hostilities between those two countries. But somehow or other considerable quantities of raw silk, silk fabrics, and porcelain still managed to reach Siam; moreover, Siam itself supplied dye woods (such as Brazil wood), aloes wood, benzoin, tin, hides, and furs.

When two Dutch merchants working for the English East India Company began to build up British commerce on the East coast of India, the Coromandel coast, the Dutch barred them from all Indian coastal towns where they had settlements. The local officials of the hinterland, on the other hand, seemed only too pleased to deal with other Europeans than the Dutch, who were apt to insist too rigidly on their privileges. They willingly granted permission to the English to set up a trading-post in Petapoli, to sell British woollen cloth and purchase major quantities of the cotton fabric, calico, which found a ready market in Bantam in Java, in Patani in the Malay Peninsula, and even in the Red Sea area and in England itself.

In Japan all commerce was firmly in Portuguese and Dutch hands. However, an Englishman by name of William Adams, travelling aboard a Dutch ship, had been stranded on the Japanese coast and decided to stay there. The ruling Shogun bestowed his favour upon him and instructed him to build a European ship—probably the first keeled ship built in Japan. Adams had sent repeated reports to the East India Company in England describing his good relations with the ruler. King James I thereupon sent a personal letter to the "Great

King of Japan" asking for trade facilities for his subjects. When the *Clove* entered the harbour of Hirado in 1613, with a representative of the Company on board, a man named Saris, the Japanese immediately put a house at his disposal. However, the English woollen cloth was not easily sold, as the country was flooded with cloth by the Dutch and Portuguese. Besides, Saris and the old sea-dog Adams did not get on

42. Processing of silk fabrics in the sixteenth century (woodcut from a later edition of the Keng Chi T'u)

too well with one another: Saris regarded Adams, who was married to a Japanese woman, as a naturalized Japanese, while Adams thought the new arrival ignorant and conceited like all Europeans. There were, moreover, factual differences of opinion between them. Adams had always maintained friendly relations with the Dutch, whereas the inexperienced Saris simply regarded them as malicious rivals. At any rate, English commerce with Japan was of short duration. During the war between Holland and England the East India Company in 1623 withdrew its trading-post. It had spent £40,000 in Japan and had received hardly any revenue in return.

Chinese merchants had been sailing to Japan, Siam, and even Java since ancient times, but in their own empire the Chinese did not permit any foreign trading-posts. Admittedly, the Portuguese were allowed to buy and sell in Macao, but only under exceedingly strict supervision. In vain had the Dutch sent their ships to Canton in 1604 and 1607. When an English ship, the *Unicorn*, was wrecked off the Chinese coast while sailing from Bantam to Japan, the Chinese authorities behaved most reasonably: the shipwrecked crew were allowed to purchase two small ships and continue their journey unmolested, but all trade was forbidden them.

The Dutch were viewing the successes of the British with growing misgivings. What right had the English to break into world trade? Until well into the sixteenth century they had left their foreign trade to Germans; after that they had bought their spices in the Low Countries, first in Antwerp and then in Amsterdam. What gave them the right, all of a sudden, to compete with the Dutch? During the difficult days of their joint war against the Spaniards the English had attracted the Dutch artisans to their country and had moved their staple from the threatened Dutch ports to Emden. So long as the assistance of British warships was needed on the high seas it had been necessary to turn a blind eye to all these infringements—but surely an end must now be put to them. Holland ruled the seas; the time had come to settle accounts with her dangerous rival.

One night, in 1623, the Dutch pounced on the small English settlement outside Amboyna. The official pretext was that the English had incited the inhabitants of the island of Ceram to rise against the Dutch at any rate, merchants and settlers were executed out of hand for high treason.

There was consternation in England. King James dared not take action against Holland in view of her supremacy at sea; he silently stomached the defeat. The English merchants evacuated Indonesia, which thus became an unchallenged Dutch possession, undisturbed by any rivals, the foundation of Dutch commerce in Asia, and the principal gold-mine of the Dutch East India Company. In Batavia there reigned a Dutch Governor General; and in that miserable swamp, beneath the scorching tropical sun, in that humid and oppressive climate, the Dutch made themselves at home. They built as they did in Holland: solid, clean, well-made houses with highly picturesque gables and brown tiled roofs, with sparkling window-panes, and with shutters.

Everything looked delightful. The town, intersected by canals, became known as the Venice of Indonesia.

The revenues of the Portuguese Crown diminished rapidly when Indonesian spices began to reach India in small quantities only and at excessive prices. After all, the wealth of Calicut and Ceylon depended on their position of entrepôts rather than on their own modest pepper crop. Even after the English had switched over to cotton and sugar they did not become rich, because competition—from Brazil, for instance—was too strong. The truth of the matter was simply that for ordinary every-day commodities the Cape route from Asia, all the way round Africa, had become too long once tropical plantations had been set up on the other side of the Atlantic. Let other nations get involved as much as they liked in the East Indies: the proud *mijnheers* of Amsterdam did not care. They had a firm hold on the two key areas of world commerce: Indonesia, the source of the really valuable spices, and the Rhine estuary, the distributive centre for Asian merchandise in Central Europe. They forged the bridge between East and West: three out of every four ships sailing the high seas about the middle of the seventeenth century flew the Dutch flag.

In order to shake their predominant position, Cromwell issued the Navigation Acts, which made it illegal to import merchandise aboard ships other than English. In bitter naval warfare the English managed, more or less, to stand up to the Dutch; they did not, however, succeed in breaking their complete supremacy in commerce.

Louis XIV's wars of aggression altered the political situation in Europe; after the fall of the Stuarts England became the ally of the Dutch, their common enemies now being France and Spain. Again piracy flared up. Freebooters, filibusters, and buccaneers furiously swooped down on the Spanish possessions in the West Indies, capturing one ship after another, looting rich ports such as Panama and Santiago, and gaining a foothold for themselves on the islands. Jamaica became British. Why should anyone engage in laborious commerce and supply merchandise when it was so much easier and quicker to get rich by force? Smuggling was rampant.

Everywhere the pirates had their agents who reported every ship promising rich booty. Unscrupulous receivers accepted and marketed the stolen goods in America—and that, at the time, almost invariably meant Spanish possessions. Above all, the pirates had to sell in the

New World the Negro slaves whom their boarding parties had seized aboard captured ships. This was easy enough, as the English were just then beginning to lay out their tobacco plantations in the southern parts of North America.

When peace was concluded, however, the English fleet at once restored order in West Indian waters, supported now by its former enemies, the Spaniards and the French.

It was no easy task to make the adventurous men who commanded the raiding ships understand that the royal charters had lost their validity, that the world no longer belonged to audacious daredevils but to peaceful merchants, and that force must at last yield to law. The pirates' lairs had to be smoked out one by one, and many an unrepentant law-breaker ended on a warship's yardarm.

I I

Paper Money, Illusions, and Speculations

IN WIDE-EYED AMAZEMENT the French fishermen gazed at the magnificent beaver furs before them; for a few knives or axes the American Indians would willingly part with hundreds of these valuable skins which were fetching such high prices in Europe. Everybody of any importance wanted a beaver hat. From La Rochelle these hats went not only to the cold areas of Eastern and Northern Europe, but also to Spain, to Brazil, and even to Africa. Indeed, the American Indians could scarcely supply enough furs, and near the coast the beaver soon became extinct. To get beaver furs in large quantities it was necessary to penetrate deeper into the country where the animals were still living undisturbed.

The French fur-traders roamed the entire North American continent. Their search for the highly prized skins took them deeper and deeper into the hinterland, and led them to enter into a new, closer relationship with the Indians. The French did not come as settlers, like the English on the New England coast, nor as proud warriors and conquerors, like the Spanish, but as friends who had definite advantages to offer to the Indians.

When the Spanish armies under Narvaez, and later under de Soto, advanced into the Mississippi basin from the south, the terrified Indians fled before them. They would rather set fire to their huts than submit to the invaders. In the end, after suffering frightful losses, the *conquistadores* were again compelled to withdraw. They carried away with them the conviction of the pointlessness of spending vast sums on conquering and opening up those territories, since they contained neither gold nor silver.

On the coast, the English settlers had robbed the Indians of their land. They were squeezing them out of their traditional hunting-grounds in order to settle there themselves. The bitter fighting along the new frontier had made the "backwoodsmen" hard and cruel. Agreement with the American Indians appeared out of the question.

But the French fur-traders, the *coureurs de bois,* had different ideas. They could not possibly trap the beavers themselves; they themselves could not collect all the skins they wanted. They depended on getting their merchandise from the Indians. What was the difficulty? Surely the Europeans possessed sufficient goods for successful barter with the American Indians?

It was no longer a case of cheating simple people, of fobbing them off with a handful of worthless glass beads, with things that were useless to them, and then expecting them to change their entire mode of living, to go out hunting and trapping in order to meet the wishes of the foreigners. If the fur-traders wanted a regular supply of skins they would have to give the Indians steel articles, knives and axes, shears and hammers. Anyway, the Indians were only too anxious to get weapons from the white men—not only swords but also firearms, especially rifles.

With these weapons they would be able to hunt the fur-bearing animals much more easily, and hence produce very much bigger quantities of furs. The Indians were ready to promise anything. But was it not too great a risk to let the Redskins have firearms? What guarantee was there that they would only be used for peaceful hunting purposes and not for war—first against rival tribes and later perhaps against the white man himself?

On behalf of the Sieur de Monts, who held the monopoly for the fur trade in the French territories of North America, the geographer Champlain sailed up the St Lawrence river and in 1602 founded the city of Quebec. Farther upstream, however, he found himself in the middle of a war between the Hurons and the Iroquois on both banks of the river. Could he remain neutral? His friends, the Hurons, who had been supplying furs to the French for many years, urged him to help them. They stood in danger of being exterminated by their cruel enemies.

Champlain let himself be swayed to intervene. He advanced as far as the lake which to-day bears his name, and, thanks to his superior firearms, defeated the Iroquois. He could not know that his intervention had triggered off a relentless feud which was to bring about the collapse of the French colonial empire in Canada.

The trade in furs had its difficulties. Time and again the Indians tried to stop the Europeans from penetrating deeper into the country lest they should seize for themselves all the advantages of the middleman. The Indians were ready enough to guide the French all the way up the rivers, as far as the lakes, but they would not allow them to establish settlements or trading-posts behind their backs—settlements which would have enabled the Europeans to deal directly with the local people. They were afraid—and quite rightly so—that they would lose the fat profits they were making from reselling the European steel tools.

The tribes of the hinterland, for their part, wanted to do business with the white men. Their hatred, therefore, was directed not against the European traders but against those Indians who interposed themselves between them and the coveted European goods and who blocked all direct trade. The European traders now had to decide: either for their old friends who had collaborated with them for many years, or for the inhabitants of the hinterland who were only too anxious to trade with them direct.

At first the French tried to shirk this decision. In vain. The Indian wars broke out all around them. The Iroquois penetrated farther and farther to the North. They drove the Algonquin from the Trent river, north of Lake Ontario, and attacked even along the Ottawa river. And, most dangerous of all, they were getting their firearms from the Dutch on the Hudson river.

The news of the rich fur trade in America had, of course, spread throughout Europe. Why should the French be the only ones to profit from it? From New Amsterdam—as New York was still then called—the Dutch fur-traders began to move into the interior of the country. They had no compunctions about supplying the friendly Indians with steel weapons, and even firearms, provided they brought them enough beaver skins. Since the French had come down on the side of the Hurons, what else could the Dutch do but support their enemies, the Iroquois? Facing each other in North America now were no longer

Redskins and Whites, but two European countries, two big trading powers, determined to achieve their ends, if need be by force.

Soon the British appeared in the arena as well. They had long been casting covetous eyes on the French fur-trading posts in the North, but they had been unable to understand the secret of the Frenchmen's success—peaceful trade with the Indians. By force of arms the British conquered the territories on the Atlantic—which were subsequently to become Nova Scotia—and parts of the Canadian mainland (1628). Four years later, however, Britain resold these seemingly valueless lands to the French. Only when the English fur-traders had begun to penetrate up the Delaware and Connecticut rivers did the official attitude change. There the traders encountered the Iroquois, the mortal enemies of the Hurons and hence now also of their French friends. In return for British help, the Iroquois undertook to divert the fur trade to the south—i.e., to the British.

No doubt the settlers in the forest clearings on the Atlantic coast, toiling relentlessly to cultivate the soil and raise crops, continued to regard the Indians as their natural enemies. But the fur-traders depended on them. They supplied them with the weapons they needed to fight their Indian and French enemies. The issue at stake was whether the fur trade would in future follow the St Lawrence to the north, or the Hudson to the south. It was an issue that would ultimately decide whether the interior of North America would one day be British or French.

Advancing down from the north, the French fur-traders increasingly pushed past the British possessions on the Atlantic seaboard. No sooner had the French received back their former possessions than Champlain dispatched a scout, Jean Nicolet, across Lake Huron farther to the west. This intrepid man travelled more than 600 miles across unknown territory never before trodden by a white man, past the Sault Ste Marie, through the narrow Mackinac Strait into Lake Michigan, then along its northern and western shores as far as Green Bay, and up the Fox river to the watershed which was only three days' journey away from Wisconsin and the vast Mississippi basin.

An enormous territory lay open before the French. It was only a question of time when they would push through to the south to reach the Gulf of Mexico. The fur-traders had opened up a route which no army could have travelled. Nicolet was travelling as the official emissary of the great fur trading company which enjoyed the patronage of Cardinal Richelieu. He regarded himself as his country's ambassador to the American Indians, with whom he entered into regular peaceful relations. It looked as though a new era in the relationship between Whites and Redskins in America was about to begin—an era of amicable co-operation. But presently the Indian wars broke out again between Iroquois and Hurons, fanned this time by the fur-traders on the Atlantic coast.

By 1650 the Hurons, the allies of the French, were all but exterminated. The victorious Iroquois, the allies of the Dutch and the British, swept on towards the north, not only to Lake Ontario but up the river courses as far as the watershed behind Hudson Bay. For twenty years they thus blocked any French advance beyond the estuary of the St Lawrence river. By the time the French troops eventually defeated the Iroquois and forced them to make peace, the British had long crossed the mountains and penetrated to the west.

With three companions and three servants, an adventurous English fur-trader, Abraham Wood, rode out from Fort Henry on the Appomattox to the Roanoke river, in order to acquire skins in the interior. A later expedition, sent out by Wood in 1673, succeeded in crossing the mountains and reaching the Tennessee, where they made friends with the Cherokee. This move aroused much indignation among the Indians on the eastern flanks of the mountains, who began to fear for their attractive profits as middlemen. The British therefore decided to deal with the Cherokee through these intermediaries; though somewhat less profitable, this was still vastly preferable to watching the skins go north, to the French. Since the end of the Indian wars the French had again been able to move more freely.

The French fur-trader Jolliet, together with Father Marquette, a Jesuit priest, had meanwhile crossed the Wisconsin river, penetrated to the Mississippi, and rowed down that river as far as where the Ohio joins it. There the local Indians warned them about the Spanish who were established farther to the south, whereupon the French travellers decided to return. But they brought back with them the news of a waterway leading right down to the Gulf of Mexico. Nevertheless, the French decided to exploit first of all the boundlessly rich fur paradise in the north.

Some time before, two *coureurs de bois*—Pierre Radisson and Grosseilliers—had made contact, setting out from Lake Huron, with the

Indians of the north. Their efforts to hire ships in New England to reach these territories from the north failed in the face of what they called the cowardice of the New England captains who were unfamiliar with the more northerly latitudes. They succeeded, however, in getting two ships from England—the *Eaglet* and the *Nonsuch*—and these they took into Hudson Bay.

Here they were then, face to face with the huge, as yet untouched rivers with their innumerable beaver dams—a goldmine which almost defied the imagination. The Indians could scarcely snatch up the steel knives and axes fast enough—let alone the rifles—and in exchange they delivered any desired quantities of skins. The French on the St Lawrence very soon noticed that their supply of skins from the north was drying up. In vain they tried to push through to Hudson Bay by the overland route. Even though the sea route was blocked by ice in winter, it was still more practicable than the laborious overland approach to the St Lawrence.

In 1670 King Charles II granted a charter to Prince Rupert and seventeen nobles for a "Company of Adventurers of England, trading into Hudson's Bay." This gave them the right to "the whole and entire trade and traffic to and from all havens, bays, creeks, rivers, lakes, and seas into which they shall find entrance or passage by water or land out of the territories, limits, or places aforesaid." That was a pretty comprehensive monopoly. Its full effect, however, was not to become apparent until very much later.

Seventy years later the Hudson Bay Company, as it was more conveniently known, maintained only four or five forts with barely 120 employees on the coast. They were content to receive the furs from the Indians and to barter them for European manufactures—knives and axes to begin with, but presently for ever-larger quantities of brandy. Back in London, the Company's critics demanded that the charter should be repealed as it was not being adequately utilized.

So long as the French in the south were trying to get the American Indians to deliver their precious furs to them, it would indeed have been difficult for the English to penetrate deeper into the continent. But when Canada fell to Britain in 1763 the number of fur-traders anxious to get their share of the wealth of the north increased considerably. Coming from the south, they moved into the territory claimed by the Hudson Bay Company for itself. As they began to clash with the

Hudson Bay Company, the traders united to form a new company, the North-west Fur Company of Montreal.

Now that the national rivalry between British and French had disappeared, the rival business interests of the traders from the north and the south clashed all the more violently. There were incidents involving bloodshed between representatives of the two trading companies; there were complaints that even gravid animals were being killed, and that far too much brandy was being foisted upon the Indians in an attempt to buy their friendship. In 1821, however, the two rival companies amalgamated.

It is scarcely possible to assess their full importance in the opening up of the American continent. In their search for new sources of furs, the companies' emissaries penetrated deep into inhospitable territories. Towards the end of the seventeenth century, Henry Kelsey travelled from Fort Nelson to Lake Winnipeg, and up the Saskatchewan river to Cedar Lake. He established peace everywhere among the Indian tribes of the plain by persuading them of the advantages of trade.

In 1789 the fur-trader Alexander Mackenzie set out from Fort Chipewyan on Lake Athabasca, across the Slave river towards the north-west, in order to open up new fur-supplying territories. By way of the river that now bears his name he reached the Arctic Ocean. Even that was not enough for the intrepid explorer, for the Hudson Bay Company—then still independent—was already trying to move its outposts up to the Great Slave Lake. Three years later we find him travelling up the Peace river and, after tremendous difficulties, cutting across country to the Pacific Ocean. He discovered the northern route across the continent, the famous North-west Passage of which explorers before him had dreamed for centuries. The fur trade alone had made his achievement possible, because it alone convinced the suspicious and hostile people that peaceful trade with the strangers could pay off. The Indians, whose economy had consisted of hunting and collecting, were now able to exchange their furs for highly prized steel tools—and, unfortunately, also for the dangerous firewater. This trade alone made it possible to overcome the mortal enmity between two races on such different levels of cultural and economic development. Thus, while the Indians of North America have largely disappeared wherever they clashed with settlers, they have most gratifyingly survived in the north, where their contacts were primarily with the fur-traders.

The government of the Sun King showed little understanding for the importance of the fur trade. It was far more anxious to establish colonies of settlers; it set up missionary stations; it appointed administrative officials. And when these efforts failed it lost all interest in Canada.

However, when the English and Dutch began to grow rich from their Asian commerce, the French Government too woke up. Why should not France be able to organize a profitable world trade? She held a number of trump cards not possessed by her rivals: a considerable industry manufacturing mainly luxury goods—fine linen, lace, tapestries, magnificent furniture, and finely wrought glass—on the basis of a domestic market of about 15,000,000 inhabitants. All these were goods for which there was keen interest throughout the Mediterranean area. From Syria, France imported Oriental fabrics and quantities of spices, from Cyprus she received sugar, from Egypt cotton and ivory, and from Russia furs; French silk fabrics from Lyons and the linen and woollen cloth made in Northern France were finding a ready market in the East. Admittedly this trade was chiefly in the hands of the Genoese and Venetians, who greatly outnumbered the French merchants. The haughty courtiers had nothing but contempt for commerce, and their intrigues and envy could easily ruin a merchant, as they did the great Jacques Cœur, who lost his vast fortune and freedom. Cœur had been the founder of France's trade with the East. He had sailed out to Damascus and introduced there French manufactures—textiles, lace, weapons, and wrought gold and silver work—articles which until then had been offered exclusively by the Italian merchants. In Syria he had purchased those Eastern goods on which the Italians had been making such high profits. Within a few years he had become so rich and respected that he was able to grant credits to the Order of the Knights of St John in Rhodes and even to the powerful city of Venice.

In 1436, during the war with England, he was appointed Director of the French Mint. When King Charles VII rode into liberated Rouen Jacques Cœur rode immediately behind him; his financial policy and his credits had ensured the King's victory. Hundreds of Cœur's ships were plying about the Mediterranean; he had trading-posts in nearly all the major towns of France, and he had 300 employees in his service. No private person in France had ever before owned such a fortune. That was what excited the envy of the courtiers. They started a rumour to the effect that Jacques Cœur had poisoned the

King's mistress, the beautiful Agnes Sorel; because of this vile defamation the ungrateful King had him thrown into prison and his property confiscated. Only after several years did Jacques Cœur succeed in escaping. He died on the island of Chios as the captain of the sixteen galleys which the Pope had sent to relieve Rhodes. France was not yet ripe for outstanding merchants of Jacques Cœur's vision.

All that was now to be changed. The young King Louis XIV wanted his kingdom great and powerful, not only militarily but also economically. His Minister Colbert, in his famous memorandum *On Commerce* written in 1664, urgently advocated the foundation of an East and West Indies Company.

43. Decorative vignette from an eighteenth-century French atlas (Paris, 1774)

Colbert's father and grandfather had been merchants and cloth-manufacturers in Rheims; he himself, unfortunately, tended to see economic affairs chiefly as a Minister of the Crown. Safety to him was the most important consideration. French commerce was to be protected by warships; markets hitherto closed to France were to be opened up by her political power.

The shares of the new companies were subscribed not by small traders, but by the great gentlemen of France, headed by the King himself and followed by his courtiers, the nobility, and the rich tax farmers who wished to ingratiate themselves with their monarch. Whenever the gentle pressure of royal favour or disfavour proved insufficient, special privileges and tax concessions were resorted to. But why, one wonders, should that have been necessary? Were the fabulous profits made by the English and Dutch not sufficient attraction? Surely, with such powerful royal support it should be possible to make even greater profits, especially as the quantities of silver needed as payment for Asian spices were easily earned in Spain. In the Iberian Peninsula sheep-breeding had been declining for some time, and in its train the wool industry; simultaneously, however, the demand for fine linen, attractive woollen fabrics, and elegant silk was going up, so that France's trading surplus with her neighbour had been growing for some time. These French exports were to be paid for with American silver exclusively; that, at any rate, was Colbert's idea.

But things did not work out that way. The Spaniards did not want to pay in silver for all their imports from France. They wanted to earn money by exporting their own agricultural surpluses and their manufactures. Indeed, all countries were reluctant at that time to allow precious metal out of their territory; they were afraid that this would lead to a paralysis of all internal trade. The dogma of 'mercantilism' was held by statesmen and scholars alike. Its basic idea was simple enough: precious metal was needed for buying spices from India and South-east Asia.

Colbert's semi-official company likewise wanted to make money by importing these spices. Its officials did not understand that France could not at one and the same time supply merchandise to Spain and prevent imports from Spain entering France by way of high customs barriers or outright prohibitions. After all, the Spaniards needed the silver themselves for buying spices. The English and the Dutch naturally also opposed the French attempts to attract all the American silver from Spain into France.

The French officials, as we have seen, were thinking in terms of barring all imports rather than promoting their own exports. The semi-official company built up an enormous machinery for realizing its arbitrary policy which was based not on economic superiority—i.e., lower prices—but on royal privileges. Economic considerations altogether played a secondary part compared with the endeavour to reflect appropriately the power and glory of the King of France.

Merchants are out for profit and more profit; they avoid all adventures which merely cost money and yield little beyond honour and glory. The "royal" companies, on the other hand, were not principally guided by these commercial ideas, even though they were supposed to do business and pay out dividends. Their officials lived magnificently, on a scale corresponding to their position. They set up fortresses in Canada, Africa, and India to buttress the power of their country. They concerned themselves with morals and behaviour, they built churches and palaces, they created a large administrative apparatus, and they held court in the grand style—costly activities which had to be paid for by the shareholders.

Similarly, when the royal companies made their purchases what mattered to them was not so much the price of a commodity as the special wishes of influential men and groups, and consideration for domestic manufacturers and for the intentions of the Government. Colbert, the great Minister on whose favour and humour a man's position might depend, personally decided what should be bought and sold, what should be imported and exported; he was "apt to turn rather ungracious if such unnecessary things as price and gain were mentioned to him." In these circumstances, would anyone dare to buy from France's Dutch or English rivals some commodity which France herself manufactured, merely because it was cheaper abroad? Or to sell weapons to the wild Iroquois in Canada, those sworn enemies of the King, merely so they should deliver cheap beaver furs? Or even to make them more amicably disposed towards the French? Rebellions could always be crushed by force of arms.

Colbert attributed the small size of his profits to the wars which his King was waging in Europe. And up to a point he was quite right. Enemy fleets had swept the French ships off the high seas; in 1702 no captain any longer dared leave the port of Nantes to sail for America. By the time peace was concluded it was too late. In Bordeaux alone thirty-two merchant-houses crashed in 1715. But was this really due only to an insane military policy? What all French colonies were suffering from was their inability to develop freely. The Minister back in Paris knew everything better. He prescribed exactly how everything was to be done: what merchandise was to be purchased and at what price, and what was to be sold in each locality. It was the same story as in France. Industry was to be 'stimulated,' but since the free entrepreneur could not of course be expected to know his own business, lengthy instructions were issued for his benefit—for instance, how tapestries were to be woven in the State-owned manufactories. All articles were to conform to definite and precise standards. An excellent idea, except that it was not practicable at the time.

Colbert was surprised that such a vast effort should yield so little fruit: the new shipyards and arsenals of Toulon and Rochefort—a base founded by him—the naval colleges of Dieppe and St Malo, and the harbour installations in Calais, Dunkirk, Brest, and Le Havre. Construction of merchant ships was encouraged by bonuses, and there were heavy penalties for the purchase of foreign ships. Yet French shipbuilding could have learned a good deal from foreign models just then. Any French sailors who, while abroad, allowed themselves to be hired for service aboard foreign ships were henceforth to be hanged.

Colbert certainly had no easy task. The King was under the influence of Louvois, his Minister of War, who was mesmerized by the Rhine frontier and had no time for peaceful commerce. Admittedly the court nobility invested much money in the royal companies, but they wanted to see quick results and large receipts; everybody was dreaming about vast profits, immense booty, and the kind of exceptionally lucky strikes as the silver-mines of Potosi and Mexico, or of such profitable commerce as the Indonesian spice trade. Nothing but illusions. When Louis XIV died France lay prostrate, exhausted by interminable wars.

Foreign trade was ruined, industry bankrupt, and the enterprising Huguenots exiled because of their faith. These Huguenots were now helping to build up flourishing industries in France's neighbour countries. Even Berlin, until then a miserable dump in the sandy heathland of Brandenburg, developed into a considerable centre of industry—thanks not to its "Prussian militarism," as is so often claimed, but because its Elector had granted asylum to the refugees whose honest hard work was bringing prosperity to the country. The harbour of La Rochelle, at one time the base of Western French shipping and the centre of the hat industry using imported beaver furs, was dead: Cardinal Richelieu had ordered it to be destroyed for reasons of religion and power politics. Agriculture, too, was in a bad way. Many peasants lived in holes in the ground, destitute; the fertile country was no longer able to produce enough food. Above all, there was no money left. The frightful wars had consumed everything. State and people were weighed down by enormous debts.

And then there appeared on the scene a man who changed the situation at one stroke, a man fired by an infectious enthusiasm and inspiring everybody with new courage—the Scotsman John Law. His magic formula was credit, his wand was paper money, and his economic method was our modern banking system. Lucidly and with complete mastery of his subject he developed his ideas to the Regent, the Duke of Orleans. France, he explained, had everything—factories, raw materials, a hard-working and skilful people, scholars and technicians, and courageous entrepreneurs. But these people could not come together because the country lacked money, and money was the driving force behind everything. The miser accumulated money to gloat over it, the private individual and the State acquired it so as to be prepared for all contingencies. The entrepreneur and producer, on the other hand, needed 'liquid' money to buy his merchandise, employ workers, and equip ships. For him money was not something to be stored and kept. Money was merely a voucher for merchandise, something needed to ensure the free running of the economy. Credit would achieve the same purpose. To the businessman it made no difference whether a certain sum of money was advanced him or a credit granted to him, whether such a credit was paid in hard cash or in paper notes vouched for by a first-class bank. It was a revolutionary idea.

Law's father, an Edinburgh goldsmith, had—in line with the custom of the day—accepted gold into safe keeping and in return given credit for it by vouching for the bill of exchange of the owner of the gold. Thus a bill in respect of the deposit played the part of money proper, the only difference being that what circulated were not banknotes but personal notes of the depositors. The Bank of Amsterdam carefully saw to it that no depositor drew a single florin more than he had deposited; on rare occasions and reluctantly it might grant credit without a collateral in gold to certain reputable firms like the East India Company. This meant that no more money could circulate in the form of banknotes or bank obligations than the precious metal locked up in the deposit, in the bank's strong-rooms. This procedure, therefore, meant a change only in the form of the means of payment, but not in their quantity.

When, during its protracted wars with France, the British Government found itself in increasingly pressing financial straits it granted the right to a number of merchants in 1694 to establish a bank of a new type. Its entire capital of 1,200,000 pounds sterling was to be loaned to the Government at once; in return the Bank of England was granted the right of dealing in precious metals and foreign bills of exchange—not, however, in merchandise—and of issuing banknotes to the same amounts. Twelve years later the privilege was extended and the capital doubled; again the entire capital had to be made available to the Government. In other words, the British Crown took out a loan, and in return permitted the Bank to issue paper money in the form of banknotes, to be used, however, only for buying money and foreign currency, not merchandise.

John Law's plans, however, went beyond. From his bank a broad stream of credit was to flow into the country, moving merchandise, stimulating the spirit of enterprise, reducing distances, and bridging the span of time between purchase and resale, manufacture, processing, and consumption. Such merchandise as was available was to start moving and to flow wherever it was wanted. Payment would be made later. After all, a merchant as a rule traded his goods not for money but, using money merely as a medium, for other merchandise. All that was needed therefore was the setting-off of accounts by a bank. And to do that a bank did not really need any capital of its own. It would make its profit from its brokerage—*i.e.,* from setting off credits and debts against one another.

But where was the capital for the credits to come from? Law's reply was: from confidence, from the confidence of those who possessed real assets—merchandise, factories, ships, raw materials, or claims. They would make deliveries against the promise of payment at an agreed date. Law steadfastly refused to make the use of banknotes compulsory by decree. Anyone accepting them as money should do so voluntarily. They offered great advantages over the traditional heavy coins: they were light and handy, and no dishonest merchant could file off or snip off any part of their value. There was only one thing they did not possess: the assured value of precious metal. Instead, the value of paper money was assured by the bank underwriting it.

Understandably enough, Law's bold idea at first met with universal refusal; in vain did the Scotsman try to make his plan palatable. Only after the death of the Sun King, when France's financial situation had become so hopeless that no straw was too weak to be clutched at, did the Regent allow his friend to set up a note-issuing bank.

The *Banque Générale Law et Cie* was founded in Paris in May 1716. Its capital of 6,000,000 livres was subscribed mostly by John Law himself and his brother William. The scheme worked. The bank-notes were readily accepted in payment not only in Paris but also in London and Amsterdam, since behind them stood the real paid-up capital of the Law brothers and not some vague promise of payment by the State, as in the case of the Bank of England. To start with, the new bank adhered strictly to the sound commercial rule of doing safe business only, in order to gain confidence. During the first two years of its operation it issued banknotes for 18,000,000 livres—*i.e.,* only treble the deposited capital. Even on this limited scale of business it made quite a good profit, if only by its international remittances which, thanks to its banknotes, it was able to perform with great ease. For transferring 150,000 German imperial talers to Hamburg—France's contribution to Sweden—another banker demanded no less than 20 per cent. commission. Law accepted the business at a far lower rate; he simply got a business connexion in Hamburg to draw a bill of exchange on his bank. The ease of this transaction so impressed the Directorate of Finances in Paris that it decreed that the notes of Law's bank were to be received as payment by collectors of taxes and that remittances from the provinces to Paris were in future to be made in such bank-notes. Throughout the country the notes circulated freely and were readily accepted. They relieved the tight money market and increased the circulation of means of payment. Everybody heaved a sigh of relief. At long last there was enough money.

Law next turned to foreign trade. France, he intended, was to become a great colonial and commercial power, with a fleet to carry the products of her industry to foreign lands and to bring back spices, tobacco, raw materials, and luxury goods. In 1717 he founded a West India Company. Politics, however, were to be his downfall. His bank was nationalized and transformed into a *Banque royale.* Before long it found itself on the slippery slope.

Whereas in the past it had issued notes only against secure assets—gold and silver, or a claim backed by some solvent entrepreneur—it now recklessly granted credits to the State and to politicians, although as collaterals these were able to provide only questionable promises for the future. Were they likely to meet their obligations as punctually as the merchants or industrialists whose reputation and financial standing were carefully investigated before an application for credit was granted?

Once again France was engaged in war. True, thanks to the credits of Law's bank it was concluded quickly and victoriously. But the anxieties of the State continued. The Sun King's heavy war debts had to be paid. As soon as the first payment of interest fell due the currency collapsed, commerce dwindled away, and the value of the silver coinage was reduced. Whereas in the past 40 livres were struck from 260 grammes of silver (a little over 9 ounces), 60 livres were now minted from that quantity. In this way the State hoped to get rid of part of its enormous debts, but all it did was to destroy confidence in its coinage. Law's bank kept aloof from such currency manœuvres. But could a flourishing colonial empire be built up with nothing but confidence?

The colonies were to be developed along entirely new lines—the cultivation of tropical crops. The plan was magnificent. Until the eighteenth century the East had supplied mainly valuables—silk, precious stones and spices, rare animals and choice fabrics. All these were articles for which a narrow circle of customers would pay exceptionally high prices—i.e., articles which carried vast profits per unit but remained insignificant in terms of quantity. By way of contrast, Law intended to cultivate in the colonies such crops as sugar, tobacco, and coffee, and to bring them to Europe; tea was not yet thought of as a possibility at that time. True, all these goods had been coming to the West for some time, but the turnover hitherto had been nothing compared with what Law believed could be achieved.

To develop colonies was beyond a merchant's financial ability. As a rule his capital would just about be enough to pay cash for his merchandise, wait for the next ship to arrive, bear the risk of the long transport routes, wait once more for the merchandise to reach Europe and be sold there. Even the capital of the prosperous merchant-houses was fully extended in these operations. Although individual settlers laid out tropical plantations on land allocated to them by the Crown these did not as a rule prosper. A great deal of capital would have to be invested, and capital was exceedingly short in the colonies. After all, the European settler had to be kept going for at least three, if not ten, years by supplies from his home country. Not till after that time could he expect to be able to pay for the implements, weapons, and the foodstuffs he had to import. Most of all, the need was for labour—not some local inhabitants who had to be driven to work and who might well run away during the harvest, but reliable Negro slaves. The plantations, in effect, depended on a sufficient number of Negroes being supplied from Africa. That, too, was a question of money. More money was wanted everywhere. Where was it to come from? Law's answer was: "I will grant credits."

In his mind's eye he saw a long chain of auxiliary measures and operations necessary for an extensive and smoothly running colonial trade. First, a ship would be equipped in the mother country—on credit—and loaded with glass beads and steel blades, which it would take to Africa, there to load slaves and carry them to America. On the other side, the settler should be able to make his purchases without having to pay on the spot; he would acquire his land from the State on credit, and cultivate it in the knowledge that for a number of years he need not worry about his livelihood or the costs of his plantation. At the end of that period he would be able to start selling his tropical produce. He would then be able to repay everything: the credit for the slaves, the purchase price of his land, and the credit for his living expenses during the initial period. In the end he would be the proud

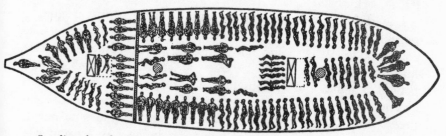

44. Loading plan of a slave ship. (From Fred Schmidt, *Sklavenfahrer und Kuliklipper*, Berlin, 1938)

owner of a flourishing plantation. He would merely have to weather the first few years. And Law wanted to help him to do just that. He would make the French realize what tremendous profits there were to be made in the long run provided one invested everything one had in the colonies from the start—human labour and supplies, and above all money. Naturally, one would have to wait for a while before one's money was returned—with interest and profit. Law appealed to all Frenchmen to bring their money to his bank. Confidence was needed, confidence in a great future and confidence in John Law. The inspired Scotsman was dreaming of building up a French colonial empire upon world commerce and the new banking system.

Needless to say, not all these ideas were conceived by John Law, visionary though he was. There had been several earlier instances of colonization. Since 1711, for instance, a South Sea Company had been established in London, which traded with Central America and invested some capital—rather cautiously and nervously at first—in the few English plantations around the Caribbean. But this did not amount to much. The English merchant, just as his colleague on the continent of Europe, was interested chiefly in buying valuable merchandise as cheaply as possible. If some stranded European settler could supply sugar or tobacco from some measly plantation at a lower price than the coloured planters of Asia, naturally one would buy his crop. But more often than not he would want credit, until the next harvest, for his Negro slaves and his implements. What was the point of putting money into these plantations so that an artificially boosted production would eventually spoil the price? Merchants, after all, were not philanthropists! The Dutch East India Company hardly knew what to do with its surplus of spices. In some years it purchased only a fraction of the harvest. The remainder it ordered to be destroyed.

Law did not think in this petty way. He believed that it must be possible, by means of credits, to boost not only production but also consumption. Why should not France be able to absorb far greater quantities than in the past? Luxuries so far had been confined to a handful of nobles and rich burghers; now they were to be made available to everybody. Tobacco, coffee, and sugar for all! The world needed only to be touched with his wand and it would pour out its cornucopia and make mankind rich and happy. Law's wand was credit.

First of all he acquired all the French overseas trading companies which, crushed by taxation and with their ships threatened by pirates, had been eking out a meagre existence—the East India Company, the China Company, and the two companies trading with Africa, the Royal Guinea Company, and the Senegal Company. In America he purchased from Crozat (who held the concession for it) the colony of Louisiana, which comprised the entire Mississippi basin, and he prevailed on the Regent to transfer to him France's tobacco monopoly. These companies did not cost much; most of them had been ruined during the protracted wars of the Sun King. In the enormous territory of Louisiana only about 700 white people were living at the time. Crozat was glad to rid himself of this millstone round his neck. But Law was calculating correctly: the colonies were offering new prospects.

It was at about that time that coffee, known in the East since the Middle Ages, began its triumphal advance through Europe. Until the end of the seventeenth century such little coffee as was drunk in the West came from the Yemen. As the demand for this stimulating black beverage grew the Yemen was unable to supply enough beans. The merchants everywhere were asking for coffee. If a settler was prepared to try his hand at growing it they would even provide him with the seed. Soon there were coffee-trees in Ceylon, in Dutch Guiana, and in Jamaica, now British—at first no more than experimental plantations, viewed sceptically by the older settlers, who did not wish to have anything to do with this new-fangled crop, but enthusiastically welcomed by the merchants, who expected profitable business in the future.

For some time the tropical plantations continued to grow their traditional sugar-cane; demand for sugar had likewise gone up dramatically. The reason was not only sugar as such, but rum. We must remember that the distilling of spirits from potatoes was still unknown and grain was expensive and in short supply. Nantes lived principally from distilling sugar-cane spirit. However, cultivation of sugar-cane did not seem to make much headway in the French colonies in the Caribbean. They lacked the cheap Negro slaves who alone were capable of working in their sun-scorched fields.

John Law was undoubtedly right; it was useless to operate with small makeshift expedients. Thoroughgoing reforms were needed. The reason why slaves were so expensive was that the Africa Company had a monopoly for the slave trade and exploited it ruthlessly in order to glean the biggest possible profit. The Company did not supply enough human labour because its penny-paring shareholders would not equip sufficient ships. As they had a monopoly they saw no reason to exert themselves. As soon as Law freed the slave trade the colonies began to flourish, and with them such import harbours as Nantes, Le Havre, St Malo, La Rochelle, and Marseille. In Bordeaux the turnover in 1721 was double the volume it had been before Louis XIV's last war.

Ruthlessly the great banker overrode the petty sectional wishes of the French industrialists. Hitherto the import of refined sugar had been prohibited in France in order to protect domestic refineries; Law simply scrapped this ban. Rum could now also be distilled in America. Rum was used by the colonists to pay for their European supplies, such as knives, axes, woollen, and linen fabrics, the African Negroes, and fish from North America. Rum was accepted in payment also by the Indians of the north-west, who supplied the beaver-skins which were in such high demand. Rum was worth as much as gold. At the time of the Sun King's death there had been fewer than 15,000 Negro slaves on the island of Martinique; during the next five years 12,000 Negroes were imported, and by 1736 their number had risen to 72,000. During the same period 200 ships from France and 30 from Canada called at the island to load rum.

From 1723 the principal crop in Martinique was coffee, while sugar was cultivated mainly in Haiti and cotton in Guadeloupe. Louisiana grew tobacco, which was then already the main source of income of the English colonies on the southern Atlantic coast of North America, chiefly Virginia. But all that was to be no more than the beginning of France's rise to economic greatness. The colonies would place major orders with French industry, they would buy hardware and clothes, lace from Valenciennes, and silk from Lyons. Ships would be built and harbours enlarged to handle the growing volume of commerce. The whole country would become rich. The debts dating from the Sun King's unfortunate wars would be repaid easily without having recourse to bankruptcy or devaluation of the currency. Such, at any rate, were Law's plans.

To realize these grand schemes, however, Law had to gain the support of those who wielded the power in the State, the great nobles and influential politicians. He spoke of credits, but they thought only of gain. To give credit a man must be able to wait patiently. To accept credit a man must be able to work hard—or else he will not be able to repay. He must produce enough for a surplus to be left after repayment of his debt, so that he can enjoy the fruits of his labours which the credit granted to him was to have alleviated.

But the men with whom Law had to deal had neither patience nor the will to work. They wanted to get rich, and, what was more, to get rich quickly. Since they occupied all the key posts it was impossible to bypass them. Law thought he might win greater support by getting them to participate in his transactions, by speaking to them of the great profits which he—in due course—hoped to make. Perhaps he was carried away too much by the fire of his own visions, perhaps he saw those fabulous successes closer at hand than they could possibly be. One thing we know for certain: he was a man who helped his friends generously and who, with all his enormous wealth, was never mean.

Everybody was now coming to him as to a miracle-worker—the

Regent of France, the Foreign Minister, the War Minister, the Minister of Finance. They all told the same tale of woe: there was no money in the State Treasury. Debts due for repayment could not be redeemed, the army and navy were in decline, foreign powers, including Spain under the great-grandson of the Sun King, were shamelessly exploiting France's weakness. Law must come to the rescue!

His bank took over the entire debts of the State, running into thousands of millions of livres. Law promised to pay the interest punctually out of the receipts from the overseas trade, an arrangement which satisfied the impatient creditors. They exchanged their war-loan bonds for bank shares which would one day yield fabulous dividends— or at least, so they hoped. But to develop the colonies Law had to have real capital. He therefore called upon the French public to bring him all their reserves of money and raw materials and to place human labour at his disposal. For this he issued shares.

Big crowds collected outside the building of the Mississippi Company, as Law called his new firm; there was not enough room at the counters for the rush of would-be subscribers. Every one wanted shares, and their quotations rose steeply. A share just acquired could be sold with a magnificent profit a few yards down the road. The short, narrow Rue Quincampoix became the Bourse. Even from the provinces people came to Paris to participate in this fabulous scramble. Everybody brought their last savings, everybody wanted to get rich quick—proud dukes, respectable merchants, shrewd notaries, rich widows, flighty servant girls, unscrupulous speculators. All France was intoxicated with the great illusion. Stock exchange quotations soared higher and higher, irresistibly, boundlessly. And with them rose the demands of the State. It needed more and more money—not to lay out plantations or build merchant ships, but to wage war and to support an enormous administrative apparatus.

More dangerous still were the politicians, the all-powerful dukes, who cunningly controlled the movement of share prices by administrative measures. At one moment they would order the old war loans to be redeemed prematurely so that too much money was in circulation, at another time they would delay repayment; shamelessly they would demand, or even extort, bonus shares. The moment quotations had reached culmination point they would sell all their shares regardless of consequences. The blissful dream was over.

Share prices now tumbled out of control; they swept the bank, the Mississippi Company, and all the beautiful projects with them into the abyss. And yet Law had operated unimpeachably and profitably. Now he was held responsible for the money which the shareholders had lost in their reckless speculations. The paper money lost its value. France, after a dazzling rise to prosperity, again sank back into poverty and destitution. The great illusion had lasted only two years.

These two years, however, had been enough to transform world commerce fundamentally. The emphasis of trade had shifted from the spices of Indonesia and the South-east Asian mainland to the crops cultivated in the Central American islands. Europe had become accustomed to sugar, coffee, tobacco, and rum, and no longer could, or wanted to, live without these new delights. The coffee-house had first made its appearance in Vienna after the war with the Turks. Now, coffee-houses sprang up in London and in the French cities. It was in Lloyd's coffee-house in London that the merchants clinched their business deals and underwrote insurance for the ships setting out on their voyages.

The entire way of life had changed. Men no longer foregathered to drink beer, which heated their tempers and made their bodies lethargic, but for a cup of hot black coffee, which stimulated and revived their minds. At the same time they would smoke American tobacco in long clay pipes and contemplate the great problems of business and life in general.

In the rural areas, on the other hand, conditions were still medieval: anything that was needed was produced locally—foodstuffs, clothing, housing, working tools, and implements. Everybody avoided having to buy things. Besides, there was hardly any cash about. Only the aristocratic landowners would earn a little from the sale of their grain and wool, but these earnings they would probably spend in town during the winter on playing at politics or amusing themselves.

It must be remembered that in the eighteenth century some nine-tenths of the population were still living in rural areas. The only trade they knew about was the hawker, who would pass rarely enough through their village. Colonial merchandise, such as sugar, rum, and coffee, were still expensive treats which one could afford only on special occasions; they introduced into the chilly West the whole seductive warmth of the tropics and the sweet ease of life in a sunny climate. For such pleasures it was certainly worth while now and again to spend a little of one's scarce and hard-earned money. The appearance of the pedlar was still an exciting event; one never knew what he would have to offer—pretty ornaments, Venetian glass, or "Nürnberg knick-nacks"—*i.e.*, clocks and watches, artisans' tools, and mechanical toys. To be on the safe side, the housewives would stock up with spices to make sure of their spiced Christmas loaf when the time came. For all they knew, the pedlar might not return.

The circle of those who could afford coffee, and later tea, was still

45. A smoker (seventeenth-century German woodcut)

limited, but it widened from decade to decade and almost from year to year. Europe became addicted. It started in the capital cities and the ports, but soon spread to medium-sized and small towns, to the country seats of the gentry, and even to the villages. Soldiers and sailors publicly indulged in the 'vice' of smoking tobacco and drinking rum, to the envious admiration of the village youths.

We have a complaint from a sixteenth-century merchant, one Andreas Ryff, to the effect that he had to ride about so much that "his saddle had burnt itself into his hindquarters." That is hardly surprising when we read that he attended thirty or more markets every year. At last the travelling merchant knew where he could place his colonial merchandise. Traders now existed even in small localities. The old distinction between the merchant and the pedlar began to disappear; in the past the pedlar had sold only 'penny goods,' articles measured with the yardstick or weighed on the scales. Oriental merchandise, spices, and incense, used to be sold by the apothecary. Sugar, coffee, and tobacco were likewise in the first place sold in the apothecary's shop; they would be sold only in minute quantities, as befitted such rare and precious commodities, and at correspondingly steep prices. Soon, however, coffee and tea were sold by the colonial merchant, just as rum was in the local tavern.

With considerable surprise the English watched the successful operations of the Scotsman John Law in Paris. Surely anything those Frenchmen could do they should be able to do better! When the Mississippi Company was at the peak of its prosperity the fever of speculation leapt across the Channel to London. The South Sea Company, at first so cautious, without another thought took on the entire debt of the British Crown, totalling over 51,000,000 pounds, against the Government's rather dubious promise that it would pay annually 1,500,000 pounds sterling in interest. The holders of war loan, who had almost given up hope of ever seeing their money again, exchanged their bonds for shares. Instead of a fixed annual rate of interest they were given a share in the business. In other words, the shareholders were to participate in the profits of the South Sea Company. The possibility of losses was not mentioned.

At first everything went without a hitch. The public had more confidence in this private enterprise than in the State, and readily subscribed whatever shares were issued. Within the first few months the shares were being negotiated with a surcharge of 29 per cent.—a very handsome profit indeed—but within six months they had soared to a Stock Exchange quotation of 1050. This intoxication with millions produced the wildest and most fraudulent deals: people were buying shares of companies which did not even exist, reputable statesmen allowed themselves to be shamefully bribed in order to help unscrupulous swindlers and to deceive gullible if reckless savers. At last the South Sea "Bubble" burst. The hangover was tremendous.

The Peace of Utrecht put an end to piracy in the grand manner—or at least to the 'honest' piracy covered by royal charter and surrounded with the halo of patriotism. Anyone still practising piracy had little hope of being commended, let alone knighted, by his monarch; sooner or later he would end on the gallows or on a yardarm. Men of adventurous mind went to the tropical plantations where money could be made most easily. They far outnumbered the Puritans who went out to the New England settlements. The number of Negroes rose steeply in the southern parts of North America as well as in the Central American colonies. It was in these areas that commerce developed most vigorously.

But what was there to buy for the settlers in the primeval forests of

't' Fort nieuw Amsterdam op de Manhatans

46. The settlement of New Amsterdam, now New York; the earliest view of the city

New England, the 'backwoodsmen'? North America as a whole was receiving from the mother country merchandise to the value of 2,000,000 pounds sterling annually; that was all. For these imports the settlers paid with the money made from their trade with the West Indian islands, to whom they supplied chiefly grain and meat, timber, wool, and ships. Without the sugar-producing islands they could not have lived at all. Only when tropical plantations had been laid out in Virginia itself did the settlers have a commodity they could sell to England—tobacco.

Trade with the West Indies had long outpaced that with the East Indies. There simply was more profit in sugar, coffee, and tobacco than there was in spices, if only because the turnover was so much bigger. The companies in London and Amsterdam, however, re-fused to acknowledge this. As if mesmerized they continued to stare at the old markets which had in the past supplied such precious merchandise. But as soon as the merchants drew up their balance sheets they realized with horror how their profits were melting away and how their losses were growing from year to year. At first they resorted to dishonest practices: they stopped publishing balance sheets, and tried to delude themselves that after a temporary recession demand was bound to go up again as soon as the perpetual wars came to an end and—when things did not improve in peace-time either—as soon as new markets were opened up. Fat dividends continued to be paid out, but no longer from profits but from capital. Not even the directors were shown the true balance sheets. To be given credit a firm had to show handsome profits and pay high dividends—a regular 19 per cent. per annum. In this way everybody was in fact deceived. When the British captured Indonesia in the Napoleonic Wars they thought they had taken a gold-mine; soon, however, they discovered the debts which had risen to 134,000,000 florins. The colony was bankrupt.

For a century the merchants in Amsterdam and London had lived by their monopoly; the apparatus of the East India Companies had been greatly inflated. Important gentlemen held posts abroad as directors or even Governors; they were officials, not merchants. They decided the local inhabitants must supply whatever they were asked and that the Europeans back home would have to buy whatever was offered them at the prices prescribed to them. Anything but free competition! Free competition would merely confuse the market, make the buyer vacillate because he would never be sure he had not overpaid, and make the producer nervous because he would always try to find some one prepared to pay a better price.

Surely plantations must be paying propositions, especially in a colony which one ruled unchecked. The order was issued to cultivate coffee and deliver it at a fixed price. However, this coffee from the plantations forced down the prices in Amsterdam. The losses were passed on to the unfortunate workers. The East India Company greatly reduced prices in the plantations. When this did not help they repeated the process in the following year. Was it surprising that by 1730 the coffee harvest had declined by half?

As, however, the demand for coffee continued to rise in Europe

pine pass: copper engraving by M. Merian. In the summer some twenty carts
velled over the St Gotthard Pass every day. During the season they carried a load of
1200 tons over the Alps

ATE XV

With dried cod from the Newfoundland Bank, the sailors from
the coasts of England and Brittany began their profitable trade
between three continents. Woodcut, about 1862

PLATE XVI

Broadsheet on the subject of British subsidies for Frederick the Great.
Hamburg merchants exchanged the British silver for merchandise
and profited both by buying and selling

...poleon's continental system was designed to hit British commerce. ...erywhere merchants were harassed by checkpoints and inspections. ...hers, such as the Rothschilds, founded their fortunes on it. The scene here is Leipzig. A contemporary drawing

PLATE XVII

The "Herring-tamer." Caricature of a small merchant of the early nineteenth century. He has done his day's work and his apprentice is allowed to help him into his traveling boots. A contemporary drawing

PLATE XVIII

The textile store of Mr Echigoya in Edo, the forerunner of the
Mitsukoshi department store of to-day. The notices inside display the name of the firm and the warning: "Cash only, no
discount." On the left, by the entrance, is a customer; in front

of her a vendor of calendars. On the right tea is served. In the
centre is an assistant carrying rolls of cloth. In the background,
right, accountants are sitting over their ledgers. Japanese colour
woodcut, attributed to Okumara Masanobu, 1686–1764

La ville de BATAVIE.
vrbs BATAVIA.

Batavia, nowadays Djakarta, the principal base of the Dutch spice trade

PLATE XIX

Novgorod on Lake Ilmen. There the Hanseatic merchants of the Court of St Peter traded Russian furs, honey, and timber, for the woven cloth of the industrial West

WELIKI NOVOGROD
ODER
GROS NA VGARD

Canton: from the seventeenth century onward Dutch and Portuguese merchants regularly called at this important port of southern China. From a travel account of Peter de Gojern and Jacob Keisern, Amsterdam, 1669

he island fortress of de Diu snatched by Portuguese seafarers from the Mohammedans
protected Goa, the most important Portuguese trading-centre

...abo, for a long
...he centre of the
... slave trade on
... African Gold
... Copper en-
...ng by Quintin
... Chedel (1705–
...) after Smith

CHATEAU ANGLOIS D'ANAMABO
A. Lieu du débarquement B. Port entre les Roches, C. Entrée du Port.

An African mar-
ket about 1670
in the town of
Lovangiri in
Lovan. From a
Dutch travel
account of 1668

PLATE XX

PLATE XXI

The most notorious slave house on the African west coast was on the island of Gorée, off Senegal. Its ruins survive to this day as a terrible memento

Inscriptions left by Portuguese sailors at Ruana Mutundi (Congo) in 1482

PLATE XXII

The Cotton Office, 1875. Painting by Edgar Dégas (1834–1917)

Warehouses—the prerequisite of an entrepôt centre. The large flour scales in the picture were used for a long time by the great merchants of Frankfurt on Main. Lithograph about 1800

PLATE XXIII

Colbert, Louis XIV's Minister of State.
A seventeenth-century engraving

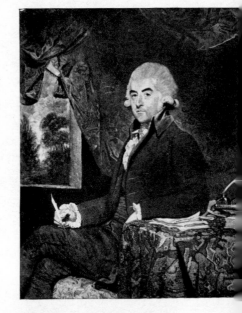

Henry Hope. Engraving by Hodges,
London, 1788, after a painting by
Sir Joshua Reynolds

The three principals of the firm of Baring studying the account of the
firm of Hope. Engraving by J. Ward after the painting by Lawrence

Fashions capture the market: a girl assistant in a Paris hosiery shop, about 1830. Coloured broadsheet

The travelling salesman. At the beginning of the nineteenth century he sold chiefly textile articles. Drawing about 1780

PLATE XXV

South Ameri
being opened up
commerce and trai
port: a high roa
remarkable for t
early nineteen
century, ran fr
Valparaiso to S.
tiago. Woodc
1859

The old Royal Exchange in London. Engraving by W. Hollar

Below: Liverpool harbour: the fourth customs house and the old dock. Painting by W. G. Herdmann

e famous Hudson's Bay Company has its trading-posts on the very frontiers of
lization: they buy skins from the Indians and supply them with every necessity for
pursuing their trade in the wilderness

PLATE XXVI

vertising—the key to success. A mechanical elephant during a Berlin exhibition in
ı spewed advertising leaflets out of his trunk. The idea met with much applause
at the time

Elegant shops spring up along the new Paris boulevards. The more exacting buying public of the mid-nineteenth century is lured into the shops by advertisements and handbills. Lithographed billhead of the reign of Louis Philippe

Left: The famous Rue de Rivoli, an elegant shopping-street, reflects the change in the appearance of cities brought about by retail trade

Harrods, one of the big London department stores, always strives to offer something special to its customers

PLATE XXVII

y Street
loscow

The new face of a
city: Fifth Avenue,
straight as an arrow,
cutting across the city
of New York

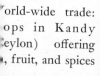

orld-wide trade:
ops in Kandy
eylon) offering
, fruit, and spices

Choice in abundance: shop-window on 42nd Street, New York

PLATE XXIX

Soviet citizens in the GUM department store

diametrically opposite orders were now issued. Production was greatly stimulated. Before long, however, it had to be throttled again. In 1744 the workers complained that the Company was buying only one-quarter of their harvest and ordering them not to sell the remainder to other dealers. It takes four years for a coffee-tree to bear fruit; any commercial miscalculation therefore takes four years to come to light. These continuous ups and downs, typical of a management by officials and politicians who had discarded purely commercial considerations and tasted the exhilarating drug of monopoly rule, undermined Holland's position in world trade.

Holland was eclipsed in the commercial field. Her supremacy was broken, not by the British Navigation Acts nor by her military defeats in the wars of 1688, but by the shifting pattern of world commerce. Britain at the same time went from victory to victory. Her troops conquered French Canada; in India they defeated the French, the Dutch, and the Indians themselves. The East India Company took over the Government of Bengal, officially as the representative of the Mogul but in fact as the ruler of the country.

The backbone of the East India business, however, was no longer the acquisition and retail of Indian merchandise but the tea trade. The tea had to be obtained in China, without military compulsion or political influence, in free commerce, and against the competition of other European nations, principally the Dutch and the French. True, the British possessed one great advantage in being able to offer to the Chinese a commodity denied to their rivals—opium. While opium-smoking was strictly prohibited in India the British supplied this narcotic to China on an increasing scale. It was only to be expected that this trade would run into opposition as soon as political conditions became consolidated in the Middle Kingdom.

But for this revenue the East India Company would have been unable to bear the heavy overheads in India. Whereas England had been a predominantly coffee-drinking country until 1730, the public, thanks to the efficient propaganda conducted by the all-powerful East India Company, switched over to tea. Britain has remained a country of tea-drinkers to this day.

Territorial conquests may have brought tremendous gain and personal wealth to the officials and generals involved, but for the finances of the Company they were irrelevant. In the last third of the eighteenth century the English East India Company stood and fell with the tea trade. Whenever business was bad the tea price was raised in England. When the State needed money the tea tax was increased. And because of this tea tax the tie linking the American possessions to the mother country was severed. A few colonists, disguised as Red Indians, tipped the tea into the sea in order to prevent importation at excessive prices; neither the Company nor the British Government could tolerate such action. The conflict led to the independence of the United States of America.

Europe was still dreaming of the rich wonderland of India, of the fabulous wealth of the Spice Islands, of the silver-mines of Peru and Mexico. The very names of these countries conjured up visions of fearless sailors, successful merchants, and great conquerors. Anyone walking along the canals of Amsterdam past the impressive houses of the merchants, anyone admiring the silver treasures of Spanish churches, anyone looking in amazement at the Port of London with its countless ships felt sure he knew where all that wealth had come from—the East Indies and the silver mountains of America. It was over those countries that the great colonial wars of the seventeenth and eighteenth centuries were fought.

Yet all the time the West Indies with their plantations were yielding far greater profits. Naturally the profit margin on a single pound of sugar, coffee, or tobacco was not very great, but the turnover of these commodities was so much bigger than that of spices or silk. After all, life in Europe had changed almost beyond recognition; luxury was gaining ground and spreading to ever wider circles. The gloomy seventeenth century with its religious wars had been followed by the light-hearted, uninhibited, self-satisfied, and pleasure-seeking eighteenth century. The princes were all busy emulating the example of Louis XIV; they were building palaces to look like Versailles and spending as much money as the Sun King himself. Indeed, some of them surpassed him.

From the Courts the new way of life spread to the capital cities, to the ports and trading towns, and even to medium-sized provincial centres. There, too, the people now wanted to drink coffee, or tea, or chocolate, enjoy a sugar titbit, smoke a pipe, take snuff, or chew tobacco. People no longer ate their meals off the traditional pewter plates, let alone from wooden bowls, but off fine crockery—stoneware at first, but later porcelain, first of Chinese and subsequently of European manufacture. Table-cloths came into fashion, and here and there even table napkins. All that cost money, which had to be earned somehow. The landed gentry, the patricians and notabilities in the country towns, and the few wealthy farmers extended their acreage under cultivation or, if that was not enough, tightened the screw on their tenants.

Reforms were badly needed. Flanders set the example. In the past most livestock had had to be slaughtered in the autumn; now, to enable the animals to survive the winter, beet and clover were planted. This 'three-field system' provided for a cropping sequence of wheat, beet, and clover or pulses. The Englishmen adopting this method as early as the seventeenth century were but few. But when the Dutch followed their King to England the "Norfolk system" spread rapidly. Success was immediate and striking: within a short time harvests were doubled. Instead of 6 to 10 bushels of wheat per acre some farmers were now gathering 20 or even 24. To introduce the new farming method, acquire the necessary implements and new seedstock, and attract expert farm workers—all that needed money. The landed gentry took out credits, got into debt with the merchants, and mortgaged the coming harvest. Money, hitherto circulating only in commerce, penetrated into agriculture and transformed it in accordance with modern views.

Men who had made a fortune from sugar-cane or from the coffee and tobacco plantations of the West Indies or North America would buy an estate in the mother country and improve it in accordance with commercial considerations. No more muddling along. The uprooted peasants—unless they moved altogether into the towns to find work in the factories which were working for export—became artisans, spinning and weaving from early morning until late at night.

The more the 'wealth' increased—if we go by the figures for Treasury revenue, for expenditure on luxuries, and for the consumption of sugar, tobacco, and coffee—the greater also became the general poverty. According to James Edward Oglethorpe, M.P., more than 4000 persons in 1730 were simultaneously in prison for debt. Famine raged in the countryside, and in the towns the proletariat was submerged in poverty and squalor. Conditions were no better in France. Was wealth then nothing but a curse? Was it only the rich who were getting richer while the poor were getting poorer still? The fact was merely that naked poverty had become more conspicuous than in the past.

The money in circulation tempted people into spending more than hitherto. Everybody was running into debt, creditors were pressing debtors, rents for homes went up, and higher rents were demanded by landlords from tenant farmers. The nobility at Court, the burghers in the towns, the higher clergy—none of them managed to live within their means now that money ran so easily through their fingers. On top of all that came the heavy taxes enacted by princes to finance their ostentatious building and military campaigns.

Visitors arriving from Central Europe at the great harbour towns of the naval and colonial powers were dazzled by the bulging sacks of colonial merchandise and the snow-white sugar cones. But the old colonies in Africa and Asia had ceased to yield profits; indeed they were now costing money. The ceaseless colonial wars consumed vast sums. The Companies raised entire armies which would remain in the field for months on end. Officials attached less importance to trading merchandise than to imposing high taxes upon the subjected people; but for that very reason they had to strengthen their military power increasingly in order to keep foreign rivals at arm's length, to intimidate neighbours, and to crush discontent within their territories. Besides, the age of great conquests was past. Some individuals, of course, might still succeed in accumulating riches, but this happened less often through commerce than by war and lucky conquest.

There were some great names in England, France, and Holland—much admired and much envied. When Clive retired in 1767, at the age of forty-two, he was reputed to be the richest man in England. The Governor of the East India Company, Thomas Pitt, had been fortunate enough to buy an enormous diamond in India for 16,000 pounds sterling which he sold to the Regent of France for 125,000 pounds. But how many people had this kind of luck? The East India Companies certainly no longer yielded such profits. They had to bear the costs of warships, troops, and the administration in India; these expenses swallowed up even the most spectacular paper profits.

Only the tea trade, which had nothing to do with conquests or proud possessions but was the subject of simple commercial calculation, yielded considerable surpluses. In 1739 the eleven ships which sailed from the Dutch Indies to Europe carried 460,000 florins' worth of tea, and coffee to the value of 304,000 florins; next came pepper (worth 212,000 florins) and sugar (worth 67,000 florins). Only then came the spices proper to which the Moluccas once owed their reputation of fabulous wealth—mace worth 59,000 florins, nutmeg worth 33,000 florins, camphor worth 30,000 florins, indigo worth 29,000 florins, cloves worth 25,000 florins, and catechu (a tanning liquor obtained from acacia) worth 22,000 florins. Obviously the spice trade alone no longer produced any great riches. The plantations were desperately competing with their West Indian rivals which were situated so much nearer to the European markets. The British realized this point and shifted the main weight of their business to commerce with China.

The victims of this decline in the East Indies were the shareholders of the great East India Companies, both in Holland and England. Nevertheless, the Powers continued to wage protracted wars over India, and for her sake governments saddled themselves with enormous debts. Under this burden the French monarchy collapsed.

12

Triangular Trade:
England, Africa, the West Indies

━━∿∿∿∿ひ◉ひ∿∿∿∿━━

THOMAS LEYLAND OF LIVERPOOL understood the signs of the times. The bigwigs of the City of London could chase after their East India business, their spice and silk trade, and subscribe as many shares of the East India Company as they liked—but he would trade with Africa and the West Indies.

The first ship with no more than fifteen Negro slaves on board had sailed from Liverpool to the West Indies in 1709. That date marks the beginning of the slow and hesitant growth of the little port whose 5000 inhabitants were crowded together on the marshy bank of the Mersey, three miles from the open sea, sorely tried by floods and severe outbreaks of plague. By the middle of the century the number of ships on the West Indies run had increased to fifty-three, with an average displacement of 100 tons. But Liverpool's real rise to prosperity came during the protracted colonial wars between Britain and France.

Lurking in the Channel were French freebooters from Dieppe, St Malo, and Dunkirk. It was the same as it had been 100 years before; the grandsons and great-grandsons of the pirates from the days of the Sun King and Cardinal Richelieu were again in their element. And the English were giving as good as they got. Commerce was languishing. Marine insurance premiums soared so high that it was hardly worth while shipping merchandise across the Channel. The Port of London was all but dead. Liverpool was situated more favourably:

ships from there sailed past Ireland to the high seas, where they were but rarely caught by the enemy.

It was then that Leyland's rise to wealth began. He made purchases on a grand style in the hinterland of Liverpool: woollen and cotton textiles in Manchester, steel blades in Sheffield, swords and guns in Birmingham. On the west coast of Africa, principally in Guinea, he traded these goods for Negro slaves. Others had tried this trade before him; the Great Elector of Brandenburg had even set up a fortified trading-post in Africa. But all these attempts had misfired for lack of the right goods to trade for the slaves. Liverpool, however, possessed that merchandise, thanks to its industrial hinterland. The West Indies were accepting any number of Negro slaves, who were needed in the sugar, tobacco, and coffee plantations. In 1765 alone the 86 ships sailing out of Liverpool carried 24,200 Negroes to America. The distasteful trade was booming. During the first ten years after the American War of Independence (1783–93) Liverpool made a tremendous, if disreputable, profit from the sale of 303,000 Negro slaves.

And that was not everything. In exchange for their human cargo, their gold dust, and their ivory, the slave traders purchased in America sugar, cotton, and tobacco. Coffee by then had lost its former popularity in England, but the other commodities from America ensured considerable gain.

The entire hinterland of Liverpool was transformed into one vast workshop. Bobbins spun, looms rattled, hammers rang in the forges and shipyards. The demand for export articles rose continuously, while at the same time colonial merchandise such as sugar, tobacco, and, above all, rum was flowing through Liverpool into the hardworking villages. No doubt they brought to the weary, grey everyday routine of incessant hard work a brief moment of pleasure and happiness. People then had to work for fourteen, fifteen, and even sixteen hours a day—men, women, and even children. But all these efforts were still not enough to meet the overseas demand. Fortunately there was an ample supply of raw materials: not only wool, but also cotton, which was being imported in Liverpool ships more cheaply than ever before. It was brought back from the West Indies to make up the load; the main cargo was still sugar and tobacco.

Liverpool's rise continued by leaps and bounds: in 1807 nearly 50,000 Negroes were taken to the West Indian plantations by 185 ships from Liverpool. This meant a tremendous profit. The sale of a single slave yielded an average profit of forty-three pounds sterling; this gain was doubled by successful deals in tropical crops. Liverpool, a small, insignificant port of 25,000 inhabitants about the middle of the seventeenth century, gained for itself the leading position in the slave trade and thus became, after London, the most important trading city in Britain.

The slave trade required a thick skin. One had to be deaf to the desperate cries of the unfortunate creatures as they were dragged from their homes and clapped into chains, and to the rattling breath of those dying from heat in the dark, airless holds of the ships. The sailors of Liverpool had learned their hard trade during the war, on savage naval raids. It had been a terrible school. During the American War of Independence 120 sea-raiders sailed out in one year alone (1778-79), armed with nearly 2000 cannon and manned by 8745 sailors. Liverpool had become a power. Its guiding spirit was its Mayor, Thomas Leyland, banker and merchant, a man of outstanding vision and determination, the richest man in Liverpool and perhaps in England.

His commercial interests, his entire way of thinking, were diametrically opposed to the ideas and projects entertained in London. London was the domain of the monopolists. They owned the East Indies and did not allow anyone to interfere. They were out to make large profits at the expense of the producer—the unfortunate farmers in Asia —and the consumers in England. They were continually obliged to wage war to defend their loot—against the Portuguese, against the Dutch, against the French, and later against the Asian rulers, starting with the Emperors of China and Japan and finishing with the Great Mogul and the maharajahs of India—always anxious to protect their artificial barriers, their customs duties, their prohibitions, and their privileges.

That way lay no future. Subsequent developments proved Leyland right: Britain's imports from India between 1750 and 1775 only rarely exceeded 1,000,000 pounds sterling in value. All attempts to step up these imports were fruitless. Even though the export of English merchandise to India, at first very slight, was doubled during that period, this was not nearly enough to balance the trade. And without money nothing could be bought. These figures were mere chicken-feed to a man like Leyland.

On the battlefields of India the great gentlemen of the East India Company advanced from victory to victory. Through the military genius of Clive the British became supreme in India—but how was this to benefit the merchants? The Company's representative in India was given the title of Governor-General—in other words, he became an official of the British Crown. But the India Office in London began to interfere in everything. One cannot really blame it; the Company as such was bankrupt and was being kept alive only by the great 'credits' from the State—subsidies which were never repaid. Behind an impressive and much admired façade there was nothing. London declined more and more. Liverpool's trade, on the other hand, increased four times as fast as the total British trade.

Things were no different in France, except that her unsuccessful military operations in India showed up the real state of affairs even more clearly. As early as 1752—*i.e.*, five years before the great defeat of Plassey, when Dupleix was still winning one battle after another—rumours were current in Paris that the French East India Company was bankrupt. And that in spite of the fact that the King had paid the Company the enormous sum of 400,000,000 livres in subsidies between 1717 and 1757—though admittedly this claim by the King has been vehemently denied by others. At any rate, the Company was deprived of its monopoly of the India trade by royal decree in 1769, and a year later it was dissolved.

Did this mean the end of France's Eastern trade? Nothing of the sort. Indeed, French trade with Asia was only now beginning to develop. Between 1725 and 1769 it had rarely amounted to more than 8,000,000 francs; during the next seven years it rose to an annual average of over 20,000,000 francs. The age of monopolies was over.

This realization was gaining ground even in the trade with America, in the face of all attempts by the great monopolists of Lisbon and Seville, who naturally were reluctant to accept the fact that the days were gone when they could dictate their prices without fear of competition. King Charles III, the Bourbon on the French throne who enjoyed the reputation of one of the most enlightened monarchs of his century, revoked Seville's foreign trade monopoly in 1765. The ports of Alicante, Cartagena, Malaga, Barcelona, Santander, Corunna, and Gijón were opened to the American trade. It was now up to the private merchant to show whether he was more efficient than the semi-official, semi-ecclesiastical monopolist association of the *casa de contratacion.*

Free competition—or, as the supporters of the old order saw it, a free-for-all—began. The reformers demanded absolute equality of opportunity. Indignantly they pointed to the organization which, quite apart from a legal monopoly, had succeeded in establishing an actual one—the Jesuit Order, or, as it was known throughout South America, the Society.

Without any doubt the Jesuits had done a great deal to develop the economy of South America. Jesuit Fathers had brought the wild Indians from the forests of Brazil and Paraguay into their 'reductions,' trained them in European methods of agriculture, and taught the girls to spin and weave and the men joinery and building. Vast estates were created where goods were produced for export—from Chilean wheat to Central American sugar. This enormous economic organism threatened to gain exclusive control of all commerce. Then came the reverse. Vast speculative transactions by the Superior of the Order in Martinique went wrong. As the Jesuit General was not prepared to stand surety for the colossal deficit of 2,400,000 livres with the property of the Order, the King banned the Order in France in 1764. That was the signal for a universal outbreak of long-suppressed hostility to the all-powerful "dead hand," and to its unfair competition. Those who under the banner of enlightenment had been opposing the Order for a long time now got their way. Within three years the Jesuits were expelled also from Portugal and Spain, their vast immovable property and extensive trading-stations were sequestrated and sold by auction, and the Order itself was prohibited. The "spirit of the century," the spirit of free competition, had scored a new triumph. It was the spirit of Liverpool.

Considerable changes had meanwhile taken place on the west coast of Africa. Commerce had shifted from the Gold Coast, or present-day Ghana, to the "Slave Coast" farther east. And this was not merely a geographical shift. Along the Gold Coast stood the old fortresses of the Europeans, from El Mina, built by the Portuguese as early as the fifteenth century, to the fortified bases of the Dutch and the French, the Danes, and—temporarily—the Elector of Brandenburg. The chieftains along the Slave Coast, on the other hand, which reached from Togo down to Nigeria, confident of their military prowess, had actually prevented the white man from setting up fortresses along that stretch of the Atlantic coast. Indeed, they did not even permit Europeans to build houses of stone or brick; only straw and reed huts were permitted, buildings at the mercy of any outbreak of fire. Nevertheless, the merchants complied—and they did not regret it. For now the Negro rulers supplied their slaves voluntarily in order to trade them for such European merchandise as woollen and linen fabrics, articles of iron and other metals, glass beads, small ornaments, and cowrie-shells.

The Portuguese had hoped for gold; they knew that part of the considerable quantities of gold reaching the Mediterranean coast from Central Africa via Morocco came from West Africa. But they had nothing to offer in exchange except inferior and expensive woollen materials and a few items of iron. That was just about enough to make modest purchases of kola nuts, West African pepper, known as Malajetta pepper, ivory, and slaves. The French, by comparison, made a greater effort. About 1720 they imported from the Senegal estuary ivory, wax, gum arabic, hides, and—needless to say—slaves to a total value of 500,000 pounds sterling.

In the seventeenth century the slave trade was firmly in the hands of the Dutch—not because they ruled the seas, but because they had built up a market for their human merchandise which was genuinely capable of absorbing large numbers and, what was more, of paying a good price. That market was the sugar-cane plantations of their Brazilian possessions and—when these were lost to the Dutch—in the West Indian islands of Curaçao and St Eustatius. Business flourished and yielded excellent profits, but it also attracted envious rivals—first of all the monopolists of the English Africa Company. It was to this Company that Spain, in the Peace of Utrecht in 1713, had to cede the *asiento*, the legal right to import 4800 Negroes into Spanish America each year. The numbers smuggled into the country were probably considerably greater. A few years later the London merchants again believed that they might gain for themselves commercial privileges by means of political compulsion: they wanted to keep all French possessions in Africa so as to eliminate French competition in the slave markets. True, under the peace treaty they had to return Goree (present-day Dakar), but that town did not play a very important part in the slave trade. But what use were all the outposts of power, the colonies, and the fortresses? Dealings with the self-assured Negro rulers along the independent Slave Coast were governed entirely by free competition. It was a matter of the highest bidder.

It was about that time that the savage tribes of the hinterland, the Ashanti and the Dahomey, penetrated from the tropical rain forests to the coast. They concluded a sinister treaty with the merchants: in exchange for firearms, which of course would give them superiority over all inland tribes throughout the vast grassy plains of the Sudan, they promised to deliver slaves in any numbers.

Until then the slave trade on the African west coast had been kept within certain limits. Chieftains had sold their own slaves: subjected tribes, inveterate debtors, criminals, and vagrants. But now the Ashanti and Dahomey organized regular manhunts. The export of slaves rose alarmingly.

A pretext for war was found easily enough, and there was always a ready market for the tragic spoils of war. Down at the coast the trade was booming. From the interior of the country came one horrible caravan after another: endless lines of unfortunate human beings, chained together, bent under the yoke of slavery, driven on with whips. No doubt they heaved a sigh of relief when they came at last to the coast. There they remained in the hands of the Negro chieftains until the white traders bought them. A doctor would examine every single slave. Not from humanitarian motives, but because it did not pay to ship 'merchandise' that was not in good health. Even strong men died like flies on the voyage. Old and weak men were useless. In demand were men between 10 and 35 years of age and girls from 15 to 25. Expectant mothers were refused by the slave traders; they would not survive the passage. As a rule, one-third of the slave transports were women. Many of the men had been killed in the fighting, frequently the strongest of them who had resisted with the courage born of despair, knowing well the fate in store for them.

In the sixteenth century about 900,000 people had been shipped from Africa to America; in the seventeenth century the number rose to 2,750,000, and in the next century it rose to over 7,000,000. And that does not include those who died on the journey and were thrown overboard.

At the beginning of the eighteenth century the price of a slave on the Gold Coast was about three pounds; by the end, it was 25 pounds sterling. But these figures are misleading, since payment was made not in money but in a number of strange currencies: on the pepper coast prices were calculated in iron bars, in Accra in cowrie-shells, on the Ivory Coast in woollen textiles, on the Gold Coast in grains of gold, on the Slave Coast in iron and copper bars, on the "oil rivers" (*i.e.,* the Niger estuary) in brass—which was in great demand mainly in Benin—and finally in the Cameroons the currency was again woollen textiles. Strange rates of exchange had come to be accepted: thus an iron bar was worth four copper bars of equal weight. The blacksmiths in the interior urgently needed iron for their tools, and this iron had to be supplied in definite dimensions.

A good deal of calculation was necessary: first the cost of the slaves in local 'currency,' then the European merchandise offered—firearms, gunpowder and lead, steel blades, short sabres, long knives, and axes, and woollen and linen textiles—not forgetting that the value of these depended on their colour. To read a Negro chieftain's mind was difficult. One day a blue material might be in great demand in one place and unsaleable a few miles farther on. Then, all of a sudden, the vogue would change: blue cloth could no longer be sold in the first locality, whereas in the other, where blue had been solidly refused the previous year, nothing but blue would now serve. The merchant had to be a good negotiator, patient and calm. The suspicious Negro chieftains would carefully examine each piece.

Monopoly or compulsion were useless in these circumstances. Besides, it was not a case of straightforward payment in gold or silver; it was necessary to supply attractive and durable merchandise if one was to be received amicably again the following year. In England thousands of human beings were labouring behind spinning-machines and looms, in forging shops and gun factories—but all that was not enough. The demand was still growing, and manufacturers were engulfed by a flood of orders.

The example of the Gold Coast was soon followed by others. London tried to regain its former importance; other ports, such as Bristol, competed for this profitable trade. The disruption occasioned by the American War of Independence was soon overcome; in 1785 some 64,000 Negroes were shipped across the Atlantic. About half this total—38,000—were sold by the British to the West Indies and North America, 20,000 were sold by the French, whose main bases were on the Volta and Congo rivers; then came the Dutch with 4000 and the Danes with 2000. The key to success was simply ability to supply the necessary merchandise demanded by the African chieftains in payment. But would England, with a population then of barely 7,000,000, be able in the long run to supply such quantities of goods?

The first commodity to become scarce was timber: the ironworks consumed what few forests there were. But how were the ores to be smelted without this cheap fuel? To import timber from abroad was far too expensive, but without wood there could be no iron, and without iron no knives, axes, or firearms—and hence no slaves. But without slaves there would be no sugar, no rum, and no tobacco. Already the gun factories in Sussex had to import both pig iron and wrought iron from Scandinavia.

Before long there was also a shortage of human labour—even though entire families, including the small children, were made to toil from early morning until late at night. Unless a miracle were to happen England's industrial production was bound to decline in spite of all her successes in the world markets.

And this miracle came to pass: the steam-engine solved all problems. It worked on coal which could be mined in the country. The steam was also used to drive the pumps which exhausted the water from the mines to prevent flooding; it drove the pit-head machinery, enabling deeper pits to be worked. Steam ultimately also saved manpower in the textile industry by driving the spinning-machine recently invented by Arkwright, and also Hargreaves's famous spinning-jenny.

The Industrial Revolution began. The spinning-jenny produced a stronger thread by twisting it harder than was possible by the human hand. Until then Europe had not been able to process cotton on its own because the thread—unlike that of the much-admired Asian fabrics—was not strong enough but required an admixture of linen. In 1779 Crompton invented the "mule" machine, which produced a considerably finer and much more elastic thread than hitherto. The road had been cleared for the English cotton industry.

Until 1775 England had imported nearly all her cotton textiles from Bengal; her own production had been so insignificant that a mere 4,700,000 lb.—*i.e.*, not much more than 2000 tons—of raw cotton from the West Indies had been sufficient. By the outbreak of the war with the French revolutionary armies English imports had risen to 33,000,000 lb.; in 1802 they reached 57,000,000 lb. But Manchester's rapidly expanding industry demanded still more. The machines devoured any quantity of cotton.

If the cultivation of sugar-cane had been greatly increased, then surely the same should be possible with cotton. There was plenty of land on the globe, and the labour could always be obtained from Africa. It was merely a matter of finding the most favourable spot. At first the Liverpool merchants thought that cotton would grow only in the West Indies, that blessed area in the tropics where the sun made all fruit mature in the shortest possible time and where the climate was bearable even for the white man. Moreover, the sea route to the West Indies was easy and cheap and the islands were not exposed to the risk of attack. The West Indies, in fact, were the most highly treasured part of the British Empire. When William Pitt introduced income tax in 1797 he mentioned that four-fifths of Britain's overseas receipts came from the West Indies. However, the West Indian islands were not big enough to supply sufficient quantities of cotton. There was not enough land there, and no number of slaves could alter that fact.

In the south of the United States, on the other hand, there was plenty of land still unused—and, moreover, in the traditional trading area of the City of London, where the Londoners had long been buying their tobacco. In vain did moralists and doctors, kings and officials inveigh against the vice of smoking. King James I wrote a spirited tract against this bad habit and flatly prohibited smoking throughout his kingdom. All for nothing. In spite of the severest penalties tobacco prevailed, not only in Europe but throughout the world from Turkey to far-off Japan. "Whenever a ship with tobacco arrives in port from foreign lands," a Jesuit noted in the seventeenth century,

the people can hardly wait for the stinking merchandise to be unloaded. They get into the nearest boat and have themselves rowed out to the ship. They order a case to be opened and a screw of tobacco to be cut off for them. They thereupon test the weed with their teeth, biting into it as if it were the choicest delicacy. If they find it to their taste, they are aflame with desire and beyond themselves with delight. Having stared at it for a long time they begin to buy and to ask the price. No matter whether a ducat or a gold florin is demanded—nothing is too much for them. They do not begrudge a single penny they spend on this merchandise. What use is money (they think) if it stays in one's purse? Money is often said to rank above virtue: but with these people tobacco ranks above money.

America

Tob...

Coffee, Su...

47. The circulation of trade
between three continents

Jesuit
Missions

Much to the sorrow of the indignant moralists tobacco was excellent business. Admittedly, its price fluctuated over the years according to the harvest. The price of five shillings, recorded at the beginning of the seventeenth century, could not of course be maintained. In 1630 a pound of English tobacco was offered at twopence, and gradually a kind of equilibrium came to be established between the steadily increasing demand and the continually increasing acreage under the crop.

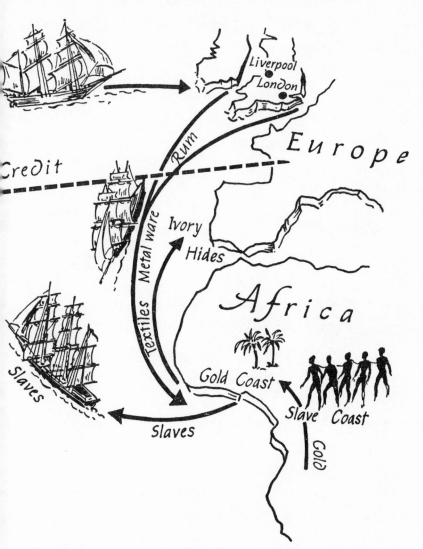

The King of Prussia founded his "smokers' circle," where he could forget the annoyances of politics over a pipe of tobacco with his friends. The kings of England imposed a high tax upon the vice. Charles II, the heir of the royal opponent of smoking, exacted a duty of 200 per cent. *ad valorem,* and his Hanoverian successor raised this to 600 per cent. Yet even so tobacco remained a paying proposition! The tobacco colonies of North and South Carolina and Georgia not only accepted slaves at high prices but also a multitude of merchandise from the English mother country. Any old rubbish, any line that did not sell elsewhere, any stuff that was piling up in the shops of London could be sold there at a good profit. Those foolish American backwoodsmen were still so behind the times! However, they were growing richer and more exacting: before long they demanded silk bonnets,

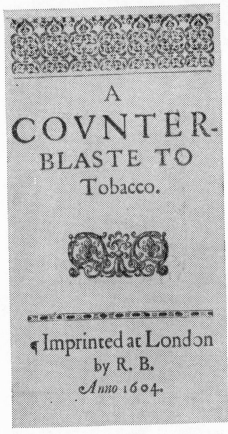

48. King James I's tract against tobacco. Printed anonymously in 1604, but included in the 1616 folio of the King's writings. The tract was also published in Latin in 1619 and again in 1689

fashionable petticoats, damask tablecloths, shoes of red morocco leather, and furniture by Chippendale and Hepplewhite—but also everyday commodities like tea, delicacies such as almonds, chocolate, raisins, and capers, and the coarse cloth of Osnabrück which was just about good enough for the Negroes. Every one of these lines was sold profitably.

This closely guarded and easy market of the London merchants was suddenly invaded by the wide-awake importers from Liverpool. Their buyers turned up in the quiet and staid tobacco ports, in Charleston and Norfolk, in order to bid for cotton. At first they had little luck. Cotton would not grow well on the light sandy soil of the inland plateau. True, there was one strain of cotton which did flourish, but it was almost impossible to gin by hand. It was therefore useless for the farmer.

The men from Liverpool, who kept hanging about the savannahs talking to the local landowners and trying to find a solution to the problem, could think of only one way—a machine would have to do the job. They found a young man of outstanding engineering ability, Eli Whitney, who constructed for them the machine they wanted. From the Atlantic to the Rocky Mountains, from the Gulf of Mexico to the Missouri river, cotton could now be grown in almost unlimited quantities. The merchants from Liverpool accepted entire harvests, they paid advances in respect of standing crops, and they supplied whatever number of slaves were wanted. Their trading-posts in Africa saw to that.

This was real business. No need to pursue a few grand ladies and gentlemen, trying to talk them into buying a precious piece of jewellery, fine silk, valuable lace, or some out-of-the-way spices. The factories in Manchester were ordering vast loads of cotton. They wanted to be sure of deliveries for weeks and months ahead, better still for several years ahead. Year after year, the machines consumed more cotton, and the merchants were hard put to it to deliver the raw material in good time. Thousands, hundreds of thousands, millions of yards of cloth were spewed out by the machines. These quantities could no longer be absorbed by Lancashire alone, nor by the whole of England, nor even by the Africans or the plantation owners in the West Indies and North America. The problem now was to find new markets.

A veritable landslide took place wherever the merchants of Liverpool threw their cotton on the market. Even in India, the homeland of cotton, where the high-quality muslins had reigned unchallenged for centuries, the Liverpool merchants offered their cheap machine-woven cloth.

The old-established wool industry in England viewed the dramatic rise of cotton with considerable alarm. As early as 1782 the worried manufacturers complained: "If the cotton-mills recently set up in the neighbourhood of Manchester are permitted to ruin our wool factories they will prove to have been the most disastrous invention ever made in old England." But time marched on. The old-fashioned enterprises with their conservative owners, who still refused to instal machinery, were simply unable to stand up to the combined effects of business initiative, technical inventiveness, and big capital.

Yet even the wool manufacturers experienced some benefits from the new world-wide business: the Liverpool merchants also imported wool, good and cheap wool from Australia. In 1787 a British ship had taken out to Australia twenty-nine merino sheep; these were the original stock of the millions which to-day populate that continent. Australia became the world's most important exporter of wool.

If the English wool industry grumbled about its dangerous upstart rival, opposition in foreign countries was naturally even more violent. But the Liverpool merchants offered their goods so cheaply that all resistance was in vain. The battle was ultimately decided by the consumers, and these would buy in the most favourable market.

In vain did guilds and old-established merchants invoke ancient rights and privileges. Their complaints were met with the slogan of free trade, free competition, freedom for enterprise. Efficient business, the free-traders were saying, was reflected in low prices. Low prices enabled Britain to conquer the Continent and eventually the world.

In 1806, however, the all-conquering Napoleon decreed his Continental System. The European market was lost.

13

Bills of Exchange open up the Continental Market

HIS BRITANNIC MAJESTY'S CONSUL was most displeased. It was bad enough that the American rebels and French freebooters were trying to break the British blockade; but that a subject of His Britannic Majesty should dare to send his ships to the West Indies against the express prohibition of the Admiralty was positively outrageous. England was fighting tenaciously against her rebellious colonies in North America.

Unmoved, the merchant John Parish listened to these complaints. After all, a man must look after himself. He was a resident of the Free Hanseatic Town of Hamburg and his ships were flying the Hamburg flag—what did he care about British laws? This impertinence provoked the Consul into massive threats: the Royal Navy would seize his ships wherever it encountered them and confiscate the contraband. "They are neutral ships protected by international law," was Parish's reply. Britain, the Consul pointed out, had not been swayed in the past when the allegedly neutral Dutch and Danes had protested to her. And the result had been, Parish retorted, that all naval powers had gone over to the Americans. Was the British Government so totally blind that it would now from sheer stubbornness ruin such little trade as had been left to it—its trade through neutral Hamburg? This threat went home. His Britannic Majesty's Consul did not even withdraw Parish's passport.

Parish knew very well who had earned him this reprimand: his own fellow-countrymen in Hamburg, those sleepy old dodderers of the Merchant Adventurers, the inheritors of the ancient monopoly guild. They had watched with envy the young upstart pull off the great deals for which they lacked the strength and the courage. During the second half of the eighteenth century Hamburg had become the great entrepôt of British colonial merchandise for Central, Eastern, and Northern Europe—ever since Emden had ceased to enjoy the exclusive right of staple for English merchandise. Via Hamburg, West Indian sugar and coffee and East Indian tea went to Germany, Poland, Russia, Denmark, and Sweden.

The business was not easy; the French were trying as hard as they could to win over Britain's customers. The French colonies in the West Indies supplied nearly all the merchandise offered by the British— apart from China tea which, except in the East Frisian islands, was of minor importance on the Continent. What Liverpool was to Britain, Bordeaux was to France: the flourishing harbour for the West Indies trade. In 1740 one François Bonaffe had come to Bordeaux from Toulouse with all his possessions in a bundle on his back. Thirty years later he owned thirty ships and a fortune of 15,000,000 livres.

Unlike Liverpool, Bordeaux lived by its brokerage; four-fifths of its imports—almost entirely West Indian merchandise—were re-exported, mostly to Hamburg. In the year when Bonaffe came to Bordeaux France imported from Canada goods worth 1,000,000 to 2,000,000 livres, from the East Indies goods worth 10,000,000 livres, and from the West Indies goods worth as much as 140,000,000 to 150,000,000 livres. These imports included 80,000 barrels of sugar, of which 30,000 barrels went to Hamburg alone. The lethargic Merchant Adventurers could not have stood up to France if they had tried. Fortunately, the Liverpool merchants stepped in. They were looking for a merchant with courage and drive, a merchant who could beat those skilful, quick-witted French. They picked on young John Parish, the son of an English sea-captain who had settled in Hamburg and ran a ship-chandler's business there.

At the age of twenty John Parish took over the firm and developed it into a top-ranking merchant house. During the Seven Years War, when Britain transmitted its subsidies to the King of Prussia via Hamburg, the firm of Parish was carried along on the crest of the wave by this new boom. Like many other Hamburg merchants Parish used the silver now available for buying colonial merchandise from England in order to sell it in Germany at good prices. Parish made considerable profits from sugar, rum, tobacco, and coffee. The conclusion of peace meant a severe setback. It was only slowly that his business picked up again. He imported West Indian merchandise via Liverpool and sold it in the Baltic ports. Just when he thought he was out of the wood, with his fortune swollen to 54,000 Marks, the Great Depression which was sweeping across Europe hit him too. Banks of standing, such as Fordyce in London, Clifford and Sons in Amsterdam, and Terner in Bremen, crashed, and their bills were dishonoured. This crash cost Parish 4000 pounds sterling. And still there was no end in sight to the depression. And then came the American War, and with it the unique business of supplying the belligerents with the foodstuffs they needed. Parish shipped Baltic grain to Western Europe and brought back the West Indian merchandise in demand—coffee, sugar, rum, tobacco, and Indian tea—from England and France. His ships, flying the neutral Hamburg flag, sailed right under the noses of the warships bristling with cannon.

For the grain Parish bought he paid with colonial merchandise, and for his colonial merchandise he paid with grain. He merely had to find some one to advance him the cash while his cargo was still at sea. Parish made out a bill of exchange which the banks 'discounted'—*i.e.,* on which they advanced money. As security he handed over the ship's papers, the 'bills of lading.' He himself bore the major part of the risk which was only partially coverable by insurance; the premium he simply added to the price of the grain and the colonial merchandise.

Business was now flourishing. Parish accepted the bills of the Baltic grain merchants against transfer of the bills of lading, and drew bills on his business connexions in England, Portugal, Spain, and France. Turnover soared; in the course of a single summer Parish handled ten shiploads of wheat. Soon he was one of the leading grain merchants in Hamburg. His transactions became increasingly risky. He began to give credit merely on the security of ships' papers in order to lay his hands on consignments before they were even at sea. He was very nearly caught out on one occasion. He had 300,000 Marks Banco with a Baltic corn merchant with whom he had a quarrel over some trivial matter. He managed to slip out of the noose only just in time; when the Baltic merchant declared his bankruptcy six months later Parish lost only 40,000 Marks.

Business with America was even more risky. Since the British Navy ruled the seas the merchandise had to be channelled by strange routes—through France, Spain, or Holland, according to which country was still neutral. But one country after another joined the war. Skilfully Parish succeeded in concealing the true nature of his deals. He drew bills on Amsterdam, Paris, Bordeaux, and London so that nobody was sure where the merchandise in question was warehoused or what was its ultimate destination. Just because these transactions were kept deliberately obscure Parish had to expect that his bills would not always be honoured punctually. On one occasion he had to take up a whole 100,000 pounds sterling of protested bills within a short period of time. On another occasion the American Minister Plenipotentiary at the Court of Madrid informed him with a shrug, at the very last moment, that he could not honour bills worth 50,000 ducats which he had accepted. Yet in spite of these risks the transactions were so profitable that by the end of the war Parish owned a capital of 203,000 Marks Banco.

Then, without any warning at all, Hamburg's biggest merchant house, Peter Hiss Sohn, crashed overnight, although until nearly the end its credit had been almost unlimited. As bad luck would have it, Parish had the previous day passed on to various brokers bills of exchange for a total of 130,000 Marks; it was possible that his customers might be swept along into disaster by the crash of the firm of Hiss, and that he, Parish, would have to meet the circulating bills. With a great deal of difficulty he succeeded in persuading the buyers of the bills—for the most part Hamburg Jews—to hold on to them and pay for them as promised. Parish himself had to make large payments on bills, chiefly for grain he had purchased in the Baltic on instructions from the British Government. How was he to find the money in the midst of a general depression? Would it be possible to place the Dutch bills, first-class as they were? Fortunately his principal creditor readily accepted from him bills for 100,000 florins in settlement of his own bills payable. It was salvation at the eleventh hour. Otherwise Parish would have gone bankrupt. The incident shows how very limited was the Hamburg market for bills at the time.

Parish fared rather worse when he tried to ship major consignments of merchandise to the West Indies. He equipped two ships of 350 and 400 tons and loaded them with beef, pork, and grain. The next two ships, which were to have carried also the 'super-cargo,' the merchant responsible for the shipment, to the West Indies, could not leave port because the harbour of Hamburg was completely frozen up that year as early as November. When the super-cargo at last arrived in Tobago —having taken ship at Ostend where unfavourable winds kept him for another six weeks—the impatient captain had long sold the merchandise at give-away prices. To complete the string of misfortunes Parish's super-cargo, instead of sending West Indian merchandise to Hamburg, misappropriated the sum realized by the captain. That was the sad end of Parish's first large-scale attempt to play at blockade-running with the aid of rather dubious characters. On the two chartered ships Parish lost some 16,000 pounds sterling, in present-day money something like $140,000. On the other hand, he made 3000 pounds on the two further ships he sent to the West Indies, even though they were both lost on the return voyage. They had been well insured.

These transactions cost Parish an overall loss of 220,000 Marks Banco —more than his entire business capital—but as he made no less than 170,000 Marks Banco on other transactions during that year, and as he moreover avoided writing off the entire loss at once, his balance sheet at the end of 1783 still showed a capital of 188,000 Marks Banco at a book loss of 15,000 Marks. These reckless deals only occasionally yielded great profits; more often they were a man's undoing. The steady, uneventful business which followed during the next six years of peace netted the Hamburg importer over 500,000 Marks Banco, but as he had to offset his earlier losses his capital in 1789, at the outbreak of the French Revolution, stood at only 321,000 Marks Banco.

Early in 1790 the French Government began issuing paper money— the *assignats*. How tempting always are the gains of inflation and how terrible and disastrous are its invariable consequences! Within a short span of time the paper issue rose from 400 to 1200 million, and still the end was not in sight. The flood of paper money rose higher and higher. Amid this insane inflation the Paris banking-house of Boyd, Ker, and Co. decided to speculate for a fall, to "sell bear," in the hope of fantastic profits; merchandise was bought for *assignats* on credit and, when payment was due, paid for with money devalued in the meantime, while the merchandise had long been sold for cash at a tremendous profit. So long as the Revolutionary Government continued to issue money in unlimited quantities nothing could go wrong with this kind of speculation.

Boyd put this attractive proposition to Hope and Co., the most important banking-house in Amsterdam, which played in the eighteenth century something like the rôle of the Rothschilds 100 years later, and also to the firms of Harman, Hoare and Co. in London, and to Parish and Co. in Hamburg.

The Paris Convention soon realized the danger of this speculation and tried to counter it by launching a large-scale speculation for a rise, a "bullish" speculation. This might well have been successful if only the very same Convention had not provided ever-new encouragement to the bear clique by its unlimited issue of paper money.

Parish, for safety, participated on both sides. In this way he thought he would reduce his risk. But when he saw that the paper issue continued indefinitely he withdrew from the bull speculation. Why should he lose his money? The bear clique, under Boyd's leadership, was about to win complete victory; the banking-house of Tourton and Ravel, who had led the opposing bull clique, crashed. Now, however, the Convention resorted to force. It instructed the police to arrest the speculators. Boyd escaped to England, where he founded a new firm, Boyd, Benfield and Co., while his son Walter tried to carry on, though more cautiously, with the Paris speculation. But he miscalculated. Robespierre was not a man to be trifled with. He had Boyd's office closed and the doors sealed. During the night three of Robespierre's agents dragged Walter Boyd from his bed and forced him to draw bills of exchange for 50,000 pounds sterling on London, for 500,000 florins on Amsterdam, and for 500,000 Marks on Hamburg, and to recommend acceptance to his business connexions. Boyd's remonstrances were in vain; the police thugs threatened immediate arrest. Every one knew what that meant.

Parish had misgivings when faced with these unexpected bills of such magnitude. He made cautious enquiries with Hope and Co. in London, who gave him a clear hint to refuse acceptance. Walter Boyd, meanwhile, had seized the first opportunity to escape to England. All three bills were dishonoured.

One of the partners of the Paris firm of Boyd, Ker and Co. was the Marquis de Walkiers, the son of a Crown banker in Brussels, whose fortune was estimated at 5,000,000 florins. His share in Boyd, Ker and Co. was 1,000,000 livres. Walkiers had ships sailing from Ostend to India on his own account, and made excellent profits from these transactions; at the same time, however, he was tempted into risky speculations in colonial merchandise. Parish was in with him on these transactions.

The very first letter shows the vast sums involved. In brevity and concision it could hardly be bettered: "Paris, January 5, 1791. Upon receipt of this letter please buy on my account and on best possible terms sugar and coffee to the value of 500,000 florins. Provide cover by drafts on Hope and Co."

The merchandise was bought and warehoused the same day. Within a month two further shiploads of the same goods, worth 800,000 Marks, arrived from Bordeaux; they were to be sold by Parish. In this way Walkiers intended to transfer the merchandise from an uncertain France to neutral Hamburg. But since in the course of these reckless transactions he frequently found himself embarrassed for money, he regularly drew bills on Parish. Parish, even though he held a certain security in the shape of the vast stores of merchandise estimated at 100,000 pounds, became suspicious when the demands on him continued to soar. When the London firm of Harman, Hoare and Co. informed him that they had accepted bills of exchange from Parish on Walkiers only for the honour of Parish, but not of Walkiers, the cautious Hamburg merchant beat a hasty retreat. When faced with new bills from Boyd, Ker and Co. for a total of 450,000 Marks he declared that he would accept them only if guaranteed by the reputable house of Hope and Co. Otherwise, with these new bills payable he would have a total of uncovered demands of 100,000 pounds sterling— far more than he could justify with a good conscience.

Hope and Co. seemed surprised. Was their Hamburg friend really worried about such trifles? With a man like Boyd? They at once provided the guarantee he wanted. Boyd, deeply offended, cursed his luck which had induced him to trust his good name to the weak nerves of a timid Hamburg merchant. How dared he doubt even for a minute that all his bills would be punctually honoured? Soon remissions of money arrived which greatly exceeded the amount of Boyd's bills. Only with difficulty was an open rupture prevented between the two business friends. All the same, before very long

Walkiers had to suspend payments. His reckless speculations had been too dangerous.

It was to this man Walkiers that Parish owed his connexions with North America. Walkiers was acquainted with the American banker Morris, the U.S. Ambassador in Paris, who stayed at Parish's house when visiting Altona, just outside Hamburg. Thanks to this connexion Parish was appointed the first United States Consul in Hamburg. This strengthened his credit. And it was badly in need of strengthening, for his insatiable enterprise had induced him to take part in increasingly reckless transactions. Enormous quantities of merchandise were then streaming into Germany. Where was capital to be found? In order to find ready money new avenues had to be explored. Parish found a way. For the large supplies which he imported in consignment from Liverpool he accommodated his suppliers, in particular the two speculative firms of Richard and Mathiesen and G. and H. Brown, with credits in advance payment. At the same time the London banking-house of Burton, Forbes and Gregory opened for him a paper credit of 100,000 pounds. This meant that the Liverpool merchants drew bills on the London bank of Burton, which they could place on the Stock Exchange at any time, while Burton drew on Parish in Hamburg. By the simple device of signing their name on these bills of exchange, the merchant houses provided themselves with vast sums of ready money without any effort at all. Thus, Parish was able to buy in Hamburg bills on Lisbon, Cadiz, and Leghorn on Burton's account; for cover he drew two-months' and three-months' bills on Burton in London. Strictly speaking, this was a case of irresponsible cross-accommodation, or what is known in business parlance as 'kite-flying,' which made almost unlimited funds available. But kite-flying is the most dangerous way of obtaining ready money, since each party is liable also for his partner and, what is more, for punctual settlement when due. This artificial credit edifice was bound to collapse the moment a single stone dropped out. Kite-flying is the quickest way for a business to go bankrupt.

Parish did not escape unscathed. When three Dutch business connexions of Burton's crashed in 1793 some other Dutchmen stepped into the breach; they paid the bills but at once drew new ones on Parish. When Burton himself began to draw bills on him Parish got seriously alarmed. He refused to accept the bills totalling 35,000 pounds and the 90,000 Marks' worth of Dutch drafts. That was the death-blow to Burton. But it was a serious blow to Parish also. His balance sheet was anything but rosy.

Parish owed 5,675,000 Marks Banco in bills—a colossal sum. Admittedly, the credit side of his business showed assets worth 8,610,000 Marks Banco. But could they be realized at short notice? The situation was exceedingly critical. Parish had bought large consignments of grain for the British Government and paid for it with bills totalling 400,000 Marks drawn on Scott, the factor of the British Prime Minister Pitt. Until the British paid up Parish was liable for these sums. In Hamburg and Altona lay merchandise worth 4,500,000 Marks, chiefly from the West Indies, for which he would have to pay in Liverpool; they included 5,000,000 pounds of coffee and over 4000 hogsheads (one hogshead equals $52\frac{1}{2}$ imperial gallons) of sugar. Three loads of sugar and coffee which Parish was to sell for G. and H. Brown (invoiced value 40,000 pounds or 500,000 Marks Banco) were still at sea; he was also expecting four similar consignments from Richard and Co. valued at 35,000 pounds (or 430,000 Marks). These liabilities were sufficient to cause any man a few sleepless nights.

And what was there on the credit side? A bank balance standing at 450,000 Marks and bills in hand worth 1,300,000 Marks, as well as still outstanding local accounts receivable in a total of 950,000 Marks. Parish therefore could count on altogether 8,000,000 Marks. But was he sufficiently liquid? Could he meet his obligations? Could he, at short notice, honour the bills he was liable for? He needed 2,000,000 Marks Banco at once, or else he might have to sell his merchandise precipitately and below value. His friend, Johannes Schuback, one of the most highly respected merchants in Hamburg, blenched when he heard what sums were involved. Surely there was not that much money to be found in the whole of Hamburg.

During the night the disastrous messages arrived from London: Burton and Co., Caldwell and Co., as well as G. and H. Brown in Liverpool, would stop payments. Quick action was necessary. At the crack of dawn Parish began to sell off his warehoused stocks. The entire coffee was sold within an hour, and moreover at favourable prices; the 1700 hogsheads of sugar were sold for cash in the course of the day.

The shattering news from England had not yet reached the Hamburg exchange, and Parish was able to get rid of a large batch of London bills to the Hamburg Jews. That was the last transaction of its kind for a whole month; once the reports of the crash of the London banks had begun to circulate no one accepted any more English bills. Parish even succeeded, through the firm of Hope and Co., in exchanging his bills on the London Government for the grain he had bought against short bills on Hamburg. In this way he maintained, throughout the critical period, a bank balance which exceeded his daily payments by at least 400,000 Marks; indeed he was able to honour in advance his own bills receivable at a later date.

His loss with Burton totalled 13,000 pounds, but some 5000 pounds of this total was due to the deterioration of the Hamburg rate of exchange by over 10 per cent. With Richard and Mathiesen, Parish had claims worth 20,000 pounds, but these were covered by four shiploads worth 35,000 pounds which were already *en route* for Hamburg. In addition, there were bills circulating for a further load of sugar and coffee, but the bills of lading for this consignment, though expected for a long time, had not yet arrived. Richard and Co. declared quite frankly that they were ruined if Parish let them down. With a sick heart Parish accepted the bills even without the bills of lading.

The situation was more precarious with regard to four shiploads for 40,000 pounds from the firm of G. and H. Brown in Liverpool, who were bankrupt already. The insurance for these ships, which were still at sea, had been underwritten partly by Browns themselves and partly by their London connexions, who were likewise bankrupt; thus, if anything happened, their creditors would impound the insurance money. French pirates were just then harrying shipping in the North Sea and did in fact succeed in capturing one of the ships. For some weeks Parish was in agony. There was no news about the fate of his shipments. He heaved a deep sigh of relief when the ships at last arrived in Hamburg.

In spite of his intensive selling Parish's warehoused stocks increased at such a rate that he had to hire eighty-five warehouse lofts; there was no space available in Hamburg itself, so that a considerable proportion of the incoming merchandise had to be stored at Altona. These stocks were worth 5,000,000 Marks Banco. Parish's own capital was somewhat over 500,000 Marks; in addition he had bill holdings of 100,000 pounds and local outstandings of 80,000 pounds. To this must be added the dishonoured bills on his bankers totalling 75,000 pounds sterling.

It was only thanks to the modern credit system, to the bills of exchange, and to the London banks, that Hamburg was able to import such large quantities of West Indian merchandise, and that this vast stream of colonial goods, especially coffee and sugar, could flow

49. Counting-house of a Hamburg merchant (copper engraving by Christian Friedrich Fritzsch, the younger, 1719-72)

through the Elbe port into the heart of Germany. Without the merchant, and without the retailer, producers would have been unable to market their continually growing harvests. Everywhere these new merchants began to deal in the fabulous merchandise of the tropics and to feed it into the widely ramified channels which soon covered the whole of Central, Northern, and Eastern Europe—Germany, Scandinavia, Poland, and Russia—like a vast network.

About the middle of the eighteenth century Hamburg still smelled of herring and blubber, of Icelandic cod and dried plaice. The merchants were little more than hucksters who got their fish from Holland and resold it by the quarter-ton, the half-ton, and perhaps occasionally by the ton, to the small shopkeepers in the provinces of Lauenburg and Mecklenburg. The business was profitable enough, provided a man worked hard and lived modestly. Only a few Hamburg merchants then imported their merchandise from far-off countries.

The most important of these was the firm of Berenberg, which was doing business with Constantinople, Venice, Milan, Genoa and Leghorn, Marseille and Alicante, Algiers, Cadiz and Lisbon, Bordeaux, Nantes, Paris and Dunkirk, Bruges and Ghent, Amsterdam and Alkmar, London and Bristol, Copenhagen, Libau and Riga, St Petersburg and Archangel, Breslau and Leipzig. This trade, however, was entirely in goods sold in small quantities: gamboge and shellac, pepper and tea, ginger, indigo and opium, rhubarb and camphor, silk and cotton from Smyrna, coffee from Mocca in Southern Arabia, saffron and capers, laurel oil and alum, Peruvian balsam and snuff, sugar and raisins from Spain, and wax from Russia. Only slowly and tentatively did the commodities appear which subsequently played such an important part—sugar, coffee, and cocoa from Martinique, coffee and cotton via London.

About the middle of the century the Liverpool merchants had not yet arrived on the scene. Hence, boldness, initiative, and willingness to take risks were still lacking. The merchants did not have enough capital at their disposal to accept bulk commodities, to warehouse them, and subsequently to distribute them in the vast hinterland. The money had to come from the banks; it was there that it accumulated, including the unproductive money of those who lacked the skill or the courage to do business themselves but who were nevertheless anxious to make more money: the landed gentry, rich widows and orphans, officials and people of independent means. Moreover, State money would accumulate in certain accounts where it would lie unproductive unless the banks pumped it into the economy.

During the Seven Years War, when Britain supported Frederick the Great with vast subsidies made available in silver, these payments had to be transferred from London to Prussia in some form or other. Since Frederick required only a small portion of those sums in ready silver for paying his soldiers and officials, his main need being for arms and foodstuffs, a profitable triangular business developed via Hamburg.

Britain was unable to supply either arms or foodstuffs, but she could supply West Indian merchandise, which found a ready market in the rest of Germany and throughout the Baltic basin. And there, in turn, it was possible to buy fish, timber, iron, and grain for Prussia. All this was organized by the Hamburg merchants; they exchanged the silver earmarked for the King of Prussia while it was still in England for merchandise from London and Liverpool—sugar, rum, coffee, and tobacco. This sounds much simpler than in fact it was. First of all, the Prussian Minister of Finance, who would have preferred to keep all the silver in his coffers, had to make the money available. Was he really to entrust his treasure to a lot of unknown rapacious Hamburg merchants who, to cap it all, demanded high commissions? On the other hand, he certainly could not risk transporting entire shipments of silver from England to Prussia. True, no commission would be payable in that case, but the costs of transport and insurance would be considerably higher.

On the Continent the Hamburg merchants traded the English merchandise for whatever the belligerents required—foodstuffs, raw materials, weapons, and ammunition. Whatever it was, they made their profit. Even when the war subsidies came to an end the business continued merrily: Hamburg bought West Indian merchandise, and Polish and Russian grain and timber on credit, in order to resell these goods at a profit.

With surprisingly small capital of their own the Hamburg merchants moved vast quantities of merchandise. That was possible only because the merchants in Liverpool, Riga, and Danzig all had great confidence in their Hamburg business partners. They delivered their goods without insisting on cash payment—all they required was a bill of exchange. With his signature the purchaser undertook to pay the sum mentioned on a certain date and in a certain place, and under all circumstances, waiving his right of objection either because the merchandise had not been properly delivered or on any other grounds which a tardy payer might put forward. If a bill of exchange was not punctually honoured it became a protested bill, a dishonoured bill; immediately any person who had added his signature to the bill became liable for it.

For a bill of exchange to be negotiable it must bear two names: the vendor of the merchandise adds his signature to that of his customer, and in this way accepts full liability. The purchaser can draw a bill on a third party by instructing him to pay the sum named on the due date. Such a third party must 'accept' the bill by writing his name across it, 'endorsing it.' If the bill is 'protested for non-acceptance' the drawer is liable. Until acceptance the holder of the bill covers himself by holding back the ship's papers, the bills of lading. A person 'drawing' a bill must be able to rely on his business friend accepting it, and, more important still, on his honouring his acceptance—*i.e.*, paying up punctually.

Solely on the grounds of their confidence in the names on a bill do banks make advances on it, or discount it. But there must also be enough ready money about to allow bills to be sold. At times of depression, when everybody is anxiously holding back with cash, even the best bills of exchange cannot be negotiated.

If the merchants of Liverpool or Danzig had insisted on cash settlement the elaborate credit edifice would have collapsed. There was not enough silver in Hamburg to pay suppliers on the nail and to accept the vast quantities of merchandise for warehousing. The firm of Berenberg and Gossler, for instance, moved merchandise worth 400,000 Marks Courant on a single day in 1799; this included the export of nearly 60,000 Marks worth of silk, of quantities of coffee, soap, wine, paper, iron, bottles, and grindstones, and imports from America of tobacco, sugar, rice, and timber. Yet the business capital of the firm was less than 1,000,000 Marks Banco.

The Hamburg merchants but rarely obtained their goods straight from the producers in their countries of origin; as a rule, the business went through the hands of local merchants. In 1792 the first ship from India entered the port of Hamburg—but not under the Hamburg flag. Not until five years later did the British permit the Hamburg merchants to send their own ships to India. The first to bring back coffee from Mokha, tobacco from Baltimore, cocoa from Surinam, and rubber from Africa was Baron von Voght.

In the Hamburg port of transhipment merchandise accumulated for resale or further processing.

Hamburg is full of warehouses, store-rooms, depositories, and cellars. Most of them are crammed full with merchandise. It cannot be said that this merchandise belongs to the Hamburg merchants: it belongs to them and the merchants of other nations who, for a variety of reasons, leave it in storage there for a short or a long period of time. Hamburg property, in turn, is scattered all over the world and from his merchandise a Hamburg merchant may derive profit or loss in areas which his foot has never trodden.

These observations were made by a contemporary, writing in 1789, a man named Hess, who sang the praises of the "manufacturists," the men who boiled sugar, turned cotton into printed cloth, cut tobacco into snuff, extracted oil from whales and seals, and made sheet-metal and wire from copper and brass. The manufacturer, Hess writes,

> is not in danger of sending his goods to a place where they are not required, or not in the quantity dispatched, or falling into the hands of a remote unpunctual payer, or being deceived by poor-content, counterfeit or tampered-with coins and bills. In the event of spoilage or damage the local broker sees to it that these shall not accrue to the detriment of the manufacturer. In this manner he achieves the best price which his merchandise can command in any region known to such experienced, knowledgeable and inquiring merchants as those of Hamburg from their present or past business.

The earnings of the Hamburg merchant were no more than appropriate compensation and commission. He supplied Germany with merchandise more cheaply and more efficiently than if it were manufactured within the country. "Frequently such goods do not come under the eyes of the Hamburg merchant at all: his ships, or the ships of another, carry the world's merchandise from one sea to another, from one nation to another."

This means that the Hamburg businessman was predominantly a merchant, a broker, a shipowner, and a carrier. The further processing of the merchandise did not interest him. This is admitted by Hess:

> His gaze is ever fixed upon the universe of world trade and his attention upon political events, accidents and their consequences, often to the point of prophecy, always intent. He knows this year's harvests of all lands upon earth, near or far, provided they concern him; sometimes he knows conditions there most accurately. He knows not only what each State requires at the moment, but also what it will require next year. Not infrequently he understands the ruling character of nations and of the men at their helm better than many a political bookworm; he knows the political weaknesses of the most respected Ministers; he knows to whose apron-strings they are tied; he knows the tortuous roads that lead to their private cabinets. Thus he learns by heart the entire compendium of their commercial conditions and is able to trim his sails to the prevailing political wind.

Towards the end of the eighteenth century Hamburg rose to the position of Europe's third most important trading city, after London and Amsterdam; it outstripped Liverpool. The Hamburg merchants found reliable helpers in the banks and insurance companies. The Hamburg bank covered the merchant against currency fluctuations. Although it did not issue banknotes it performed its calculations in a currency of its own, known as "Mark Banco," which had a fixed value based on silver. All other currencies were computed in Marks Banco according to the rate of exchange of the day as soon as an account holder wished to have cash in one currency or another. Most financial transactions were performed within the bank by 'setting off'—always in Marks Banco.

Insurance could, up to a point, cover a merchant against unforeseen contingencies—shipwreck, enemy raiders, or warehouse fires. No one, however, could relieve him of the purely commercial risks. These sprang principally from a judgment of the market and the customer. A man buying merchandise on credit cannot be certain of selling it in time—*i.e.*, before payment of the purchasing price is due. This un-certainty becomes even greater when the merchandise has been bought for an inexorable bill of exchange. Yet to manage without bills of exchange was impossible, since a merchant's own capital would not be nearly sufficient. Credit is tied to the bill with its strict time-limit because the supplier, for his part, has not enough money either to weather far-flung business transactions. He, too, has to go to his banker to convert the bills into ready money as quickly as possible.

Merchants in all trading-centres would seek bills of exchange in order to settle their debts in other towns, to accept merchandise in foreign ports, and to make various payments. A Riga merchant who had ordered sugar in Hamburg would first of all need a bill on Ham-burg. Or he might accept a bill on Liverpool if his Hamburg business friend happened to be looking for a bill on England. Again, the Baltic merchant might sell the English bill in Hamburg to a fourth merchant and pay his Hamburg connexion in ready money. The bill-brokers—frequently Jews—would have other people's bills discounted by banks or merchants, either locally, or in Amsterdam, or in London, Bordeaux, or Leghorn. They would buy bills on other people's accounts—*i.e.*, they never signed their own names on the bills; they made their profit from the discount. Whenever large quantities of merchandise were moved a great many bills would be offered on the Stock Exchange. At a time when no one was ordering merchandise bills would be in short supply. Accordingly the discount would rise or fall—*i.e.*, the percentage which a banker deducts from the amount of the bill and which is held to cover his risk and to include his interest.

Whenever an operator like Parish imported several million Marks' worth of merchandise from the West Indies and from the Baltic the brokers would have a field day. They would run around trying to get the bills discounted which Parish had accepted. This means they had to find banks prepared to finance the vast quantities of warehoused goods in one form or another. If they held back—or if their financial strength was not sufficient to join in this hectic operation—the discount would go up. The cautious merchant would realize that things were becoming dangerous and money was getting short. Evidently one could not count on the warehoused goods finding a ready market. Better not to order any more. Then, suddenly, orders would begin to come in from Stockholm, from Danzig, from St Petersburg, from Berlin and Magdeburg, from Frankfurt and Leipzig. The market would revive, warehoused stocks would diminish, and further supplies would be urgently needed from Liverpool. To be able to order them bills of exchange would be needed. Once again the brokers would get busy, this time seeking bills and offering increasingly high prices; now the banks would content themselves with a smaller discount.

The Stock Exchange would sense the excitement; it would note the revival of demand, the increase in the turnover, and the rise in prices. The warehoused stocks would yield an excellent profit. With this lively demand interest could easily be added to prices. Speculation would begin, ever new orders being placed as the general surge of optimism swept away all prudence. Everybody would want a share in the boom. And indeed, all would go well. Speculation in Hamburg would act as a stimulus to the merchants inland. Sugar was getting short, it was said—sugar was going up. One should buy up sugar before it was too late. And thus the wave rolled over the land.

Perhaps Liverpool saw the speculation coming. In that case instructions would have gone out to the West Indies: everything to be bought that was offered, even if it meant buying a less attractive consignment and paying a higher price—only buy, buy, buy!

A Hamburg merchant had to be able to act quickly—from one day to another, from one hour to the next. Strong nerves were needed when dispositions had to be scrapped in a matter of minutes and new decisions made. At all this Parish was a past-master, which was why he grew rich. The old-established merchant-houses kept aloof from such speculations; they wanted to turn over only what they could finance by their own means, what they were fairly certain of reselling within a reasonable time. Naturally, with their modest turnovers they could not stand up to the young men and their large-scale transactions. Thus the old firms disappeared as new ones rose to prosperity. One such man, Jacques de Chapeaurouge, had come to Hamburg in 1764 with one single *louis-d'or*. When he died in 1805 he left roughly 1,500,000 Marks. Others, it is true, lost their shirts in the wild speculations.

Hamburg became rich. When Napoleon started his Continental System there were in Hamburg, according to a contemporary estimate, 41 persons or firms with a property of more than 1,000,000 Marks Banco (totalling 67,000,000 Marks), 33 persons with more than 500,000 Marks (totalling 19,000,000 Marks), 83 persons with a property between 200,000 and 500,000 Marks (totalling 19,600,000 Marks), and 65 persons with more than 100,000 Marks (totalling 8,900,000 Marks)—in all 222 persons or firms owning a total of 114,500,000 Marks. Parish figures on this list with a fortune of 2,500,000 Marks. The list is headed by the merchant Averhoff with more than 6,000,000 Marks; but his principal business was banking—*i.e.*, money transactions rather than purchase and sale of merchandise.

These were fortunes beyond the wildest dreams of the Hamburg merchants of only a few decades before, at the time when they used to import overseas merchandise against cash payment in order to store the modest quantities in their warehouses. Indeed, Germany's overseas trade then scarcely deserved the name. About the mid-century it still yielded rather less profit than the hucksters' trade with fish and blubber. True, the "wholesale and overseas merchant" would turn up his nose at the herring-tamer—and not merely because of the pungent smell of brine—but he had to concede that the fish merchant was earning more than he was. Only when Hamburg had become the great entrepôt of Central, Northern, and Eastern Europe did the great fortunes begin to accumulate.

They were the fruits of the courage shown by three business partners: the Hamburg merchant, who, by comparison with his own capital, was purchasing excessively large quantities of colonial merchandise; his business partner abroad, who would supply this merchandise, waiting patiently—though at times no doubt anxiously—for payment to be made; and finally the banker who would bridge the long period of waiting by financing the bill of exchange bearing the two signatures—that of the Hamburg merchant and that of his foreign supplier.

None of the three had enough capital himself: each of them would try to extend his credit to the maximum, to open up ever new sources of money. The bills went from hand to hand; the more signatures they bore the more secure they became and the more easily could they be converted into cash. The whole business, in the final resort, depended upon the Hamburg merchant selling his merchandise to the final consumer in good time—even though such "good time" might have to be bought at an increasingly distant date by the prolongation of bills, by the drawing of new bills, or by risky credit manipulations. Once the chain was broken the Hamburg merchant was caught out. The whole credit edifice would collapse. The supplier would be held liable, and eventually the banker would have to come to the rescue. The venture consisted in the fact that the Hamburg merchant would order the vast quantities of merchandise at his own risk. But without that risk, without the firm and solemn assurance of payment on a definite date, without the bill of exchange, the Liverpool merchant would have been unable to supply the merchandise to him.

The Hamburg merchant, in turn, could not content himself with warehousing his West Indian sugar or his Virginian rum and tobacco and waiting patiently until a business connexion in Leipzig or Berlin would buy the goods from him and pay in silver. Since there was no silver available either in Germany or in Eastern Europe, he had to stock up with merchandise which could be sold in England or perhaps even in the West Indies—in other words, he had to buy grain and timber. In the last analysis, the bills on Hamburg could be paid for only by bills on London and Liverpool.

Because Prussian grain could be sold to Holland and England the large State-owned estates in Prussia began to flourish. And because wool found a reliable market in England sheep-breeding in Mecklenburg and Prussia received a powerful impetus. Indeed that was the only way in which the trade could be balanced. With silver alone these countries would never have been able to pay for their imports of tropical produce. To achieve this trade and payments balance was no easy task. To have achieved it was the great and lasting merit of the Hamburg merchants.

The eighteenth-century mercantilists, such as Colbert in France and the Great Elector of Brandenburg, resented every taler which they had to spend on imports; the fact that their fellow countrymen and subjects should spend money on such short-lived pleasures as sugar, tobacco, and coffee distressed them profoundly. But Hamburg demonstrated clearly, for the first time, that exports are stimulated by imports, and that exports give an impetus not only to commerce but also to production, especially agricultural production.

All that was needed was courage and confidence in oneself and the merchandise one was offering for sale. The imported colonial merchandise extracted from the country, as it were, the raw materials and foodstuffs which alone could pay for its importation. Productive forces began to stir because merchants everywhere—from the big merchants in Danzig, Riga, St Petersburg, Warsaw, and Berlin down to the small pedlars travelling from village to village, accepting wool, hides, or spun flax in payment—wanted to market West Indian produce. Once this exchange had got going on a sufficiently large scale the country was able to stand up even to unforeseen accidents springing from politics.

During the Seven Years War it had been difficult enough to transmit the British subsidies; during the Napoleonic wars this transmission of money presented no difficulty whatever. In the winter of 1794–95 British troops were established in Osnabrück, cut off from their mother country, since Holland was occupied by the French, and Prussia, Britain's former ally, had concluded a separate peace. The French might march into Hamburg at any moment, and the Elbe was blocked by ice.

In exchange for bills on the Government in London, Parish paid to the British Consul in Hamburg the sum, in gold, of 50,000 *louis-d'or*; he had the bills discounted with his business friends in Hamburg and his suppliers in the Baltic basin, even though navigation was at a standstill because of the weather. During that single winter Parish accepted altogether bills for the unprecedented amount of 2,300,000 pounds sterling, the equivalent in purchasing power of about $21,000,000 to-day. This netted him 11,500 pounds in commission. Not a bad brokerage, but worrying—even if the name of the British Treasury was a guarantee that the bills would sooner or later be honoured. But could anyone ever tell what politicians would suddenly take it into their heads to do? The events of 1806 were a case in point.

Napoleon prohibited all trade with Britain. Around the entire European continent, from the Portuguese and Spanish coasts up to Scandinavia and East Prussia, he erected a customs barrier which did not allow through any British merchandise. He likewise sealed off the Mediterranean coasts of France, Italy, and Austria. Albion, the hated enemy, would be forced to its knees. Neither its superiority at sea, nor its magnificent merchant fleet, nor yet its possessions in America, Africa, and Asia would be of the least avail. Britain would no longer be able to market her merchandise. With this single blow England would be defeated. That, at any rate, was the plan of the Corsican dictator. But things turned out differently.

Napoleon's brutal measures cut off the flow of merchandise that was everybody's livelihood. Admittedly, the British lost their market for tropical merchandise and industrial products. But, on the other hand, they were no longer able to buy the surpluses of the Continent—neither French grain nor French wine, neither fruit nor vegetables, neither olive-oil nor fine woollens or lace. The French merchants were ruined, and with them France's agriculture. The price of wheat dropped by 60 per cent., while the prices of sugar, coffee, and tobacco soared to vertiginous heights—assuming, of course, that the goods were available at all.

Cautiously the French Minister of the Interior yielded; in consideration of a special tax of 30 to 40 *louis-d'or* merchants were permitted to engage in trade with Britain after all, selling French manufactures in exchange for tropical produce or for timber and hemp—*i.e.*, merchandise from the Baltic. In 1807 alone the French Government issued 18,000 licences which riddled the Continental System. During the two years of 1809–10 Britain was able to import French grain worth nearly 1,500,000 pounds quite apart from the extensive illicit trade which was flourishing side by side with the licensed one.

Before long France's allies—Italy, the Hanseatic towns, and Danzig —demanded the same rights. They too received licences because Russia was insisting emphatically on selling her timber, grain, and flax in exchange for West Indian merchandise as she had done in the past. The Continental System, inaugurated with such grand promises, threatened to become no more than a customs barrier, a fiscal burden upon commerce. The increased taxes were passed on by the merchants to the consumers who were quite prepared to pay the high prices in order to obtain any merchandise at all. Britain experienced no marketing difficulties in spite of the increased prices; she knew that the continental public would not easily give up their sugar or coffee.

Napoleon, however, was not prepared to yield to economic considerations. He simply revoked all licences and blocked all frontiers. Only the smugglers slipped through the mesh of the vast net with which the Corsican had surrounded Europe. The merchants were squeezed out of business; in Hamburg and Amsterdam, in Bordeaux and Marseille, in Danzig and Leghorn the harbours lay dead and deserted. Although Hamburg merchants would try to run the blockade, they only rarely succeeded in doing so. In the end the losses became too great and business too dangerous. In 1809 the firm of Parish—to which his sons had by then succeeded—still received from America more than fifty shiploads, worth altogether some 3,000,000 dollars. On one occasion the French seized a large consignment in Holstein, and it was only with great difficulty, by mobilizing good friends in Paris—and by paying an appropriate bribe—that the firm succeeded in getting its impounded merchandise released.

Yet the customs barrier was by no means the greatest obstacle. How was imported merchandise to be paid for? What use was a fat bank account if no merchandise could be sent to America or even into hostile Britain? Certainly, the smugglers who sailed their little boats under cover of darkness and fog from British-owned Heligoland into the Elbe or Weser estuaries occasionally took a valuable bale of silk with them, carefully wrapped in waterproof material so it should not get wet on the stormy crossing. But what use were such small quantities?

But even in those turbulent times a lively mind could find opportunities for world-wide business. In America lay the great silver hoards of Mexico and Peru; over there the silver was useless, and to ship it across the Atlantic was impossible so long as Spain was Napoleon's ally. Britain, on the other hand, urgently needed silver in order to support her troops and her allies on the Continent. France, for her part, was still waiting for the promised payments from Spain, but without American silver Madrid could pay nothing. David Parish, the youngest son of John Parish, had a brilliant idea.

He proposed that the Mexican silver should be transferred into the neutral United States and there exchanged for merchandise. The silver should be set off against the 72,000,000 francs which Spain was under an obligation to pay Napoleon each year. Next, the American merchandise, principally cotton, was to be shipped to England. After all, it would be the merchandise of a neutral State! From Britain the goods would then go to Germany by the devious route through the Baltic.

David Parish had good connexions. Through Messrs Hope and Co. in Amsterdam, his father's old business friends, the threads led to the London banking firm of Baring Brothers and Co., in which Hopes had a decisive share. In Paris, on the other hand, Parish knew the all-powerful Talleyrand, whose acquaintance he had made in Hamburg when Talleyrand was in exile. Finally, Parish's father had been on friendly terms with the influential banker Morris in New York. Connexions were everything—even then.

All that was needed was a special permit from Napoleon. Talleyrand was the only man who could obtain it; the great army supplier and grain merchant Ouvrard had to be involved in the operation. Everything went smoothly. David Parish directed the operation from Philadelphia, saw to the countless permits and licences, to the transport of the silver, to the purchase of the merchandise, and to the ships for England. He made not a bad profit: a round million dollars. The lion's share, however, was pocketed by Hope and Baring, who paid out the Spanish subsidies in cash in Paris; they made a profit of 860,000 pounds sterling after deduction of all overheads. "David Parish is the matador, the pearl of the Atlantic Ocean, one of the most accomplished men I ever knew"—this was the fulsome praise bestowed on him by Friedrich Gentz, Prince Metternich's secretary, who knew all the leading merchants of his day.

When Napoleon grasped the full extent of the business he furiously confiscated Ouvrard's entire fortune. He would tolerate no trade whatever with hated England. The Tsar, however, refused to be drawn into this commercial warfare which showed no consideration for friend or foe and did almost as much damage to one's own merchants and farmers as to those of the enemy.

Napoleon's Continental System collapsed on the snow-covered plains of Russia.

14

Machines need New Markets

――――∿∿∿∿∿/⊙/∿∿∿∿――――

NAPOLEON had been defeated. No longer did French customs officials guard the North Sea coast, ready to arrest any merchant who dared to import coffee or sugar.

With their pencils poised over their order-books British merchants once more visited their old customers on the Continent, in Antwerp, Amsterdam, Frankfurt, Cologne, and Hamburg. For seven years they had been cut off from them. Now they were able to sit together again, exchanging reminiscences, telling stories about life under the blockade, and about adventurous and dangerous smuggling exploits. Many a worthy merchant on the Continent had been inside a French prison. Every one had been tricking the detested Corsican in some way or another, buying or hiding contraband, making prohibited payments, or harbouring smugglers.

Now it was all over and commerce could at last emerge again. It was positively bound to boom, if only because of the prices which had until quite recently been paid for prohibited sugar, coffee, tea, cotton cloth, and tobacco. Now everything would become cheap again. Business surely would soar to unprecedented heights. That, at any rate, was what the British thought. It was also what the great merchants in the continental ports expected, in spite of their deep-rooted caution. Order-books were filling up rapidly; the whole world expected an unparalleled boom. But instead there came a painful setback.

Europe was impoverished. Only now did it become plain how much she had suffered during the difficult war years. Britain was passing through a grave economic crisis: the interminable wars had left her

300

with a debt of millions of pounds sterling. The Continental System and the war at sea had inflicted terrible losses upon the merchant-houses and the shipowners, losses which could not be offset by Britain's overseas trade, by her business with America and Asia. But these losses were as nothing compared with the devastation suffered by the Continent, where armies had marched from Spain to Moscow, fighting battles, trampling down crops, looting cities, and paralysing all trade.

The consumers certainly were eager enough to buy. After all, behind those enforced customs barriers, who had not dreamed of drinking once again some genuine coffee instead of the chicory infusion which served as a substitute; who had not longed for a pipe of real Virginia tobacco instead of the pungent (and by no means cheap) weed on sale during the war? And did not the sugar made from sugar-cane taste sweeter than the stuff now extracted from beet juice? The English cotton cloth came as something of a revelation to the women on the Continent: such colour and beauty, and above all such low prices! Compared with the English cottons the coarse stuff worn during the terrible years of blockade seemed dull and drab, besides being shockingly expensive.

But how was continental Europe to pay for all these splendours? During the long years of the Continental System new conditions had come into being: domestic manufacture had been extended, re-orientated, and adapted. Britain had lost not only her market for colonial merchandise but also her suppliers of foodstuffs and timber. Producers everywhere were trying to prevent merchants from importing cheap goods from abroad.

In 1815 the English landed gentry achieved a total ban on imports of wheat so long as the price was below eighty shillings per quarter. How were they to pay off their crushing mortgages if the grain price were to drop to nothing under the impact of continental competitors? No matter how much the population of the rapidly growing cities, such as Manchester and Birmingham, lamented about the "hunger bill," the Conservative majority in the Commons remained adamant. The result was impressive: the price of wheat rose to 120 shillings per quarter. Within fifteen months many farming estates were able to quintuple their receipts. But the trade with the Continent was killed dead.

Because Britain prohibited the import of wheat the price soon dropped on the Continent. In France it declined from 36 francs per hectolitre in 1816 to 24·60 francs, and before long to 18·42 francs. France now similarly cut herself off from outside, and in turn passed on the agricultural depression to the East. Germany did not know where to export her surplus in order to pay for the colonial merchandise that was wanted so badly.

The Hamburg merchants, meanwhile, were stuck with the supplies they had bought in the first fine flush of rejoicing. They could not hold out for long, since the capital of even the wealthiest firms had been greatly reduced by the colossal war levies imposed on them as recently as 1813. But all that might have been bearable if only business got under way again. As the prices of agricultural produce suddenly collapsed the purchasing power in town and country dwindled away.

The manufacturers of industrial goods were now likewise clamouring for 'protection,' for customs duties and import prohibitions. The French prohibited the import of all iron and steel from Britain, of silk from Italy and India, and of woollen blankets and shawls. They greatly increased import duties on cotton and woollen goods. At the same time, the French manufacturers demanded from their Government large-scale export aid; the country was being choked by its own over-production.

Everybody—Germans, Swedes, Dutch, Spaniards, Russians, and even the young republics of America—barricaded themselves behind colossal customs barriers. As if disaster could be averted that way! No one had learned his lesson and no one was prepared to learn. Governments clung to the fetish of the home market as though it were a cake from which slice after slice could be cut off for the domestic producers. However, this home market proved to be a mirage: it shrank and faded away. One by one, the merchant-houses had to suspend payments; one by one, the factories had to close. Workmen were hanging about the streets, unemployed, while their wives and children were starving at home. There was no shortage of men willing to work, nor of raw materials, nor yet of manufacturing enterprises. All that was lacking was a market.

The producers dominated the field. But the measures they proposed merely made things worse. "Buy as little as possible from others and sell them as much as possible" was the slogan coined by the French Minister of Commerce Saint-Cricq. First ruin your customer—and then expect him to buy! In the course of a single year (1826) some 7000 French merchant firms crashed. The French Revolution had brought freedom: political freedom by the overthrow of the monarchy and the foundation of the Republic; legal freedom by the liberation of the peasants. To that was added economic freedom: all trades had been declared free, and every person was entitled to engage in whichever vocation he chose regardless of guilds or trade associations. No longer did a peasant have to toil hard for his feudal lord; no longer did the peasant women and girls have to spend the long winter evenings spinning at the manor. If they did so they had to be remunerated, and, what was more, in ready money—money which they could spend on whatever they chose. That was something previously unknown in the countryside. Peasants and their womenfolk had always worked for themselves and for their master. In return they had received their daily bread, their clothes, their footwear, their farming implements, their cottage and their beds, feathers for their eiderdowns, and hams for the winter. Cash was almost unknown to them. In sixteenth-century England a ploughman—the most valuable man in the field—received fifty shillings a year. That did not leave much for purchases. But then, most of what he required he received on the estate. Now he was being remunerated in cash, just as the maids and the spinning women. At last he would be able to afford all manner of things. But all these hopes were bitterly disappointed: there was no work for him because the squire did not have enough ready money.

Itinerant merchants and pedlars would offer the most dazzling merchandise: colourful printed cotton cloth, known as nankeen, sugar, coffee, and tobacco—but only few people would reach for their purses. True, prices were temptingly low—but there just was no money about.

Under the old feudal organization of the big estates no one had asked for money. A man would wait until a job was finished, the harvest gathered in, a piece of workmanship completed. Then the squire or his lady would set up beer and bread, harvest festivals would be celebrated, and every man or woman rewarded according to his work—with the fruits, in part, of his own labour. Now the small farmers were complaining that their landlords had ceased to look after them and abandoned them to their fate, no matter whether they went hungry or lay sick. The landowners, for their part, complained just as bitterly: farm hands would no longer work, they had become lazy and rebellious, and grumbled about their low wages. Yet they were charging the most fantastic prices for any service performed for the landowner! Small wonder. When a man took his horse to be shod he now had to pay cash to the blacksmith; when a shoemaker sold a pair of boots he demanded good money. If a man's worn-out clothes needed replacing a veritable small fortune was needed. There was nothing to be had free; nothing was given away as a present.

Were conditions any different in the towns? In the past a man would have his adolescent son apprenticed to a craftsman or a merchant. There he would be safe for five years. He would get his bed and board, he would be clothed, and if he should fall ill his employer's family or servants would look after him. He was thus relieved of all anxiety. On the other hand, he could buy next to nothing during those years—for he was given no cash. If his employer's wife was stingy, then he would go hungry. To buy additional food, say a loaf of white bread or a stick of candy sugar, was a dream only rarely realized. Discipline was old-fashioned and strict. "Don't disgrace us, boy!" his guardian said to young Hudtwalker—later to become a highly respected Hamburg merchant—when he took him to be apprenticed to a herring merchant.

The apprentice shared the servants' table with the maids, eating whatever was set before him—and that, according to his own account, was not much. During the day he had to work in line with the herring-packers; even if he had cut his finger he had to dip his hand into the smarting brine; in the evening, when the other workmen went to their homes, he had to do office work in the counting-house. He was not allowed to go out without permission. In the morning he cleaned not only his master's shoes but also those of the firm's servants. The one thing that got him down, to the point of tears, was having to carry the filthy refuse of the house across the street. His apprenticeship lasted four years. He had very little pocket-money.

This very strict discipline, which survived in many places until the middle of the nineteenth century, was described also by Bernhard Reemtsma, the founder of the big German cigarette firm. One night, during his apprenticeship, his hunger had become so unbearable that he sneaked out and walked home to his parents, a distance of several miles, to tell them how miserable he was. Without a single word his father took him by the arm and walked back with him the whole distance to hand him over to his apprenticeship master for punishment. He was given no food at home.

A merchant can make a sale only if his customer has money, or if he is likely to have money in the near future. Credit can be given only if one is sure that money—*i.e.*, cash—will be available at some future date. A country, similarly, can sell goods to another only if it will also buy from it—not the other way round, as the over-clever French Minister imagined. But the moment a merchant supplied cheap merchandise the local producers would clamour for protection. In the 1820's the colonial merchants were still the only ones of any account— at least in so far as turnover was concerned. Before long, however, drapers' shops appeared in the major towns, selling no longer artisan-made articles, but factory-produced goods. The artisan, who preferred to sell his own products, looked with disfavour and alarm on the merchant who was robbing him of his livelihood by offering cheap goods made elsewhere—"factory-made rubbish." The new-fangled stuff was certainly pleasing to the eye, but would it stand up to a thorough test?

During the age of the rococo most manufactories had been working for the nobility and the rich burghers; they alone could afford the heavy brocades, the lace jabots, and the magnificent tapestries. The rest of the townspeople contented themselves with watching the elegant world on the great feast-days—and the oppressed unfree peasants did not enter into the picture at all. Now the machines were available but the consumers were hanging back. Was it really practical and cheap to buy clothes and articles from the merchant? The artisans were up in arms, proclaiming against the poor quality of factory-made goods; family men were alarmed at the thought of having to produce more house-keeping money because "everything was so expensive nowadays." Why was it suddenly necessary to buy so many foreign-made goods? The authorities chided the 'extravagance' of the broad masses who insisted on smoking tobacco, drinking coffee, and eating sugar titbits, and who were finding their wages no longer adequate. Perhaps all these unnecessary luxuries should be taxed so heavily that people would lose interest in them? But the good old days were gone. A new wind was blowing across Europe.

The merchants were offering the prettiest and most alluring materials at very reasonable prices, thanks to the machines and—let us not forget it

—thanks to the abominably low wages paid to the workers. But would it have been possible, without those low prices, to break the old-established habit of buying practically nothing and making everything at home?

Commerce meant work, bread, and money not only for the urban worker but also for the farmer who could send his produce to wherever it was well paid. Bismarck's father was always in a good humour when he could sell wool to England. If only there had been no customs duties!

Anyone travelling from Hamburg to Frankfurt at that time had to cross 144 customs frontiers, some territorial and some urban. At every one of them a customs official would collect some form of impost for the merchandise the traveller was carrying with him—customs duty or road toll, excise duty or consumer tax—and every time it meant a delay, lengthy argument, and sometimes annoyance. How could trade prosper under these circumstances even within a limited economic area? In 1816 Prussia abolished all customs duties on the boundaries of her provinces and cities. Only on her national frontiers was duty to be levied in future. Moreover, instead of the forbidding rates which had arisen during the war years, the maximum duty now was to be 10 per cent. *ad valorem*. There were no restrictions on imports or exports, and all commerce within the Kingdom of Prussia was open to anyone. Merchandise passing through Prussia—*i.e.,* to be re-exported—was not subject to customs duty upon entering the country. The smaller German principalities were likewise compelled to exempt transit goods for fear that trade would otherwise bypass them. But the centrally situated Electorate of Hesse could not be bypassed, and it alone kept up its transit toll. Twenty-five years after the Congress of Vienna the German States amalgamated to form an economic union. The German Customs Union had at last become a fact.

But who would protect the artisan and the newly arising industries from competition? Britain was anxious to dump her industrial goods—cotton cloth, woollen textiles, iron and steel articles, and machinery—as well as her West Indian tropical produce, such as sugar, rum, tobacco, and coffee, on to the European market. In exchange she would have to accept continental goods—no matter what her worried domestic producers said. The struggle for 'free trade' began.

Skilfully the free traders denounced the high corn prices and mobilized public opinion against protective tariffs. Certainly, they said, British agriculture must be assured of a 'fair' price. But as soon as the price of grain rose above sixty shillings per quarter the tariffs would have to be lowered to allow foreign grain into the country—until the domestic price had again dropped to the standard level. France was once more allowed to export silks to Britain; Britain also lifted the strict export prohibitions on machines and raw wool.

50. Political cartoon on the abolition of tariffs against the opposition of the House of Lords (English woodcut, about 1840)

The effect of this more liberal commercial policy was surprising: during the ten years from 1820 to 1830 British imports rose from £30,000,000 to £46,000,000, and exports from £38,000,000 to £60,000,000. If the country wanted large-scale commerce, the free traders were saying, the merchants must be given a free hand. Price, and price alone, must govern foreign trade. In that way the most efficient man would succeed. Anyone maintaining his business thanks only to high protective tariff barriers would fall by the wayside. Initiative and efficiency would bring their reward.

Richard Cobden of Manchester, a former merchant in fine cottons, unfurled the banner of genuine free trade. Manchester was the place where the new wind of free enterprise was felt most clearly; Manchester manufacturers had the best machines, and the Manchester merchants with their low prices were squeezing the monopoly traders of the old East India Company out of all world markets. It was in Manchester that the enterprising spirit of the port of Liverpool had created a modern industry. Manchester became a concept. It stood for freedom, for both peaceful and fierce competition, for industrial progress. In all arguments about trade policy, about the cushioning that should or should not be given to the domestic producer, about the extent to which a nation's prosperity depended on fixed prices, about methods of labour and production—the name of Manchester invariably stands for free trade. It embodies the idea of the merchant in opposition to protective tariffs, to a protectionism which all too frequently, if not always, protects the producer at the expense of the consumer.

In 1846 Cobden was victorious; the British corn taxes were abolished, and a few years later free trade encompassed all branches of British foreign trade. At last the idea that a country could not sell anything unless it also imported had gained acceptance. Manchester did not need silver or gold to buy merchandise in the East or West Indies; it supplied the cheap cotton goods which were in greater demand than any precious metal. If the State wanted to impose taxes and duties upon its subjects that was its own business—but the public should not be compelled to buy merchandise from manufacturers working with outdated methods and with inadequate machinery, producing articles which did not stand up to fierce competition because they were too expensive. Why should the cultivation of grain and other crops be protected when these could easily be replaced by imports from other parts of the world? Especially if a worker could earn higher wages in the factories than by toiling in the fields.

The French were not convinced. It was all very well for the British to hold those views, but their industry was technically superior to that of France. If France opened her frontiers surely she would be swamped with cheap goods and so ruined. Impossible, replied the free traders. Britain was bound to import as much as she exported—how else was she to pay for her imports? It was, of course, possible that one domestic producer might be favoured at the expense of another, the Lyons silk-weaver, for instance, at the expense of the Normandy farmer; a particular industry might even be ruined if it proved unable to stand up to foreign competition—but on the national scale one country could never benefit at the expense of another. No country could ever export unilaterally without importing at the same time.

Who then was to decide what the population in a country should consume—the Government by its customs barriers or the customer by his reaction to the price?

The fiercest struggle for protective tariff barriers was put up by the French cotton manufacturers. They were joined by the sugar-refiners and the wool manufacturers, and before long support came also from the ironmasters. What use were the Finance Minister's bitter complaints about monopoly tendencies? The middle-class entrepreneurs allied themselves with the landed gentry in stubbornly opposing any reduction of tariffs. Against this resistance even the "enlightened" Government of the Bourbons was powerless. At least, the merchant was able to move freely within the frontiers of France; all internal customs barriers of provinces and towns had been abolished. Not until after the fall of the Bourbons, in 1836, were the first tariff reductions made—33 per cent. on wool and 25 per cent. on iron. But that was all. Only in the overseas markets could a merchant sell his merchandise without difficulty, for to the European merchant the tropical produce was as good as ready cash. Since the planter could easily sell his own crops he was also prepared to buy European industrial goods. Besides, who was to object to imports there?

What had once been achieved by Liverpool should not be beyond the powers of the Hamburg merchants—to build up a domestic industry by way of the world market. The Spanish colonies in America —with the exception of Cuba—had broken free from their mother country; they were receiving the German merchants with open arms. Provided they bought their sugar, coffee, and tobacco they would buy their German textiles and German craftsmen's tools. The Hamburg merchants went out to America, to Africa, and to Asia. The independent republics of America would rather supply their coffee, sugar, tobacco, and cocoa direct to Hamburg than send it via England; they readily accepted German textiles and hardware. From 1823 to 1825 some 40 to 50 ships called at Hamburg each year from North America, and 70 to 80 from the West Indies; the number of ships from South America soared from 63 to 130.

Trade agreements were concluded with the young republics, prepared and negotiated, as a rule, by merchants from the Hanseatic
towns. The bigger German States, like Prussia, were holding back.
Two-thirds of all firms which opened settlements overseas were Hanseatic merchant-houses. They had a tough fight on their hands against
British and U.S. competition, but they established themselves firmly—
not by any means because German industry was superior to that of the
Anglo-Saxon countries, but simply because the German merchants
represented a vast continental market for tropical produce.

In continental Europe people were only slowly switching from the
old and familiar woollen and linen materials, or the linen-cotton
mixtures like fustian, to the new-fangled cotton fabrics. Even the lower
prices made little difference at first. A housewife would view the new
cloth with suspicion: Would it last? Would it do for her daughter's
"bottom drawer"? Would a skirt made from it still be good in ten
years' time?

The farmer in Georgia and the Creole in Buenos Aires were less
choosy—so long as the merchandise was cheap, handsome, and colourful. In the New World cotton went well. All one had to do was sail
out there and seek customers, and find out at the same time what those
foreign countries produced and whether it would pay to import their
manufactures to Europe. About the year 1845 there were nearly 400
German business houses overseas—137 of them in North America,
98 in South America, 48 in Mexico alone, and 35 in Central America.
Without a sea power or a unified country to back them these men were
prepared to compete against the all-dominating British trade.

World commerce at that time was tantamount to British commerce.
England could scarcely be beaten; she possessed the best machines, a
well-balanced banking system, with boundless capital and rich experience; moreover, her merchants knew the whole world. Nowhere
could cotton or wool be bought so favourably as in Liverpool or London, nowhere were tariffs so low, nowhere was as much coal mined as
in Britain, nowhere was as much iron smelted. What chances had
Hamburg got? Commerce, however, is not a one-way street; anyone
wishing to sell must also buy. Anyone seeking a customer must try to
please him. Since England needed the German market she had to
cultivate the Germans: she had to lend them capital, make machinery
available to them, and buy anything that could be further processed or

re-exported. The more solvent the customer, the more he will buy, and the more business will prosper. Britain did all she could to build up a modern industry on the Continent and to stimulate trade. English merchants were working hand in hand with German merchants; English banks discounted the bills of the Hamburg merchant-houses, English insurance companies underwrote a considerable part of the risks. London remained the centre of an all-embracing world trade.

But, still the sinister slave trade was flourishing on the African coast. Indeed, it had increased tremendously. How else was a Negro chieftain to pay for the weapons, the alcohol, the pearls, the fabrics, and even the cast-off generals' uniforms, unless with "black ivory"? The southern states of the U.S.A. and Brazil were clamouring for this 'merchandise.'

In 1806 Britain had prohibited the slave trade and had moreover urged France, Holland, and Denmark to cut off this trade. But this did not have much effect because the Portuguese and U.S. merchants now appropriated the business. True enough, Portugal prohibited the trade in human beings in 1836 and the Brazilian Empire followed suit in 1850; the United States of America had issued a bill against the slave trade as early as 1820. Those laws, however, existed only on paper. There were plenty of greedy, ruthless, and unscrupulous men who cared little about laws, or about British men-of-war, let alone about "the commands of humanity." On the coast of Dahomey a certain Don Francisco de Souza was established; he was the son of poor people from Rio de Janeiro with African blood in his veins. He could neither read nor write, but he supplied woollen materials, iron articles, pearls, and, above all, weapons to the Negro king in exchange for slaves. Since superstition prevented the king from ever going near the sea, Souza administered the coastal area as his 'Resident.' His house in Widah positively sparkled with silver vessels. There he would receive his European visitors and discuss lawful commerce with British merchants. Offshore, however, on the high seas, the British warships intercepted the sailing-ships which Souza sent to America loaded with wretched negroes. Although thirty-four fully laden ships were thus intercepted in the course of a few years Souza grew richer and richer. It was not particularly surprising: between 1836 and 1840 the slavers still exported more than 100,000 slaves from West Africa each year.

Farther north, in Sierra Leone, lived a Spaniard named Pedro Blanco, a retired sea-captain from Malaga. All round his house were the hutments which housed between 1000 and 2000 slaves; moreover, he had a number of trading-stations strung out as far as Digby. His look-outs were posted along the African coast, watching the British blockade ships through telescopes. As soon as they spotted a gap in the line, the slave ships would slip out on a dark night to gain the high seas. Finally the British lost their patience; they simply burned down all the trading-posts. The cunning Pedro, however, had meanwhile escaped to Havana, in Cuba, where he became a reputable merchant dealing in European industrial articles and in sugar. When he died he left a round million dollars.

In Africa Pedro's shady business was continued by a certain Canot, a Florentine by birth. His slave station was in the land of the Krumen, in what is to-day Liberia. He even founded a colony of his own which he offered to Britain; he laid out plantations and engaged in legitimate trade—in short, he tried to give the impression of a reputable merchant. Nevertheless he was caught in the end, while taking a slave ship to the New World under the American flag. He died in poverty. They were strange and colourful characters, the men who controlled commerce on the African coast, the men with whom the honest merchants from Britain and Hamburg had to work whether they liked it or not, if they wanted to engage in commerce there at all.

In 1834 the Hamburg shipowner Georg Heinrich Wappäus sent the brig *Brazil Packet* to Africa under the command of Captain Hinrichsen. His instructions were to reconnoitre from Gambia where ivory and gold, as well as pepper and rice, might be purchased most favourably. On no account was he to turn into the Niger estuary since "that river was unhealthy"; instead he was to look out for dye-woods, arrowroot, and ebony. Above all, he was to trade linen for ivory. He was instructed not to sail beyond Angola because, in the opinion of the prudent merchant, "further down it is dangerous and no business to be done." The British, suspecting Hinrichsen of having dealt in slaves, arrested him without much ado; however, he was able to prove his innocence. The German trade with Africa developed surprisingly quickly, and before long surpassed that of France.

Yet Britain continued to hold the key position in world trade. It was from Britain that most of the tropical produce was bought—sugar, coffee, cotton, but also British cotton fabrics, iron, machines, and so on. From Britain came the new manufacturing methods, the "industrial age." By 1812 France already had 11,000 Jacquard looms, which controlled the threads by means of punched cards and produced magnificent silks in unlimited quantities. Entrepreneurs installed new machines, modernized their undertakings, and employed steam-power to save human labour.

Marketing, on the other hand, encountered well-nigh insuperable difficulties. The small shopkeeper was unable to sell the vast quantities which the manufacturers were putting out. At the beginning of the nineteenth century the European public—almost as in the Middle Ages —still made its purchases in the market, in the square before the cathedral, in front of the town-hall, by the bridge, or during Church fairs, when merchants would come from far afield. Food was brought to the towns by the peasants of the neighbourhood.

Anyone wanting to buy anything in between markets had to go to the huckster or small shopkeeper, who would sit in his narrow ill-lit shop, frequently a basement, crammed full of all kinds of merchandise from barrels of salted herring and sugar-cones down to linen and wool-len materials. There was hardly room to move in the confined space among the piles of haphazardly stacked goods. But the regular cus-tomers were not put out by that: they knew exactly what there was and where it was to be found. As these 'general stores' had to keep all kinds of merchandise they were, of course, unable to offer much choice. A customer had to accept what he was offered: paper and writing materials, sewing equipment for the womenfolk, needles and thread, but also spades, chains, scythes, and whips for the peasants who might come to town to shop, besides spirits and all kinds of junk which some itinerant dealer might have talked the shopkeeper into buying—neck-laces, rosaries, an occasional porcelain figure or a fine china cup.

Herring continued to be part of the popular diet, at least during the winter and during Lent in the Catholic countries. But it was in demand also with other European nations because it kept well and was easily transported in the barrel. Little wonder that the nickname of "herring-tamer" came to be applied to the small shopkeeper generally on the continent of Europe.

Since the collapse of Napoleon's Continental System colonial mer-chandise such as coffee, tea, cocoa, tobacco, and sugar were stocked also by the general store. The days were gone when these pleasures had been confined to a small circle and when a well-meaning authority had severely punished smoking in public, especially in public squares and parks. Only in the Tiergarten Park in Berlin was the ban on smoking kept up until 1848. Its abolition was one of the achievements of the March Revolution. Now anybody might buy as much tobacco, coffee, and sugar as he wished—or as he could afford.

In the small crowded general store there simply was no room for textiles; besides, the valuable fabrics were too easily soiled among the jumble of mixed merchandise. Until well into the nineteenth century textiles were sold by the wholesale merchants—both in the bale and as garments, trousers, jackets, dresses, and overcoats for individual customers. As a rule, however, material used to be bought at the tailor's. Under the pressure of factory-made supplies a significant change was now coming about: the general store began to specialize. Shops would stock either colonial merchandise or 'home produce,' or textiles, or iron articles.

The 'victualler's shops' were based on the assumption that fewer and fewer housewives would get their food from the patch of land they might own outside the town walls. Only few would now kill a pig to keep the family in ham, bacon, and sausage throughout the winter; housewives no longer pickled *sauerkraut* or dried beans; they no longer stored apples and pears. Indeed, they did not even go to the weekly market regularly any longer but bought whatever they needed in the shop. All domestic produce was stocked by the 'home-produce merchant.' There the townsmen and farmers could also try a glass of spirits, a quarter of open local wine, or a tankard of beer.

The drapers' shops stocked colourful printed cottons, especially nankeen, as well as English cotton cloth, occasionally also some genuine Indian material, muslin, or silks from Lyons made now on a Jacquard loom, haberdashery, gloves, and modish bonnets. Here the ladies would always find some novelty; the commercial travellers going from town to town, trying to sell their wares, saw to that. At the end of the eighteenth century out of the 165,000 people employed in Prussia in trade and industry, 151,000, or 92 per cent., worked in the textiles industry, with linen manufacture still accounting for more workmen than the woollen and cotton industries taken together. But after the collapse of the Continental System British cotton goods began to flood the German market. The fierce struggle between linen and cotton was on. With the courage of desperation the linen-weavers resisted their more powerful rivals. Surely their customers would not forsake the durable, sound linen materials which were so ideally suited to being handed down from one generation to another and which could be bought years ahead for one's daughter's marriage portion without deteriorating by prolonged storage.

Hardware merchants often adjusted themselves entirely to the needs of the farmers, stocking ploughshares, hoes, nails and screws, hammers and axes from Sheffield or Solingen. They also kept whips, saddles, harness and carts, barrels and hoops, much to the annoyance of blacksmiths, wainwrights, coopers, and saddlers. The hardest hit by these changes were the pedlars and hucksters, who used to roam over the country without any competition, selling all kinds of junk and knick-knacks, as described by Jost Ammann in his *Book of Estates* printed in 1568: "Spices, sugar and brandy, looking-glasses, handbells, combs, needles, gingerbread, lace and spectacles." In order to display his specialized and more extensive range of goods a merchant needed more spacious premises, preferably on the ground floor. But to meet the high rent he must have a big turnover. He could no longer wait for customers to walk in on their own account. Instead, he would have handbills distributed in the street, advertising the merchandise he happened to have in stock. The artisans were outraged by these new importunate methods of publicity, which ran counter to all custom and indeed to good manners. The freedom to practise any trade, brought by the French Revolution and the reforms of Stein-Hardenberg, was evidently breaking up the traditional principles of business morality. Surely, the artisans told themselves, the quality of a hand-made article must speak for itself. But instead, those shopkeepers were advertising their factory-made rubbish by excessive claims, noisily announcing their low prices, and generally behaving like vulgar mountebanks at a fair! Surely a respectable merchant should know better. Soon fences and walls were no longer sufficient: about the middle of the century Litfass set up pillars at street corners to accommodate all the posters. Some of these pillar hoardings survive in France to this day.

Now that the merchant stocked also craftsmen's manufactures, such as clothes, shoes, carts, knives, etc., he had to have some knowledge of these articles or else his customers would go back to the old master craftsman who, as it was, kept telling them that anyone buying articles at the shop was merely throwing away his money. Only the expert, they said, could provide the right article, and the only expert was the man who manufactured it. But how was a small shopkeeper who stocked everything under the sun and who spent all his waking hours in his shop to acquire any expert knowledge of his goods?

The manufacturers sent out their travellers with the latest samples—fashionable cottons, sound woollen materials, precious silks, plain sheets. Their job was to sell, to bring back orders so that the "iron angels" could be employed profitably. There were the representatives of small manufacturers from Coventry and Schmalkalden, from Nürnberg and Stuttgart; there were the travellers of the great merchant-houses in Bremen, Amsterdam, Le Havre, and London, offering coffee, cocoa, sugar, tobacco, and tea.

They would all harangue the small shopkeeper, praising their goods, bent on selling as much as possible. They would offer credits, they would raise all sorts of hopes to make their customer place an order. He could turn away all those who came later, so long as he could be talked into making his purchase now. Balzac has portrayed for us one of those highly skilled salesmen, the great Haudissard, whose persuasive powers overcame all resistance; he sold everything he took with him on his journey. They were the battles which brought victory for modern capitalism.

Inventors had created the steam-engine, spinning-machines and looms, blast furnaces, railways and steamships, the ginning-machine for cotton, and the first machine tools. Entrepreneurs had built their factories, installed machines, recruited labour in the countryside, and produced their goods in overwhelming quantities. However, for marketing their products they continued to be dependent on the retailer. But how, from his modest little shop, was he to attract customers and persuade them to buy factory-made articles instead of making everything themselves?

To begin with, there was a shortage of ready money. The average weekly wage in English cotton-mills was 25 shillings, but during the subsequent years declined again as the cost of food dropped. About the middle of the century the average wage was 22 shillings a week. There was not much a worker could buy for that money. And yet wages in the cotton-mills of the flourishing industrial towns were relatively good.

The average wage of a fully employed worker in England in 1795 was no more than 13*s.* 6*d.* The wage increase during the war was more than offset by the rising cost of living. Then came the difficult years leading to the depression of the 1820's. By 1850 the average wage had again declined to 17 shillings a week, yet the price-level then was much the same as it was, later, in 1913.

The rural population, which still made up nearly four-fifths of the total in Germany, France, and Italy, and nearly two-thirds in England, had very little ready cash. How, then, was the small shopkeeper to persuade these people that it was cheaper and more advantageous for them to buy everything in his shop?

The problem seemed insoluble. First of all, the public had to buy merchandise at the shops so that the factories could work to full capacity; but to do this they needed ready cash, and that had to be earned somewhere. Manufacturers were spurring on their travellers; desperately they were looking for 'crack salesmen.' But no retailer could buy from them more than he was able to resell. Surely, the shopkeeper would argue, the demand of a small town was constant. Before long, booths selling spirits to the workmen sprang up outside the factory gates on pay day, and stalls where women and girls would be persuaded to part with their hard-earned money on some trinket or other. In this way their purchasing power for the whole week was absorbed—to the detriment of the local shops and, ultimately, the factories which needed a big turnover.

In Britain the workers united in consumer co-operatives in order to cut out the 'expensive' middleman, in the belief that here lay the solution of the problem. The turnover, however, was still far below the greatly increased volume of production, simply because there was no adequate distributive apparatus. This, in turn, placed industry under the pressure of intensified competition, and this pressure it passed on by paying lower wages. But just because these wages were so low there was great poverty and hardship in the industrial areas and, consequently, the turnover there remained small. Only if the distributive apparatus was extended and fundamentally reorganized would the industrial age have a clear road ahead. Was this at all feasible within the narrow confines of Europe? In 1858 there were, in the whole of Prussia, 39,300 independent commercially active persons with 22,900 employees. In other words, only every other merchant had an employee.

In a few cases there might be an apprentice as well as an employee, but for the most part a shopkeeper would run his business merely with the help of his family.

He would stand behind his counter, chatting with his customers, all of whom he would know personally. They would endlessly haggle with him about prices, since each article was a little different from another and there was always something to be found that might justify a discount. How, in these circumstances, was a shopkeeper to find the time and energy for introducing a new line, for talking his customers into buying a new article, as those grandiloquent travelling salesmen expected him to? The small shopkeeper could not afford to go in for brash advertising. In spite of his legal 'freedom' he was still very much in the grip of the traditional guild outlook. His customers expected the same sound merchandise that they had bought from him for many years and which they knew from their parents and grandparents. The manufacturers could find some one else to market their new-fangled junk!

The harassed manufacturer could not possibly market his large output on the old continent of Europe. Overseas, however, where there were no obstinate artisans making a fuss about their quality work, and no middle class stubbornly clinging to old habits, it should be possible to find a large-scale market. Lancashire cotton cloth positively flooded the Indian market. The result was disastrous. Under the onslaught of the factory-made goods India's age-old crafts collapsed. Even the Indian spinner with his modest hand-operated spinning-wheel could not produce as cheaply as the steam-driven iron machines; even the indigent Indian peasant could not supply cotton as cheaply as the Alabama planter with his ginning-machines and his Negro slaves. The collapse of India's crafts meant the collapse of an important part of her economy. The country became impoverished.

Wherever European industry was seeking a new market, in India or Africa or the South American republics—everywhere its superior competitive power ruined the local crafts and, with them, the potential customers for Europe's ready-made goods. After all, the poor people of Africa and Asia had even less ready cash than the Europeans. The only truly receptive market was the United States of America.

I5

The Beginnings of Global Economics

━━━━ᴧᴜᴧᴜᴧᴜᴧ/◉/ᴧᴧᴧᴧᴧᴧ━━━━

AN UNENDING PROCESSION of covered wagons was laboriously moving through the wilderness. Ever since Daniel Boone, the prototype of James Fenimore Cooper's "leather-stocking" hero, had crossed the mountains which separated the coastal strip along the Atlantic from the measureless plains of the Mississippi basin people had been moving into the interior of the country to make their fortunes. They were not after gold, they did not expect to find mineral wealth—all they wanted was land. Did they fully realize what was in store for them?

From Cumberland on the upper Potomac the road wound its way through the mountains to Wheeling on the Ohio—a rough, narrow track, cut by watercourses and huge fallen trees, over rocks and through deep sand. Until about 1840 most of the arrivals in the West came by the famous Cumberland trail. Once he had left Cumberland behind him a man had to depend on himself alone. And with the coast he would leave behind him all ties with world traffic, with the rapidly growing cities and the flourishing factories. Alone he would penetrate into a world yet undeveloped, a world without roads and bridges, without towns and villages, indeed without houses or huts. There was nothing. Everything had to be created from scratch. The vast territory was void of human beings. Only a few wild Red Indian tribes roamed the plains—Indians resisting the influx of the white man and desperately attacking him. They had to be pushed back by force.

The development of the Mississippi basin would depend entirely on whether the settlers succeeded in trading their surpluses of wheat, maize, and meat for weapons, axes, gunpowder and lead, for nails, textiles, and cooking-pots.

The men who arrived in the West through the narrow bottleneck of the Cumberland trail saw before them the vast plains as yet unclaimed, plains which seemed only to wait for a hard-working farmer, to receive the seed and then to yield crops a hundredfold. But did these men consider that in future every rifle, every ounce of gunpowder, every knife, and every needle would have to be imported along this same road and that these articles would have to be paid for by their own agricultural produce which, in its turn, would have to be taken eastwards along that same lengthy and laborious route?

The question was not merely one of transport but also of who was to accept these agricultural surpluses. After all, there was still plenty of unused land between the coast and the mountains. The original forest had long been cut down in Massachusetts and New York, so that the inhabitants of those areas could now feed themselves from their own land. Who, then, was to buy the grain whose price must inevitably reflect the high costs of complicated transport? There was no doubt that the farmer putting his plough to the wide open spaces of the Ohio basin was undertaking a considerable risk.

The people who emigrated from the Old World of Europe left behind them also the traditional social order. At the head of the State was the King; the people were divided into three estates—the clergy, the nobility, and the common people. The peasant, tied to his land and unfree, served the nobility, toiling in the fields of his feudal landlord, doing whatever his master told him. He was not even free to choose his religion. "A subject takes the religion of his overlord"—that was the formula thought up by jurists at an earlier date. This oppressive social pattern did not always end even when a man landed on the American coast. There were still far too many laws and regulations, officials and feudal landowners. But in the West, beyond the mountains, there was freedom. If a man found his fellows irksome, if he felt they were trying to impose on him their way of living, their religious beliefs and their political views, exact taxes from him, or impose on him distasteful tasks, he need only pack up his belongings and with his covered wagon move farther to the West, towards the frontier which, year after year, advanced farther into the unexplored wilderness.

Most immigrants arrived in America practically penniless: they were lucky if they had been able to pay for their crossing and bring with them enough clothing and seeds for the first few months. A payment had then to be made to the Government for one's land. Only rarely would an immigrant's means go beyond that. But what about the farming equipment that was necessary, or the tools which would enable a man to pursue his trade? As a rule the merchant would advance the money for wagons, implements, cattle and horses, seeds, and even food. In the autumn he would take over the harvest in order to resell it on the coast.

In the small communities there was one inexorable law: a man had to pay his debts, he had to keep his word, he had to discharge his obligations, deliver the goods he had promised, accept and punctually pay for the goods he had ordered. His neighbours would see to that. Even before they built their church or their town-hall they would erect in the village square the pillory for tardy debtors. They had their reasons. Survival in this boundless vastness of America depended on the merchandise supplied by the merchant—from rifles and axes down to the rum for the Red Indians. Not to mention such welcome luxuries as tobacco for a man's pipe, tea for the cold winter evenings, or sugar, salt, and spices to make the daily fare more palatable. After all, there was little variety in a mid-Western farmer's diet; he ate only what he grew. Occasionally a welcome change might be provided by the animals he hunted or the fish he caught.

In every small settlement there was a merchant—the most important and most powerful man in the village. His store would look odd enough: barrels of syrup standing on the floor, sausages hanging from the rafters, mice scurrying about, nibbling the sacks of flour, plough-shares and scythes stacked against the wall, knives of every size, bales of cotton, woollens and linens, paper, nibs, and ink. Anything a farmer needed he would find at the store. The shopkeeper himself was away most of the time. He might be riding his mule from farm to farm, offering cloth or buying up grain; he might be taking his covered wagon along the bumpy Cumberland trail to Philadelphia, New York, or Baltimore to stock up with ploughshares or to sell wheat. He would always grant credit. He would chalk up a man's debt. Accounts were settled when the harvest was in. As a rule his customers would pay not in cash but in kind—with the grain or the wool they had produced and which the merchant would accept against the farmer's inflated debts.

The merchant was variously regarded as a benefactor or as a usurer under whose avarice and graspingness the village community groaned—according to whether he happened to be giving credit or relentlessly collecting debts. Anyone not paying punctually was mercilessly declared bankrupt: he would lose everything he owned, he would be driven out of his house and home or clapped in the pillory to be mocked by the village youths, a cautionary example to all and sundry.

To be a merchant in the 'Wild West' required a considerable stock of courage and confidence, as well as a hard and inflexible will. Everybody wanted credit, far more than they could ever hope to repay; everybody got into serious difficulties when the time of settlement arrived. The harvest—not unnaturally—did not always turn out as good as had been hoped in the spring, and prices rarely reached the figures one had anticipated; besides, who would have thought that a man's debt could grow so rapidly? Every glass of rum, every tot of whisky increased it. Or had the merchant cheated? What use was the neatly made-out bill with its numerous entries? It meant nothing to the simple borderman who felt entirely at the mercy of the cunning merchant and usurer. Often enough a hand would reach for the gun to square accounts in that way.

A good deal of psychology was required for granting the appropriate amount of credit to the right man, firmness to turn down requests, a thick skin to withstand all laments and threats, a friendly, open manner to hold one's own in the community, good humour to keep on amicable terms with those wild characters and so as not to lose one's customers, a good head for business in order to stock the most favourable merchandise at all times and to pay the appropriate price for agricultural surpluses—and, above all, a strong personality which would not panic even in the worst confusion and trouble. It may not be fortuitous that three Presidents of the United States of America had at one time been merchants out West—Andrew Jackson, Abraham Lincoln, and Harry Truman. All three, admittedly, made a failure of their commercial careers. The merchant in the Middle West was only a minute wheel in the great machinery of American economic life. He possessed neither the capital nor the necessary overseas connexions to develop trade in the new areas by his own resources. The real wire-pullers were down by the coast—the big merchants with their ties with Europe, the West Indies, Africa, and even Asia. They, in turn, gave credit to the small Mid-Western shopkeeper; they supplied whatever he had ordered, they instructed him to buy up an entire harvest, they fixed the prices which so often infuriated the disappointed farmers.

America was rich not only in farmland but also in mineral deposits such as coal, ores, and—though still unsuspected at the middle of the century—oil. From London and Liverpool, from Lille and Paris, from Hamburg and Chemnitz, came the buyers who took everything that was being produced—first the cotton, which was getting increasingly short in view of the growing number of mills it had to feed; then grain, which had been finding a ready market ever since Britain abolished its corn duties; and finally bacon and lard. The Cumberland trail had long ceased to be sufficient; merchandise was now shipped to the Gulf of Mexico down the Ohio and the Mississippi. In 1817 the first steamship sailed from New Orleans to Cincinnati; two years later as many as sixty flat-bottomed paddle steamers were plying between Louisville and the mouth of the Mississippi. As a result transport costs were halved. The merchants in Philadelphia, Baltimore, and New York watched their customers moving away. What use was it to them that large numbers of immigrants arrived in their cities only to set out on the great trek to the West? Once they had crossed the Allegheny Mountains they were lost to the merchants on the Atlantic seaboard. They were absorbed in the rival transport network which was based on the rivers of the Mississippi basin.

In 1817 the New Yorkers began the construction of the Erie Canal, which provided a direct link between the Atlantic coast and the Great Lakes. As a result, transport costs from New York to Buffalo dropped from 100 dollars per ton to 8 dollars. Philadelphia and Baltimore likewise tried to drive canals towards the West—in vain. With redoubled vigour they therefore turned to the building of railroads. Within a few decades the iron rails ran from the Atlantic ports over the mountains to Pittsburg and Cincinnati, carrying vast quantities of grain from the interior to the coast and taking immigrants and European industrial goods to the newly opened territories.

World trade was increasingly shifting away from the eastern shores of the Atlantic, the Mediterranean, and the Indian Ocean towards the coast of the United States. An ever-growing volume of merchandise was passing through the American ports from Boston to Baltimore. The merchants resident there were no longer content—as their fathers and forefathers had been—to act as agents for the great, all-powerful merchant houses of London and Liverpool. They wanted to have their own share in the world trade, independently of Britain.

Ever since the eighteenth century the New England states had been supplying to the West Indies the products of the temperate zone—fish, timber, grain, and meat—either in exchange for their sugar and rum, or merely to earn the pounds they needed to pay for the import of British industrial manufactures into North America. The scope of the fishing industry grew as consumption in the interior of the country increased. Moreover, the extensive fishing grounds of Newfoundland offered an unlimited field of activity. As a result, there was an adequate supply of experienced sailors and skilled skippers. That was the basis of what eventually was to become a world-wide shipping trade.

New England's magnificent oak forests, unmatched anywhere in the world, were her principal asset in shipbuilding. They enabled the building of sailing ships that developed a hitherto unparalleled speed.

During the long war years, which continued until 1815, the heaviest possible merchantmen had been necessary—ships powerful enough to carry cannon to ward off enemy attacks. Safety had been more important than speed. Yet even before 1812 sailing ships had been built in Baltimore on a new system: a relatively narrow beam and the greatest possible sail-carrying capacity. Thus a long, slender vessel was born, with a sharp long bow, and the three masts slanting backward and carrying rectangular sails.

The first great clipper for the high seas was built in Baltimore in 1833: it attained the then exceptional speed of eighteen knots. It simply left all other ships standing. This advantage became particularly marked when the clippers were used on long runs. Their great age coincided with the discovery of gold in California and Australia. The early pioneers had struggled across the American continent on their slow covered wagons, over impassable tracks, across turbulent rivers, constantly menaced by nature itself, by arid deserts and towering mountains, as well as by hostile Indians trying to prevent them from occupying their land. Their journey often took many months.

And now the swift clippers took their fortune-seeking passengers to the Isthmus of Panama, where they disembarked them, or later even round the tip of South America and then all the way up the coast to San Francisco. Some 80,000 people were carried by the clippers during the first year of the Californian gold rush. And when news reached Britain of the gold finds in Australia, the clippers carried 400,000 passengers from the mother country to the colony in the southern hemisphere. No wonder that 160 clippers were built during the first four years of the gold rush. They yielded enormous profits.

But when the freight rates began to drop, when it was no longer a case of carrying people rapidly to where they hoped to make their fortune but of carrying merchandise which could not support such high tariffs, the shape of the ships underwent a change. The very slender vessels were replaced by a somewhat broader type, the "medium clipper," capable of carrying more cargo. Though no longer quite so fast, it was still faster than most. The principal field of the medium clipper was the China trade.

The English consumers could discern at once whether their tea had been rocked across the tropical seas on an old-type, slow, lumbering East-Indiaman, or whether a fast clipper had brought it quickly to the temperate zone. They refused to accept any but the best tea—that which had best kept its delicious flavour. The dealers on the London tea exchange were outbidding each other in purchasing the freshest tea and offering it to their clients. They offered high rewards to the first ship to reach England from China with the new tea harvest.

The names of the ships taking part in the race were on the lips of every tea-drinker. The British public's sporting instinct was roused. There was, for instance, the famous *Nightingale* which was built in 1851 and which sailed the seas for fully forty years. Another tea clipper was the *Witch of the Wave*. There was tremendous jubilation when the *Cutty Sark* (built 1869) covered the distance from China to England at an average daily speed of 363 nautical miles—a record for a tea-clipper.

Because they were so fast, the clippers practically left standing the men-of-war whose task it was to arrest the slave trade from West Africa to North America. Once these fast ships had gained the open sea no warship could possibly catch them. That was why they were used also for the illegal trade in opium. The faster the journey, the smaller the risk. Before long, the merchants generally were unwilling to wait for their regular merchandise as long as they had done in the past.

They instructed their agents in China, India, Australia, or South America to dispatch the local products by clipper whenever possible. It was a revolution in the maritime freight business.

Clippers were now sailing all the seven seas. They shortened the journey between New York and San Francisco from 160 to about 90 days. The *Sovereign of the Seas,* built in 1852 and the biggest sailing ship ever to be launched, covered 411 nautical miles in a single day—an average of 17 nautical miles per hour. Only the *Lightning*, built by the American Donald McKay, surpassed that speed.

The British stood helpless in the face of the superior American vessels. They complained that their great sail-ships were hanging about week after week in the East Indies waiting for cargo, while one American clipper after another sailed out to England with their holds filled to capacity. Were the British to watch helplessly as the trident, that symbol of the dominion over the seas, passed from British to American hands? As the tonnage of the American merchant fleet kept rising, Britain's continued to decline alarmingly. Then, suddenly, came the turning point. The British began to build steamships.

In 1835, the famous engineer Brunel, then only twenty-nine, had proposed to the Great Western Railway Company the construction of a steamer, made of iron, to provide a passenger service between Liverpool and New York. Three years later this vessel, the *Great Western,* built under Brunel's direction, made her first voyage across the Atlantic. Brunel was not yet satisfied with her performance. He conceived the idea of propelling the ship not by paddle-wheels but by means of a screw. The *Great Britain,* the first long iron ship driven by a propeller, made her maiden voyage from Liverpool to New York in 1845. But Brunel was still not satisfied. He wanted a bigger and faster ship yet.

In 1858 the *Great Eastern* was launched—a huge ship with a gross tonnage of 19,000 tons, or fourteen times more than the *Great Western* (1340 tons) which only twenty years previously had been admired as one of the great wonders of the world. But the new ship was ill-fated from the start. To begin with, she stuck fast on the slips. Brunel was having her launched sideways, because of her enormous hull, but he checked the movement so much that the ship got stuck and could not be made seaworthy for another three months. The shippers went bankrupt as a result. The next firm to take over the *Great Eastern* also suffered heavy losses, as they could not find sufficient cargo for the enormous vessel. The outsize ship had to be withdrawn from ordinary shipping and used only for cable-laying in the Atlantic.

Commercially this large steamship may have been a failure, but as an engineering feat it represented a crucial turning-point. Steam rapidly supplanted sail; iron ships took the place of wooden ones; and the British once more outstripped the Americans in the shipping trade. But before long the American shippers also ordered steamships to be built. American engineers, too, went in for bold new ideas, and the United States Government paid out subsidies in order to keep the Atlantic shipping routes under the U.S. flag. One American ship-owner, E. K. Collins, operated a regular service to Europe: his *Adriatic*, of 3670 tons, developed a speed of $13\frac{1}{2}$ knots. However, after two accidents the government withdrew its subsidies. Cornelius Vanderbilt made one last effort to organize a trans-Atlantic service at his own expense, but soon gave up the race. The American paddle-steamers were no match for the British propeller-driven ones.

During the next thirty years the Americans confined themselves to letting their steamers ply on the rivers or in coastwise traffic: they left the high seas to the British. As a result, Britain alone profited from the tremendous upsurge in world trade about the middle of the nineteenth century. British vessels handled the vast shipments of passengers and freight over all the seas. British ship-owners made all the profits. They carried the raw materials—principally cotton from the southern states of the U.S.A. to supply the English textiles industry; they brought home the foodstuffs to feed the ever-growing population in the industrial areas. The world's industrial production was increasingly concentrating in Britain. Would the Americans let themselves be beaten in this field too?

In order to promote a native industry the coastal States imposed a high protective tariff on imported textiles and ironware. Why should the British exclusively supply the American market? Anything Manchester and Birmingham could do the Yankees in the New England states must surely be able to do as well. As it was, all the profits went to the high and mighty British firms which were established in the harbour towns and were graciously granting credits. What America needed was manufacturing industries, not merely trade.

But the farmer out West wanted to buy cheaply in order to export cheaply. His customers were for the most part in Europe, and it was

from there that he wanted to import his machines, his farming implements, and the textiles which were largely woven from his own cotton,
by people nourished by his grain. In 1832 the cotton state of South
Carolina arbitrarily forbade its officials to collect the monstrous tariffs
decreed by the Federal Government. But this piece of disobedience did
not go down at all well with President Andrew Jackson.

"Old Hickory," as he was known to his friends, hated the big

51. New York stockbrokers, 1866

merchants of the great coastal cities who had ruthlessly declared him
bankrupt in his younger years; his anger was above all directed against
anything to do with banking and credits. The honest farmer, it seemed
to him, might toil as hard as he could, but in the end the rapacious
merchants would fleece him and then cast him off like an old glove.
Banks, to Andrew Jackson, were the personification of those anonymous, dangerous, and uncanny powers of commerce; they would
arbitrarily fix prices, they would decide whether the sun of prosperity
should shine from the sky or the icy wind of depression shrivel all life.
They were all-powerful. Thus it came about that Andrew Jackson, at

one time the representative of the borderman's interests and the champion of States' rights against an over-powerful Union, enforced protective tariffs. Henceforward these tariffs were only to be raised, never to be lowered. The farmers had to foot the bill.

The reaction came very promptly. In 1837 the United States was swept by an economic depression without parallel. Although Europe's demand for cotton and grain kept increasing, American supplies were growing even more quickly; her surpluses were a drug on the world market.

Were there any shortages at all in this country of unlimited possibilities? What about human labour? Millions of immigrants were arriving from the Old World. In defiance of all prohibitions and of British warships slavers were still importing Negro slaves from Africa. Naturally, these were a good deal more expensive now. Whereas in 1832 a young, vigorous Negro slave could be had for some 500 dollars, five years later, shortly before the depression, the price had risen to 1300 dollars.

The cultivation of cotton continued to be expanded. The manufacturers literally snatched the cotton out of the merchants' hands. The price of cotton rose to over 17 cents per pound; the cotton exchanges were in a fever. Then, suddenly, the wild speculation collapsed. Between 1845 and 1848 the price of cotton dropped to eight cents; even for a top-quality slave a planter would now offer no more than 650 dollars. Many merchant-houses were unable to survive the depression.

No sooner had a factory closed its gates for lack of customers, or of a financial backer, than the merchants would persuade some other entrepreneur to take over the factory; as an inducement they would promise orders and advances. A merchant could make a profit even at low prices: he would buy more cheaply in order to sell more cheaply.

The North American farmer was no peasant wedded to a century-old tradition, suspicious of all change and progress. He was a business-man who knew how to calculate; he knew his overheads, he knew the approximate value of his coming harvest, and he knew the price offered him by the merchant. Any farmer distrustful of that price could sell his grain as a standing crop or else sell it on the exchange for future delivery; there were always merchants willing to contract for future deliveries and manufacturers anxious to assure themselves of long-term supplies of raw materials.

Provided a farmer had courage enough he could expand his acreage under crops as much as he liked. After all, land was available in unlimited quantity—the best possible, highly fertile soil. Year after year the railways thrust deeper into the continent; wherever they arrived the virgin land opened up as to an "Open sesame!" of the Arabian tale. Along the new iron roads trains filled with wheat and maize, with pork and lard, and, in the south, with cotton, rolled towards the coast; laden with machinery, ploughs, and clothing they returned. Transport had become cheap. The only shortage in this headlong expansion was one of human labour. Even an over-populated Europe could no longer supply a sufficient number of immigrants.

The merchants organized a human trade of a new kind. Their agents would travel from country to country, from village to village, collecting the sturdiest and most adventurous men for shipment to America; they promised them land, they advanced them the passage money, they granted them credits for seedstock, cattle, and farming implements. Behind the settlement companies stood the railway com-panies to whom the State had given free of charge a wide strip of land on both sides of each new railway line. Certainly America's agri-cultural production need not, for any lack of land, fall short of what an overpopulated Europe required.

Into the vast, empty spaces of North America the merchants pumped tremendous quantities of rails, locomotives and rolling stock, mowers and threshing machines, ploughs and axes, houses complete with all household effects, furniture and clothing, luxury foods like sugar, coffee, tobacco, rum and tea, soap and glassware, books and musical instruments. A farmer need only go to his local store and express a wish—and pay. But money to him meant his harvest.

As soon as the harvest was gathered in the buyers would appear with their well-lined wallets, bidding for wheat, maize, livestock and cotton, rice, sugar, and tobacco. Their firms would keep them informed about prices, according to the state of the market on the big corn ex-changes. The farmers might hesitate. Was the price good enough? Might they not achieve a better price in winter when the first rush of buying had died down? On the other hand, there were their accu-mulated debts of the past year. New seed had to be ordered, new ploughs and wagons had to be bought; stocks had to be laid in for the coming months in case heavy rains or snow cut communications with the outside world.

In this to and fro, in this free interplay of supply and demand, prices found their own level. There was no question of a 'fair' price, or of a 'food-growing class' that had to be pampered and feather-bedded, or of some 'organic integration' of town and country. If a man could not supply at the ruling market price he had better get out of American agriculture. It had no permanent, divinely ordained market, nor a government with consideration for the much-harassed farmer's wife. On the other hand, American agriculture was free to sell anywhere in the world because it produced on more favourable terms than any other country. When at last the corn tariffs were abolished in Britain her people lived more cheaply than ever before. There was ready employment to be found in the Birmingham steelworks which supplied railway rolling stock to America. The Old World and the New supplemented each other ideally: the former had the factories, the blast furnaces, the scientists, and the engineers, while the latter had the wide, open farming areas with their hard-working people who urgently needed machines and technical equipment. The new steamships now carried across the ocean very much larger cargoes in a much shorter time. In 1860 Britain exported merchandise worth £300,000,000; one-third of this total went to the British Empire and one-sixth to the United States. The list was headed by cotton cloth with nearly 40,000,000 pounds sterling, followed by iron bars, machines, and coal; woollen cloth, once the mainstay of England's foreign trade, ranked only fifth. Finally there was pottery, glass, weapons and ammunition, knives, soap, books, and stationery. British imports consisted almost exclusively of foodstuffs and raw materials, headed by the eagerly demanded cotton. Thanks to this commerce American agriculture and Britain's heavy industry both flourished simultaneously—the iron foundries of Birmingham, the engineering factories of Northampton, the shipbuilding yards of Glasgow, and the cotton-mills of Manchester.

Division of labour meant the choice of the most favourable location, and production under the most favourable transport and working conditions—in short, acceptance of no other yardstick than price. Why was that not possible in continental Europe? There each nation was barricaded, suspiciously, behind its customs barriers: nothing must be bought that could be manufactured at home, no matter under what conditions and at what cost! Why throw away good money on some foreign manufacture when it could be given to a fellow citizen as a reward for his trouble and work? But modern economics cannot be run like a medieval farmstead. Efficient production, low prices, consequently higher consumption, bigger production, and a higher standard of living! That was the new slogan of the merchants about the middle of the nineteenth century.

When the young Bonaparte, who had attentively studied the new doctrine in England, became the Emperor Napoleon III he tried in vain for a long time to introduce free trade in France. In the French parliament his words fell upon deaf ears. The farmers' league and the over-timid industrialists stuck firmly together. Only with great difficulties were the import duties on wheat and flour lowered slightly during the years of famine, and, during the years of industrial strain, the duties on coal, iron, steel, machines, and wool. In principle, however, France clung to protective tariffs. Napoleon III therefore conducted secret negotiations with Cobden, the British Minister, and in February 1860 a surprised world was informed of the conclusion of a trade treaty. All import bans were revoked and duties greatly reduced. Raw materials were to be imported entirely free from duty and finished articles subject only to a moderate rate. Britain, for her part, made considerable concessions: French silks and fashion goods were to be completely exempted from customs duty, and that on wine and spirits would be very slight. "Wherever soil and climate produce natural wealth, such wealth should be enjoyed by all nations"—that, in the words of a contemporary, was the principle underlying the trade treaty. It inaugurated a new age, the age of free trade.

Four hundred dismayed French industrialists requested an audience with the Emperor in the hope of making him realize the danger which threatened French industry from that of Britain. The Emperor did not even receive them. There would be no more misguided consideration for manufacturers muddling along in the old way, for backward producers or inefficient farmers! Prices should rule unchecked. Anyone unable to supply at the current price in the world market would have to get out of the race sooner or later. Only he who could produce cheaply had any prospects. Close co-operation between Britain and France was bound to benefit both nations, even if some individual or other suffered. The Emperor was proved right.

In the single decade between 1857 and 1866 French foreign trade was doubled: it rose from 3,100,000,000 francs to 6,200,000,000 francs, and by 1869 had increased to 8,000,000,000 francs. To everybody's surprise the French textile industry survived successfully in the face of British competition. And indeed why not? In the face of danger the French had made a supreme effort: they had invented new patterns, new machines, new colour effects. For centuries they had been the leaders of fashion. Why then should they now be defeated by the British? They could import their cotton at the same prices as their British rivals—the merchants of Liverpool saw to that as much as those of Rouen, Paris, or Lille. The workmen contented themselves with the same wages, especially as wheat was now imported cheaply and the cost of living had correspondingly declined.

True, Britain was able to step up its woollen cloth exports to France considerably, but in exchange she now imported French silks which, until recently, had been almost prohibitively expensive because of the high import duty. In the 1860's British exports of cotton cloth to France did not yet exceed those to the Netherlands. At the great World Exhibition in Paris in 1867 Gladstone remarked with surprise, "Britain has derived comparatively little advantage from the trade treaty, while agricultural and industrial production in France has undergone a remarkable increase." The other European countries were still reluctant to accept the idea of free trade, but they lowered customs tariffs and slowly—so as to harm no interested party—integrated themselves in world trade.

In 1862 Prussia signed a customs agreement with France which envisaged much lower tariffs than hitherto; the duties on the import of cotton goods were greatly reduced, and so were those on iron, silk, leather, and textiles. The State was anxious to open a wider market for its growing industry, and it felt strong enough to compete with France and even with Britain. Reluctantly the remaining members of the German Customs Union followed suit.

The heart of this world-wide business was the city of London. Every day, indeed every hour, ships arrived in port from all over the world—for the most part windjammers, but also, more and more often, steamships making fast in the new docks. The West India Docks, much admired at one time, were surpassed by the St Catherine Dock. A ship of 3000 to 4000 tons was now turned round within a week, whereas at the beginning of the century a whole month or even six weeks had been needed for unloading an East Indiaman of no more than 500 tons.

Along the docks stood the vast warehouses where huge quantities of sugar, rum, coffee, tea, tobacco, silk, wheat, wine, wool, cotton, linen, copper, tin, lead, spices, timber, coal, iron and steel, ivory and ostrich-feathers accumulated. Everything was warehoused there. Since 1803 it had been possible to store merchandise in bond; without special dues these goods could be kept there in order to be imported either into England or resold abroad. Anyone needing merchandise in a hurry would turn to London. There he would find whatever he required.

The banks paid advances on these warehoused stocks. Just as all the world's important shipping firms had to be represented in London, so the City contained all the big banking firms or, at least, their agents. There were the big private banking-houses like that of Rothschild; since 1834 there had been additionally the first big share-issuing bank, the London and Westminster Bank. The London banks granted short credits all over the world; they discounted bills, and accepted deposits which could be withdrawn at any time. The banks were backed by the Bank of England, which, since 1830, also accepted foreign bills.

The big insurance companies provided cover against every conceivable risk—fire and water, accidents in transit and theft, shipwreck or confiscation on the high seas or in foreign lands. Powerful life assurance companies accumulated a vast capital which they put at the disposal of commerce. The biggest of them all was Lloyd's, who, against an appropriate premium, would relieve other insurers of part of their risks by way of re-insurance.

The Stock Exchange was the hub of the City: there the shares of the most important companies, international loans, and bills of exchange bearing the names of prominent merchants anywhere in the world were dealt in. Should a new railway be built in the United States? Could Brazil afford a new port? Should new blast furnaces be blown in in the Ruhr? All that was decided, more often than not, on the London Stock Exchange. It was there that all great financial transactions were discussed, that countries, entrepreneurs, and firms were weighed and appraised, and their credit assessed, approved, or rejected. A hint was enough for the Stock Exchanges of Frankfurt, Amsterdam, Paris, Vienna, or Berlin to show reserve. A warning was enough for the

52. Morning scene at Billingsgate market, London (wood engraving by Gustave Doré, 1872)

Rothschilds or the Bleichröders to keep off a particular loan, a particular credit or a particular share.

On the commodity exchanges—the wool exchange, the iron and steel exchange, the coal exchange, and the Baltic exchange—the world market prices were discussed and fixed which might bring the small farmer in the United States to the verge of despair, which might decide the fate of a sheep-breeder in Patagonia, or the future of a copper-mine high up in the Chilean Andes. It was in London that all the news accumulated which alone made it possible to form a true picture of what was really going on in the world. To fix prices one had to know everything: the condition of the crops in Wisconsin as much as in Southern Russia and France, the size of the harvest of sugar-cane, tea, and coffee, the production of the coal-mines in Britain, in the Ruhr, and in Pittsburg, the volume of copper manufacture in Utah and in Chile, the development plans for the zinc-mines of Upper Silesia and the tin-mines of Bolivia.

Was there going to be a revolution in the Argentine? Was the Tsar getting ready to pounce on the Turks? Would the Paris Government fall? Was the Vienna Government letting itself in for risky adventures in the Balkans? The Stock Exchanges would buzz with reports and rumours, with official and private assessments of the situation. More and more accurate statistics became available. Nowhere were even the smallest details studied with such eagerness and close attention as on the London commodity exchanges. And nowhere were the first signs of a political earthquake noticed sooner than on the London Stock Exchange. The flow of information had greatly improved since Reuter founded his great news agency in 1849. In every important centre on earth his representatives and correspondents were gathering the latest news.

All the world listened to London in order to form a picture of the world situation. And rightly so. For it was in London that all threads met—those of commerce and those of politics. London was the hub of an empire which girdled the whole world; British ambassadors and consuls were continually sending home reports from all major capitals and trading-centres. Now and again the Government would tip off the Stock Exchange or the big banks—secret information based on an intimate acquaintance with a foreign country, information that might foreshadow measures to be decided in the Cabinet Room.

London was the great 'clearing centre' of international trade, a vast pot into which one might confidently throw any demand or asset in order to pull out, in exchange, those currencies or bills which one happened to need at the moment, since all transactions were effected via London. Nowhere on earth were savings deposits, money reserves, claims, or Government securities as secure as in England. The currency stood unassailable. "Safe as the Bank of England" was a phrase which stated no more than the truth. Jealously the City of London saw to it that the reputation of its banks remained untarnished. It kept an eye on all bills discounted in the City, indeed on all bills drawn anywhere in the world. If any were noted for protest, the foreign representative would at once report to his firm's headquarters in the City. Were other firms likely to be affected? An occasional protested bill here or there did not, of course, matter greatly. Some speculators, mostly small fry, might occasionally bite off more than they could chew; inevitably some merchant or other might go bankrupt. But if protested bills were to accumulate, if even solid firms and old business friends should begin to totter, the greatest caution would be indicated.

The City of London had the best overall picture of the situation—the quantities stocked in its warehouses, the number of bills drawn, the amount of merchandise insured against fire or theft, the shipments still at sea. Perhaps the harvest in Eastern Europe had been a failure, but that in America had been good—appropriate steps would have to be taken at once. Perhaps the American railways required large consignments of steel rails which Germany's young steel industry was in a position to supply. Offers would go to and fro, prices would fluctuate upward and downward.

It was a daily struggle. Even though statistics were now providing reliable data for assessments, the practical merchant nevertheless liked to keep his ears open for what he could pick up on the Stock Exchange. What was its mood? What were the brokers saying? Were customers settling promptly? What were suppliers demanding? Were prices steady or were they unsteady? It was on the London Stock Exchange that the world market price was settled. The price was at the centre of all business. Throughout the world calculations were made in pounds sterling to facilitate comparison of quotations on the Stock Exchanges of Buenos Aires, Singapore, and Berlin. The pound sterling was firmly based on gold. The nineteenth century trusted blindly to the promise of the Bank of England to exchange a pound note for its full value in gold at any time. The Latin Mint Union—France, Italy, Belgium, Spain, and Switzerland—gave up its so-called silver currency in favour of gold: one franc equalled eighty German Pfennig. From 1872 the Mark was a gold currency.

The international Stock Exchanges were not interested in tariffs.

Each country could tax its consumers as it chose; the London Stock Exchange practised its world-wide free trade outside all customs barriers—free on board ship for outgoing freight, and inclusive of freight costs and insurance in the port of destination for all incoming freight. "Fob" (free on board) and "Cif" (cost insurance freight) became internationally accepted concepts.

Everywhere, tremendous changes were brought about by this worldwide business. New railroads traversed the Middle West, the Argentine pampas, and Southern Russia. That meant new orders for rails, locomotives, and rolling stock. Steamships were now sailing on all the oceans. The steamship enabled Britain to recapture her supremacy in shipping which she had temporarily lost to the Americans with their fast-sailing clippers. Steamships of 3000 to 5000 tons were built on the Mersey and on the Clyde. The *Great Eastern*, built by Brunel, had the then unparalleled displacement of 19,000 tons. New blast furnaces had to be built and blown in, factories had to increase their output of machines, cotton cloth, and chemicals.

Suppose these elaborately woven threads of world trade were to come apart? The first shock came with the American Civil War. Ruthlessly the Northern States blockaded the rebellious South. There was no cotton coming on the market; it was rotting on the plantations in the Southern States while the industrialists of Manchester, Mulhouse, and Saxony were anxiously wondering how long their stocks would last.

All over the world cotton was being purchased—in the East Indies, in the West Indies, in South America, and in Africa. New plantations were laid out. No sooner had the shortage been overcome than peace came. Within a few years the cotton plantations in the devastated South were as prosperous as ever—even without slaves.

The population of Europe increased tremendously during the nineteenth century: from 187,000,000 in 1800 it rose to 266,000,000 about 1850 and to 401,000,000 by the end of the century. And there was nothing of the famine or starvation which the English author Malthus had prophesied for the rising flood of humanity. But then, what did Malthus know about world commerce?

Foodstuffs were imported by merchants from all over the world. The merchants would have their agents in Chicago, in Buenos Aires, in New York, in Cincinnati, in Odessa, and in Hamburg. Carefully they would study Stock Exchange quotations and turnovers, harvest figures and consumer statistics, money in circulation and the amount of bills offered. They would study market analyses, orders, and requirements. Where was anything in short supply? Where were unsaleable quantities of grain, wool, or cotton accumulating? Where did the supply of iron, steel, and wool exceed the demand?

The flood of orders continued to rise and prices to soar. In 1873 came the collapse. It hit the world of commerce with tremendous force: thousands of merchant-houses, many bearing old-established and venerable names, crashed overnight, many a speculator vanished from the scene, and industrial production dropped dramatically.

World-wide economics are an exceedingly complex piece of machinery—each little cog passes on its motion to its neighbour. The money spent by a consumer in, say, Dresden reaches a *fazendeiro* in São Paulo by a long, roundabout route. Along that route lie countless transactions. Only rarely was it possible to trade one commodity directly for another now that raw materials for industry accounted for such a large portion of world trade. The textile mills needed cotton, but the cotton-planters needed tractors and machines.

Commerce had so stimulated agricultural and industrial production throughout the world that the resulting low prices positively demanded a reorientation to new suppliers. Neither for their food supplies nor for their industrial raw materials did nations any longer rely on their own native territory. But was the European peasant to compete with the American farmer who employed the latest harvesting machines in his enormous fields, or with the Chinese coolie, the Egyptian fellah, or the American Negro? Could a manufacturer in the Rhineland supply as cheaply as the mammoth trust in Pittsburg which sold its steel at ruinous prices in order to crush its poor competitors? Were all workers and peasants to leave their homes and to move to wherever better and cheaper production was possible? "Free competition is a menace!" was the new cry that went up in Europe. Protective tariffs were the new order of the day.

Industrialists allied themselves with the farmers in order to regulate and stabilize the home markets and freeze prices behind high customs barriers. In the world markets it was impossible to sell at cost price. There one had to sell at the ruling market price, or indeed at a competitive price much below that in the home market. The bill, of course, had to be footed by the domestic consumer. His support as a voter, however, was gained by appealing to him as an interested party—as a farmer, as an industrial worker, or as an entrepreneur. Not because commerce had failed, but because of its triumph through low prices did the call for protective tariffs now ring out. In Le Havre the Americans were selling their beef and pork, as well as mutton from the Argentine, at half the price demanded by the French farmers. Wool from Australia and the Argentine effortlessly undercut that from Silesia, Mecklenburg, and Saxony. In 1885 the price of wheat in France dropped to 165 francs per ton. In 1879 Germany went over to protective tariffs; France followed suit two years later. The road to disaster had been chosen: every decade the tariffs were raised. To each protective tariff decreed by one country another would reply with tariffs of its own, in order to protect its native producers. No concessions anywhere along the line! Each individual customs issue must be separately negotiated. Every concession meant a loss to some domestic interested party. Indeed, if one was not careful prices at home might drop! And that was a terrible thought!

Friedrich List wrote in 1840:

> Commerce is productive of values in an entirely different way from agriculture and manufactures. These produce goods, while commerce merely organizes the exchange of these goods. Commerce does not care what effect the goods imported by it will have on the nation's morals, welfare or power. It imports poisons and medicines. It undermines entire nations by opium and brandy. In wartime it supplies weapons and ammunition to the enemy. It would, if only that were possible, gladly sell fields and meadows to foreign countries and, the last patch of land sold, would take ship and export itself. . . .

Another author, Méline, the spokesman of France's opposition to free trade, declared in 1891:

> How can they compare the privileged agriculture of the young nations with our own unfortunate farmers? Ceaselessly, with prodigious efforts and considerable sacrifices they must rejuvenate a soil weakened by centuries of cultivation. And all the time they are crushed by heavy taxes and the harsh necessity of military service. Is it really so unfair to demand from foreign agricultural produce an equalization of this injustice, for which our own farmers, surely, are not responsible?

"Kneel down in humility before the simple woollen stockings of the peasant!" he called upon the Minister of Finance. "Protect the poor wretch!"

Only in the United States did the farmers side with the free traders because they wanted to market their vast surpluses in Europe. In

Europe, on the other hand, the peasants allied themselves with the industrialists in order to force protective tariff bills through their parliaments.

The small backyard workshops, the countless family-owned coal-mines, the small manufactories which had been only too pleased to have a big merchant pre-empt their entire production, advance them the cost of their raw materials, and pay cash upon delivery, had grown into gigantic enterprises of world-wide fame, technically efficient, financially independent, managed by captains of industry who knew the world and had mastered the rules of banking as much as of market-ing, and backed by the powerful banks whose representatives sat on their boards of directors.

Business secrets existed no longer. The leading industrial nations sent their consuls to all foreign countries; everywhere the big European banks had their representatives—the British, the Germans, the French, the Spanish, the Italians. And in all those countries they found fellow-countrymen who had been washed up there by some destiny or other—as settlers, as soldiers, as scientists, or as merchants. They founded their colonies where all new developments, in the ports and in the capital, were discussed among themselves.

Whenever an industrial firm received an enquiry about a product it would obtain from its country's consul, from the bank, or from one of the newly founded Chambers of Commerce, some information about the commercial standing of the enquirer. Manufacturers' agents no longer had to ask the export firms whether any orders had been received from overseas. An industrial enterprise which supplied wholesale, or which built bridges, port installations, electric power-stations, under-ground railways, tramways, or skyscrapers would send out its own representative who would work for them exclusively. As a rule they would also send along a technician, so that expert advice could be given on the spot to a prospective customer.

Before very long it became generally known that the German manu-facturers were glad to deliver even without the mediation of an ex-porter. Foreign merchants began to come to Germany, to inspect the latest products for themselves, and to place orders. The fairs in Ger-many changed their character. Merchandise itself was no longer dis-played for sale, but only samples; after the fair a factory would fulfil any orders 'as per sample.' Thousands, tens of thousands, hundreds of thousands of foreign customers would visit Leipzig twice a year in order to stock up with merchandise. A manufacturer with whom an order had been placed in Leipzig would then make tactful enquiries with the banks, the Chambers of Commerce, and the big international information bureaux whether Mr So-and-so in Buenos Aires or Singapore or Shanghai was good for credit. The postal system was delivering letters faster and faster, eventually also by aircraft. The telegraph could flash messages at lightning speed to any part of the world.

Whereas in the past a manufacturer's name had usually remained unknown—the Hamburg exporters used carefully to remove all names of firms from the merchandise they handled—present-day industry attaches much importance to the trade-mark. It guarantees quality, measure, and weight, and frequently prescribes the price. The names of big manufacturers—Ford, Coty, Borsalino, or Zeiss—are known the world over. Thanks to advertising the public has come to know the slogans of each make.

A large part of commerce soon consisted of marketing. A manufacturer's marketing apparatus became of decisive importance; astonishing successes were achieved by some manufacturers through skilful advertising. They might seize a large, possibly the overwhelming, part of a particular market. They would create new markets for merchandise hardly dreamed of even by the technicians a few decades earlier. The centre of commercial life shifted from trade to production. In Pittsburg, in Newcastle, in St Gobain, in Milan, in Essen, in Höchst, in Frankfurt, in Berlin, and in Pilsen vast enterprises grew up which supplied their products to the whole world. The industrialist everywhere had gained in standing and influence; he might now employ thousands or tens of thousands of workers who owed their livelihood to his business efficiency. All eyes were centred on men like Rockefeller and Carnegie, Schneider-Creuzot and Skoda, Pirelli, Krupp and Bayer. The merchant was being eclipsed.

Wealth was concentrated in a few hands; it belonged almost exclusively to the big entrepreneurs, the big factory owners. Before the Civil War the United States had five millionaires; there may in fact have been a few more. By the end of the century the number had grown to 3800. Nine-tenths of the national wealth belonged to one-tenth of the population in this democratic country which knew no class distinctions, where newsboy might rise to millionaire. His ascent, however, would be more often by way of industry—*i.e.*, by way of production.

In all countries the governments were being urged to ensure a market for the rising industries. By far the best thing would be to divide up the home market, to keep it free from ruinous competition. Cartels and trusts were formed to fix quotas and regulate prices. Competitors were to be eliminated—or else bought up and incorporated in the giant trust, the steel trust, the oil trust, or the tobacco trust. Once all rivals had been absorbed the markets could be regulated at will.

The free world market was getting smaller and smaller. Britain alone upheld the banner of free trade, but there too an increasingly vocal group of interest began to oppose it—not only the spokesmen of her badly neglected agriculture, but also the industrialists who were watching enviously as their competitors in America and Germany built up an increasingly powerful industry behind high customs barriers. Joseph Chamberlain demanded protective tariffs for the British Empire. Even in the free markets political influence was to ensure advantages over one's tiresome rivals. Trade agreements and tariff regulations were becoming almost more important than competitive prices and quality.

Each power was trying to secure the largest possible territories as markets for its industries. The mailed fist was breaking down locked doors. As early as 1853 an American fleet of warships compelled Japan to admit foreign merchants; shortly afterwards the British and French jointly stormed the Taku forts. China had to permit the establishment of Legations in Peking and of Consulates in all the major towns—but it was not until 1853 that the first foreign Ambassador was received in audience by the Emperor.

The Chinese market was open once more—the much-admired empire of the many millions of human beings. But would they prove to be as many consumers? In the sixteenth century the emperor had expelled the Portuguese when their colonists in Ning-po had behaved improperly. The Dutch had had to be content with sitting in Formosa and dealing from there with Chinese traders from Canton; the country itself had remained barred to them. Such considerations were alien to the new age. Industries lived by finding new markets. And since the world market was made up of separate home markets each nation had to stake its claim wherever it was strong enough—or believed itself

53. The Chinese market is opened up. Quay and harbour of Shanghai, 1860
(contemporary wood engraving)

strong enough. This was demonstrated by the British, when, in the Opium War, they compelled China to admit the drug. Power was everything! Thus, the age of protective barriers gave birth, almost inevitably, to the age of imperialism.

With the end of free trade the prolonged period of peace also came to an end—the *pax Britannica*, the period when merchants had measured the goods of the whole world by one yardstick alone—price.

16
The Art of Selling

———— ᴠᴠᴠᴠᴠᴠ◎ᴠᴠᴠᴠᴠᴠ ————

IN 1852 Aristide Boucicaut opened the first department store in the heart of Paris. It was a tremendous success.

The comparatively small shop became crowded with women. They all wanted to see the Bon Marché. Naturally, the same articles might be bought at any of the large, old-established shops, the *magasins de nouveautés,* but everybody wanted to see for themselves how Boucicaut displayed his materials, how he treated his customers, how he made his sales. And the low prices he charged! It was all rather bewildering.

What a merchant needs most is ideas. And courage. Boucicaut drastically reduced his profit margin. Whereas the Paris retailers would charge, on an average, 40 per cent. above their purchase price, Boucicaut contented himself with 20 per cent. His calculation was simple enough: provided his quick turnover allowed him to keep his general overheads below 15 per cent., he would still be able to make a net profit of 5 per cent. In this way he could be 20 per cent. cheaper than his competitors.

No self-respecting artisan, let alone an elegant shopkeeper, would have stood behind his counter from morning till night for a measly 5 per cent. Surely for the sake of such a meagre profit a man could not take the risk of his materials going out of vogue and remaining unsold—especially now that fashions were changing so quickly. And besides, so many customers expected credit!

As if it mattered how much a merchant made on a single item of merchandise! As the turnover increased so would his profit—and 5 per cent. on brisk sales might yield a great deal more than 40 per cent.

with a slow turnover and losses from unsold stock. Boucicaut had calculated correctly: his overheads did not in fact exceed 15 per cent.

Another idea of his was fixed prices. Boucicaut would not even consider bargaining; he marked all his goods with their final price and declared flatly that on no account would that price be reduced—not even if an indignant customer flounced out of the shop.

No customer had a price reduced by as much as a centime—however much she pleaded, hesitated, or feigned indecision. No matter whether the customer was a celebrated opera star, a noble baroness, or the wife of an all-powerful minister: at Boucicaut's they had to pay the same price as the wife of a minor civil servant. They were all customers.

Every customer could see for herself the price of every article: it was prominently displayed above each counter. At leisure, unhurried and unworried by assistants, the customer could make up her mind whether a purchase was really worth while. In point of fact it nearly always was; after all, Boucicaut's price was well below the ultimate figure to which some other shopkeeper might be 'beaten down' after endless bargaining.

But was not the very charm of shopping lost as a result—that duel of flattery and lament between purchaser and vendor? And was not every discount allowed by the vendor to the customer a token of courtesy, of respect for the customer's name, position, or even just youth and personal charm? Was Monsieur Boucicaut really so ungallant as to decline to discuss price altogether?

As recently as the eighteenth century retailers used to be punished for distributing handbills offering articles at fixed prices, because such advertisement ran counter to the rules of the guilds and the spirit of commerce.

Nonsense, said Boucicaut. If after protracted haggling a customer had at last got a particularly fine length of material at a reduced price she would leave the shop much pleased. But the news would spread round. Immediately her neighbour would burst in, full of indignation, and throw a frightful scene; what else could a merchant do but reduce the price for her as well? And before he knew where he was all his women customers would be haggling for hours. No—only by charging fixed prices could all customers be kept satisfied in the long run. Nobody was obliged to buy anything in his shop, Boucicaut announced. Anyone could spend as long as he or she wished inspecting his displays and studying his prices. A lady should never feel under an obligation to buy even the smallest trifle. Why not walk right in, ladies? No over-zealous assistant will pester you. We like you to see everything for yourselves. Everything is openly displayed.

In the old type of shop all materials used to be kept at the back on high shelves. The assistant would ask in detail what precisely his customer desired; he would consider carefully what colour and which pattern would be most suitable. He would then climb up a ladder or perhaps descend into the basement in order to produce some carefully wrapped bale or other. "This is the very thing for you, madam!" As if a lady could make up her mind so quickly! But the assistant would not let go. The fish was in the net and must not be allowed to escape. For that very reason customers would sometimes rather not enter a shop at all.

Boucicaut caught his fish not in the net but with the bait of cheap prices, of irresistibly beautiful materials and brilliant colours. He knew the power of his bait: it would bring a customer back even after she had left the shop. Never harangue a customer. The lady must ask herself whether she can afford to miss this unique opportunity. She must be allowed time to day-dream a little; this magnificent turquoise cloth with its flowing folds would suit her magnificently. What a tempta-tion! And the low price! The price, Boucicaut knew, would allay all doubts more readily than the most eloquent salesman.

His materials were to be displayed well spread out, so that a customer could see more of them, make a better choice, and become really enthusiastic at the magnificent sight. First of all the curious had to be drawn into the shop—and nothing did that more effectively than the reassuring, though deceptive, knowledge that there was no need to buy anything and that one could always walk out again.

Boucicaut declared himself ready to take back any merchandise with-out question, either exchanging it for something else or by repayment of the price in full. No customer of his was ever to regret a purchase merely because she had allowed herself to be carried away too readily and now was finding herself landed with something she did not really want. If she discovered some other material which she liked better she need only say so. Instantly Boucicaut would exchange it. No need, ladies, to suffer torments of indecision. Make your choice, take your goods, pay your money. If you regret your purchase or if you are not satisfied with what you have bought, or if you can get it cheaper else-where—Boucicaut will gladly take it back.

In vast numbers the curious Parisians streamed into his shop. They saw, they admired, they bought; only very few thought of changing their purchases. They might have entered the shop mistrustfully or doubtfully, but they were swept off their feet; the ladies were positively burrowing among the piles of material. Boucicaut's sales in 1852 were worth 500,000 francs; in 1860 they totalled 5,000,000. Bon Marché became the model for department stores everywhere.

Boucicaut had started with materials and haberdashery; before long he added dresses and skirts, and eventually underwear, accessories, and shoes. He was a man of ever new ideas—so much so that his partner was getting cold feet. He sold his share. That obsessed merchant Boucicaut could make his experiments by himself—surely, that kind of thing could bring no good in the long run. But it did. In 1870 his turnover reached the downright fantastic sum of 20,000,000 francs. Boucicaut's profit was a full million. At first there had been mockery and sneers, then excited opposition by retailers, indignant criticism, and eventually imitators. Chauchard and Hériot opened a department store for a somewhat more exacting clientele—the Louvre. Jaluzet, at one time the manager of a department in Boucicaut's firm, founded the Printemps, which became an irresistible magnet for all visitors to Paris. Every one would go there to see with amazement what surprises and attractions the city of lights, the centre of the second empire, had to offer.

The face of Paris was changing rapidly. The wide boulevards which the Emperor had laid out through the old narrow quarters brought light and air into the city centre. An elegant, leisured public would stroll down the wide streets to watch other passers-by and to view the new fashions and the shop windows. The day of the old tiny shops was gone, shops which were sometimes housed in basements with only a miserable lantern throwing light on a dismal room, on merchandise piled higgledy-piggledy on primitive wooden racks, stacked unlovingly, out of fashion and crumpled. The customer had to content himself with what there was. If he did not find what he wanted the shopkeeper would let him walk out unmoved; fussy customers with requirements out of the ordinary were only a nuisance.

This pattern of trade had its advantages and its drawbacks. A small merchant could rely on his circle of customers. He would greet his customers like old friends, he would ask how the family were, and there would be some discussion of the latest news before getting down to business. The customer would rely on getting good sound merchandise which would keep for years. The customers, who would normally know one another, made or marred a merchant's reputation. No merchant would try to lure away another's customers. The mere idea was indignantly repudiated. The eighteenth-century police regulations of the city of Mainz stipulated expressly that "no man shall take away

54. The Magasin du Printemps department store in Paris, 1883

another man's sale or increase the price of a merchandise by higher bidding; no man shall intrude upon another man's bargain or drive so hard a bargain himself that another citizen is ruined thereby." Until the middle of the nineteenth century a retailer believed that to sell in a way damaging to his fellow citizen would not be profitable to him in the end.

While a business was run by its owner—who might have had an assistant or two, although these did little more than fetch and carry—a customer could always argue about the price. The merchant had to make certain concessions to a well-established customer or a lady of standing merely because they invariably came back to his shop. In these circumstances, naturally, there was no need for any special 'display.' The well-known customer would state her wish, and the shopkeeper would at once know what she wanted. From some corner of his shop he would produce the merchandise which was exactly what his customer had in mind. Or else he would produce a big surprise, some material or implement which a traveller had only recently offered him. Though, strictly speaking, he had had that particular customer in mind even at the time of buying it.

At the beginning of the nineteenth century the retail shops in Berlin—and no doubt the same applied to all European cities—were still divided into two main categories: the ones where merchandise was weighed (principally foodstuffs) and the ones where it was cut (textiles). Only later did the shops arise where goods were sold by number: ironmongery, glassware, fancy goods—all those things which are covered in France by the term *quincaillerie*.

All that was no longer in line with the splendour of Paris under the second empire. Marshals and generals, senior ministerial officials, the landed nobility, and wealthy manufacturers all wanted luxury. Napoleon III wanted his Court and his people to enjoy riches and splendour.

In Lyons Jacquard's mechanical looms were producing silks in almost inexhaustible quantities. Artists were vying with each other in ever new designs. Everything hinged on the ability to sell—on bringing the merchandise to the notice of the elegant ladies and on pricing it in such a way that the ordinary womenfolk of the country could snatch for themselves a small portion of the general luxury. It was so much easier to make one's prudent husband part with his money if one strolled past those magnificent shop-window displays. Behind the large window—the glass industry had also made much progress—there was an enchanting new model; who could resist the temptation?

Visitors came from far afield, attracted by the reputation of the Paris fashions and by the great World Exhibition of 1867. They came, they saw, they admired, and they imitated—not only the dressmakers and manufacturers, but also the retailers. Boucicaut's success swept away all doubts. This, clearly, was the way to handle one's customers, to compute one's prices, and to organize one's sales if one wanted to achieve a big turnover and to make real money.

In America, Macy founded his first department store in New York in 1858; Wanamaker followed suit in Philadelphia in 1861; Marshall Field came next. In London, the department stores of Harrods, John Lewis, Whiteleys, and Selfridges appeared in 1909. In Germany the first department store was opened by Karstadt in 1881. Shortly afterwards, three big department stores sprang up in Berlin one after another, all of them in Leipziger Strasse—Jandorf, Wertheim, and Tietz.

All department stores firmly adhered to Boucicaut's four principles: big turnover, fixed prices, no obligation to buy, and generous exchange. On one occasion a wealthy customer acquired an expensive chandelier at Wertheim's; six months later he died. His heirs, having no use for the ostentatious piece, enquired at Wertheim's whether they would buy back the chandelier at a reduced price. The firm immediately declared themselves ready to reimburse the full purchase price. It was a good advertisement.

Advertisement! That was the secret of this great success. To begin with, the customers had to be lured into the store. For that purpose it needed a continuous succession of new 'hits,' articles which 'went' because of their exceptionally low price. They might come from a particularly favourable bulk purchase, perhaps from bankrupt stock or from an experimental consignment offered at a special price; or perhaps a buyer might have discovered a new line which was the result of some technical innovation, of a new invention or a new process. A tremendous stir was produced, for instance, by the first sewing machines, and later by the first electric appliances. That was exactly what industry needed. Under the old system of retail trade, when shopkeepers could not afford experiments, it had been impossible to increase sales quickly enough. The public had to be made to buy, and to buy more. Now whatever the machines produced had to be sold. If at first industry had supplied poor-quality articles the quality was now improving from year to year so that, before long, machines were working more efficiently, more cheaply, and often even more durably than the small craftsmen.

Besides, the ladies wanted variety. The small shops had called themselves *magasins de nouveautés*; Printemps was an even more seductive name. Better still was the name which Émile Zola gave to the department store of his novel, *Au Bonheur des Dames*. Provided the ladies could be won over to the new materials, provided they could be educated to move with the fashions, and every spring and every autumn to look out for whatever was new on the market, then the manufacturers need worry no longer. From the fashionable capital city with its dazzling shops the new spirit radiated outward, and with it the public's higher demands and a livelier style of living—first to the suburbs, to engulf the middle class and the *petit-bourgeoisie*, then to the provinces, and eventually to the young countries beyond the seas. One day the new fashions would penetrate even to the 'savages'; their demand, too, would be stimulated, and they too would be engulfed by the restless bustle of the industrial age.

The department store was the pacemaker of that age. On its vast floors, amid the throng of customers, during the great seasonal sales the fashionable new materials and articles emerged victorious over old habits, over prejudice, over traditional customs which had stubbornly survived until then. The great cities grew at an astonishing pace. New means of transport—tramways and later motor-cars—brought new groups of customers from the suburbs, from neighbouring villages, and from provincial towns. Technical progress favoured the development of the department store.

At first the shopkeepers complained that the department stores were robbing them of their customers by selling rubbish, the cheapest kind of factory-made article, whereas they themselves had to demand appropriately high prices for good craftsmanship—in other words, they could not even begin to compete. They painted a picture of a ruined middle class. But in actual fact the number of shops increased. In Prussia, for instance, there had been only 97 independent merchants per 10,000 of the population in 1843; by 1895 the number had risen to 240. In Saxony, more highly industrialized, it had risen from 256 to 637.

Fixed prices relieved the owner from serving in his shop himself; he could now leave most of the selling to his employees and devote himself to organization, calculation, buying, and advertising. From a craft—in the Middle Ages it was still a guild—retail trade developed into big business, into a specialized, highly ramified undertaking. The merchandise was artistically displayed in the shop-windows so that every customer could see and choose. Nowadays many retailers owe nearly half their turnover to a well-arranged window display. Even if a customer does not want to buy what she sees in the window, the model displayed may nevertheless induce her to step into the shop and make further enquiries. Once she is inside the greatest obstacle is overcome. So as to lure even the hurrying passer-by into a shop many big firms nowadays build huge arcades with continuous window displays along both sides; for the sake of this they gladly sacrifice a considerable part of their floorspace even though each square foot costs a great deal of money in the big shopping streets. Once the passer-by feels "inside the shop," even for a moment, half the battle is won.

Thus the second half of the nineteenth century witnessed the rise of the famous shopping streets which attract visitors to this day—the Rue de la Paix in Paris, Regent Street in London, Leipziger Strasse in Berlin, and the Galleria Vittorio Emanuele in Milan. Industry sees to it that ever new goods are offered for sale and that fashions change.

The high rents in the city centre can be met only if turnover increases correspondingly. To increase the price of the individual piece of merchandise, to charge some fabulous figure, does not pay if a customer can buy the same item at a lower price a few yards down the road. An annoyed customer is a customer lost. A merchant must calculate precisely and give the most courteous service to each of his customers.

Now the customer is queen. She may stroll from shop-window to shop-window, viewing the luxuries displayed, comparing the price-tickets. She may enter a shop, without any embarrassment, ask for a particular item, inspect a whole mountain of patterns and models—and walk out again to consider her purchase carefully once more. A shopkeeper must remain polite and obliging; he must never show his irritation. Perhaps that exacting customer will come again one day when he has the right material or the pretty little hat she covets, and if its price is competitive.

Inwardly a shopkeeper may often groan under the excessive demands of his customers: goods of the most awkward and intractable shape are to be packed up neatly and conveniently, even the smallest package is to be delivered to the customer's home. But if a merchant does not keep abreast of the times he will lose his customer, for his rival at the next corner makes up very tidy parcels and naturally has everything delivered to a customer's house. It is a far cry from the days when a housewife would carry home all her shopping in a large basket or when she took jugs and jars with her if she went to the grocers.

That kind of thing no longer fits into the elegant boulevards of Paris, into the affluent streets of the big cities. The paper industry supplies high-quality wrapping-paper, smooth, plain white, or in pastel colours, and pretty string or tape is supplied by the cord-making industry. These things used to be precious luxuries, but have now become a matter of course.

More and more novelties are stocked in the shops. Only a well-run specialized shop can now carry the thousands of different articles which an exacting customer may demand. And there is no end to those demands. And if a customer is not offered the thing she has asked for she will go straight to one's competitor. The widest possible range of goods must be carried. Stocks have become the retailer's nightmare. Anything that is not sold quickly becomes out of date.

At first slow selling lines could still be sold without great loss in the provinces because there the fashions were months, if not years, behind Paris. By the time the styles of Paris, London, or Berlin had spread to the provinces they had become *passé* in the big cities. Boucicaut, however, introduced big sales in Paris itself. The sales of his day were like great battles, with customers fighting furiously over unique bargains.

They were occasions no one could afford to miss. There were always some articles which were 'dumped' well below cost price— some delicious soap, a pretty handkerchief, or a delightful silk remnant. This bait invariably paid for itself; the delighted customer would take with her so many other things. And, more important still, she would come back regularly. In Boucicaut's emporium all merchandise was openly displayed, the prices were clearly marked, and the assistants had to do no more than wrap up the goods bought and hand them over to the customer. That kind of selling could be done by any young girl from the country; she merely had to be taught to be courteous and pleasant to the customer and never to lose her patience.

All customers were equal. The servant-girl might rub shoulders with the countess, the charwoman with the wife of the Minister. They all paid good money and were entitled to be treated as customers. A shop's clientele was composed of thousands and thousands of simple people; these together would spend far more money than a few high-born ladies who came to buy the most expensive lace. Quantity matters, was Boucicaut's motto, not a high profit margin on an individual article. The main task was to gain a mass clientele, to flatter the customer and give her courage to enter an exclusive shop filled with elegant ladies.

Slowly and laboriously a modern merchant educates his public. Dazzling shop-windows, attractive displays, clearly marked fixed prices, to save a customer the embarrassment of first asking and then being told that the hat in the window, a pair of gloves, or some delightful handkerchiefs are well beyond her reach, and courteous service—all these have but the single purpose of giving the customer self-assurance. At first the ordinary public fought shy of the elegant shops. They had always been told: these things are not for the likes of you, they are for 'the quality.' In modern conditions the art of salesmanship no longer consists of a soft, persuasive voice, of skilful argument, and of countless little psychological tricks of the trained salesman. What matters is that a merchant should stock the right goods, demand a reasonable price, be able to give reliable advice so that a customer buys only what will really give her pleasure—for then she will return. The old-style small shopkeeper who merely weighed or measured his merchandise had to yield to the properly trained modern shop-assistant, who must be thoroughly acquainted with the goods he sells, be able to answer all questions with lucidity and assurance, and to distinguish between various manufactures and explain the advantages and disadvantages of the one compared with the other. A customer nowadays expects expert advice when he enters a specialized shop.

Even the small shopkeeper, until recently looked down upon, gained in esteem and social standing. Respectable citizens at first shook their heads over the 'showy' shop at the corner, its big shop-windows and its expensive fittings. Who was going to pay for all that? The buying public? Never. The over-ambitious shopkeeper, they thought, was bound to come to grief before long. But they were wrong. Customers came by the dozen, they convinced themselves that prices in the lavishly equipped shop were no higher than in the miserable basement premises they had patronized in the past.

In order to cover the overheads of expensive displays the turnover must remain large—or, more correctly, it must go on increasing all the time. Now and again a retailer might make some suggestions for the benefit of the manufacturer when ordering from the travelling salesman. This idea in itself completely upset the traditional views about the functions of the retailer. The retailer, it used to be held, had to buy his goods from the wholesaler; and he would receive credit only so long as he bought hundreds of different lines of articles. Now a retailer would deal directly with the manufacturer, inform him of his wishes, and occasionally give him a tip or two. A manufacturer is always glad of a good idea.

In 1882 Oscar Tietz, then 24, opened a small draper's and haberdasher's shop in Gera, with some assistance from his uncle Hermann. He decided to buy his stock straight from the manufacturer. His uncle shook his head; his nephew's ideas, which also included fixed prices and cash payment, must surely wreck the business in no time. After a mere fortnight uncle Hermann withdrew from the partnership, leaving the business to his reckless nephew. Some years later Oscar Tietz owned 10 department stores, several smaller shops, and a number of industrial works. More recently, Horten had a similar success with his stores in the Rhineland and the Ruhr.

A good idea was always worth a fortune. In Utica, in the state of New York, a 27-year-old merchant offered every article in his shop at 5 cents. Every customer could take what he wanted. Surely that idea was bound to work! But it proved a failure. A distrustful public did not respond, and the shop was forced to close down. During the very same year the young man opened another shop in Lancaster, Pennsylvania, where he offered all articles at 5 or 10 cents. This time it worked. When Frank Winfield Woolworth died in 1919 he left 27,000,000 dollars. As early as 1912 his firm owned nearly 600 of these uniform-price shops in the United States; by the middle of the twentieth century their number had risen to 2000 and their turnover to 600,000,000 dollars.

Everything hinges on the art of selling. A great many customers do not like personal service or being harangued by assistants. They know exactly what they want; they merely cast a quick, expert glance at merchandise and price, and hurry out of the shop again. To meet their demands fruit, vegetables, butter, and cheese are wrapped in weighed quantities marked with the price, ready to take away. Self-service saves time and speeds sales. In 1946 some 60 per cent. of all food sales in the United States were made in self-service stores, compared with only 31 per cent. in 1929. In chain-stores up to 80 per cent. of all food sales are made in self-service departments, compared with 43 per cent. in the case of independently owned shops.

The retail trade is spending more and more on advertising. Hand-bills are distributed, entire pages in the daily press are taken up for advertisements, huge posters are put up on hoardings. Articles are extolled and customers lured to the great emporia in the town centres. But is it right that the retail trade should be so concentrated in a few locations?

The answer was provided by the chain-stores. Chain-stores, spread out over a whole town or even a whole country, all stock the same articles at the same prices. A customer should be able to get his cigars, his coffee, or his butter at the next corner without having to make a long journey into town. In the United States there are now about 1100 firms whose chain-stores stock only foodstuffs. In 1929 the independently owned shops accounted for 68 per cent. of all food sales against 32 per cent. in chain-stores; two years later the proportion had changed only slightly in favour of the chain-stores; it stood then at 66 to 34 per cent.

Automatic vending-machines are not tied to shop hours. Day and night these 'dumb salesmen' are ready to give service. In Germany and many other countries it was the chocolate industry that first put up such automatic vending-machines at railway stations and other places where large numbers of people passed through. A small coin would buy a sizeable bar of chocolate. The idea conceived by industry was presently adopted by the retail trade. Before the Second World War there were 400,000 automatic vending-machines in Germany. In the United States their number had risen to 2,500,000 by 1946, with a turnover of 500,000 dollars. Half a century ago Bob Greene, the President of the National Automatic Merchandising Association, accumulated a vast fortune out of the 10-cent pieces which were dropping into his vending-machines day after day and hour after hour.

But even automatic vending-machines require careful organization, sound judgment of customers' demands, likes, and habits, and careful consideration of where the machine is to be located and what it is to be filled with. The machines are not cheap, and can yield profits only if prime investments are written off quickly before technical development renders a machine obsolete.

The key to success is buying—*i.e.,* the gift of anticipating customer demand. In Germany many food merchants nowadays entrust their buying to a buying co-operative; this ensures for them the advantages of

55. Office routine revolutionized by the first typewriter. "Opposition to such novelties is unlikely to abate," a Berlin periodical remarked in 1899

bulk buying with the corresponding discounts. Each member of such a buying co-operative still remains fully liable.

In an ever new variety of forms, commerce is trying to discharge its tasks—in the American supermarkets, by way of mail-order stores, by buying syndicates. Anyone with a good idea which might increase turnover, attract customers, or save costs can make a fortune.

Strolling down our modern brilliantly lit shopping streets it is difficult to think ourselves back to the days of our grandparents or great-grandparents, to the towns with narrow, ill-lit, and badly cobbled streets where shopkeepers sat in stuffy little shops and craftsmen were working in dark basements. It may well be said that the modern city began with Boucicaut.

17

The State takes over Distribution

━━━━━ᴧᴧᴧᴧᴧᴧ◯ᴧᴧᴧᴧᴧᴧ━━━━━

IN MOSCOW'S RED SQUARE stands the vast department store GUM, its three enormous halls linked by wide light-shafts. Displayed on the counters are rolls of woollen, cotton, and linen cloth, in red, blue, black, and white. There are lamps, chandeliers, radio and television sets, pots and pans, electric irons, buckets and brooms, furniture, typewriters, washing-machines, boots and shoes, hats, silk scarves, toys, apples from Belorussia, grapes from the Black Sea, wine from the Caucasus, champagne from the Crimea, and silks from China. All these are for sale.

Wide-eyed with amazement, the peasant women from the Volga and the Tartar herdsmen from Siberia shuffle through the brightly lit rooms. They can hardly believe that they can feast their eyes on everything and choose to their heart's delight. Even the visitor from Western Europe admires the variety of the goods offered; the scene, in fact, is much the same as at Boucicaut's, or at Wertheim's in Berlin, or at Selfridges in London. In the GUM department store the Soviet citizen is made to feel a customer—flattered and wooed, the master of his own money, which he can spend freely. All appearances of a commercial enterprise are carefully preserved: lay-out, service, range of articles. Anybody can choose what he likes, everything is for sale; there are no restrictions on a customer other than his own purse.

And yet a whole world divides the Russian department store from Boucicaut's or Wertheim's. GUM is set up by the State. GUM sells, or more correctly distributes, whatever the State supplies. It is, in fact, no more than a small cog in the great distributive machinery. The

359

purpose of GUM is not so much to induce people to buy as to demonstrate to an astonished world the achievements of the Soviet economic system. Boucicaut's, Tietz's, Macy's, or Selfridges continually bring out tempting new merchandise, for they know that their profit depends on their turnover, and their turnover on their success in attracting customers. GUM, on the other hand, sells only what the State-owned factories are supplying in accordance with the plan. It has its scheduled range of articles and these simply have to do for the public. No special effort is made to produce articles of particular appeal to the customer, since for the State authorities there is no such thing as a customer. As if anybody could produce all the things some people might like to have! They should be satisfied with what there is!

Competition is unknown. State-owned enterprises produce whatever a Five-year Plan or Seven-year Plan prescribes for them. Their output goes to the State retail organizations or direct to the GUM department store. They do not have to worry whether a new article will 'sell.' Anything leaving the factory gate is as good as sold. The distribution is taken care of by the State apparatus. There are no customers, only 'standard consumers.'

Even if all visitors to GUM were to pounce on one and the same article, say, some colourful material or a convenient kitchen stove, no one in the store would dream of ordering larger quantities of that article. It would simply be sold out. The assistants would shrug their shoulders and explain that there was no more in stock. Perhaps next month, or perhaps next year. After all, a lot of things are in short supply in the vast land of Russia. The people ought to be thankful for all the things they are able to buy.

What industry produces is determined not by the customer but by authority—the State, the Five-year Plan, or the Seven-year Plan. The choice is determined by 'higher' considerations than the fancy of the buying public. The socialist development of the country must come first—defence, heavy industry, hydro-electric power-stations, and the opening up of the vastnesses of Siberia. The State Planning Commission knows what it wants. The consumer is allocated whatever is good for him, whatever he 'really' needs. He will have to wait a little; by the end of the current Seven-year Plan, or quite certainly by that of the next, he will be able to choose from an unlimited abundance of goods, far more even than the pampered customer in America. But first of all production must be stepped up: new steelworks, new engineering factories, new electric power-stations, new coal-mines, and new oilwells.

The merchant's mind works differently. He acts in accordance with consumer wishes. At the same time he will look around for new articles which he might make attractive to his customers and which might at the same time yield him a profit. Publicity to him is an important means of stimulating demand. He places his orders with the factories, which in turn place orders with the engineering industry, with heavy industry, and with the basic materials industry. From the consumer a wave of orders rolls into the economy; as soon as it stops or ebbs away orders peter out; and then textile factories as well as engineering works will be idle and the workmen unemployed.

The First World War severed the threads which world commerce had woven throughout a hundred years of peace. The British fleet barred the oceans to the Germans. No neutral was allowed to supply 'contraband' to Germany or Austria—and almost anything came under the heading of prohibited strategic supplies! All foodstuffs, all basic raw materials, all industrial manufactures. Trade with the enemy came to a complete standstill. Very little was left for private consumption. Customers would implore a merchant to "try and get them" some potatoes, cabbage, bread, or meat, a pair of shoes, or a warm overcoat; they would gladly pay a good price. In 1917, when the big cities and industrial areas such as Saxony and the Ruhr were already suffering from famine, there were still sufficient foodstuffs left in the farming areas of the more remote agricultural provinces.

The buyers from the hardship areas, however, excited the hostility of officials in the more favoured provinces. Were they to permit those merchants to carry away their last reserves? They issued export prohibitions, closed the frontiers of the provinces, and instituted checks on the railways.

Commerce might be justified in normal times; in an emergency other means had to be adopted to ensure that supplies for the population were equitable and sufficient. The authorities themselves took over distribution. Grain and potatoes, meat and butter, leather and textiles were taken over by the State, which thus was able to form a picture of what supplies were available. A retailer was allotted a definite quantity for distribution. He was not allowed to sell anything except against an official food-ration card. In this way an end was put to food hoarders and profiteers. Prices were "frozen" and the law of supply and demand suspended. Any person offending against these regulations was a "racketeer" and a criminal.

Money had lost its purchasing power in respect of the most important everyday articles. In order to buy anything a person needed coupons. These coupons, however, were issued by the State not in exchange for a definite service but in accordance with need. Money had ceased to be money in the strict sense of the word; in order to make a purchase a customer also needed his ration cards—unless, of course, he wanted to buy prohibited goods at preposterous prices in the black market.

The hungry urban population used to wander out into the country-side in hordes in order to induce the peasants to part with a small portion of their generous "food producers' allowance" in exchange for silver spoons or Oriental carpets.

The Government intensified its regulations and decreed heavier penalties. Academic economists thundered against "racketeers and criminals who flouted the official directives." The urban masses grumbled because not enough food was supplied to the towns. Surely the farmers were being paid a fixed price and the wholesalers were allowed a sufficiently generous profit margin for storage, transportation, and losses through deterioration? The retailer had his prices prescribed for him and his customers were listed on official registers. From an entrepreneur he had been turned into a civil servant. But surely in times of emergency the State had to take control?

Only in times of emergency? Surely a powerful, just, and socially minded State would solve distributive problems more efficiently, more equitably, and more fairly even in ordinary times than the avaricious merchant. Why should everything in this world be ruled by money? Socialism would see to it that every person received what he needed and what was his due on the grounds of fairness and equity. The planned economy of wartime was to be succeeded by the State-controlled planned economy of peacetime. The Bolshevik Revolution in Russia realized this grand dream.

Nowhere had chaos been greater or suffering more appalling than in Tsarist Russia just before its collapse. Revolution further aggravated the chaos and exacerbated the famine in the great cities. Why should there be famine in such a vast agricultural territory? Surely the reason must be that the merchants had failed the public. By decree of October 1918 all commercial enterprises, large and small, were closed down, and their stocks and premises handed over to consumer co-operatives or State distribution centres. The peasants, on pain of severe punishment, were ordered to hand over whatever they did not consume themselves.

Conditions, however, did not improve. The peasants simply did not deliver all produce; they neglected their fields and formed themselves into rebellious groups whenever officials came to collect the harvest. To make matters worse, the harvest of 1920 was a failure; millions of people died of starvation.

Lenin realized that matters could not go on like that. In March 1921 he proclaimed the New Economic Policy, known for short as NEP. The independent merchants were again permitted to buy whatever they wished, to pay and demand what prices they chose. Provided only they produced the goods—bread, meat, milk, honey, cabbage, no matter at what price, so long as people did not starve to death. The result was startling. As if by magic, shops filled with goods sprang up in towns and villages. Everything was available again, though at very high prices.

In order to keep up its own retail centres in competition with the privately owned shops the State granted them numerous privileges on the railways, as well as various tax concessions. It made no difference. The merchants were undeniably superior. In 1924 some 90 per cent. of all public stalls belonged to private merchants, who accounted for two-thirds of the turnover.

Consumers in Moscow no longer had to take the overcrowded "potato trains" to the countryside in order to carry home on their backs the week's supplies for the family. The small shopkeeper at the corner had woven his threads; he knew what he had to offer the peasant. By this kind of barter he would get from him far more food than would a Bolshevik official with his threats of police action.

Stalin believed that the root of all difficulties lay with the producers, the peasantry. In 1928 began the first Five-year Plan, which organized the peasants into State-controlled collective co-operatives, the *kolkhozes.* The rich peasants, or *kulaks,* were expropriated, imprisoned, deported to Siberia, or even executed. The NEP era was at an end. Anyone now buying food from the peasants in order to resell it at a high price to urban consumers was severely punished as a black marketeer.

In 1931 the co-operatives still accounted for 65 per cent. of the urban turnover and 85 per cent. of the rural turnover. Then the Party decided to act against them too. To begin with, they were forbidden in the towns, and in the countryside their share in the total turnover declined to 38 per cent. in 1934 and to 26 per cent. three years later. A collective farmer was permitted to sell freely only such produce as was in excess of prescribed delivery quotas—milk and butter from his personally owned

56. A Russian black marketeer arrested by Red Army soldiers. A propaganda leaflet of 1920

cow, grain grown on his privately owned patch of land, the chicken he was allowed to keep, and the eggs it laid for him.

Instantly the small middleman appeared on the scene—oppressed, intimidated, and hunted, yet he transacted his little deals, buying something here and something there in order to resell it elsewhere. At night he would come to the back door of the farmhouse to collect the promised side of bacon or loaf of bread. Under his overcoat he would bring a saucepan for the farmer's wife, a kitchen knife or a soup ladle—precious rarities for many years. True, there was the risk of heavy penalties, but then most people lived by fooling the police in one way or another.

Thanks to this illicit trade a collective farmer could exchange his surpluses for things he really needed. He had only to compare the things he obtained by this illicit barter with the official prices he was paid for his compulsory deliveries of grain for any doubts to be cast aside. With the merchant he could choose, demand, and refuse; in the big, official, distributive machinery he had to accept whatever the State doled out to him. With the roubles paid to him by the merchant he might be able to buy at the GUM department store those wonderful things which did not exist in the provinces simply because no merchant made any effort to bring them there. Even the high fares seemed worth while.

The town-dweller was hardly better off. All foodstuffs were rationed —first of all bread, then all other foods, then all industrial consumer goods, clothes, footwear, pots and pans, plates, knives and forks. Everybody was issued with purchase vouchers or food cards, which he had to produce at the official retail centres—without any assurance whatever that the items specified on the coupons were in fact available. If he wanted something special he would go to the weekly market, where peasant women would offer for sale apples from Belorussia or grapes from the Crimea in order to make a little money on the side. What else could anybody do? So long as this last remnant of trade survived money still had some value.

All complaints by consumers drew the same reply: saboteurs were preventing the country's rise to prosperity; the fascists throughout the world were compelling the Soviet Union to spend her substance on armaments. There was always some one else to blame when the State failed to achieve what the small shopkeeper had accomplished during the NEP era. Things would be better after the next Five-year Plan. In 1936 Stalin changed the entire distributive system; trade was organized centrally by the Torg, the retail trade trust. The 'open' shops were now joined by the new restricted ones, reserved for the privileged classes— visitors from abroad with foreign currency in their pockets, high functionaries, activists, scientists, and artists. The State itself, as it were, took over the black market. Rationing was abolished. The normal consumer had to watch in silence. And watch in silence he did, for once again a frightful wave of purges was sweeping through the Soviet Union.

The rest of the world, however, was staring as if mesmerized at the tremendous 'successes' of the Communist system. Production statistics were soaring at a time when the capitalist countries were in the throes of the Great Depression, when millions of unemployed crowded the streets, when huge stocks of unsaleable raw materials were accumulating in the producer countries overseas, when prices in the world markets slumped to a third or less.

Strangely enough, it was poverty springing from over-abundance. The effects of the First World War had been overcome astonishingly quickly. Whereas in the past production had for a long time been unable to keep pace with the growing demands, thanks to technical progress it was now outpacing demand with giant strides. Instead of shortages there now was a surfeit. While countless statesmen and economists were still considering ways and means of reviving and promoting production, vast surplus stocks were already accumulating overseas: coffee in Brazil, wheat in Canada, wool in Australia, cotton in the U.S.A. The supplies forced down the prices in the world market.

The merchants were trying to market these vast stocks in the industrialized countries. But wherever a merchant appeared with his low-priced commodities the native producers, unable to compete with these prices, were up in arms. Unless they were to be reduced to poverty this dangerous foreign competition must be stopped. They demanded higher customs duties, or, if that did not help, import prohibitions. As for the roots of the evil—excessive reparation payments, the magnificent technical equipment in the factories of some countries, the starvation wages paid to the workers in others, the dumping practised by Japan, who was building up a State-subsidized industry, the ruthless under-selling by the Soviet Union—all these did not interest the producer. He saw only one thing: his work was not being adequately remunerated and his products were no longer bought. He was driven from house and home by his creditors, and his factory had to be mortgaged. He could not see beyond the merchant who was offering merchandise at prices which were low beyond all reason and bore no relation to his own high prime costs.

What had gone wrong? Distribution had broken down. The merchant was simply no longer able to channel the flood of merchandise to the consumer. And all the time millions of human beings in every continent were dying of starvation. Why did not commerce see to it that enough bread was being eaten, enough coffee drunk, enough homes built, and enough pots and pans bought?

The merchant operates by means of money; only when his customer has money can he sell and, hence, also buy. What does he gain by offering his goods cheaply? Once the equilibrium between purchasing power and goods has been disturbed, as it inevitably is after a frightful war, the situation is beyond the merchant's control. He cannot re-organize the finances of the whole world. That is why he must 'fail.'

The merchant who is not bound by any plan directs his goods to wherever they achieve a good price. His competition invades the last remote islands of tranquil economic life. His low prices ruin the local crafts, so that people lose their work and livelihood and are thus eliminated not only as producers but also as consumers. Needless to say, a stop must be put to the merchant at once, before he causes any further damage. Again, those threatened turn to the State. The State, surely, would be able to cope with this super-abundance more easily than it did with shortages! All unsaleable stocks are henceforward with-drawn from the market; they are warehoused or, if perishable, destroyed at public expense. In Holland cauliflower was allowed to rot in the fields, in Brazil coffee was tipped into the sea, in Canada wheat was burned in railway locomotives, and in the Argentine the gasworks were fired with maize.

When that, too, proved ineffective the next step was to throttle pro-duction: the Roosevelt Administration mercilessly ordered the closing down of oil-wells. Wherever the owners of oilfields refused to comply, State troopers appeared on the scene. Farmers ploughed up a third of all wheatfields and cotton plantations where the new crop had just begun to sprout. Surely there ought to be no difficulty in mechanically holding down the volume of production to that of actual consumption!

Price rivalry by manufacturers was eliminated by laws and regula-tions: cut-throat competition was to be supplanted by trusting co-operation. Manufacturers who undertook to sell at a 'fair' price, to pay decent wages, and not to dismiss any employee needlessly were permitted to pin the Blue Eagle of the New Deal to their factory gates. In return the State granted them long-term credits at a low rate of interest.

Most important of all, the State stopped imports. It impounded all foreign monies and claims, blocked all payments to foreign countries, and introduced strict "foreign currency control"; to all effects and purposes the State took over the entire foreign trade. Goods were no longer imported because they were cheap, but only if they were essential.

Producers had greatly enlarged and extended their enterprises—and now they were short of orders. Nothing could be expected from the merchants: after the frightful knocks they had taken during the depression they could not and would not take any risks. The old method of dramatically reducing prices in order to revive demand failed. The more the prices were reduced the less people were buying: factories had to close down, workers lost their jobs, industrialists, wholesalers, and terrified retailers greatly cut down on their stocks. They did not want to lose even more.

The millions of unemployed, the hundreds of thousands of small and medium entrepreneurs, the vast numbers of peasants and farmers—all had lost confidence in 'the economy.' If anyone could help at all in this situation it was the State.

The State was interested not in marketing but merely in consumption. Governments were spending more money than they were making. The political parties which made the biggest promises were returned to power. Why should they pay large subsidies to exporters? Enormous domestic orders would revitalize economic life. They built roads and bridges, they drained swamps and seas, they paid out subsidies for big housing schemes. Above all, they invested gigantic sums into armaments. In its most extreme form this attitude was practised by the National Socialist Government in Germany, which showed a total disregard for all commercial considerations. Work at any price was its slogan. No imports! Only thus could prices for agricultural produce be raised again.

The merchant was everywhere being restricted, bypassed, eliminated. In Soviet Russia it was by State-run retail organizations; in National Socialist Germany foreign trade was put under State supervision by means of currency regulations, export compensation, agricultural subsidies, and an internal Market Order, by a campaign against department stores, the stabilization of wages, and the 'fixing' of prices. In 'liberal' England it was done by fighting the depression according to the Keynes recipe, and by the customs tariffs of the Ottawa Agreement; in democratic France by way of foreign trade contingents and the prices policy of the Popular Front; and in the South American republics by way of foreign currency control and large-scale subsidies for raw material prices. Everywhere the State was acquiring the decisive say. The State wanted to reorganize the world. It wanted to give work and bread to the unemployed, to protect the producers, and to ensure fair prices. For that it did not need the merchant, that ruthless profiteer who would not understand economic causes and effects on a world-wide or even on a national scale, and, what was worse, who showed so little patriotism.

If he drove up prices he was a usurer and an oppressor of the poor; if he forced prices down he was a saboteur engaged in unfair competition and damaging his fellow citizen—to wit, the manufacturer who seemed incapable of reducing his high overheads. If he allowed his goods to rot and spoil rather than selling them cheaply he committed a sin against the starving; if he closed his factory gates because he could not market his products he was reviled as incompetent. If he carried on, risking the future of his enterprise, he was a reckless gambler. The State alone could afford to do all those things! The State could do no wrong: it enjoyed the support of academic economists, public opinion, and, of course, the politicians who were only too eager to see themselves in the rôle of captains of industry and directors-general of nationalized enterprises.

The one thing these officials could not understand was why their surpluses could not be sold. Surely there must be a buyer somewhere! No business deal should fall through because of the price alone. In nearly all countries the governments granted considerable subsidies to exporters. Manufactures were marketed far below their production costs. Only in the home market was the price anxiously maintained, so that the producers should suffer no disadvantage.

What the economic officials would not see was that their own tariffs, currency regulations, and import quotas had ruined the foreign customer by preventing him from marketing his manufactures. If he was unable to sell his products, where was he to find the foreign currency for his purchases? The foreign currency restrictions had put an end to purely commercial credits, since even the most solvent and willing debtor was now unable to pay unless he first obtained the consent of some official or other; without a rubber stamp on a foreign currency application payments across frontiers had become impossible.

The home market was languishing for different reasons: manufactures were too expensive because prices of raw materials and wage rates were being maintained artificially at a level which barely allowed a producer to recover his own costs. Hence—the officials concluded—goods must not be marketed so cheaply. Instead of adjusting prices to actual market conditions and eliminating those factories which were no longer competitive, an official Market Order was introduced with rigidly fixed minimum prices and protected by import barriers. Needless to say, this arrangement acted as a brake on sales. A peasant could no longer sell his pigs; hence he could not afford to buy a harvesting machine; hence the factory had to dismiss workers; and with their meagre dole these unemployed workers could no longer afford expensive food such as pork. Savings were disappearing, mortgages had to be called in. The banks were getting nervous and demanded repayment of their loans. Farmers could not get credit anywhere. Thus the depression sped towards its climax.

The governments tried to pull themselves out of the morass of economic depression by their own bootlaces. Thousands of millions of dollars, pounds sterling, Reichsmarks, and other currencies were spent without any cover on paying unemployment benefit to millions of workers for doing nothing, or on building roads and draining seas. Yet at the same time production was being artificially throttled, and imports ruthlessly choked down until all wholesale and retail stocks had been consumed.

The merchants realized that this trend must lead to disaster. Surely one day all the money that was being pumped into the economy by the banknote presses must appear in the form of purchasing power: the public, in fact, would demand merchandise. The governments would find themselves crushed under a mountain of debts, and foreign trade would be short of currency. Hence prices were bound to rise.

While the politicians were still talking about social welfare, public works, the buttressing of prices, import controls, and protection for the home producer, the merchants acted. They were buying and stocking up. The boundless waste of money had aroused their mistrust. By an irony of fate it was this mistrust that saved the politicians—not because of, but in spite of, their senseless economy of public expenditure.

This was clearly shown in Germany. The National Socialist Government announced proudly that during its first fiscal year 1933–34 it had spent 2000 million Reichsmarks in order to revive the country's wrecked economy. But what was that compared with the 6000 to 8000 million Reichsmarks spent by the German retail trade between July 1, 1933, and June 30, 1934, on increasing its stocks?

Hitler did not concern himself much with economic problems;

economic difficulties, he believed, could be dealt with by the same methods as political ones—by discipline, order, and commands. To him it was all a matter of will-power. When everything went well he declared with satisfaction that the German nation had "taken fresh courage." He shut his eyes to the fact that in the summer of 1934 a very dangerous situation had arisen when, owing to the unfavourable foreign trade balance, supplies of the most essential raw materials to German industry were being seriously held up, and even butter was in short supply, as well as to the fact that the country's gold reserves were dwindling. Moreover, Germany's racial policies cost her a substantial portion of her merchants, especially in the field of foreign trade. Foreign contacts were likewise affected, as many old friends turned away from Germany with disgust.

And then came the great surprise. During the most critical years, between 1935 and 1939, German foreign trade expanded considerably. The reason was that most foreign merchants were not interested in politics; they merely wanted to do business. So long as Germany was buying they did not care whether she paid with foreign currency or gold, or by way of special accounts and German exports. Above all, the countries supplying raw materials were wooing the German customers —South Africa, Australia, and Canada with their wool and wheat, India with her jute, Japan with Manchurian soya beans, Brazil with its coffee, and the Argentine with its grain and linseed.

Within a few years the volume of Germany's foreign trade had surpassed that before the Great Depression—in the face of all boycotting. Many South American countries imported more goods from Germany than from the U.S.A. and Britain.

In spite of the close mesh of regulations and formalities merchants in Germany were able to operate within limits. If a merchant imported some goods from abroad he would pay the amount into one of the new special accounts for foreigners; some other merchant would export German manufactures against payments from that account. In this way ever more foreign merchandise was flowing into Germany—but it was all consumed by Hitler's armament drive. Before long there was a shortage not only of imported raw materials but also of German export articles. All exports became subject to specific permits from the authorities.

Abundance once more gave way to shortages. In spite of technological advances production was unable to keep pace with the insane gallop of rearmament. Needless to say, the situation further deteriorated upon the outbreak of war. In this war the State assumed from the very outset full control over production and distribution. All prices were fixed regardless of supply or demand. There was no longer any "trade" —only State-controlled distribution.

On the surface things did not change very greatly: a housewife would continue to go to her little shop every day in order to buy her foodstuffs, household needs, or clothes. Although she would still be buying these articles in the same shop and from the same shop-keeper, the 'merchant' had nevertheless been reduced to the part of a 'distributor,' permitted only to hand over his merchandise against coupons or 'points' from the customer's food or clothes ration book. Even so, all stocks were sold out instantly and soon long, dismal queues formed outside the shops. At the beginning of the war a number of articles were still freely available because the authorities assumed that but a few customers would be interested in them; but they too disappeared from the shops. Since the public were unable to spend their money on what they would have liked, they were prepared to buy anything there was, from winkles and seagull's eggs to elegant tail-coats.

All life was ruled by the war machine. With an alarming speed this 'military thinking' gained ground in all directions. The precise order, permitting of no contradiction, appeared to be a wonderful way to get things done—and it was so simple and cheap. Everywhere the wartime economy became an economy of military orders, an economy in which there was no place for merchants. Merchants were only a nuisance, and while they were allowed to meddle in the economy any planning was impossible. The entire 'civilian sector' was suspended.

When the war was over this mental attitude remained firmly rooted in the heads of soldiers, officials, Party functionaries, several politicians, and even some economists. Surely the wartime production statistics were convincing evidence? The world was in ruins; how could it be built up again except by planning, under the firm direction of the authorities? The individual was not allowed to dispose either of his property or of his own labour. Only the State knew what was right, what was good for each citizen, and how much work could or should be expected from each member of the community.

Gigantic organizations were supplying the whole world with consumer goods. They added up all available wheat, fats, and meat, and allocated it all 'fairly.' All accounts were settled direct among the authorities, and the balance—thousands of millions of dollars—was paid by the U.S. tax-payer.

After eighteen months the benevolent statesmen were beginning to realize that their principle of fair shares had certain disadvantages: although the distribution of controlled goods was functioning more or less smoothly nothing was being done to restart production. If a producer was obliged to surrender his produce—foodstuffs or industrial manufactures—at a low price he naturally did not over-exert himself. Initiative and the spirit of enterprise were lacking.

What could be done was revealed by the black market which flourished side by side with the official allocation system. Hungry townsmen were streaming out into the countryside to barter their last bicycle inner tube for a side of bacon; smallholders would keep chickens, goats, and sheep in order to get a little coffee in exchange; shoemakers would work late into the night to earn a few cigarettes. What was happening on a small scale within the war-ravaged countries was duplicated on a large scale in the international sphere: the Argentine supplied its wheat not to the international bodies set up by the United Nations, but to the 'rich' neutrals, who not only paid higher prices but could deliver such goods as watches, machines, and ships.

Was the merchant to be left to supply merchandise, to place his orders, and to choose his customers merely on the strength of their solvency or otherwise? Or should the State continue to distribute the available goods in accordance with a plan, purposefully, equitably, and in a spirit of social justice? In the latter case one would have to content oneself with the quantities which the producers, under a system of officially fixed prices, were prepared to deliver. Should prices again be allowed to decide what was manufactured, or should one continue to cling rigidly to official "plans"? Should merchandise go to the customer who could pay for it or to him who needed it? Should everybody be allowed to buy as much as he could afford, or should the yardstick of social justice be applied? Finally, who was to decide what was to be produced, manufactured, and consumed, or, more important still, who was to consume what, who was to live well and enjoy himself? Party functionaries, the soldiers, the civil servants, or the merchants?

Two economic systems, two different ways of thinking, were opposing one another: planned economy and free-market economy. Each nation had to make its own choice. Admittedly, various attempts were made to combine or reconcile the two systems, to find a middle road, to adopt from each of the two systems their positive features. As if that were possible! Fire and water will not mix.

The United States of America abolished all economic controls in 1946. Prices and wages were allowed to find their own level—even at the cost of prices doubling and widespread strikes breaking out throughout the economy. Within a few months, however, the United States once more experienced a boom which, though checked now and again by slight recessions, has continued to this day. On the other hand, many countries embraced the principles of the "welfare State": wages were officially regulated, the State paid out large subsidies, prices were fixed by the authorities, rents were controlled, and housing was taken over by the State, which allocated the new homes in accordance with 'priority' categories.

The Soviet Union kept its coercive economy. In China the Communist system resulted in 1958 in the establishment of "people's communes"; the working day was extended to ten, twelve, and more hours. Families were separated, and all private life came to an end. Money likewise lost its meaning; the working people were fed free of charge. But they had to work wherever they were needed—on the construction of canals or at primitive steel-furnaces. One's personal wishes counted for nothing.

What is the yardstick of success? Is it to be the absolute volume of production regardless of the sacrifices and rewards of the individual? Does a human being accomplish more when he is ordered about, when he is handled firmly and ruthlessly, and when he is threatened with imprisonment, deportation, or even death? Or is he to be left to his own devices—either to die of starvation by the roadside or to hire himself out for money? Must not some one be responsible for him? Who was to give employment and bread to the starving except a solicitous State or an all-powerful party?

The Allied Occupation Powers could not understand how, in that devastated, divided, and impoverished Germany, anybody could even think of abandoning a coercive economy. When Erhard ended the control of industrial production, when he scrapped purchase vouchers, and allowed prices to find their own level, the supporters of coercive economy all prophesied disaster. They implored the "professor in the ivory tower" to keep State controls. Otherwise, they said, chaos and famine would be inevitable. Were people really to be allowed to buy freely anything they wanted? And where was the merchandise to come from? The German factories had been destroyed by bombing or stripped by the victors of their machinery. In order to produce at all, foreign raw materials were needed—and where was industry to get them from? Exports had been non-existent for nine years. Because of their fear of German competition the victorious Powers had made exports subject to the control of an official body known as the JEIA—the Joint Export Import Agency—in which soldiers, bureaucrats, and commercial rivals had the decisive say. Under these circumstances, how could the free interplay of supply and demand be expected to produce sensible prices? How could Germany penetrate into the world markets when she was faced everywhere with political barriers?

In the end even the politicians of the victorious Powers realized that their policies cost them a lot of money and ultimately hit their own economy. True, Germany had been eliminated as a competitor—that much the victors achieved—but she had also been eliminated as a customer. Who was going to buy the cheese and vegetables the Dutch were offering? Brazil wanted to supply coffee to Germany in order to buy German machines. By throttling German machine-construction the Allies were damaging the production of coffee. How were the U.S. tobacco-growers to market their tobacco if their potential customers were barred from exporting anything themselves? The recipients of Marshall Aid had used the money to build factories making export articles. Everybody would benefit if German merchants were again given a free hand. The Western Powers relented.

Erhard had no faith in State control; he trusted the entrepreneur and the merchant. Not from pure idealism or from any sense of public duty, but for the sake of plain, brutal profit the entrepreneurs could be relied upon to work, plan, organize, and take risks. If some one was able to offer a good article let him achieve the highest price the 'market'— *i.e.*, the customer—was prepared to pay. If his profit was high production would increase; if it was too low then the factory would have to close down. At least it would mean an end of the manufacture of rubbish and the elimination of all entrepreneurs producing useless stuff. Without licences, permits, or raw-material vouchers the factories began to manufacture. As though by magic the shops were filled with goods. The black market collapsed almost overnight.

With amazement the whole world was watching the "German miracle." How was it possible for industrial production to soar in that devastated country while it made such slow progress in the victorious states? The Germans appeared to be possessed by a blind fury for work: after normal working hours, and even on Sundays, workmen would toil at building-sites and at their lathes. There were no strikes. What was the secret? In the shop-windows there were all the wonderful things they had been without for years—from an ordinary glass tumbler to a radio set. Anything was available, but it cost money. And money could be had only in return for work done.

Merchants went abroad again to weave new threads, to restore confidence in Germany, to offer manufactures, and to purchase raw materials —on credit, of course, but that was readily granted because they had sound manufactures to offer at reasonable prices. Entrepreneurs were able to rebuild their factories because their goods were finding a ready market. Workmen worked many hours of overtime because at long last they were able to buy with their money the things they needed.

Whereas in 1949 Germany's imports still exceeded her exports, German exports have for many years now been greatly in excess of imports. The pitiful factories dug out of the rubble of the air raids have long been transformed into superbly equipped modern enterprises— without State intervention, guidance, directives, subsidies, or any other form of interference.

Whereas the socialist countries are concerned principally with production, the countries practising a free-market economy are interested mainly in consumption. Prices are determined by sales. The most impressive production statistics are meaningless if expensive or inferior manufactures remain unsold, or are sold only with State aid.

The new nations, on the other hand, anxious to catch up as quickly as possible with the lead of the industrialized countries, are reluctant to be guided by price. They want to manufacture as much as possible themselves, regardless of cost. Instead of importing the cheapest steel on the most favourable terms, they are setting up their own giant steelworks—often in the middle of the jungle. They close their frontiers by high customs barriers in order to protect the home producers. They are not alone in this practice. The industrialized states, too, have closed their frontiers against import of articles at price levels below those of their own manufacturers in order to protect the wages of their own workers against competition from cheaper foreign labour. But in doing so they have been forcing up the general price level year after year, by some 2 or 3 per cent.

Once a country sets aside commercial considerations, once politics are governed by regard for domestic producers or other interested groups, the currency begins to be undermined. The State can then either maintain its price structure by means of protective tariffs and import prohibitions or else it can allow its currency to slide. But in the world markets there are no such things as artificially maintained rates of exchange. There gold remains the inexorable yardstick. It is against gold that each nation's prices are measured. If they are too high that nation's exports must decline. But the volume of those exports must inevitably determine the volume of imports.

The countries with a controlled economy are at the parting of the ways: are they to adhere to their system in the face of the evidence of Germany's success? Are they to cast their principles to the winds and make price once more the ultimate arbiter?

They promise everybody social security. The State looks after its own like the father of a family. Except that a father also bears the entire responsibility for earning his family's livelihood. But who works for the State? In the long run only compulsion can make one individual work for another. But where there is compulsion human beings will invariably rebel against it; hence compulsion must be intensified for it to be maintained. There is no half-way house between freedom and servitude.

Though at times of crisis it may threaten his very existence, the merchant lives by freedom. He takes the risks. He has to come to terms with a changing market and with his customers, whose wishes can never accurately be predicted. His customer enjoys freedom of choice. Without that freedom he becomes a mere standard consumer.

At times when prices everywhere appear to fluctuate chaotically, when all forecasts prove false, when one business house after another crashes—then indeed the merchant may curse his freedom and long for the security of the pensionable civil servant, for a centrally regulated market order, and for the protection of a benevolent State. But with the freedom of the merchant there disappears also the freedom of the customer. Goodwill is supplanted by words of command. The merchant, now as ever, stands for freedom.

Epilogue

TO-DAY THE MERCHANT is faced with new tasks. Once again he is expected to open up new markets. But he no longer needs to venture out into remote, unknown corners of the earth, to battle against wind and waves, or to cross deserts. To-day he travels in a comfortable aircraft, which, in a matter of hours, takes him safely to his destination. And yet his efforts to do business are beset by obstacles scarcely less formidable than those of past ages.

Nations everywhere are endeavouring to seal off their entire economies against the outside world—and hence also against the foreign merchant —by means of customs barriers, foreign-currency restrictions, import contingents, and, last but not least, political considerations. They distort and, indeed, prevent all free competition by banning such imports as they consider unnecessary. Each state tries to protect its own producers, to preserve its foreign-currency holdings, and to organize its domestic market in accordance with its own ideas. But present-day economics cannot be forced into a straitjacket of restrictions.

So that they should not atrophy behind these all-too-narrow customs barriers, several states have combined to form larger economic units. Within these enlarged units the customs duties are abolished or at least greatly reduced. On the continent of Europe six countries have banded together to form the Common Market; they are opposed by the European Free Trade Association of the outer seven.

All this, naturally, alters the market conditions. Where in the past a native industry or agriculture used to satisfy domestic requirements undisturbed by foreign competition, a neighbour suddenly appears on the scene, anxious to do business for himself. Countries previously able to count on reliable customers in a closed market now find themselves at a disadvantage against a competitor from a most-favoured fellow member of the Common Market or the Free Trade Association. They begin to lose their market. The merchant is compelled to readjust himself: he must seek new customers to make up for the ones that have been lost to him. Whether trade shall flourish or stagnate depends on his commercial skill.

The governments are trying to help him to open up new markets and to shield him against unfair discrimination in the old ones. Britain has taken the first step towards bridging the gulf between the two emerging economic blocs. Hers is not an easy task. Britain is unwilling to sacrifice her traditional trade with the great family of her Commonwealth. Will this entail the surrender of her interests in the European market?

The task of the merchant is even more difficult in a country whose economic system rejects free competition, where production and consumption are planned and controlled by a centralized official agency, and where economic considerations are determined not by the price of an article, or even its production cost, but by political aims, production targets, controlled distribution, and the ultimate economic objectives of the State—as in the countries of the Eastern Communist bloc.

There the merchant has no choice before him but to emphasize very patiently his favourable terms, the excellence of his goods, and his readiness to fill gaps and to accept other deliveries in payment. He must think on a big, nationwide scale, and his propositions must carry conviction. Political considerations must be set aside, and industrial and commercial arguments must be advanced and pressed home. The rôle of the bazaars, where foreign merchants used to display their wares, has been taken by the great national exhibitions with their vast political, cultural, and statistical trimmings. Their aim is to show what a country's economy can do.

The forms of trade may have changed, but the task of the merchant has remained the same—to win a hesitant, undecided customer by making him realize that the deal proposed is also to his advantage.

Acknowledgments

——◅∿∿∿∿◍∿∿∿∿▻——

Archiv, II (*bottom*), III (*top*), VIII (*bottom*), XI (*top*), XI (*bottom left*), XV (*top*), XIX (*top*), XXIII (*top*), 24, 37, 40, 48; Archivbild, XII (*bottom*), XIV, XVI, XVII (*top*), XXV (*centre*), 8, 9, 14, 19, 31, 39, 41, 50, 54; Archivfoto, V (*top*), V (*centre*), XIX (*centre*), XX (*top*), XX (*bottom*), XXI (*top*), XXI (*bottom*), 46; Archiv für Kunst und Geschichte, Berlin, I (*bottom*), VIII (*top*), XX (*centre*), XXII (*bottom*); Bechtold-Archiv, Neckargemünd, III (*bottom*), V (*bottom*), VI (*top*), VII (*centre*), XVII (*bottom*), XXIV (*top*) XXVI (*bottom*), 6, 11, 12, 27, 55; Berlin Museum, 5; Bibliothèque Nationale, Paris. Cabinet des Cartes et Plans, 17; British Museum, 18; Diocesan Museum, Trier, II (*top*); Fuggerarchiv, Dillingen, VI (*bottom*), XII (*top*), XIII (*top*), XIII (*bottom*), 25, 26; F. u. G. Fuggersche Stiftungen, Augsburg, 32; the Firm of Hope, Amsterdam, XXIII (*bottom*); Kunstarchiv Arntz, Haag i Obb, I (*top*), IV, VII (*top*), VII (*bottom*), X, XV, (*bottom*), XXV (*top*), XXVIII (*bottom*), 16, 28, 42, 49, 51, 52, 53; Land Museum in Braunschweig, IX; Professor Eva Lips, Leipzig, XXVI (*top*); Museum of Nordic Antiquities, Copenhagen, 38; G. Oberländer, 10; Picton Library, Liverpool, XXV (*bottom*); Public Library, New York, 46; Rietberg Museum, Zurich, VII (*bottom*); State Museum, Berlin, X; Ullstein XXIX (*bottom*)

Index

ABDULLAH MOHAMMED OF VALENCIA, 106
Abu Abdullah, Sultan of Tunis, 119–20
Accra, 269
Adams, William, 226–7
Aden, 59
Adrianople, 108
Adriatic (steamship), 327
Advertising, 315, 342, 351, 357
Aetolia, 108
Africa Company, 267
Aghena, 97
Agra, 214, 224, 225
Agriculture: American, 320–1, 327–31; French, 297; Greek, 51; reforms in eighteenth century, 259; Roman laws on, 76
Aigues-Mortes, 116
Akbar the Great, 224, 225
Al-Khowarizmi, 99
Albrecht of Brandenburg, 166–7
Aleppo, 108, 208, 210
Alesia, 79
Alexander IV, Pope, 107
Alexander the Great, 56, 58, 63, 89
Alexander (Greek merchant), 85
Alexander of Pheræ (pirate), 46
Alexandria, 52, 61, 62, 63, 72, 79, 86, 104, 105, 210
Algeria, 93
Algonquin Indians, 233
Almaden mercury-mines, 171, 185
Almagro, Diego de, 186
Almeria, 106
Alps, 153–4
Alsace, 153
Altai, 51
Altmark, 131
Altona, 284, 285
Amalfi, 105–6
Amboyna, 218, 220, 223, 228
American Civil War, 338

American War of Independence, 263, 264, 269, 277, 279
Ammann, Jost, 315
Amphoræ, 54, 61
Amru, General, 86
Amsterdam, 145, 198, 199, 216, 258; banks, 243, 244, 282, 292; rise to power, 217, 222, 256
Andalusia, 73
Ango, Jean, 185, 204
Anhilvada, 95
Animals, as gifts, 101, 113
Antimony, 32
Antioch, 52, 56, 61, 72, 106
Antwerp, 145, 151, 160, 186, 188, 196, 198, 199; and Fuggers' Asian trade, 165, 166, 169, 170, 172, 173, 175, 193; sack and decline of, 175, 193
Aparaturios, 50–1
Apollodorus, Admiral, 47–8
Appomattox, 235
Apprenticeship, 304
Apricot, 58
Aquileia, 82, 103
Arabs, 104; Chinese and Asian trade of, 97–101, 183–4; empire of, 84–9, 94; Indian trade of, 56–7, 58, 59, 85, 89, 92–6, 178, 180–1; keel ships, 29
Aral, Sea of, 98
Aramæans, 90
'Arbitrage,' 163, 166
Archangel, 206
Arezzo, 70
Arles, 107
Armenia, 108, 110, 112
Artisans, 55, 101, 128, 129, 305; of Augsburg, 154, 155–6; Dutch, 228; Flemish woollen, 205, 207; Florentine, 119, 123, 124; Hanseatic, 137–8; peasants become, 259; slaves as, 70
Arts and crafts, Italian, 115–16, 119, 123
Ascension (English ship), 223

Ashanti tribes, 268
Assignats, 281
Assyrians, 34, 56, 105
Athens, and grain trade, 43–52
Attica, 46
Augsburg, 18, 148, 150, 151, 154, 155–157, 158, 160, 171
Augustus, Emperor, 69, 101
Axes: bronze, 28, 31; stone, 29
Ayuthia, 226
Azores, 40
Azov, Sea of, 51
Aztecs, 18

BACTRIA (Balkh), 57, 89, 90, 92
Bætica (now Andalusia), 73
Baghdad, 99
Baku, 99
Balance of payments, 54, 55, 137, 295–6, 308
Balkh (Bactria), 57, 89, 90, 92
Baltic Sea, 126, 130, 139–40, 146, 147, 205, 206, 220
Baltimore, 323
Banana, 58
Banker, earliest record of, 43–4
Banking, 163; Florentine, 117–19, 123–5, 163, 166; Law's system, 242–6, 248; Spanish, 189, 192–3
Bankruptcy: French, 241, 242, 303; South German, 198–9; Spanish, 188–92, 198
Banks, 282–7, 288, 292–3, 334, 337, 341; Amsterdam, 243, 244, 282, 292; Hamburg, 288, 292–3, 295
Banque Générale Law et Cie, 244–6, 252
Bantam, 218, 220, 223, 225, 226
Bantchoa (Hwang Tchao), 100
Bardi bankers, 118–19
Baring Brothers and Co., 299
Barlow, Roger, 206
Barter, 16–22, 29–30, 31, 200, 201, 207, 232, 233, 236, 237, 249, 267, 269
Baryzaga, 82
Basle, 154
Basra, 86, 89, 213, 214
Bastianenzoon, Cornelis, 218
Batavia, 220, 228
Batchian, 220
Bavaria, 158–9

Bazaars, 93, 94–5
Beaver skins, 231, 232, 233, 236, 242, 249
Beirut, 105
Bengal, 94, 257
Benin, 269
Berenberg and Gossler, 288, 290
Bergen, 128, 133, 139
Berlin, 137, 242; shops in, 350, 351, 353
Bielefeld, 130, 155
Bilbao, 199
Bill-brokers, 292–3
Bills of exchange, 124, 193, 243, 245, 279, 280, 282, 283, 284–7, 289–90, 292–3, 295, 296, 339
Bills of lading, 279, 286, 290
Birka, 130
Birmingham, 301, 331
Biscay, Bay of, 140, 142, 146
Black market, 362, 363, 364, 365, 373
Black Sea, 40, 43, 44, 47–8, 51, 53, 61, 89, 107, 108, 109, 114, 130, 153, 208
Blanco, Pedro, 312
Boats, early, 28–9, 30–1, 38
Bodeck, Johann von, 198–9
Bombay, 221
Bonaffe, François, 278
Bordeaux, 241, 249, 278
Bosporus, 61, 114
Boston (Lincs.), 147
Boucicaut, Aristide, 345–8, 351, 354
Boyd, Walter, 282, 283–4
Boyd, Ker and Co., 281–3
Brandenburg, 131, 166–9, 242
Brenner Pass, 154
Breslau, 146, 160
Brest, 242
Brewing, 131, 137
Bristol, 269
Broach, 82, 93
Brokerage, 278, 296
Bronze, 26, 31, 38
'Brotherhoods,' 130
Brown, G. and H., 284, 285, 286
Bruges, 129, 142, 144, 145–6, 148, 165, 173
Brunel, Isambard, 326
Brygus, 70
Buda, 169
Bukhara, 89, 92, 208

Burgundy, 145
Burma, 214
Burton, Forbes and Gregory, 284-5, 286
Buying co-operatives, 357-8
Byblos, 27-8, 29, 30-1, 33, 35, 38
Byzantium, 103, 104, 105, 107, 114, 130

CABOT, JOHN, 203, 206
Cabot, Sebastian, 181-2, 183, 206
Cadiz, 73, 284
Caesar, Julius, 66, 68
Cairo, 210, 211
Calais, 242
Calculation, 121-3
Calico, 226
Calicut, 218, 229
California, 324-5
Cambrai, League of, 163
Cameroons, 269
Campania, 70-1
Canary Islands, 40, 178
Cannæ, battle of, 65
Canot (slave-trader), 312
Canton, 228, 343
Cape Horn, 216
Capital, 117, 123, 160, 246
Capua, 65, 70-1
Caracalla, Emperor, 79
Caravanserai, 87-8, 90-2, 93, 94, 96, 98, 109-12
Caribbean Sea, 184-5, 248, 249
Cartagena, 195
Cartels, 343
Carthage, 40, 52, 66, 86
Caspian Sea, 208, 209
Cassiodorus, 102, 103
Castile, 191-2, 214-15
Catalonia, 154
Cattaneo, Silvestro, 188
Cavallis, Antonio de, 162
Cedar Lake, 237
Cedars of Lebanon, 26, 30
Cembalo, 115
Centurioni, Ottavio, 191
Ceram, 228
Cerco, 115
Ceylon, 89, 97, 178, 229, 249
Chæronea, battle of, 49, 55
Chain-stores, 356, 357

Chaldeans, 32
Chamberlain, Joseph, 343
Chambers of Commerce, 341, 342
Champlain, Samuel de, 232-3, 234
Channel Islands, 40
Chapeaurouge, Jacques de, 294
Charlemagne, 118
Charles II, 236, 273
Charles III of France, 265, 266
Charles V, Emperor, 150-3, 165, 166, 169, 170, 174-6, 182, 185-6, 187, 188
Charles VII of France, 238
Chauchard and Hériot, 348
Cherokee Indians, 235
Cherry, 58
Chibchas, 18
Chile, 183, 186
Chios, 239
Chorasmia, 89, 92, 94, 98, 99
Chowaresmia, 89
Christian I of Denmark, 140
Church feasts, 101, 104, 128, 129
Cincinnati, 323
Clippers, 324-6
Clive, Robert, 260, 265
Cloth trade, 154-6; English, 165, 205-7, 208, 214, 226, 227; Flanders, 144, 145
Clove (English ship), 227
Co-operatives, 317-18; buying, 357-8; Russian, 363-4
Coal-mining, 270
Cobden, Richard, 307-8, 332
Cochin, 218
Cœur, Jacques, 238-9
Coffee, 248-9, 250, 252, 253, 254, 256-7, 263
Coffee-houses, 252
Coinage, 119-20
Colbert, Jean B., 239-42
Colchis, 51
Collective co-operatives, 363-5
Collins, E. K., 327
Cologne, 129, 135, 138, 142
Colonization: English, 247-8, 250, 260, 277; French, 245-52, 260, 278
Columbus, Christopher, 16, 17, 178, 179-80
Commercial travellers, 314, 316, 317
Commodity exchanges, 335

Common Market, 379, 380
Communes, Chinese, 374
Compass needle, 99–100, 105
Consolato del mare (maritime lawcourt), 105
Constance, 154
Constantinople, 108, 109, 110, 210, 211
Consulates, 341, 343
Consumer, 301, 339–40, 361; co-operatives, 317–18; Russian, 360, 363, 365
Continental System, 276, 294, 297–9, 301, 313, 314
Controlled economy, 359–78
Convoys: Athenian, 47–8, 54; Spanish, 195
Cook, Captain, 22
Copper, 33, 34, 38; Hungarian, 160–1, 162, 168–9, 170, 173; Sumerian use of, 25–6; Swedish ore, 147
Cordoba, 195
Corfu, 108
Corinth, 66, 67
Corn tariffs, 308, 331
Coromandel coast, 97, 226
Corunna, 183
Corvo, 40
Cosmetics, 31–2
Cotton, 93, 310; American, 263, 323, 328, 329, 338; Egyptian, 57, 155, 171; Indian, 57, 82, 171, 173, 208; Syrian, 214; Venetian monopoly, 155, 156; West Indian, 263, 270, 271
Cotton cloth, English, 270–1, 275–6, 310
Counters (trading agencies), 105, 133, 134, 142, 144, 147, 165
Cracow, 110, 146, 153
Credit, 199, 334; and Continental market, 279–87, 289–90, 292, 295; Fuggers and, 150–3, 156–63, 166, 170–1, 175–6, 185–6, 187, 188, 189, 191; Italian, 118–19, 123, 124; John Law and, 242–6, 248, 251–2, 256; Spanish, 185–6, 187, 188–95; in Wild West, 322–3
Credit, letter of, 43–4
Credit standing, 123, 124, 245
Crete, 33, 37–9, 108
Crimea, 108, 109, 114
Croatia, 107
Crockery, 258

Cromwell, Oliver, 229
Crusades, 108–9
Cumberland trail, 319, 320, 321, 323
Curaçao, 267
Curiel, Juan de, 189, 190
Currency, 337; Florentine, 119; Genoese, 197–8; Hamburg, 292; in slave trade, 269
Currency devaluation: French, 245–6, 250; Roman, 79–80, 83
Curzola, battle of, 115
Customs barriers, 302, 306, 308, 309, 331, 338, 339–40, 343, 377, 379; Napoleon's, 297–8, 300, 301
Customs duties, 156, 160, 332, 333; ancient Indian, 58–9; Italian, 117; Turkish, 210, 211, 225
Cutty Sark (tea-clipper), 325
Cyprus, 33, 39, 92

Dahomey, 311; tribes, 268
Dakar, 267
Dalmatia, 104, 107, 108
Damascus, 238
Danube, river, 107, 153, 160, 161
Danzig, 139, 141, 182, 220, 289, 290, 297
Dee, John, 213
Delos, 52, 61; and slave traffic, 65–8
Demetrios Poliorcetes, 54
Demosthenes, 45, 48
Denia, 106
Department stores, 345–8, 351–8, 359–60
Depression, Great, 366–8, 371
Deventer, 145
Dieppe, 185, 204, 205, 242
Diocletian, Emperor, 83
Discount, 292–3
Domitian, Emperor, 76
Dordrecht, 144
Dragon-tree, 40
Drake, Sir Francis, 202, 207, 210, 213
Drapers' shops, 314
Dunkirk, 204, 205, 242
Dupleix, Marquis de, 265
Dutch East India Company, 199, 217–20, 221, 226, 228, 248, 256–57, 260–1
Dutch Guiana, 249
Dyeing, 115, 116

EAST INDIA COMPANY, 222–8, 256, 257–8, 260–1, 262, 308
Edward III, 118
Einbeck, 131
Elizabeth I, 205, 207, 209, 213, 222
Embargoes, 134, 136, 146, 194–5
Emden, 199, 207, 228
Emporos (merchant), 49, 54–5
England, Bank of, 243–4, 245, 337
Entrepreneur, 362, 375, 376; French, 241, 243, 245, 309, 313
Epirus, 66, 108
Erasso, Francisco, 188
Erhard, Ludwig, 374
Erie Canal, 323
Erythræan Sea (Indian Ocean), 57, 85, 89
Estates: Roman, 70, 72–3, 76, 82, 83; South American, 266
Eubœa, 108
Euphrates, river, 39, 90
European Free Trade Association, 379, 380
Ezekiel, 41–2

FACTORY-MADE GOODS, 305, 314–16, 318, 351, 352
Fairs, 101, 128, 129, 165, 192, 198, 199; German, 341–2; Spanish, 189, 191, 193; Swedish, 126–7
Falsterbo, 126–7, 128
Farmers, 303, 315; and free trade, 340; in Mid-West, 320–1, 327–31
Farming, and commerce, 259
Fashion trade, 332, 333; French, 350
Feodosia, 114
Feudalism, 303
Finch, William, 225
Firm, as distinct from association, 160
Fish trade, Baltic, 126–7, 128, 129
Fishing: Greek, 51, Newfoundland, 203–4, 324
Fixed prices, 346, 351, 352
Florence, 115–20, 121–5, 155, 163
Florin, 119
fonduks (foreign quarters), 105
Font de Gaume, 29
Foreign merchants, special quarters for, 56, 105

Formosa, 343
Francis I of France, 169, 174, 175
Frankfurt on Main, 198–9
Frankincense, 32
Frederick the Great, 278, 288–9
Free competition, 62, 256, 266, 276
Free trade, 62–3, 306–9, 332–3, 338, 339–41, 343–4
Free-market economy, 374–8
Freedmen, Roman, 70–2, 74–5
Freight charges, 61, 116, 117
French Africa Company, 249
French China Company, 248
French East India Company, 248, 265
French Revolution, 281–2, 303
Frescobaldi bankers, 166
Frisians, 139–40
Frobisher, Sir Martin, 209
Fruit, 57–8
Fugger, House of, 155, 156–76, 182–3, 185, 188, 189, 190, 191, 192, 197, 198
Fugger, Andreas, 156
Fugger, Anton, 150–3, 169, 170, 174, 175–6
Fugger, Georg, 157, 160, 162
Fugger, Hans, 155
Fugger, Jakob, 152–3, 156, 157, 172, 174
Fugger, Jakob II, 157–9, 160, 161, 162, 163, 168–70, 182, 183, 187
Fugger, Lukas, 156, 158
Fugger, Ulrich, 157, 158, 160, 161, 162
Fur trade: medieval, 131, 132, 134, 142, 144; North American, 231–8, 249; Russian, 206, 208
Fustian, 155–6, 171

GABES, 93
Gades (now Cadiz), 73
Gama, Vasco da, 23, 180
Gambia, 312
General stores, 313–14
Genoa, 117, 123, 154, 155; bankruptcy, 190, 191, 198; and Eastern trade, 114–15, 121, 238; fairs, 197–8; power in Western Mediterranean, 106–7, 114, 116
Gentile, Agostini, 188
Gentz, Friedrich, 299
Georgia, 273
Gera, 356

German Customs Union, 306, 333
Gernsheim, 166
Ghent, 145
Gibraltar, 89; Straits of, 52
Glasgow, 331
Glass manufacture, 105, 115
Goa, 213, 215, 219, 221, 222
Gobi Desert, 89
Golconda, 214
Gold, 267; Egyptian, 33; Roman payments in, 82
Gold Coast (now Ghana), 266, 268–9
Gold rush, 324–5
Golden Hind, 210
Good Hope, Cape of, 217
Goree (now Dakar), 267
Gothland, 126, 130
Graben, 155
Grain, 131, 136, 170, 191; American, 323, 328, 329; Athens and, 43, 44, 47, 49, 51, 61; Baltic, 279; in China, 100; Flanders, 139–40, 142; Prussian, 295
Great Eastern (steamship), 326, 338
Great Slave Lake, 237
Great Western (steamship), 326
Greene, Bob, 357
Grimaldi, Nicolo de, 190, 191
Grosseilliers (coureur de bois), 235–6
Guadeloupe, 250
Guanajuato, 184
Guatemala, 18
Guilds, 128, 135, 153, 155, 156, 165, 205, 276, 278; Florentine, 119; Roman, 77, 78
GUM (Moscow), 359–60, 365
Gumpeltzhamer, Dr, 199
Gun factories, 270
Gunpowder, 99

HADRAMUT, 32, 59, 85
Hadrian, Emperor, 74–5, 76
Haiti, 250
Hakluyt, Richard, 213
Hamburg, 131, 135, 142, 199, 245, 309–11, 342; banks, 292; and Continental market, 278–96, 302; position and wealth of, 207, 277, 278, 291, 294
Hangchow, 97
Hannibal, 65

Hanseatic League, 126–49, 165, 171, 172, 173, 202, 205, 206–7
Hardware merchants, 315
Harman, Hoare and Co., 282, 283
Haro, Cristobal de, 181, 183
Harrods, 351
Harun al-Rashid, Caliph, 93, 101
Hausham copper-mines, 161
Havana, 312
Hawaiian Islands, 22
Hawkins, Sir John, 201–2, 225
Hector (English ship), 225
Henry VII, 202
Herodotus, 35, 40–1, 51, 60, 89
Herring trade, 126–7, 129, 132, 144, 313
Hesse, 306
Hinrichsen, Captain, 312
Hippalos, 59
Hirado, 227
Hitler, Adolf, 370–1
Holbein, Hans, 149
Holstein, 131, 298
Honey, 153
Hope and Co., 282, 283, 286, 299
Hopewell Indians, 19
Hopi Indians, 19
Houtman, Cornelius, 216
Huancavelica mercury-mines, 186
Huantchi (Sumatra), 101
Hucksters, 288, 294, 315
Hudson Bay, 235, 236
Hudson's Bay Company, 236–7
Hudson river, 233, 234
Hudtwalker (Hamburg merchant), 304
Hundred Years War, 144
Huron Indians, 232, 233, 235
Huron, Lake, 234, 235
Hwang Tchao (Bantchoa), 100
Hyderabad, 93

IBRAHIM IBN YAACUB, 100
Import-export business, 295–6; Hanseatic, 137; rôle of merchant in, 54, 55
Imports, 264, 270, 278, 301–2, 307
Incas, 17
Incense, 32
Income tax, 271
Indian Ocean, 57, 85, 89
Indians, American, 16–17, 19–20, 231–6

Indigo, 93, 116
Indonesia, 226, 228-9, 256
Indulgences, trading in, 167, 188
Indus river, 58, 59
'Industrial age,' 313
Industrial empires, 341-2
Industrial Revolution, 270-1, 316
Industry: American, 327; English, 269-70, 275-6, 331; French, 238, 241, 243, 249, 250, 332-3
Innsbruck, 150, 151, 152
Insulinde Islands, 221
Insurance, 292, 334; marine, 116, 117, 262, 286
Iron-ore, 147
Ironfounding, 269, 270
Iroquois Indians, 232-5
Isabella of Castile, 178, 179
Istria, 102, 104, 107
Itil, 99
Ivan III of Russia, 144
Ivan the Terrible, 206
Ivory Coast, 269

JACKSON, ANDREW, 322, 328-9
Jahangir, Emperor, 225
Jakarta, 220
Jaluzet, M., 348
Jamaica, 249
James I, 226, 228
Jandorf store (Berlin), 351
Java, 24, 215, 220, 223, 225, 226
Jenkinson, Anthony, 208-9
Jesuits, 266, 271
Joachimsthal, 161
Joint Export Import Agency (JEIA), 375
Jolliet (French fur-trader), 235
Joppa, 107
Joseph, 30, 32
Junk, Chinese, 29

KABUL, 96
Kaffa (now Feodosia), 114
'Kanfu' (?Hangchow), 97
Kara Kum desert, 90
Karakorum, 110, 112
Kashgar, 92
Kattigara, 85, 89
Kaukamali, 97

Kazakhstan, 89
Keel ships, 28, 29, 34, 38, 226
Kelsey, Henry, 237
Khasvin, 209
Khotan, 92
Kirchberg, 162
'Kite-flying,' 284
Kublai Khan, 110, 112-13
Kula, 21
Kwakiutl Indians, 19-20
Kyat, 98

LA ROCHELLE, 205, 231, 242, 249
Lace-making, 115
Lagash, 36, 37
Lancaster (Pennsylvania), 356
Lancaster, Captain, 222
Landowners, 303
Latin Mint Union, 337
Laudanum, 32
Law, John, 243-51, 254
Law and justice, growth of principle of, 34-9
Lawsuits, Athenian, 45-6, 49-51
Le Havre, 185, 242, 249
Lebanon, cedars of, 26, 30
Leghorn, 117, 284
Leipzig, 199, 342
Lemberg (now Lvov), 140-1, 153
Lemon, 57
Lenin, 363
Leocrates, 55
Letter of credit, 43-4
Levant Company, 210, 212-14, 222
Lewis, John, 351
Leyden, 144
Leyland, Thomas, 262-3, 264
Liberia, 312
Lightning (clipper), 326
Lincoln, Abraham, 322
Linen trade, 59, 130, 155-6, 315
Linschoten, Jan Huyghen van, 215-16
Lisbon, 165, 171, 181, 182, 193, 196, 284
List, Friedrich, 340
Liverpool, 262-4, 265, 271, 275-6, 278, 284, 285, 288, 289, 290, 292, 293, 295, 308
Lloyd's, 252, 334

Loaysa, Garcia de, 183
Local traders, 129, 254, 290
Lombards, 103, 105
London, 139, 146, 179, 244, 269, 274–5, 284, 295; City of, 271, 333–7; coffee-houses, 252; department stores, 351; docks, 333–4; and East Indian Company, 222–4, 256, 258; shopping streets, 353; Steelyard, 133, 146, 147, 172, 205, 207; Stock Exchange, 334, 336–7; world trade centre, 211, 333–7
London and Westminster Bank, 334
London Hansa of Germans, 135
Louis of Hungary, 167–8
Louis XIV of France, 239, 242
Louisiana, 248
Louvain, 156
Lübeck, 127, 132, 135, 137, 140, 142, 207
Lucullus, 58
Ludwig of Brandenburg, 127
Lüneburg, 127, 131, 140, 146
Luxury, increasing, 258–9
Luxury goods, 82, 83, 88, 95, 154, 214, 238, 240, 246, 248, 305
Lvov, 140
Lykon (Athenian merchant), 46
Lyons, 350

MACAO, 228
Macedon, 47
Macedonians, 65–6
Mackenzie, Alexander, 237
Mackenzie river, 237
Macy's (New York), 351
Madagascar, 24, 88
Madeira, 179
Magdeburg, 138
Magellan, Ferdinand, 181, 182
Magellan, Strait of, 216
Mainz, 84, 166, 349
Malabar, 218
Malacca, 214, 215–16, 219, 221, 222
Malachite, 26
Maldive Islands, 97
Malines, 145
Malmesbury Abbey, 205
Malta, 34
Manchester, 270, 275, 276, 301, 308, 331
Mansfeld copper-mines, 199

Manufacturers: distinct from merchants, 30, 55, 128–9; dominance of, 342–3; and world markets, 309–18
Manufactures: English, 269–70, 275–6; French, 238, 241, 302; Italian, 115, 117
'Manufacturists,' 291
Maps, ancient Greek, 52–3
Marcus Aurelius, 79
Marketing, 342–4
Markets, 16, 18, 99, 313; beginning of, 101
Marks Banco, 281, 292
Maronia, 48
Marquette, Father, 235
Marseille, 249
Marshall Aid, 375
Marshall Field, 351
Martinique, 250, 266
Matchian, 220
Matelief, Cornelius, 218–19
Mathematics, 99
Maug family, 197, 198
Mauritius, 218–19
Maximilian, Emperor, 156, 157, 159, 160, 161–3, 165–6, 169, 175
Maximum prices, 192
Mayas, 17
Mazadachen, 98
Mechelen (Malines), 145
Mecklenburg, 131, 295
Medici family, 118, 163
Mediterranean Sea, 25–8, 30, 32, 34, 35, 37, 39, 43, 52, 57, 72–3, 82, 85, 88–9, 107, 114–16, 129, 180, 208, 209–13, 238
Méline, Félix, 340
'Mercantilism,' 240
Merchant Adventurers, 146, 205, 207, 208, 278
Mercury, 171, 185, 186
Metal-working, 38
Mexicans, 17–18
Mexico, Gulf of, 234, 235, 323
Michael Pæolologus, Emperor, 114, 115
Middelburg, 144, 145
Middlemen, 76, 128
Midnall (Levant merchant), 224–5
Milan, 173, 353
Millionaires, 342

Minorca, 106
Mississippi basin, 319–20, 323
Mississippi Company, 251, 252, 254
Mohammed, 86
Mohave Indians, 19
Mokha, 226
Molossians, 66
Moluccas, 24, 182, 183, 216, 223, 261
Mongols, 109–13, 154
Monomatapata, 97
Monopoly, 62, 264; decline of, 265–6;
    Dutch, 256, 257; English in Mediter-
    ranean, 210; herring, 127, 128; of Hud-
    son Bay, 236; Portuguese, 214, 217,
    220; Venetian, 108–9, 123, 155
Morris, Gouverneur, 284, 299
Moscow, 206, 209, 359–60
Mulberry-trees, 93, 103
Müller, Thomas, 192
Murano, 104, 115
Muscovy Company, 206–7, 208–9
Muslims, 104, 105, 106, 107, 110, 112,
    115, 117
Muslin, 103, 275
Muziris, 82
Mycenæ, 33, 39
Mysians, 39

Nahr Feidar, 25
Nahr Ibrahim, 25
Nantes, 249
Napoleon, 276, 294, 297–9, 300
Napoleon III, 332
Narbonne, 107
Naucratis, 56
Naukleros (shipowner and carrier), 49
Navigation, 100, 106, 202–3
Navigation Acts, 229
Neidhard, Sebastian, 174
Neusohl, 160, 168
New Amsterdam (now New York), 233
New Deal, 367
New Economic Policy (NEP), 363, 365
New England, 255, 324, 327
New Orleans, 323
New York, 233, 323, 326, 351
Newbury, John, 212–14
Newfoundland, 203–5, 324
Nicolet, Jean, 234–5

Nicostatos (Athenian merchant), 46
Nicoya, Gulf of, 18
Nightingale (tea-clipper), 325
Nile river, 26, 29, 53, 61
Ning-po, 343
Noort, Olivier van, 216
Norberg, 147
Norfolk system, 259
North Carolina, 273
North-West Fur Company of Montreal,
    237
North-West Passage, 209–10, 237
Northampton, 331
Nova Scotia, 234
Novgorod, 105, 108, 130, 133, 139, 142,
    143, 144
Nürnberg, 199

Officials: Byzantium, 104; and colo-
    nialism, 257, 260; French, 239–42;
    Portuguese, 195–7, 217–18, 219–21;
    Roman, 74–5, 76; Spanish, 192, 193,
    195
Oglethorpe, James Edward, 259
Ohio river, 235
Oil, 103; American, 323
Oleron, Isle of, 140
Olive oil, 73, 76
Omar, Caliph, 86
Ontario, Lake, 235
Opium, 257, 325, 344
Orange, 57
Ormuz, 213, 221
Ortega de la Torre, Juan, 193
Osnabrück, 296
Osney Abbey, 205
Ottawa river, 233
Otto the Great, 84
Outriggers, 22, 28
Ouvrard, Gabriel Julien, 299
Over-production, 366–8

Packaging, 353–4, 356
Padua, 103
Palmyra, 39
Pamirs, 89, 90
Panama, 184, 207
Paper, 100
Paper money, 242–6, 252, 281–2

Paris, 345–50, 353, 354
Parish, David, 298–9
Parish, John, 277, 278–86, 293, 294, 296, 298
Parmenides (Athenian sea captain), 50–1
Parthians, 85, 90
Pasion (Athenian banker), 43–6
Patani, 226
Paul, St, 72
Payment in kind, 118
Pazzi banking house, 118, 119
Peace river, 237
'Peace ships,' 137
Peach, 58
Peasants, 15–16, 18, 320; become artisans, 259; French, 303; and protective tariffs, 339, 341; Roman, 73, 76, 79; Russian, 362, 363–5
Pedlars, 252–3, 254, 315
Peking, 112, 343
Pepper, 165, 223
Perfumes, 31–2
Petapoli, 226
Petra, 85–6
Petronius, 71–2
Philadelphia, 323, 351
Philip of Macedon, 47, 49, 55
Philip II of Spain, 186, 188, 195, 205, 207, 213, 214, 215, 217
Philip VI of France, 119
Phœnicians, 35, 39–42
Phrygians, 39
Piracy, 39, 43, 254; Caribbean, 184–5, 195; Cossack, 209; Elizabethan, 207–8, 210, 211–12, 222, 224; off Flanders, 144–5; Mediterranean, 43, 46–8, 54; Newfoundland, 204–5; in West Indies, 229–30
Piræus, 43, 46, 47
Pisa, 116–17
Pitt, Thomas, 260
Pitt, William, 271
Plantations, 247–50, 255–9, 262, 263, 267
Plassey, 265
Pliny, 40, 56, 57, 58, 72–3, 82
Plum, 58
Polo, Maffeo, 109–14
Polo, Marco, 17, 24, 112–14, 115
Polo, Niccolo, 109–14

Polynesians, 28, 30
Pomerania, 131, 140
Population increase, 338
Porcelain, 98, 226
Potlatch, 20
Potosi silver-mines, 19, 171, 184, 185, 187, 242
Pottery, Roman, 70
Poundage dues, 137
Poverty, eighteenth-century, 259–60; Russian, 361–3
Prague, 142
Precious stones, 103, 109
Price calculation, 120–2
Price fixing, 335–6, 337, 343, 346, 351, 352, 369–70, 372, 373, 377
Prices, 100, 330–1, 332, 339–40; falling, 366–7; rising, 191–2, 196, 301–2
Priests, as protectors of early merchants, 32
Prime cost, 120, 121
Privileges, Hanseatic, 128, 135, 136, 139, 147, 148, 205
Processing, 291
Profit, 13–15; of Arab traders, 96, 98; department stores, 345, 348, 354; Florentine, 123–4; French, 240–2; Hanseatic, 139; Venetian, 123–4
Protection, 332, 333, 339–41, 343–4
Protectionism, 305, 307, 308, 309
Prussia, 131, 136–7, 288–9, 295, 296, 306, 310, 317, 333, 352
Ptolemy IV, 61
Pyron of Pherai, 45–6

Quebec, 232
Quesada, Jimenez de, 186

Radisson, Pierre, 235–6
Rafts, 28
Railroads, 323, 330, 331, 338
'Rami, land of the,' 97
Rattenberg, 161
Ravenna, 102–3
Ravensburg, 154
Red Dragon (English ship), 223, 225
Red Sea, 28, 32, 40, 226
Reemtsma, Bernhard, 304
Regensburg, 160
Representatives, 341

Resins, 31
Retailers, 287, 345–8
Reuter's, 336
Rhine estuary, 229
Rhineland, 135
Rhodes, 49, 52–4, 61, 238, 239; law of sea, 54
Rhône valley, 153, 154
Rhubarb, 208
Rice, 57
Richard and Mathiesen, 284, 285, 286
Riga, 289, 292
Roanoke river, 235
Rochefort, 241
Rome, 65–83; agriculture, 76; estates, 70, 72–3, 76, 82, 83; officials, 74–5, 76; peasants, 73, 76, 79; sack of, 175; slavery, 65–71; social structure, 70, 73–4, 75–6; suppression of merchants, 75–9, 83; taxation, 78–9, 80; trade gap, 82
Rothschild, house of, 334
Rouen, 185
Royal companies, 236, 240–1, 242
Royal Guinea Company, 248
Ruhni (now Bengal), 94
Rum, 249–50, 254, 263
Ryff, Andreas, 253

SAFFRON, 154
St Eustatius, 267
St Gotthard Pass, 142, 154
St Lawrence river, 232, 234, 235, 236
St Malo, 185, 204, 242, 249
Sales, bargain, 354
Salt, 18, 19, 127, 140, 144
Samarkand, 89, 92, 100, 110
San Francisco, 325, 326
Santo Domingo, 195
Saris (East India Company agent), 227
Satyricon (Petronius), 71–2
Satyros I of the Crimea, 44–6
Saxony, 352
Scanderoon, 210
Schetz, Balthasar, 187
Schmalkalden, League of, 151, 175
Schonen, 127, 128, 139, 140
Schuback, Johannes, 285
Schwaz silver-mines, 158–9

Scudi di marchi, 197–8
Sea, Rhodes law of, 54
Self-service stores, 356, 357
Selfridges, 351
Senegal, 267
Senegal Company, 248
Septimius Severus, 79
Settlements, trading, 105
Seven Years War, 278, 288, 296
Seville, 182, 183, 189, 192, 193, 198, 200, 215, 265
Share issues, 251–2, 254
Sheep-breeding, Spanish, 191, 192, 240
Shipbuilding, 105, 182–3, 194, 241–2
Shipping, 202–3; American, 324–7; British, 326–7; Netherlands, 220–1; Venetian, 125
Ships, 222; early, 28–9, 30–1, 34, 38; increasing size of, 61, 131
Shirvan, 209
Shopkeepers, 313–18, 321–3, 343–58
Shopping, 345–58
Siam, 226
Sicily, 89, 106, 107
Sickingen, Franz von, 170
Sidon, 39, 106
Siena, 117
Sierra Leone, 312
Sigismund, Archduke of Tyrol, 158, 162
Sigtuna, 130
Silk, 85, 92, 93, 98, 103, 104, 115, 208, 209, 332, 333
Silk route, 89, 92, 208
Silver: declining purchasing power, 196; payment in, 82, 224, 239, 240, 288–9; 295, 298–9; South American, 184–8, 189, 193
Silver-mines, 19, 158–60, 161, 171
Sinai peninsula, 26
Skanör, 126–7, 128
Slave Coast, 266–8, 269
Slave trade: African, 200, 201, 204, 207, 210, 212, 246, 247, 249, 250, 266–70, 275, 311–12, 325, 329; Dutch, 221; Roman, 65–8; Russian, 98, 99; West Indian, 230, 262, 263–4
Slavery, Roman, 65–72, 75
Sluys, 134
Smythe, Thomas, 222

Soame, Sir Stephen, 222
Soest, 130, 135
Sofala, 23, 24, 96
Sohn, Peter Hiss, 280
Sokotra, 225
Soldaia (now Sudak), 115
Sopaios, son of, 44-6
South Carolina, 273, 328
South Sea Company, 247, 254
Souza, Don Francisco de, 311
Sovereign of the Seas (clipper), 326
Speculation, 251-2, 254, 281-6, 293-4
Spice Islands, 182, 210, 218, 220
Spices, 56, 97, 103, 163-5, 171, 182, 196-7, 208, 209, 210, 213, 220, 223, 224, 228, 229, 240, 242, 248, 252, 255, 261
Spinning-jenny, 270
Spinola family, 190, 191
Stalin, 365
Staple, Merchants of the (Staplers), 205, 207
Staple rights, 141, 144, 145-6, 160, 278
State control, 61-4; ancient Rome, 82-3; German, 368, 370-2; Russian, 359-60, 362-6, 368, 374; Spanish, 192-5
Steam-engine, 270
Steamships, 323, 326-7, 331, 333, 338
Stock Exchanges, 293, 334, 336, 337, 358
Stockholm, 130, 139, 148
Strabo, 53, 57
Stralsund, Peace of (1370), 128
Strasbourg, 154
Stratocles (Athenian merchant), 43-4
Streets, shopping, 353, 358
Stumpe, William, 205
Subsidies, 265, 288, 296
Sudak, 108, 109, 115
Sugar, 56, 92, 97, 103, 153, 179, 249, 250, 263, 267, 278
Suleiman (Arab merchant), 93
Suleiman the Magnificent, 208
Sumatra, 97, 101
Sumerians, 25-6, 35-7
Sunium, Cape, 47, 48
Surat, 225
Swabian League, 169
Syndicate, first German, 161

Syracuse, 52, 65
Syrians, 32, 37, 39, 54, 63

TABLEWARE, 258-9
Tadmor (later Palmyra), 39
Tahmasp, Shah, 209
Takla Makan desert, 89-90, 92
Talamone, 117
Talleyrand, 299
Tamono, 115
Tangier, 117
Tarentum, 65
Tariffs, 211, 307, 308, 309, 327-9, 332, 333, 339-41, 343-4
Tarim basin, 91-2
Tarraco (now Tarragona), 73
Tartessus (Tarshish), 34, 40, 41
Tashkent, 92
Tax farming, 78, 192
Taxation, 78-9, 98, 108, 113, 188-9
Tea, 253, 254, 257-8, 260-1, 278, 279, 325
Technicians, 341
Tennessee river, 235
Tenochtitlán, 18
Ternate, 220, 224
Teschen (now Těšín), 160
Textiles, 82, 103, 105, 115, 192; English, 146, 205-7, 208, 214, 223, 226, 227, 270-1, 275-6, 333; Flemish, 129; German, 154-6, 157, 171, 314-15; Italian, 115-16, 117, 119
Thasos, 48
Thebes, 32
Theophrastus, 58
Thorn, 141
Thorne, Robert, 206
Thrace, 48
Three-field system, 259
Thurzo, Georg, 169
Thurzo company, 160, 161, 168
Tidore, 224
Tietz, Oscar, 356
Tietz store (Berlin), 351
Timber, 26, 30-1, 104, 131, 270
'Tin islands,' 40
Tobacco, 248, 250, 252, 253, 255, 263, 271-5
Tortosa, 106
Toulon, 241

Trade agreements, 98, 106, 108, 115, 310
Trade fairs, 341–2
Trade-mark, 342
Trading-posts, 133, 207; Dutch, 218–19, 220; English, 210, 226, 227,
Trajan, Emperor, 26
Trebizond, 208
Tripoli, 210
Trobriand Islands, 21
Troy, 33, 39
Truman, Harry S., 322
Trusts, 343
Tunis, 108
Turkestan, 85, 98
Turnover, rapidity of, 345, 348, 351, 353, 355
Tylos, 57
Tyre, 39–42, 106, 107, 115
Tyrol, 158–9, 161–2, 163

UGARIT, 39
Unemployment, 302, 366, 368, 370
Unicorn (English ship), 228
United Gothland Traders of the Roman Empire, 135
Urban II, Pope, 106
Urgench, 98
Urukagina, King of Lagash, 36, 37
Utica (New York), 356
Utrecht, 145; Peace of (1713), 254, 267

VALDEMAR IV OF DENMARK, 126, 127
Valencia, 106
Vander Hagen, Admiral, 218
Vanderbilt, Cornelius, 327
Venafrum, 73
Vending-machines, automatic, 357
Venezuela, 183
Venice, 102, 112, 113–14, 117, 120–1, 123, 124–5, 161, 165, 173, 238; arts and crafts, 115; colonies, 108; decline of, 171; Eastern trade, 103–5, 106, 107, 108, 109, 115, 121, 154, 158; monopoly, 108, 123, 155; position of, 107–9
Vera Cruz, 200, 201, 207
Vespucci, Amerigo, 18, 181
Victuallers' shops, 314
Vienna, 159, 252
Village-to-village trade, 128

Vines, 60–1, 73, 76
Virginia, 250, 255
Visby, 126, 127, 130–1, 135
Vittoria brothers, 193
Voght, Baron von, 290
Volga river, 98, 99

WAERWYCK, WYBRAND VAN, 218
Wages, 304, 305, 306, 316–17
Walkiers, Marquis de, 282–4
Wampum, 19
Wanamaker store (Philadelphia), 351
War loans, 251, 254
Warehousing, 286, 288, 290–1, 293, 295, 334
Warthe river, 141
Wealth: concentration of, 342–3; increase in, 258–9
Weissenhorn, 162
Welfare State, 374
Welser firm, 18, 169, 171, 174, 181, 182, 183, 198
Wendish towns, 127, 140
Wertheim's (Berlin), 351
West India Company, 245
Westphalia, 130, 135
Wheat, price of, 301–2
White Sea, 207, 208
Whiteleys, 351
Whitney, Eli, 275
Wholesalers, 314, 316, 356
Wild West, development of, 320–3, 327–30
Window display, 348, 350, 352–3, 355
Wine, 103, 134, 153, 194
Winnipeg, Lake, 237
Wisconsin river, 234, 235
Wismar, 131
Witch of the Wave (tea-clipper), 325
Wittenburg, Johann, 127
Wood, Abraham, 235
Wool trade, 115–16, 133–4, 136, 146, 155, 191, 192, 205–7, 208, 214, 223, 226, 227, 275–6, 331, 333
Woolworths, 356
Workers, 302, 303–4, 306; and co-operatives, 317
World Exhibition (Paris, 1867), 333, 350

XANTEN, 82

YAACUB, IBRAHIM IBN, 84
Yemen, 249
Ypres, 144, 145

ZACCARIA, BENEDETTO, 115

Zagros mountains, 26
Zanzibar, 94
Zapatecas, 19
Zenon (Greek merchant), 60, 62
Zieriksee, 144